Mr. Market Miscalculates

Mr. Market Miscalculates

The Bubble Years and Beyond

James Grant

for Patricia

Axios Press
P.O. Box 118
Mount Jackson, VA 22842
888.542.9467   info@axiospress.com

Distributed by NATIONAL BOOK NETWORK.

Library of Congress Cataloging-in-Publication Data

Grant, James, 1946–
     Mr. Market miscalculates : the bubble years and beyond / James Grant.
          p.   cm.
     Includes index.
     ISBN 978-1-60419-008-3

     1. Speculation—United States. 2. Stock exchanges—United States. 3. Finance—United States. I. Title.

HG4910.G753 2008
332.64'273—dc22

2008031189

Contents

Foreword

MR. MARKET, THE hero and anti-hero of this volume, is the flighty anthropomorphic invention of Benjamin Graham. Teacher, author and investor, Graham lived through the roaring 1920s and the sinking 1930s (and into the inflating 1970s). It puzzled him that stocks and bonds commanded such radically different valuations from one phase of the investment moon to the next. Graham would invite his students at Columbia University to imagine going into business with a manic-depressive, a certain Mr. Market. When the sun shines, this strange duck pesters you to sell him your share of the business. But when darkness falls, he begs you to buy his interest. Price is never an object; he just wants in, or he wants out. You, the sane one, could get rich just by availing yourself of the opportunities served up by your unbalanced partner.

Any resemblance between Mr. Market and the calculating and even-tempered human being who features in the economics texts is, therefore, purely accidental. Homo economicus would never be a party to anything so irrational as a financial bubble. Mr. Market, on the other hand, can't seem to help himself. What gets into the head of Graham's creation is the thematic glue of this anthology.

Mr. Market and I have had our differences. In the mid and late-1990s, we were at daggers drawn over stock prices; and we had a second falling out in the early 2000s over house prices and mortgage-backed securities. These essays chronicle the strange events of the bubble years, including the boom-like rise in the reputation and prestige of our celebrity central bankers. Especially was Alan Greenspan, chairman of the Federal Reserve Board from 1987 to 2006, invested by his credulous fans with powers very close to clairvoyance. In the old days, gold stood behind paper money. Nowadays, reputations do. *Grant's Interest Rate Observer* favors gold.

The Internet boom and the mortgage crackup shouldn't have happened, according to a literal reading of the theory of efficient markets, one of the bedrock ideas of modern-day academic finance. Proponents of the idea of investment efficiency posit that Mr. Market is just as sane as the next fellow. If he seems to hold extreme views, it's because the facts support them; and if he changes his mind, it's only because the facts change. And because he knows everything that can possibly bear on stock prices as soon as that information becomes available, there is no point in trying to second-guess him.

An elegant theory, and a highly influential one. No less than a third of institutionally managed funds today are invested passively, through indexing. The investors who deploy their money in this fashion accept at least the basic tenets of market efficiency. They choose to take no view of the valuation of individual securities but rather to buy a basket of them, such as the Standard & Poor's 500 stock index. Believing that markets are efficient—or, at least, efficient enough—they decline to try to outfox them. To a high-church exponent of the efficient-markets proposition, Cisco Systems deserved every dollar of its $485 billion stock-market capitalization at the peak of the high-tech craze in early 2000. And it just as richly deserved its $85 billion capitalization at the bottom of the bear market 18 months later. So it goes for debt securities, mortgage-backed instruments included, and real estate. To the adherents of perfect market efficiency, there was nothing to fear in the fact that, at the culmination of the post-millennial real-estate frolic in the spring of 2006, a family earning the median income could afford just 1.8% of the houses sold in Los Angeles without recourse to a fancy, new, save-the-bad-news-for-later mortgage. After all, calculating humans had incorporated every known relevant fact into the quoted prices.

The articles in this collection first appeared in *Grant's Interest Rate Observer*, the twice-monthly journal I founded 25 years ago. I had initially planned to focus on the bond market and the Federal Reserve, but I quickly shifted my attention to the cycles of lending and borrowing and to Mr. Market's curious personality. I noticed, for instance, that the terms and conditions of lending seem always to be on the move, shuttling between the opposite poles of stringency and accommodation. At one extreme, you can't seem to get a loan against the collateral of a gold bar. At the other, you can hardly open your mailbox, stuffed as it is with letters pleading with you to borrow (no questions asked) against collateral real or imaginary. What are lenders thinking about over the course of this cyclical journey? And what comes over the investors who feel an irrepressible urge to buy stocks when the market is up but to sell them when the market is down?

The reader may now reflect on his or her own approach to life's financial problems. Perhaps, like so many others, you are alternately informed and ignorant, risk-averse and risk-tolerant, steadfast and wavering. Perhaps you do not always process information (especially information about so emotionally charged a topic as money) with computer-like speed and detachment. Perhaps, in short, you are heir to mankind's weaknesses of the spirit and of the flesh. How, then, one may ask, can crowds of human beings be held to expectations of cool efficiency that few individuals can meet? Actually, a newly-formed school of behavioral finance is looking into the matter. Pending a final report from the scholars, however, I submit Graham's famous dictum: "In the short run the market is a voting machine, but in the long run, it is a weighing machine." In other words, in the long run, value will out, though the wait can tax the net worth of even the patient rationalist.

No doubt, the Federal Reserve has contributed more than a little to this instability. Its North Star, after all, is "stability,"—in prices, in business activity and in the financial markets. It won't put up with too much inflation, it says. Neither will it suffer too little. Too little? That the nation requires a decent modicum of currency debasement happens to be one of the principle tenets of modern central banking. Ben S. Bernanke, Greenspan's successor, made the case for just a little inflation in 2002 and 2003. *Grant's* argued against it, but Bernanke carried the day (he seemed not to hear us), and the Fed drove its interest rate all the way down to 1% in 2003. If success is defined as averting a bout of inadequate inflation, the Fed assuredly succeeded, though at the cost of facilitating a wave of speculative borrowing by home buyers and Wall Street financiers alike. Here I check myself, however. There were speculative bubbles in America long before the Fed was legislated into existence. And there were speculative bubbles in Europe long before the apparatus of modern finance took shape. To create a proper speculative riot, the only essential ingredient is a quorum of human beings.

Markets may not be perfectly efficient, but neither are they reliably inefficient. It's a tall order to second-guess them with profitable consistency. Certainly, by the peak of the Nasdaq market in early 2000, high-tech stocks were absurdly overvalued. But, then again, they were only a little less overvalued in 1999 and 1998. Indeed, to the kind of person who was attuned to that absurdity, the same stocks looked grotesquely overpriced in 1997 and 1996. I myself thought the market was a little high in 1992. (For my persistent and unprofitable bearishness, I earned pride-of-place in a 1997 *Wall Street Journal* report on the slow learners of the great bull market. The story appeared under the page-one headline, "Bears Will Be Right On Stocks Some Day, Just You Watch—So They Missed 5,000 Points, It's No Reason They Ought To Stop Prognosticating.") Indeed, though *Grant's* has been bullish on many stocks and on many markets, and although I have invested professionally in Japan for 10 years without making one short sale, *Grant's* has never—not in 25 years—had a constructive thing to say about the S&P 500. Some day, we're going to astonish people.

It wasn't false modesty that led me to choose to word "observer" for the banner of my 12-page journal, rather than, say, "soothsayer" or "prophet." The truth is that I can't forecast interest rates, and neither can many other people. Yet the temptation to forecast is ever-present, for the only thing the world really seems to want to know about the not-inherently fascinating subject of interest rates is, "Where are they headed?" Where they have been is a legitimate field of study (the late Sidney Homer wrote a superb, non-best-seller on the subject) but it is not one calculated to bring its devotees fame or fortune. Though I have tried to hold fast to the founding observational principle, *Grant's* wasn't in business for nine months before I gave in to temptation. It was the spring of 1984, and the bond market was in a shambles. Long-dated Treasury securities were offered for sale at a yield of almost 14%. To the 21st century generation of savers, who have had to accustom themselves to pygmy interest rates, such a return is unimaginable. What was the catch? The catch was the deep-rooted memory of 35 years of mainly adverse returns in the fixed-income markets. Bond yields had been going up—bond prices had been going down—with only irregular intervals of relief since the spring of 1946.

Since the late 19th century, rates have tended to rise or fall in generation-length cycles. Thus, in round numbers of years, they fell in the last quarter of the 19th century and rose in the first quarter of the 20th century. They fell until 1946 and, for the next 35 years, zigzagged higher. At the end of that long trek, the prime rate topped 20% and 30-year U.S. Treasurys fetched almost 15%. Nobody had ever seen the likes of it.

Those Alpine peaks in rates coincided with the Great Inflation of 1970s, and, though the inflation receded, the fear of inflation persisted. The Consumer Price index registered an increase of

14.8% in March 1980. Four years later, it was rising by just a little over 4%. But many doubted that inflation was whipped or, in a social democracy, ever could be. As if to anticipate a return to double-digit price increases, the market pushed bond yields up almost to 14%. That an equity-like return was available on government bonds at a time of moderating inflation was, from the strict efficient-markets standpoint, impossible. Yet it happened. It seems that Mr. Market was watching his own long and scary shadow, not taking a clinical view of the future. To many who had lived through the interminable postwar bear market in bonds, these high-yielding Treasurys were not God's gift, but, rather, as the saying went, "certificates of confiscation." *Grant's*, screwing up its courage and violating its self-imposed mission to observe interest rates but not to predict them, urged "Buy bonds." And that was as good as our career in interest-rate prophecy ever got.

These essays span years of even greater mispricing and grosser miscalculation than those served up in the 1984 bond market. The curtain rises on the technology-stock bubble of the late 1990s and falls on the worldwide mortgage and credit debacle of the late 2000s. In between came the bankruptcies of Enron and World-Com, the dissolution of the accounting firm of Arthur Andersen, the ignition of economic growth in the so-called emerging markets, the reignition of the bull stock market, the debut of the euro, the changing of the guard at the Federal Reserve, the seeding of what would prove to be the credit and mortgage crisis of 2007–08 and the worst residential real estate market in memory (i.e., one's grandfather's memory).

Curiously, these millennial scenes of financial miscalculation took place at a time of bounding worldwide prosperity. "The entire human race is getting rich, at historically unprecedented rates," Robert E. Lucas, a Nobel Prize-winning economist, declared in a 2003 address before the Federal Reserve Bank of Minneapolis. "I have said that total world production has been growing at over 4% since 1960. Compare this to annual growth rates of 2.4% for the first 60 years of the 20th century, of 1% for the entire 19th century, of one-third of 1% for the 18th century." And global growth was accelerating even as Lucas was speaking. By 2006, according to the International Monetary Fund, world GNP was expanding by 5%. Nor did the rising rate of growth tell the whole bullish story. With the annexation of China, India and the former captive states of Eastern Europe into the world economy, faster growth was occurring on a larger base than ever before.

Only once before in modern times had world growth been faster than the rates seen in the first decade of the new millennium, and that was in the early going of the 1970s. In 1970–73, planetary output in inflation-adjusted terms averaged 5.4% a year. It is interesting to contemplate the timing of this gust of prosperity. It took place during the transformation of the dollar from a gold-backed currency into a paper, or faith-based, one. In that day, as in our own, commodity prices were climbing, and inflation was on the rise. The sharpest increase in prices since the Korean War coincided with America's decision to stop exchanging dollar bills for gold at the $35-per-ounce statutory rate.

Financial markets exist to channel scarce capital into profitable outlets. If they can't distinguish true value from ersatz, what good are they? The answer, or one part of it, is that identifying a value-laden investment is easier said than done. What kind of value do you prefer? The value in plain sight, i.e., that registered on the balance sheet? Or the value in prospect, i.e., that projected by forecasts derived from profits recorded on the income statement? To the disciples of Benjamin Graham, value is all in the seeing, not the imagining. The future is a closed book, the value tribe asserts. To armor themselves against adverse contingencies, they strive to buy good assets at a steep discount from their inherent value—dollar bills for 50 cents, as the expression goes. This is the *Grant's* approach to investing. It exactly suits the temperament of the editor. Yet you can find professional investors, very rich ones, who have made their fortunes by figuratively buying dollar bills for $1.01, and up. Growth is their mantra. Value investors like growth, too. They're just not willing to pay for it.

Identifying true value is further complicated by the rules of financial score-keeping. The principles of accounting are not hard and fast. They are, in fact, remarkably subjective, even in so seemingly straightforward a matter as the totting up of a company's top line. They are still less certain when it comes to assigning a value to complex or infrequently traded debt securities (as so many have discovered to their cost during the continuing mortgage mess). What is revenue? When and how should it be recognized? What is net income? And what, pray tell, is a collateralized debt obligation? Even after the accountants have reckoned the value of these flows and structures, there remains the question of defining the unit in which the values is expressed. So, then, what is a dollar?

It's a testament to the world's abiding faith in the United States currency (despite its long-running depreciation against the euro and, indeed, most other monetary assets, from gold to the Iraqi dinar) that that question is so rarely asked. We know what the dollar used to be: It was a legally defined weight of gold. And we know that that it is not what it is today. The fact is that, today, the dollar is undefined and, like every other currency, uncollateralized. It is whatever Mr. Market says it is. That this piece of paper, or electronic impulse, of no intrinsic value is accepted the world over as a means of payment and a store of value must stand as one of the greatest, and most improbable, monetary achievements of all time.

The dollar is not the first currency to pass as good money the world over. But previous claimants to the title of the top global monetary brand had something behind them besides the expressed good intentions of the issuing central bank. The pound sterling, which ruled the roost from Napoleon to Hitler, was exchangeable into gold at the rate of £3.17s.9d. an ounce, or roughly £3.9 in contemporary terms. If you didn't trust the paper, you could demand the metal. Britain left the gold standard at the outbreak of World War I. It went back to gold in 1925 but gave it up, once and for all, in 1931. At this writing, an ounce of gold carries a price tag of £460.

The essence of the gold standard is the idea that in monetary affairs, too, the rule of law should apply. Money should be lawfully defined. The government that issues it should protect and defend that statutory value. A gold-standard country should balance its external accounts. No nation, however powerful, should be permitted to consume much more than it produces for years, or even decades, on end, as the United States has been privileged to do under the post-1971 non-gold standard.

To strike off a half-ton of new currency on a printing press takes no great skill. The history of inflation attests to it. Digging up gold out of the earth is a much harder proposition, which is exactly what commended the gold standard to our monetary forebears. Now, according to the consensus of enlightened economic opinion, the world has outgrown it. Far better for the government workers called central bankers to fix interest rates and/or to regulate the supply of new money and credit than to trust in the self-regulating and impersonal processes of the international gold standard. These modern ideas, however, I doubt, as the readers of these pages will soon see. In any case, on Aug. 15, 1971, President Richard M. Nixon pushed the world into the modern age by transforming the dollar into an uncollateralized piece of paper; the $35-per-ounce gold price at that moment was erased from the statute books. At this writing, the price is closer to $900. The gold price, in the *Grant's* view, is the reciprocal of the world's faith in the stewards of paper money. Late in the 1990s, as Greenspan was riding the crest of his popularity, less than $300 bought you an ounce. In March 2008, as the Fed-organized rescue of Bear Stearns took shape, the price topped $1,000.

What makes Mr. Market tick is a question to which I have devoted more than a quarter-century's rumination. And I believe I have hit on the answer. What makes him do what he does is his evident love of paradox. Every novice investor comes face-to-face with this essential truth when, to his surprise and disappointment, his favorite stock seems not to rally on good news but—all too frequently—to sink. "The news was in the price," a wise head will explain to him. So known facts are not worth knowing; it's the undiscovered truths that make you rich.

Paradox is a motive force in central banking, too. Imagine an economy at room temperature, a perfect 72 degrees: Low interest rates, high profit margins, full employment, contained inflation, moderate growth, accessible credit, rock-solid faith in the currency. Here is a central banker's idea of paradise. And it might be paradise, too, except for the human beings who inhabit it.

Basking in this radiant setting, profit-seeking individuals would proceed to ruin it. They would build factories, houses, offices, shopping centers and securities portfolios. Many would finance their acquisitions with borrowed money. The most confident and aggressive would use little besides borrowed money. After all, we have assumed that debt is cheap and the sky is blue. Trusting the Fed to smooth out the financial or macroeconomic rough patches, people would incur an extra increment of risk. Into this pellucid air, great towers of debt would start to rise.

Not everyone would see them. And the few who did see and warn against them would no doubt speak too soon—I have had some experience along these lines—and their warnings would go unheeded. Professional investors would certainly see the growing risks in excessive leverage. Of all people, they understand the tendency of profit margins and equity valuations, for example, not to keep getting wider and lusher but, eventually, to snap back to the their long-term averages. Capitalism itself obviates the possibility of any "new era" of permanent, uninterrupted, above-trend profitability. Over-large profit margins fetch up new competition, and new competition tightens profit margins. Yet these knowing professional investors have jobs to keep. The Cassandra industry is not so remunerative as the hedge fund business, so the professional investors and bankers stay in the race, taking the kinds of risks that their better judgment tells them to avoid.

"What have I learned in life? I have learned this:
If you are down by 70%, then up by 70%,
you have not broken even."

The Federal Reserve seeks—above all things—stable prices
in a growing and dynamic economy. But capitalism is an unstable form of economic organization. Invention itself is disruptive. Prices tend to fall as the cost of production falls, or when
new regions of the world are opened to productive enterprise.
The last quarter of the 19th century was one such era of innovation and expansion. The time in which we are privileged to live is
another. In the closing decades of the 19th century, average prices
fell because the cost of production declined. But no such drop in
prices has been allowed to occur in America around the turn of
the 21st century. Bernanke, joined by Greenspan, served notice
in 2002–03 that the Fed would not suffer falling prices. Indeed,
they promised to counter any sag in the price level by printing up
the requisite volumes of inflationary dollars. Bernanke colorfully
vowed to drop scrip out of helicopter doors, if necessary, to keep
the specter of deflation (as he called it) at bay. In fact, no heli-

copters were launched, but the Fed did push down the federal funds rate to a level not seen since the dollar was exchangeable into gold at $35 to the ounce.

Just as the Fed intended, the American price level did not sag but resumed its familiar upward creep. However, as the Fed did not apparently intend, a gigantic bubble of mortgage debt inflated. To a degree, the mortgage bubble was itself an offshoot of the digital revolution. It would take an army of clerks to collect, sort and service the hundreds of thousands of individual mortgages that constitute the typical residential mortgage-backed security. Computers make it easy. And it would take a pretty persuasive salesman to put across the dubious proposition that, structured just so, $1 billion of subprime mortgages could assay $800 million of triple-A rated MBS. Armed with a computer, however, Wall Street's quants persuaded investors the world over that just this alchemy was attainable. *Grant's* refused to believe it, and we went on an analytical crusade to enlighten a credulous and ill-served world (you'll find a sample of this output in the chapter headed "Mortgage science projects"). If we'd had 100,000 or so additional subscribers, we might have made a difference to the macroeconomic outcome. As it was, the alchemists brought high finance low.

The shocking breakdown in ratings and risk management on Wall Street during the mortgage bubble (the worst such performance "ever" in the judgment of the Swiss banking giant UBS) dealt hundreds of billions of dollars worth of losses worldwide and badly rattled the American financial system. Economists and bankers pronounced the dislocations the most severe since the Great Depression, a judgment as curious as it was chilling. Depression-like financial strains had surfaced without a confirmed recession, let alone a Hoover-scale collapse. It wasn't Mr. Market's finest hour.

Then, again, the best investors don't waste their breath deploring the foibles of this erratic man. Rather, they pounce on the opportunities he presents to them. Mispriced assets—absurdly low or farcically high—are the old gentleman's gift to the patient opportunist. John Paulson, president of Paulson & Co., who made more in 2007 by anticipating the mortgage mess than Rwanda earned in gross domestic product, reminded attendees at the Spring 2008 *Grant's* Conference that the secret to generating outsized returns lies in investing when Mr. Market is most unhinged, either giddy or inconsolable. Paulson himself had sold the ears off the mortgage market when there was little to lose and—as his results duly showed—a fortune to gain if only common sense prevailed. Eventually, Paulson told the crowd, he expected to have the opportunity to buy the same kind of mortgage detritus he had so successfully sold short. But the time was not yet ripe: "We're nowhere near the bottom," he said.

One of my favorite opportunists was the co-founder and guiding light of Teledyne, the 1960s-era conglomerate. His name was Henry Singleton. An MIT-trained electrical engineer, Singleton made his mark as a deployer of capital. He did what we all should do, that is, to buy when Mr. Market is selling and to sell when Mr. Market is buying. Singleton did well what so many corporate managements today do badly: When Teledyne shares were richly valued, he used them as a currency with which to make acquisitions. But when the cycle turned and the shares got cheap, he repurchased and retired them. Tendering for his company's own stock between 1972 and 1984, as you will see for yourself in the first chapter of this collection, he reduced the Teledyne share count by 90%. Singleton took no options awards and bought his own stock with his own money. He sold none of his personal holdings. A model capitalist, indeed!

So let the theorists of market efficiency publish their tracts. Mr. Market takes no notice of them. Buying high and selling low, losing his head at the top of the market and his nerve at the bottom, he is Every Man. He invites us to become rich at his expense. May these essays help a relative few, at least, to take him up on his offer.

I am the founder and editor of *Grant's*, and its rewrite man besides, but it would be a meager publication without our superb staff. Ian McCulley and Dan Gertner contribute financial analysis and investment ideas. Hank Blaustein draws the cartoons that decorate our pages (and these) and Ruth Hlavacek edits the copy. Del Coleman, John McCarthy and Eric Whitehead oversee circulation, computer design and office operations, respectively. Adam Rowe conducts historical research, and John D'Alberto handles the telemarketing. I wish to thank, as well, the analysts who contributed so much to *Grant's* in its earlier years. They include Jay Diamond, Ken Shirley, Joshua Kahn, Peter Walmsley, Rose Ann Tortora and Eric Fry. Sue Egan, who ran the office and managed the conferences for more than 10 years, has embarked a well-deserved retirement. I thank her and her immediate successor, Susan Lhota.

And what would a book be without its publisher? I am grateful, indeed, to Axios Press, and to Emma Sweeney, Hunter Lewis, and Jody Banks for making it seem to work so effortlessly.

Chapter One
Gallery of the Immortals

First There Was J. Pierpont Morgan

April 9, 1999

THE MARCH 30 edition of *The Wall Street Journal*, with its unique page one makeup and exultant "Dow 10,000" headline, fairly jumped off the newsstands, and the quotes of the bullish equity strategists almost leapt off the page. "Top American corporations will command even higher valuations in the future," said one, "because they constantly reinvent themselves." "What price do you want to pay for a Matisse?" he asked.

Henry Clay Frick, turn-of-the-century steel titan, earlier compared another financial asset to the works of a different Old Master. "Rembrandts of investment," pronounced Frick, referring to railroad bonds. Although mistaken about the senior securities of a fast-maturing industry, Frick did die rich.

"But while stocks never before have been so richly valued," wrote a reporter in the same *Wall Street Journal* Collector's Edition, "neither has the U.S. ever enjoyed so long a period of economic growth with declining inflation."

Possibly, the writer did not remember the last three decades of the 19th century, when the annual rate of growth in real GNP averaged some 3.83%, and the consumer price index registered an average annual decline of 0.87%.

The perfect antidote to the suggestible millennial press is the wonderful new biography of J.P. Morgan, *Morgan: American Financier* by Jean Strouse (Random House, 796 pages, $34.95 at retail). Morgan's life is testament to the importance and inevitability of financial and economic cycles, as well as to the possibility of becoming very rich while spending half the year in Europe collecting art. A Morgan partnership in the late 19th century was almost regarded as a death sentence, Strouse relates, so overworked were the principals at 23 Wall Street. Yet Morgan somehow managed to find the time to run the firm, rescue the credit of the United States, reorganize the railroads that had issued too many "Rembrandts," create trusts, intervene to stop recurrent financial panics and, yet, to organize his personal life in such a way that his second wife and he were not often together on the same continent, let alone under the same roof.

"What's really driving the market is peace," another brokerage-house employee was quoted in the March 30 *Journal*. "Nobody's talking about the peace dividend."

The United States was at peace from the close of the Civil War, in 1865, to the start of the Spanish-American War, 1898 (which lasted only about as long as a modern bear market). Yet, over that span of years, creative destruction raged, panics swirled and interests clashed. Feckless and overleveraged optimists periodically came to grief, low interest rates and the absence of a federal income tax notwithstanding.

There was no central bank in those years, either, but Morgan, de facto, almost seemed to fill the office himself. Even before he played Atlas in the Panic of 1907, he was widely viewed as the

"J.P. Morgan dresses down."

indispensable man. In 1902, when Morgan was 65, the historian Henry Adams wondered "What would happen if some morning he woke up dead?"

The year of Morgan's death, 1913, was also the year of the passage of the Federal Reserve Act. "The king is dead...," a perceptive New York banker wrote of Morgan's passing. "There are no cries of 'Long live the king,' for the general verdict seems to be that there will be no other king; that Mr. Morgan, typical of the time in which he lived, can have no successor, for we are facing other days."

Now they say, "Thank God for Alan Greenspan," and many wonder what would become of the charmed stock market if the chairman left office (his term expires in 2000). What followed Morgan's death was unimagined change. A peaceful Edwardian world went to war, governments formerly limited in their taxing power became rapacious, a gold standard turned to paper and the Rembrandts of investment (which, in truth, had been in a bear market since the turn of the century) went on depreciating. History is bigger than individuals, and there is no permanent high plateau of prosperity. On a more hopeful note (now we are thinking of Asia), there is also no permanent low plateau of depression.

Emulate Henry Singleton

February 28, 2003

Something went haywire with American capitalism in the 1990s, and we think we know what it was. There weren't enough Henry E. Singletons to go around. In truth, there was only one Singleton, and he died in 1999. He could read a book a day and play chess blindfolded. He made pioneering contributions to the development of inertial navigation systems. He habitually bought low and sold high. The study of such a protean thinker and doer is always worthwhile. Especially is it valuable today, a time when the phrase "great capitalist" has almost become an oxymoron.

Singleton, longtime chief executive of Teledyne Inc., was one of the greatest of modern American capitalists. Warren Buffett, quoted in John Train's *The Money Masters,* published in 1980, virtually crowned him king. "Buffett," Train reported, "considers that Henry Singleton of Teledyne has the best operating and capital deployment record in American business."

A recent conversation with Leon Cooperman, the former Goldman Sachs partner turned portfolio manager (he's the managing general partner of Omega Partners), was the genesis of this essay. It happened in this fashion: Cooperman was flaying a certain corporate management for having repurchased its shares at a high price only to reissue new shares at a low price. He said that this was exactly the kind of thing that Singleton never did, and he lamented how little is known today of Singleton's achievements as a capital deployer, value appraiser and P/E-multiple arbitrageur. Then he reached in his file and produced a reprint of a critical *Business Week* cover story on Teledyne. Among the alleged missteps for which Singleton was attacked was his heavy purchase of common stocks. The cover date was May 31, 1982, 10 weeks before the blastoff of the intergalactic bull market.

The wonder of Singleton's life and works is the subject under consideration—admittedly, a biographical subject, as opposed to a market-moving one. We chose it because Singleton's genius encompassed the ability to make lemonade out of lemons, a skill especially valuable now that lemons are so thick underfoot.

Singleton was born in 1916 on a small farm in Haslet, Texas. He began his college education at the U.S. Naval Academy but finished it at M.I.T., earning three degrees in electrical engineering: bachelor's and master's degrees in 1940, and a doctorate in 1950. In 1939, he won the William Lowell Putnam Intercollegiate Mathematics Competition Award. In World War II, he served in the Office of Strategic Services. At Litton Industries, in the early 1950s, he began his fast climb up the corporate ladder: By 1957, he was a divisional director of engineering. In 1960, with George Kozmetsky, he founded Teledyne.

Anyone who was not reading *The Wall Street Journal* in the 1960s and 1970s missed the most instructive phase of Singleton's career. When the Teledyne share price was flying, as it was in the 1960s, the master used it as a currency with which to make acquisitions. He made about 130. Many managements have performed this trick; Singleton, however, had another: When the cycle turned and Teledyne shares were sinking, he repurchased them. Between 1972 and 1984, he tendered eight times, reducing the share count (from high to low) by some 90%. Many managements have subsequently performed the share-repurchase trick, too, but few have matched the Singleton record, either in terms of market timing or fair play. Singleton repurchased stock when the price was down, not when it was up (in the 1990s, such icons as GE, IBM, AOL

Time Warner, Cendant and, of course, Tyco paid up—and up). He took no options awards, according to Cooperman, and he sold not one of his own shares. Most pertinently to the current discussion of "corporate governance," he didn't sell when the company was buying (another popular form of managerial self-enrichment in the 1990s).

The press called him "enigmatic" because he pursued policies that, until the mists of the market lifted, appeared inexplicable. For example, at the end of the titanic 1968–74 bear market, he identified bonds as the "high-risk asset" and stocks as the low-risk asset. Accordingly, he directed the Teledyne insurance companies to avoid the former and accumulate the latter. To most people, stocks were riskier, the proof of which was the havoc they had wreaked on their unlucky holders during the long liquidation.

Some were vexed that, for years on end, Teledyne paid no dividend. The master reasoned that the marginal dollar of corporate cash was more productive on the company's books than in the shareholders' pockets, and he was surely correct in that judgment. Teledyne's stable of companies (many in defense-related lines, others in specialty metals, offshore drilling, insurance and finance, electronics and consumer products, including Water-Pik) generated consistently high margins and high returns on equity and on assets.

Singleton made his mistakes, and Teledyne's portfolio companies made theirs. A catalog of some of these errors, as well as not a few triumphs misclassified as errors, appeared in the *Business Week* story. We linger over this 21-year-old piece of journalism because it illustrates an eternal truth of markets, especially of markets stretched to extreme valuations. The truth is that, at such cyclical junctures, doing the wrong thing looks like the right thing, and vice versa. In the spring of 1982, few business strategies appeared more wrongheaded to the majority of onlookers than buying the ears off the stock market.

On the *BW* cover, the handsome Singleton was portrayed as Icarus in a business suit, flying on frail wings of share certificates and dollar bills. The article conceded that the master had done a pretty fair job for the shareholders, and it acknowledged that the share repurchases had worked out satisfactorily—to date. They had, in fact, boosted per-share earnings "and also enabled Singleton, who held on to his own Teledyne shares, to amass 7.8% of the company's stock." He was the company's largest shareholder and its founding and indispensable brain.

Yet the magazine was not quite satisfied, for it perceived that Singleton had lost his way. For starters, it accused him of having no business plan. And he seemed not to have one. He believed, as he later explained at a Teledyne annual meeting, in engaging an uncertain world with a flexible mind: "I know a lot of people have very strong and definite plans that they've worked out on all kinds of things, but we're subject to a tremendous number of outside influences and the vast majority of them cannot be predicted. So my idea is to stay flexible." To the *BW* reporter he explained himself more simply: "My only plan is to keep coming to work every day" and "I like to steer the boat each day rather than plan ahead way into the future."

This improvisational grand design the magazine saw as the "milking" of tried-and-true operating businesses and the diverting of funds to allow the chairman to "play" the stock market. A *BW* reader could imagine Singleton as a kind of Nero watching Rome burn while talking on the phone with his broker. He didn't invest in businesses, the magazine suggested, only in pieces of paper. He either managed too little (as with the supposedly aging and outmoded operating companies) or too much (as with the insurance businesses, where, according to *BW*, he managed to no great effect). His reserve was "icy."

Singleton's disdain for the press was complete and thoroughgoing: The *BW* article just rolled off his back. It puzzled him that his friend Cooperman would bother to draft a nine-page rebuttal, complete with statistical exhibits. Why go to the trouble? Cooperman, who has fire where Singleton had ice, wanted the magazine to know that, during the acquisitive 1960s, Teledyne's sales and net income had climbed to about $1.3 billion and $58.1 million, respectively, from "essentially zero," and that during the non-acquisitive 1970s, profit growth had actually accelerated (with net income of the 100%-owned operating businesses rising sixfold).

As for those share repurchases, Cooperman underscored an achievement that appears even more laudable from the post-bubble perspective than it did at the time. "Just as Dr. Singleton recognized [that] he had an unusually attractive stock to trade with in the 1960s," wrote Cooperman, "he developed the belief that the company's shares were undervalued in the 1970s. In the period 1971–1980, you correctly point out that the company repurchased approximately 75% of its shares. What you did not point out is that despite the stock's 32% drop from its all-time high reached in mid-1981 to the time of your article, the stock price remains well above the highest price paid by the company (and multiples above the average price paid) in this ten-year period." And what Cooperman did not point out was that none of these repurchases was earmarked for the mopping up of shares issued to management. He did not point that out, probably, because the infamous abuses of options issuance still lay in the future.

Business Week, however, was right when it observed that nothing lasts forever and that Singleton couldn't manage indefinitely. In 1989, he formally relinquished operating control of the company he founded (and, by then, owned 13.2% of). Even then it was obvious that the 1990s were not going to be Teledyne's decade. Appended to *The Wall Street Journal*'s report on Singleton's withdrawal from operations was this disapproving note: "The company hasn't said in the past what it plans to do. It doesn't address analyst groups or grant many interviews. Teledyne's news releases and stockholder reports are models of brevity. Some securities analysts have given up following the company because they can't get enough information." Imagination cannot conjure a picture of Singleton on CNBC.

The dismantling of Teledyne began in 1990 with the spin-off of the Unitrin insurance unit (later came the sale of Argonaut, another insurance subsidiary). Singleton resigned the chairmanship in 1991, at the age of 74. Presently, the financial results slipped, the defense businesses were enveloped in scandal and Teledyne itself was stalked as a takeover candidate. Surveying the troubles that came crowding in on the company after the master's departure (and—unhappily for the defense industry—after the fall of the Berlin Wall), *Forbes* magazine remarked: "For many years Henry Singleton disproved the argument that conglomerates don't work. But it turns out Teledyne was more of a tribute to Singleton than to the concept."

In retirement, Singleton raised cattle and became one of the country's biggest landowners. He played tournament chess. "Most recently," according to a tribute published shortly after his death (of brain cancer, at age 82), "he devoted much time to computers, programming algorithms and creating a fine computer game of backgammon. . . ."

To those not attuned to the nuances of corporate finance, Singleton's contribution appeared mainly to concern the technique of share repurchases. Thus (as an obituary in the *Los Angeles Times* had it), Teledyne was the forerunner to the white-hot growth stocks of the Clinton bubble, including Tyco International and Cendant. Singleton knew better. To Cooperman, just before he died, the old conglomerateur confided his apprehension. Too many companies were doing these stock buybacks, he said. There must be something wrong with them.

Inside Isaac's Head

March 12, 2004

"We had a genuine debacle in the portfolio, which cost us 200 basis points last month." In such a confessional vein begins the year-end report to investors of Arbiter Partners, a $45 million hedge fund managed, part time, by Paul J. Isaac. The discussion of the two percentage points of calamity occupies more than 25% of a letter that stretches to 21 pages. Yet, news of the 2003 return to investors fills just one paragraph. "Obviously," writes Isaac of the year's investment performance, "these returns bear no resemblance whatever to the likely long-term returns of Arbiter and should be taken as random good fortune, if not an indication of the risk of future sub-normal returns." For the year, the partnership was ahead by 133%.*

What manner of investor would dwell on a trifle while passing lightly over a triumph? Before delving into this mystery, we have an interest to declare: Isaac is a fast friend and longtime business associate. The unfolding essay may be many things, but it is unlikely to be objective. At least, it is unlikely to be so clinically objective as Isaac is about himself.

How would he appraise his own fund, he was asked the other day, if it were one of the several hundred hedge funds he checks up on every year in his capacity as fund-of-funds analyst for Cadogan Management, in New York? "The manager is entertaining and opportunistic," he writes of the man named Isaac, "but he is spreading himself too thin even for an opportunistic manager." As for the fund itself, with its heavy concentration of illiquid securities and its multitasking general partner, it falls squarely in the "three-F" bracket—a "friends, family and fools fund." Most definitely, while wearing his Cadogan hat, Isaac would not hire Isaac.

---

* Arbiter Partners returned 40.3% to its investors in 2004, 34.9% in 2005, 37.6% in 2006, 75.4% in 2007 and 12.3% through May 2008. Altogether, a brilliant run.

As for that 200 basis points of loss, they will serve as our portal into the investment portion of Isaac's head. The loss stemmed from Parmalat, in which Arbiter had purchased a small equity position. When the price doubled, Isaac chose not to sell, but to wait until the shares qualified for long-term capital gains treatment. However, before they could reach the IRS finish line, it came to light that Parmalat was not entirely truthful about its finances. "I wish I could say it will never happen to a larger position," Isaac confesses, "but I can't."

In retrospect, it is obvious that Parmalat was crooked enough to meet itself coming around a corner. In prospect, it was not so clear, and it is this fact that most concerns Isaac—and ought to concern us all. The company's capital structure may now seem incriminatingly complex, he observes, "but most firms Parmalat's size, especially with extensive Third World holdings, have complicated arrays of subsidiaries. . . ." Parmalat supposedly had $5 billion of cash and securities. "That seemed a very large amount," Isaac notes, "but given large operations in countries subject to exchange control and exit taxes, such as Brazil and Argentina, and the company's supposed propensity for buying back its own debt, it seemed peculiar but not especially worrisome."

Also forestalling suspicion was Parmalat's bond rating (investment grade, by a hair) and the fact that the company "had undertaken numerous recent bond issues through several well-regarded underwriters, each of whom would presumably have done their own due diligence on basic financial and reporting issues. Both the bond ratings and the audits were reviewed in the aftermath of the heightened sensitivity engendered by the Enron and WorldCom scandals."

As the bad news broke, the stock plummeted to about Arbiter's cost. Isaac, who was abroad, reasoned that the banks would try to avoid bankruptcy and that there was probably enough value in the business and on the balance sheet to support the common. So he kept the stock. "Worse," he admits, "when the bonds plummeted to the mid-40s, and I could buy a questionably senior status convertible issue at under 40 cents per dollar of claim, with some incremental upside under a favorable scenario, I committed an additional 120 basis points of capital to buy some."

As the full scope of the fraud emerged, Isaac sold the bonds and marked the common to zero. It only remained to commit to paper the lessons learned, including:

1. Nothing is an absolute protection against fraud. Ironically, fraud is often associated with smoother surface appearances and higher valuations than prevailed with Parmalat....

2. When there are incomprehensible reasons for unusual business practices, e.g., Parmalat's purported concurrent maintenance of large liquidity and debt balances . . . the valuation needs to be truly compelling and the justification credible....

3. There is a reason foreign situations need to be a lot cheaper than American opportunities and not all foreign countries deserve the same haircut....

4. Arbiter is a concentrated fund. . . . Our three largest positions are 20%, 11% and 10% of capital, respectively. I don't believe any of them could be frauds, but I was shocked by Parmalat as well. All three started out as 200–400 basis-point positions and reached their large current size via appreciation; but it wouldn't hurt any less if we lost it all from this level as opposed to the initial cash outlay. In general, going forward, I will be less inclined to let something run much past 10% of the fund's NAV, no matter how much I like it, for just that reason.

Isaac thanks his limited partners in advance for the sympathy and encouragement they are certain to shower on him—after all, despite Parmalat, December was a profitable month and the year was one for the record books. However, he needs no shoulder to cry on, but rather a moment of introspection: He is checking himself for signs of the hubris that often accompanies feats of money-making.

"All corporations, especially large complex ones," the letter goes on, "are subject to considerable risk of retroactive adverse restatement of earnings or balance-sheet re-characterization." The name Isaac gives to this predilection is "corporate accounting bulimia," and its increasing incidence has an important implication for investing. It means, says Isaac, that investors should prefer known accounting sinners that have confessed their faults to "those organizations of business genius whose marathon water walks are the wonder of adoring *Business Week* profiles."

Many are the hedge-fund managers who would have stopped writing after the incandescent phrase "up 133%," but Isaac instead ranges far and wide. Valuation is one of his best subjects. "I leaf through *Value Line* occasionally," he writes. "I am struck by the number of very good companies, many of which have continued to grow, albeit at reduced rates, which managed to hit very high valuations 5 to 15 years ago and are still below those peak quotations." Berkshire Hathaway, before its 2004 lift-off, was selling at a price not much higher than the $80,000 seen in 1998.

"Please contemplate that for a moment," Isaac bids us. "One could have invested directly in Warren Buffett, the pre-beatified 'greatest investor ever,' at a time, one might add, when it was foolish to assume he could have more than 15-20 years remaining in his career, and still have zero returns over five years, including dividends (of which there were none). Moreover, this occurred when Buffett was widely see as on a roll. . . ."

Or consider Coca-Cola, "the greatest brand name extant," trading down to $50 a share from $85 in 1998. At its peak price, Isaac reminds his partners, Coke was selling for almost 50 times earnings: "Therefore, a 45% decline in the share price over six years has only been offset by cumulative earnings equal to less than 14% of the peak share price, or less than a third of the price drop. A company purchased at 10 times earnings which suffered a similar depreciation would have had cumulative earnings equal to about 130% of the price decline. At some point, either the

Employee of the Month

growth of the cheaper company's per share equity or the profit growth from its reinvestments or repurchases of shares would be likely to either stanch the stock's decline or lay the groundwork for a renewed advance."

Such reasoning often meets with the objection that you get what you pay for: A cigar butt at 10 times earnings fails to measure up to a growth stock at 40 or 50 times earnings, people will say. It falls short in terms of franchise value, business prospects and rates of internal reinvestment. Isaac disputes such a rule. However, just for the sake of argument, he is prepared to concede that the Cokes of the world do have attributes unmatched by the typical value stock. Still, he writes, "I doubt that their characteristics are superior by a factor of four to five times."

Isaac is an investment generalist, and Arbiter is an eclectic hedge fund. It buys long and sells short, deals in foreign as well as domestic markets and traffics in bonds and options and equities. With Isaac, therefore, it is never so simple as being bullish or bearish. One must always ask him, "On what?" With that said, he reports that he is "starting to set up bear weighted trades in big-cap, very expensive, growth-type names," taking care not to overpay. This is especially advisable on the short side of the market, he advises, because the world has a way of not coming to an end. The so-called unsustainable economic imbalances that are supposedly going to knock the market for a loop have a way of being sustained. On form, they are sustained for at least as long as one's puts have to run.

Though not a professional bear, Isaac has the characteristic tenacity of the most successful short sellers. In 2001, its first year, Arbiter was down by 7%. It was down by 6% in 2002. From inception through September 2002, it was down by more than 30%. All of which was mere scene-setting for last year's stupendous gain. "The volatility in adverse markets was too high," writes Isaac, rapping himself on the knuckles.

However, the general partner is not unreasonable. He is prepared to draw a distinction between a permanent and temporary loss: "Parmalat was especially galling because it entailed over 200 basis points of definitive, absolute and irrecoverable loss"—he might as well have burnt the money in the backyard grill. But, as Isaac proceeds, "We actually 'lost' twice as much in December from a 10-point plunge in Millicom shares, which I contemplate with relative equanimity. We were holding the shares for good reason; I think the company trades inexpensively relative to the market and its comparables, and the underlying business continues to grow. That is not a definitive loss and I assess its likelihood of being permanent as low."

If Isaac played baseball, Millicom International Cellular (MICC) is the kind of home run that would cast him under suspicion of steroid use. Alas, he tells *Grant's*, there aren't many Millicoms around just now. "[T]o the extent you do find opportunities," he says, "they are historically reasonable companies, often reasonably good companies at historically reasonable P/Es." The trouble with reasonably valued investments is that they are priced to deliver reasonable returns. One puts them together in a portfolio with the hope of beating a certain hurdle rate—in Isaac's case, 15% a year. Which means, absent the occasional Millicom, one must have a pretty high rate of being right. Isaac says he liked it better when he was collecting a bunch of "positive sum lottery tickets," the kind of orphaned securities that littered the ground in the summer and fall of 2002, for example (when, to judge by his monthly returns, Isaac was fast going out of business).

However, one must take the world as it is. What is Isaac doing about it? He is investing more overseas, in Japan and South Korea (but not in China, because, he says, he doesn't know where to put his money). Domestically, he's bullish on health care and biotech, but is leaving the stock selection to Dan DeClue (*Grant's*, October 24). He is bullish, too, on oil- and gas-exploration and production companies, a group that Mr. Market refuses to warm to. He mentions Devon Energy, quoted at four times cash flow and seven times run-rate earnings. Not a bad price, says Isaac, for a company that "has grown its compounded cash flow per share on a three-year trailing average of 20% a year over the past 15 years through a wide variety of oil markets. It seems to me a very financially disciplined management; I don't see why they're going to start getting stupid all of a sudden."

The favorite flavor in the S&P 500 this season is financial, with banks, credit-card companies, mortgage purveyors, etc. carrying a 21.7% index weighting (information technology, yesteryear's darling, is second with 16.8%, followed by health care with 13.5%). Isaac does not share the excitement. Financial companies are dealers in debt. And debt, though an indispensable institution, cannot continue to grow "infinitely relative to the income stream that supports it. We have a very large stock of private debt. It cannot grow indefinitely at a much faster rate than the aggregate of after-tax incomes."

One important spur to the growth of indebtedness has been the tumble in nominal interest rates; the lower the cost of borrowing, the more that can be borrowed. But Isaac is a doubter about rates continuing to trend lower: "I think they will trend higher over time."

Rising rates per se may or may not be bearish for the run-of-the-mill financial institution. However, a narrowing in the spread between the rates a lender charges and the rates it pays, after operating costs, would certainly be bearish. Bearish in a subtler way is the ever-plunging cost of communications and data processing. As technology improves, Isaac proposes, geographic barriers to lending fall. "Ergo," he goes on, "one would expect competitive spreads to diminish." For now, net spreads are "maintained by aggressive cost-cutting, improvements in liability management, more aggressive balance sheets and growth in lending, including to lower-quality credits." But these things can be pushed only so far. "I question whether these trends haven't been largely exploited and, therefore, competitive pressures are likely to press on aggregate lenders' profits going forward. That, in turn, means that they can't, in the aggregate, grow, which, in turn, should compress their multiples. Taken to an extreme, financials should shrink as a portion of the indices. In a flat market, that could well imply an extended period of little or no appreciation. I therefore prefer consolidatees rather than consolidators."

It was Isaac who, at the top of the gold-stock bull market in 1987, contributed a satirical piece to *Grant's* suggesting that someone ought to just bury some bullion, call it a gold mine ("Golden Recycle" was the suggested name) and do an IPO at the then sky-high valuations. So it is no gold bug who last week said, "I think gold is very interesting here." By "very," Isaac says he meant a future price two to five times higher than today's $400 "under a scenario of people becoming progressively worried about a generally reflationary climate." This is for the future, however. Isaac says that the idea is yet unimplemented.

At the Bank of Graham and Dodd

February 11, 2005

The prior issue of *Grant's* featured a bearish critique of Commerce Bancorp of New Jersey, the hell-bent-for-election outfit headed by Vernon W. Hill II. Now unfolding is a bullish review of Monroe County Bank of Forsyth, Ga., an institution in no particular hurry, which is owned and chaired by Karl B. Hill. Possibly no two banking Hills have ever had less to talk about than the unrelated Vernon and Karl. Then again, Karl is a banking industry original. His remarkable success owes less to adherence to present-day ideas than to the business-building philosophy associated with George F. Baker (1840–1931), guiding light of the old First National Bank of New York. As a banker, Baker emphasized securities operations over lending and wealth creation over earnings growth (never mind stair-step, perfectly predictable earnings growth to please the analysts). Baker, like Karl Hill, often stumped the federal examiners who tried to understand his business.

Inconveniently for his admirers, Hill owns every share of the Country Bank Co. (CBC), and CBC, a one-bank holding company, owns every share of the Monroe County Bank (MCB). So a bull on the bank must be content to be platonically bullish. A few *Grant's* readers may believe that an investment analysis without an appended ticker symbol or CUSIP number is no analysis, merely a word salad. However, if ideas are a prerequisite to success, Hill, a fount of unconventional thought and action, is a worthy object of study. Just before Christmas, he committed his ideas to writing in an essay entitled, "Out Of Step In Banking: One Bank Holding Company And Its Subsidiary Bank."

Many will wish they had been out of step in the ways enumerated by the essayist. Hill writes in a tone of ironic bewilderment. Why can't others figure out what he, an "aberrant rural redneck," has so profitably discovered? It's so easy! In recent years, Hill has bought

TIPS and euro-denominated bonds. He has invested in gold and gold-mining shares for his employees' pension fund. Now, in anticipation of rising interest rates, he is issuing long-maturity, fixed-rate CDs with heavy early-redemption penalties. In anticipation of rising loan losses, he is reducing the bank's loans (as a percentage of assets) and increasing its loan-loss reserves. And, in anticipation of a bust in the house-price boom, he is cutting back on residential real estate lending.

Hill, age 75, was graduated from the University of Chicago in 1949 and from the Harvard Law School in 1960. He holds master's degrees from Chicago (philosophy) and Harvard (social anthropology). He is a veteran of the U.S. Army. He was editor in chief (indeed, at the time, the only editor) of the Beacon Press, Boston, and an original functionary at the U.S. Department of Housing and Urban Development (newly established by President Lyndon B. Johnson in 1965). Early in 1968, Hill came home to Forsyth, 50 miles south of Atlanta, to take over the reins of the Monroe County Bank from his 86-year-old father. At the time, the bank, which was founded in 1908, had $4 million of deposits, $2 million in loans and $320,000 in equity. It was sinking. A dozen of its stockholders were all too happy to sell young Karl the 60% of the shares not already held in the Hill family.

Karl's first big idea was not to try to lend to the local textile barons but to seek out the business of "struggling, starting, risk-taking entrepreneurs." By 1999, six of the seven former textile mills had vanished, and two of the local banks that depended on them had sold out to regional banks. In that same year, Hill could claim banking dominance in the automobile-paint-and-body-shop, sawmill, building-supply-store and contractor-and-builder segment of the Forsyth economy. In 1999, the Monroe County Bank had $40 million in assets; now it has $82 million.

Today, the significantly understated tangible book value of bank and holding company together adds up to $14.7 million; over the past five years, it has grown at an average rate of 18.47%. Between

1999 and 2004, the little Monroe County Bank defined-contribution pension fund, which Hill himself manages, produced annual
compound returns of 37.6% (significantly enlarged by an up-208%
performance, paced by junior gold-mining stocks, in 2003). "I have
the investment advantage of not owning a television," is the country
banker's partial explanation for this singular investment success.*

Hill lives a life of ostentatious frugality. He drives a 1990 Lincoln
Town Car, dresses as if he had something else on his mind beside
his clothes and types his own letters on an electric typewriter,
pushing the margins all the way out to the edges of the pages so as
not to waste paper. He lives in the same house he bought when he
came back to town in 1968. Last summer marked a personal financial milestone, Hill relates, deadpan. For the first time, he felt "rich
enough to have carpenters come in and add a second bedroom."

Hill has made a profitable habit of not doing what others do,
and of doing what others couldn't imagine doing. For example,
after deciding to diversify out of the dollar, and persuading the
state bank regulators to let him, he proceeded to build the maximum non-dollar exposure allowed by law (i.e., 15% of equity
capital). This was in August 2003. It astonishes him that, as of
December 2004, not one of the other 271 state-regulated banks
in Georgia had applied to do the same. Similarly with the Treasury's inflation-protected securities, a.k.a. TIPS, which made
up the Monroe Bank's principal securities holding in 2002–03.
In this, too, Monroe appears to have been virtually alone. "The
distance in financial sophistication, and probably in financial
risk, between the vast majority of banks, and the few monster
nationwide banks, is huge; like the distance from one nebula to
another," he reflects.

---

* In June 2008, Karl Hill furnished this update: "Our bank's growth has been slow, but
our internally managed employee pension fund, invested in microcap mining stocks, has
achieved such dramatic investment gains that its size now almost equals the bank's stated
capital. . . . We hold no mark-to-model assets, no financial derivatives, no structured
mortgage tranches and not even any government agencies, only Treasurys for liquidity."

Hill is a thoughtful and prickly dissenter from almost everything that passes for orthodoxy in finance today. His departures from standard procedure run the gamut from investing at the holding-company level to lending at the bank level; from the duration of assets and liabilities to the proper level of loan-loss reserves. Not that he is infallibly contrary. He tried, but failed, to operate an MCB branch in a grocery store.

As an investor, Hill shows highly volatile returns, the kind that would cost him his job if he were running a hedge fund. In one five-year period, 1994–98, MCB's defined-contribution pension fund was down four years out of five. But over the past 10 years, according to unaudited results, it posted a compound annual return of 12% (before dividend reinvestment, the S&P 500 compounded at 10.2%). Hill invests in stocks, chiefly micro-caps.

Hill and the president of the bank, Bill Bazemore, are preparing for heavy weather. At 2.64%, loan-loss reserves are more than twice the average for state-chartered Georgia institutions. "Why?" Hill poses, and he answers his own question: "We feel the U.S. economy is in trouble, with major weaknesses and unpleasantness ahead. Whether inflation or deflation or some kind of both lies ahead, we believe many borrowers will be unable to repay their loans as scheduled, as a consequence of: Low or nonexistent net saving in the U.S., weakening household financial conditions, and starving industry for the main source of capital investment, savings; and, low capital investment in manufacturing capacity, with much of industry's investment in short-lived and rapidly depreciating software instead of longer-lived and slower depreciated capital equipment, and with the illusion that consumer binging on housing is 'investment.' With low capital investment few jobs are created, and bank borrowers need jobs to repay loans, and high paying jobs to repay loans at rising interest rates."

Hill, whose intellectual approach to banking and investment is to begin with a big idea and work his way down to smaller ideas, believes that a bear market in bonds began in the spring of 2003.

And he has acted on that conviction by reversing the usual practice of borrowing short and lending long; Monroe County Bank today tries to borrow long and lend short. As far as Hill knows, he is the only banker in the county to implement this strategy; as far as we know, he is the only banker in the country to do it.

The yield curve, though flattening, is still positively sloped, short rates being lower than long ones. To generate the maximum net interest margin, banks like Commerce and North Fork gather short-term, low-cost deposits. Hill, because he expects rates to rise, seeks out long-dated liabilities; 60% of his certificates of deposit run 3½ years or longer, "many of them seven or eight years, with the average remaining duration of all our CDs around four years." By the same reasoning, he regards short-dated assets as more desirable than long ones; he reports that 4.8% of Monroe County Bank's assets take the form of cash and deposits, 33.9% are in Treasury or agency securities maturing inside of one year and 55.4% are in loans, mainly short-term ones.

Hill is the first to admit that the long-liability, short-asset business model is an unhandy one. "It is far easier to get a short-term deposit than a longer one," he notes, "and far easier to get a long-term fixed-rate loan than a short-maturity or variable-rate loan. Depositors have a liquidity preference, and borrowers a predictability/stability preference. So on both sides we concentrate on getting what is harder to get, sometimes to the detriment of current profit spreads, knowing we can easily get short-term deposits or long-term loans by simply 'buying' them at an incremental-to-market interest rate."

More than unhandy, Hill's method is also, for as long as the curve remains positively sloped, costly. The Monroe County Bank earned $800,000 last year, or about 1% on assets. Conventionally managed, with an emphasis on short-dated liabilities, it might have earned $1.4 million, Hill estimates. Like other bankers, Hill prefers a higher net interest margin to a lower one, and a more efficient operation to a less efficient one. But, he insists, profitability at MCB is not so much a product as a byproduct. It is the residue of considered risk taking. "We feel," he declares, "that profits will sooner or later ensue if risks and losses are reduced, if the market value of assets increases, and if liquidity is maintained to take advantage of unexpected profit opportunities. Market value of assets trumps reported profits."

The financial asset value dearest to Hill's heart is the value of the 2,498 shares of Community Financial Services. CFS is the holding company for the Bankers Bank of Atlanta, a profitable and fast-growing service company for banks in the Southeast. Hill's bank is the biggest, and almost certainly the happiest, stockholder in this bankers' cooperative. Acquired over 20 years at a cost of $1.7 million, the shares, on Sept. 30, 2004, had a market value of $5.3 million. All told, unharvested gains in the securities portfolio of Monroe County Bank come to $3.8 million, two-thirds of the bank's stated book value of $5.6 million. Hill likens this unrecognized profit to the "hidden assets" without which old-time German bankers would have felt undressed. He relates the story of the bank examiner who clucked at the quality of Monroe County Bank's earnings one recent quarter. Except for some gains on sales of securities, the examiner pointed out, the bank would have shown a profit lower than that of its peer group. Hill protested that the wealth of unrealized gains on the Monroe County balance sheet meant that the bank could peel them off at the same reported quarterly rate for each of the next 10 years. The examiner yielded. But his suspicions were well-founded, Hill allows:

> A growing number of banks are in the opposite situation, having unrecognized security losses masked by using held-to-maturity instead of mark-to-market accounting, and having inadequate loan reserves, while reporting profits. Maintaining and growing the real market value of assets is MCB's policy, which in the long run produces real profits.

Hill is bearish on bonds. He expects interest rates to rise for the familiar litany of reasons (he reads *Grant's*), but especially because of the deteriorating external financial position of the United States.

Unlike the typical corporate interest-rate prophet, however, he acts on his convictions. And unlike the overwhelming majority of corporate executives, he commits his own money, which he is loath to lose. "There is presently such a dearth of both attractive lending opportunities and attractive bond investment opportunities," he says, "that rather than arbitrage present deposit rates against present income-producing opportunities, we will instead arbitrage present liquidity against future lending and investment opportunities. Interest rates on loans and bonds could get much higher and more attractive. A collapse of the housing bubble could result in widespread foreclosures producing far lower prices and better value in houses than now. Sufficient devaluation of the U.S. currency, especially if U.S. savings and investment rates improve, could produce some revival in U.S. manufacturing, presenting banks with more and better commercial/industrial lending opportunities than at present. MCB is strong enough to wait for better opportunities."

Hill is at his most analytically pungent on the subject of residential real estate. He wants to have as little to do with it as possible. (Investment real estate is another matter; he owns 1,300 acres in Henry County near Atlanta, among other parcels. "I like to add to land; I never sell land," he says.) "Home prices, home lending as a percentage of bank lending, home mortgage debt as a percentage of home values and homeowner debt service as a percentage of income are all at cyclical highs, indicative of trouble ahead," he laments. "Home mortgages were 30% of commercial bank loans in 1980, and are now over 60%. Concentration of lending to housing is even greater when one considers the large portion of 'commercial' loans which are to residential land development, building supply, furniture etc. We keep tabs, through publicly available FDIC call reports, on activities of the 40 banks closest to us in middle Georgia, large and small. Currently, the median of these 40 banks has 78% of loans in 'real estate,' mostly homes or land development for homes, and only 9½% in 'commercial' loans, some of which are also indirectly dependent on homebuilding. MCB, in comparison, has only 47% of loans in 'real estate' and 40% in 'commercial,' most of which is unrelated to homebuilding in our case."

The bank finds itself with a worrisome shortage of eligible borrowers. Few of the leading American industries seem to need a loan on terms that the Monroe County Bank would find attractive. Hill observes that the most successful industry in the 50 states is the lawful printing of dollars destined for export. But this stupendously profitable activity is funded by the taxpayers. Next follow distribution ("of products made abroad, mostly in Asia," dominated by the big chains, which do not need a loan from MCB), home building (an industry so far safe from Asian competition), manufacturing ("in steady decline") and, finally, "miscellaneous local businesses which cannot easily, or cannot at all, be shipped in from Asia: Restaurants, automobile repair, public safety, legal and accounting services, etc." This last category is the "industry" to which MCB has lent and continues to lend. But it, too, is increasingly tied-in with the house prices that Hill judges dangerously and unsustainably high.

If Hill had his way, loans would be self-liquidating; the debt itself would finance its own liquidation. From the files of the Monroe County Bank, he produces the beau ideal of a self-liquidating loan, a note in the sum of $387 to finance the harvesting of a cotton crop in 1914. Collateral consisted of two wagons, two cows, a horse and three mules. The mules were named Mack, Kate and Lillie. "That was much better loan collateral than we are accustomed to see in banks in 2005," the banker grumbles.

A rich man living in a simple house is unlikely to hold a high opinion of an illiquid man living in a grand house. Hill does not, although—in fairness—he does not seem to consider himself an especially rich or successful capitalist. ("A REAL CAPITALIST" is his note in the margin of the D.R. Horton 10-K report, in which the eponymous chairman observes that the $3,000 in equity with which he started the company in 1978 had grown, as of Sept. 30, 2004, to $4 billion.) "To pierce through the mirage that a luxurious home solves all household financial problems," he writes, "I several years ago devised a simple 'active ingredients' test of individual, household and sole-proprietor balance sheets. The analogy is that in chemical solutions mixing various elements and compounds, some ingredients will be inert, having no influence on the acid and basic active ingredients whose interaction will make the whole solution acidic or basic. A balance sheet has debts, which are extremely 'active' in that their required principal reduction and interest payments must be made, and may have income-producing assets such as stocks, bonds, mutual funds, bank accounts and investment real estate, all of which are 'active' in producing interest, dividends or saleable market value appreciation."

A house, Hill continues, is not to be confused with these active, income-producing assets. Even though it may appreciate in value, it produces no income. It may, indeed, be considered a kind of "debt," a use of cash rather than a source of cash (think of bursting pipes, property taxes, etc.). "Thus," he says, "on all applications for sole pro-prietor business loans, and on most larger home loans, at MCB we look at two versions of the applicant's balance sheet: One with the house included as an asset, and one revised to remove the lived-in house from the assets. This second 'houseless' balance sheet reveals the balance or imbalance of the borrower's 'active' debt payments and income, reveals a clearer picture of his liquidity and also paints a meaningful portrait of the borrower's financial psychology."

But, of course, Hill does not speak for the financial mainstream. Ameriquest, the nation's No. 1 subprime mortgage lender (and sponsor of Sunday's Ameriquest Super Bowl half-time show), not MCB, is the institution with the up-to-the-minute business model. Hill says that the present-day U.S. economy reminds him of a mythical Nation of Home Building. How would the inhab-itants of such a country generate cash flow? They would have to borrow it. They would borrow from each other until the store of domestic savings ran dry; then they would borrow abroad. "Much of our meager savings and massive borrowing has gone into U.S. housing," Hill muses. "How convenient it would be now if mansions and subdivisions could be exported, to improve our foreign trade balance. Since they cannot be exported, perhaps the foreigners who own our massive debts can be repaid by coming to live in our McMansions, with homeowners serving as houseboys and house maids to the visiting Japanese and Chinese owners of our debt."

Pending this epiphany, Hill relates, MCB "is running as lean a ship as practical. While many banks are responding to the reduced availability of mortgage refinancings and other loans by lowering standards and increasing loan-sales personnel, MCB's president, I believe prudently, has reduced our lending personnel and branch personnel to better match present demand."

Vernon Hill, please copy.

Thomson Hankey was Right

May 30, 2008

The governor of the Central Bank of Luxembourg raised some eyebrows when he questioned the integrity of the fast-expanding balance sheet of the European Central Bank. Yves Mersch, a member of the ECB's governing council as well as the Ben S. Bernanke of the Grand Duchy of Luxembourg, introduced the subject at a gathering of the International Capital Market Association in Vienna two weeks ago. Insofar as a currency derives its strength from the balance sheet of the issuing central bank, the euro is unsound and becoming more so, as Mersch did not quite say. We, however, will say it for him. In fact, we will say the same for most of the leading monetary brands, that of the United States not excluded. The mortgage mess is the immediate cause of the new debasement. A long-held article of central banking dogma is the remote cause.

Mersch landed on the front page of the *Financial Times* by acknowledging that the ECB is accepting a dubious kind of mortgage collateral in exchange for loans to the world's liquidity-parched financial institutions. In so many words, Mersch charged that the commercial banks are gaming the central bank, a situation he called of "high concern." Reading Mersch, we thought of Thomson Hankey.

Mersch has the look of a comer in world central-banking councils. Hankey, though he served a term as governor of the Bank of England in 1851 and 1852, is known today, if at all, as a sparring partner of the great Victorian Walter Bagehot (say "Badge-oat"). It was Bagehot who laid down the law that, in a credit crisis, a central bank should lend freely against good collateral at a high rate of interest. Hankey emphatically disagreed, and he answered Bagehot in a little book entitled, *The Principles of Banking*, first published in 1867 in the wake of the famous Overend Gurney run (the one to which the 2007 Northern Rock panic is sometimes compared). Way back then, the Bank of England was an investor-owned institution conducting a conventional, for-profit commercial banking business. It had but one avowed public purpose, and that was to manage the workings of the international gold standard. It stood ready to exchange currency for gold coin, and gold coin for currency, at the statutory rate of £3.17s.6d. to the ounce, or £3.89 in metric terms, no questions asked.

For Bagehot, the Bank of England was no ordinary deposit-taking institution but the lender, or liquidity provider, of last resort. Actually, Sir Francis Baring had anticipated Bagehot in that judgment. In the crisis year of 1797, Baring had fixed the Bank with the name, "*le dernier resort.*" Neither Bagehot nor Baring seemed to anticipate that, before many hundreds of years would pass, the Bank—indeed, many central banks—would become, so to speak, "*la premier resort.*" Anyone with good collateral should expect to find accommodation at the Bank's discount window at a suitably high penalty rate, Bagehot said. What passed for good banking collateral in the mid-19th century was bills of exchange, i.e., short-dated, self-liquidating IOUs. Mortgages, inherently illiquid, were inadmissible. Hankey liked to quote a relative of his, one C.

Poulett Thomson, on the art of banking. It wasn't very hard, said Thomson, as long as the banker "would only learn the difference between a Mortgage and a Bill of Exchange."

By now, a busy reader of *Grant's* might be wondering why the editor is reaching back to 1866 for actionable ideas on the 21st century monetary situation. Medical science has made a certain amount of progress since Dr. Strickland's Pile Remedy, Constitution Life Syrup and Webster's Vegetable Hair Invigorator represented state-of-the-art therapeutics. Neither has monetary economics stood still—has it?

You be the judge. Hankey, in a losing cause, marshaled two principal arguments against the Bagehot doctrine. No. 1, moral hazard: Let profit-maximizing people come to believe that the Bank of England will bail them out, and they themselves will take the actions, and assume the leverage, that will require them to be bailed out. No. 2, simple fairness: If Britain's banking interest can claim a right to the accommodation of the Bank of England, why shouldn't the shipping interest, the construction interest, the railroads "and, last of all, the much-maligned agricultural interest" do the same? Shouldn't all economic actors "be equally entitled to benefit by any favors for which the public have a right to look from such an institution as the Bank of England?"

At this writing, the Federal Reserve, the ECB and the Bank of England are taking extraordinary measures to accommodate the demand for liquidity by the institutions that couldn't seem "to learn the difference between a Mortgage and a Bill of Exchange," or between a triple-A corporate bond and a triple-A mortgage, which is a slightly different kind of confusion. To bail out these slow studies, the central banks are lending government securities against the inherently illiquid mortgage collateral that never had a place on the balance sheet of a properly run monetary institution in the first place. In fact, in Hankey's day, it was a breach of good form for a central bank even to acquire government securities (the preferred assets were commercial loans, foreign exchange and gold). How far the world has come: Gold, the most liquid of monetary assets, is today officially demonetized, whereas mortgages, the least liquid of banking assets, are now—all of a sudden, because there seems to be no choice—being embraced, or, at least, tolerated. They are certainly being monetized.

"Ready money," writes Hankey in a passage on liquidity that seems to speak directly to the post-Bear Stearns world of 2008, "is a most valuable thing, and cannot from its very essence bear interest; everyone is therefore constantly endeavoring to make it profitable and at the same time to retain its use as ready money, which is simply impossible. Turn it into whatever shape you please, it can never be made into more real capital than is due to its own intrinsic value, and it is the constant attempt to perform this miracle which leads to all sorts of confusion with respect to credit. The Bank of England has long been expected to perform this miracle; it is the attempt to force the Bank to do so which has led to the greater number of the difficulties which have occurred on every occasion of monetary panics during the last twenty years."

So Hankey would have every banker, trader, merchant and speculator watch out for himself, proceed with prudence, not overreach, not overborrow and—above all—not depend on the Bank of England for emergency accommodation. About 150 years later, Northern Rock and the Bank of England are both in the arms of the British government (the Bank joined the public sector in 1946). The Bank has just rolled out its Special Liquidity Scheme to exchange the government's gilts for the private sector's mortgages, and the gold price, expressed in sterling, stands at £468.2 an ounce, up from £3.89 in Hankey's time. From 1867 to date, the annual rate of debasement, sterling against gold, comes to 3.3%.

Hankey's ideas did not go down to defeat for no reason. The gold standard was as hard as it was clean. When the price level fell, as it did in the final quarter of the 19th century, it just fell. No gold-standard central bank resisted the trend with newly created credit (as every major central bank does, or would do, today).

"It's really no fun when the market's closed."

A certain kind of person—*Grant's* knows the type—takes it to be a good thing that, under the monetary arrangements of Hankey's day, no monetary-policy committee fixed interest rates or sized up the money supply or regulated the price level or supervised a return to macroeconomic equilibrium when imbalances appeared. Rather, as Hankey observed, interest rates moved and macroeconomic adjustments took place more or less spontaneously. No government commanded them. To judge by all that has happened since the gold standard bit the dust, we would have to say that the people have registered their collective preference for the comforting sight of a Bernanke or a Mersch at the helm of a central bank. There is something pleasing to many, or to most, about a government functionary taking responsibility for interest rates, the price level and/or the labor market, whether or not such an individual can actually make the magic demanded of him (we are sure he or she cannot).

Nowadays, the consensus of belief has it that America fills the bill of a "market-based system," whereas Europe is closer to a "bank-based system." But the truth is that the worldwide mortgage mess has pushed America away from markets and Europe away from banks. Both systems are moving closer to a state of government or central-bank control. And both currencies are, therefore, moving even further away from an orthodox notion of soundness (not that either was within hailing distance of it before the credit clouds rolled in last summer).

In the United States this election year, the galloping socialization of the mortgage market proceeds with hardly a peep of discussion, let alone protest. Thus, mortgage originations by the government-sponsored enterprises reached 81% of overall originations in the fourth quarter of 2007, up from 37% in the second quarter of 2006. In the first quarter of this year, Fannie copped a 50% share of originations, double its take in calendar 2006. But in comparison to the biggest GSE, Fannie and Freddie might as well be standing still.

In Boston, before a Mortgage Bankers Association audience on May 6, the chairman of the Federal Housing Finance Board, Ronald Rosenfeld, noted that the Federal Home Loan Banks, which his agency supervises, are closing in on $1 trillion in outstanding loans, or "advances" ($925 billion are currently outstanding, up by $300 billion in just 12 months). "The FHLBs," Reuters reported of Rosenfeld's remarks, "are facing increased risk due to the concentration of loans to big financial institutions that recently 'decided to become very involved in the FHLB system,' Rosenfeld said. Those banks include Countrywide, Washington Mutual Inc. and Wells Fargo & Co., he said. The top borrowers of the FHLB system account for 37% of all advances, he said. 'That's an astonishing amount of concentration,' he said. The FHLBs can continue to provide money for their commercial bank members as long as demand persists in the market for agency debt." Foreign central banks can't seem to get their fill. In the 12 months through March, according to a recent Home Loan Bank slide show, central banks took down

40% of the system's debt issuance, the top investor group it tracks. Russia's central bank has shown a particularly strong appetite for the GSEs: 21% of Russian monetary reserves are parked in the obligations of Fannie, Freddie and the Home Loan Banks, according to a May 19 *Bloomberg* report.

Taking an evolutionary view of present-day monetary disturbances, we see a kind of grand comeuppance. Embracing Bagehot and rejecting Hankey, central bankers have pushed aside the classical doctrines of liquidity. In the way that financial ideas seem always to be carried to an extreme, they have pushed too hard. Under their noses, the global credit apparatus froze up, and now it falls to them to thaw it out. A measure of the difficulty of that work is the huge volume of lending that the Bank of England and the ECB, especially, have chosen to undertake; over the past 12 months, the balance sheets of the ECB and the Bank of England have grown by 21% and 19.4%, respectively. (In comparison, the Fed is a model of restraint.)

In his critique of the Bagehot doctrine, Hankey understandably failed to imagine how the financial engineers of the future would respond to the opportunities presented to them by ambulance-chasing central banks of the 21st century. According to the *Financial Times*, investment bankers the world over are bundling up mortgages to place in the special liquidity facilities created by the ECB and the Bank of England. "The Bank of England," the paper reported on May 16, "recently created a facility for UK banks to access funding for mortgages and the *Financial Times* has learnt that almost £90 billion ($175 billion) worth of bonds are being created to be placed there—almost twice the £50 billion initially expected when the scheme was launched only three weeks ago. . . .

"Investment bankers who work in securitization," the *FT* went on, "say that their main business is structuring bonds that are eligible for ECB liquidity operations. Some analysts have concerns about whether the bonds being created will ever be saleable if markets recover."

We believe that more analysts ought to be concerned about the risk that these monetary exertions will result in a new cycle of currency debasement. For ourselves, we expect it. A brilliant man was Walter Bagehot, but Hankey had the foresight.

Chapter Two

On Planet Stock Market

Crisis of the Big Guys

March 26, 1999

R EMARKS BY JAMES Grant before the American Council of Life Insurance, in Tucson, Ariz.:
I have a big subject to address, and big shoes to fill. As you know, I am here today only because Peter Bernstein couldn't be. Peter, who is ailing, literally wrote the book on risk—his splendid *Against the Gods* appeared in 1996. You'll agree that anyone who could make an international best-seller out of the history of risk in the speculatively charged 1990s must be a very formidable intellect indeed.

Peter's timing was admirable. This is a risk-fraught juncture in finance; in my opinion, among the most perilous ever. I know that I have said this before, too many times, and I understand full well that my association with a bearish message does not necessarily enhance its news value. I have resolved to do better during the next once-in-a-lifetime boom.

The tricky thing about risk is that it is more threatening as it seems less obvious; and less threatening as it seems more obvious. If you concede the truth of this paradox, you are bound to agree that America is dangling by a thread, financially speaking. Rarely has risk seemed less obvious to the majority of investors than it does today. Although not actually eradicated by modern science, it is, like polio, thought to be in full retreat. *Time* magazine crystallized the spirit of the age last month when its cover featured a picture of Alan Greenspan, Robert Rubin and Lawrence Summers, collectively identified as "The Committee to Save the World." The story inside implied that no financial risk is so great that it cannot be neutralized by a committee of enlightened public servants.

Like many other financial ideas, the concept of risk is forever being redefined. Its definition varies with financial and economic circumstances, and it has recently undergone a bull-market transformation. For a professional money manager in 1999, the riskiest asset isn't necessarily interest-rate derivatives, commodity futures, Russian sovereign debt or even domestic small-cap equities. It is probably Treasury bills. Cash is the one asset class that is positively guaranteed not to double in value in the next fiscal quarter. It is the investment that is certain not to keep up with the S&P 500.

For me, the all-cycle definition of risk is the chance of loss. It is not the risk of falling behind the S&P or of not retiring, like everyone else in one's neighborhood, at the age of 49 to Boca Raton. (Nor, it seems to me, is the volatility of a particular security in relation to an index. If a good business can be purchased at a compelling valuation, of what significance is the flight path of its stock price?) The value investor Seth Klarman has thought long and hard on the subject. "Unquantifiable in prospect," he writes, "risk is (surprisingly) no more measurable in retrospect. You can, of course, measure the outcome of an investment. But you cannot easily evaluate what failed to transpire, all of those seeming risks that were somehow avoided as well as those that were never even imagined."

"What's the valuation? What's the valuation?
The market's going up. THAT'S the valuation!"

I think Seth would be the first one to concede that thinking about risk has lately not been the way to get rich, or to become richer. The trouble is that the risk-averse investor is competing with people who might be described as risk-oblivious. They can imagine no conceivable way in which there could be a loss—the subject has never dawned on them. I used to pity these innocents—they didn't even have the good sense to subscribe to *Grant's*. Now, I suppose, they pity me. In such a paradise as this one, the argument goes, the only relevant risk is that of underperformance—of not keeping up with one's brother-in-law, the Internet trader. I fearlessly predict that this will change. In fact, to judge by the weakening net inflows into equity mutual funds as well as by the great and growing disparity between the chosen few stocks and the unwashed mass, it seems to be changing already.

In his book, Peter observes that the science of risk management itself introduces risk. Thus a normally prudent driver might not pay his customary heed to a patch of ice if his new car is equipped with a seatbelt and airbags, front and side. Similarly, a conservative investor might become slightly less conservative after watching the Federal Reserve chairman and the other members of the Committee to Save the World in action.

The suit of armor that encases the average premillennial investor is an idea—the belief that, over the long run, no real harm will come to a diversified holder of common stocks. Or rather, I should say, no diversified holder of American common stocks in this cycle. Plenty of harm has come of late to long-term equity investors in markets outside the United States and, at home and abroad, in eras preceding this one. The theory that stocks excel in the long term, regardless of how they are valued at the time one buys them, has become secular gospel. Variations on the theme that this is the kingdom of heaven are featured almost daily on the editorial page of *The Wall Street Journal.* However, it seems to me, it isn't the theory itself that the mass of investors find most persuasive; it's the profitable investment experience that inspired the theorists: The almost unchecked, apparently unconditional returns on the S&P.

Like champagne, bull markets remove inhibitions. This fall will mark the 25th anniversary of the bear market of the early 1970s. Since 1974, the prevailing direction of equity prices has been up (with occasional, temporary setbacks, of course—"buying opportunities," as they are known). A quarter century leaves a powerful impression. Contrast, please, the span of years that separated the 1929 Crash from the 1954 breakout to new, post-Crash highs. Those 25 years in the investment wilderness conditioned an earlier generation against excessive risk-taking—indeed, against risk-taking of any kind. To convey a flavor of the bear-market orthodoxy, I will quote a horror-struck Frederick H. Ecker, chairman of the Metropolitan Life Insurance Co., in his testimony in the fall of 1941 on the advisability of changing the New York State life insurance regulations to allow life companies to invest in common stocks. Although, "unquestionably, many common stocks are sound investments," Ecker allowed, a company like his was better advised to own bonds.

"... [I]f the stock is sound," the chairman continued, "the obligation [i.e., the bond] of that company is more sound; and our belief is that we are wiser in adhering to the practice of buying the obligations rather than the equities in corporate enterprise." Notice that this verdict was rendered without regard to valuation (at the time, stocks outyielded bonds). Observe, too, that Ecker's remarks were dated about six months before the stock market made its decisive 1942 lows, lows that would not be seen again for the rest of the century. Now, of course, latter-day Frederick Eckers want to demutualize their life insurance companies so that they can be paid in stock, or stock options, the new coin of the realm.

For the editor of a publication with "Interest Rate Observer" in its name, I realize that I am spending what may seem an inordinate amount of time on the stock market. This isn't because I'm confusing myself with Barton Biggs, but because the stock market has become perhaps the biggest feature of the U.S. economy. In finance, it sets the speculative tone, the analytical tone and the intellectual tone. I don't mean to discount the contribution made by low interest rates to the great boom. They have changed the valuation parameters. But rising stock prices have changed the macroeconomic, social and political parameters. The stock market nowadays is nothing so prosaic as a mirror to the secular growth in corporate earnings. It is rather a cornucopia, showering wealth on day traders, Internet entrepreneurs, 401(k) plan investors and former President George Bush, who had the foresight not to take a recent $80,000 speaking fee in cash but rather in shares of a private communications company, Global Crossing, that would presently light up the tape. Incidentally, I have contracted to receive my $80,000 speaking fee in cash. The bull stock market has changed the way companies report their earnings and pay their employees. It has changed the way people think about the future and the way they save (or don't save). And it will change, profoundly, the relationship between the middle class and the government, come the day it stops going up. I now have a mental image of the forthcoming federal hearings into the collapse of the stock market and the Clinton administration's $1 trillion equity rescue package (widely judged to be inadequate). I visualize Richard Grasso, chairman of the New York Stock Exchange, explaining to members of the Joint Economic Committee what is meant by "price/earnings ratio," "book value" and "dividend yield." These technical terms appear new to them.

It's the stock market that sets the speculative tone for every market, including the credit markets. Thus, under cover of steadily rising equity prices, the credit quality of American corporations has become decidedly weaker. Moody's notes, for example, that the percentage of issuers with senior unsecured debt below investment grade late last year stood at 41.8%, an all-time high. Similarly in bank lending: the share of syndicated lending earmarked for leveraged M&A transactions climbed to more than 30% last year, up from 10% in 1993. Leo Brand, an analyst at Standard & Poor's who helped to conduct a survey of corporate borrowing in 1998, summed up the results of the study in a remark to the *American Banker* the other day: "Credit quality is in bad shape," he said. Certainly, a recession or a bear market wouldn't improve things.

Watching "Wall Street Week" and reading *The Wall Street Journal*—especially the very accessible "C" section—the public has recalibrated its investment expectations. If the S&P delivers 20% a year, year in and year out, people ask, why settle for less? Why settle for a paycheck when one can elect to receive stock options? And if five million Americans (according to *Forbes*) are day-trading for fun and profit on the Internet, why settle for professional money management?

The Little Guy may be thriving; not so the Big Guy. The professionals to whom I speak (and I admit that I don't move in mainstream circles) are frankly miserable. Suddenly the rate of return on the skills that made them successful has fallen to next to nothing. They say it would be better if they didn't bother to read the footnotes on the balance sheet any more (as if they could help themselves). It is surely no accident that some of the most accomplished professional investors are logging the worst fiscal quarters of their careers as hot stocks take flight on the extraneous news that there will soon be two shares for every one.

How the daytime soaps stay on the air is beyond me. Everyone seems to be speculating or watching others speculate. I use the word "speculate" advisedly. An investment is a speculation to the extent that its success is contingent on a forecast of uncertain events. Thus an arbitrage involving two securities in the same capital structure is very probably an investment, as the outcome has so little to do with the cosmic things that nobody is able to predict very well. On the other hand, an outright purchase of the S&P 500 is a rank speculation. At prevailing levels of valuation, its success depends critically on the continued unfolding of what might conservatively described as a state of worldly perfection.

What is the risk if, instead, there were imperfection? Steven Leuthold, Minneapolis-based financial thinker and doer, calculates that a return to median basic valuation measures would imply a drop of about 52% in the S&P 500. He adds that downside risk is considerably smaller for small-cap stocks, as depressed as they already are; he puts this at 10%.

It should give pause to the millions of American speculators that the Federal Reserve itself—alleged bulwark against down cycles and bear markets—is apparently no better at divining the unfathomable future than they are. Thus, looking ahead to 1999, the staff of the Federal Open Market Committee in February 1998 projected real GDP growth on the order of 2% to 2 ¾% (it turned out to be 4.1%) and consumer price inflation of 1 ¾% to 2 ¼% (the actual number was 1.5%). Never mind that the Fed was pleasantly surprised. This is a Federal Reserve Board that operates almost entirely on what is known in the interest-rate profession as "Kentucky windage." It follows no known set of rules. If, under Paul A. Volcker, there was a "cigar ash" standard, today, under Alan Greenspan, there is the intuition standard. So far, so good, but what if the chairman intuits incorrectly?

Not the least of the risks facing the U.S. financial markets is that the Fed will fail to live up to its exaggerated press. We at *Grant's* have done our best to deflate the central-bank bubble. For example, we have noted that the temporary seizing up of the U.S. capital markets last fall was not a willful act of monetary policy. The Fed didn't cause it to happen. And when the Fed tried to restore liquid, two-way credit markets by a succession of cuts in the federal funds rate, it succeeded mainly in restarting the stock market (although, in fairness, the Fed has at least helped to foster a two-way equity market; as big-cap has levitated, small-cap has languished).

The measure by which we have failed to win our point on the Fed is the frequency with which the name of the Federal Reserve and its chairman are joined with the word "God," as in, "Thank God for Alan Greenspan." It is the mirror image of the chronically poor press received by gold bullion, the monetary asset that competes (unsuccessfully for quite some time) with managed currencies. Recall, for instance, the common juxtaposition of the words "Nazi" and "gold" last year, e.g., "Swiss deny Nazi gold role."

Probably, today, the greatest risk to the market is the market itself. The very popularity of equities has given rise to a culture, or cult, of options compensation, one that—owing to accounting and tax quirks—serves to exaggerate reported corporate profits. "The effects of employee stock options are now so large that they influence the macroeconomy," concludes a new study by Smithers & Co. "The relationship between published profits and capacity utilization has changed, tax anomalies have arisen and the discrepancy between GDP and gross domestic income is getting larger." Adjusting for the effects of options activity, according to Smithers, the price/earnings ratio on the S&P 500 at the end of 1998 "is likely to have been between three and five times its long-term average."

"In 1952," wrote Paul Gigot in last Friday's *Wall Street Journal*, "just 4% of Americans owned stock—the consequences of depression and war. And even as recently as 1981, the dawn of the Reagan era, only 16% of American adults owned shares. A decade later 24% did. But by 1997, more than four in every 10 adults had an ownership stake of one kind or another in corporate America." Would it be even more stupendously bullish if 100% of Americans owned equities? It would not, it seems to me—unless, that is, a national margin facility, perhaps financed by the Federal Home Loan Banks, could be established to increase the per-capita exposure. It is interesting that Gigot picked 1952 as a reference point. In the March 24, 1952 issue of *Barron's* was an article that tried to poke holes in the buy-and-hold school of investment. The author's method was to compare prices of the leading stocks in 1929 with the prices prevailing at year-end 1951. Radio, for instance, was 23½, down from 50 on October 31, 1929; General Electric was 59½, not yet back to 63, where it had been at the time of the Crash. "The moral is plain," wrote Thomas F. Willmore. "If an investor does not convert a considerable part of his paper profits into cash profits before the current bull market is over, the consequences are apt to be unpleasant." In fact, the moral was not at all plain, as the postwar bull market had only begun. The same issue of *Barron's*, incidentally, noted that General Motors was trading at 9½ times earnings and yielding 7½%. Long-dated Treasurys were priced to yield about 2.70%. Risks were obvious—war and depression, as Gigot noted. Not by accident, therefore, were valuations compelling.

The capitalists who created U.S. Steel in 1901 were enlightened men, and they wanted to share the benefits of equity ownership. When they offered all employees the chance to buy preferred stock at a concessionary price on the installment plan, the response was gratifying—10% of the company's unskilled workers, who earned less than an average of $550 a year, signed up. Anticipating Gigot, the journal *Finance and Commerce* ventured that the Steel experiment would convert the country into "a nation of conservative Bourbons."

The conversion is farther along today than ever before, but I doubt that the faith of the bull-market capitalists is unwavering. On form, it is highly contingent on continued satisfactory investment performance—say, 20% a year on indexed equity mutual funds. One of the fundamental shifts of the past decade, observes the economist Gert von der Linde, has been the migration of American pension management from a defined benefit system to defined contributions. More and more American employees—today's conservative or not-so-conservative "Bourbons"—are managing their own money. They are buying into the most fabulously valued bull market in history. Is this, therefore, the end of history?

It is not. As socialists failed to create a new human being in the image of their own ideology, so too will the capitalists. When it is good and ready, the incredible bull will finally wander off the field, and the concept of risk will come in for cyclical redefinition. Let me make my submission now: "Risk is the chance of loss." I thank you.

The Economic Consequences of Air Conditioning

June 4, 1999

On Wall Street's authority, the Internet is the most important innovation of all time. The brokers and bankers say this without qualification, and they would have us invest in the same spirit. In general, they advise the purchase of Internet stocks without regard for price or valuation on the ground that, to them, the principal long-term financial risk associated with the worldwide web is not being invested in it. Amazon.com, eBay, Priceline.com, E*Trade, Charles Schwab et al. have purportedly already conquered the future, even though they haven't seen it yet. There are no visible competitive threats to these companies, the bulls contend. Supposedly, in fact, they are already as deeply entrenched in the U.S. economy as DuPont, General Motors and Procter & Gamble ever were.

We didn't believe these claims in cold weather. At the start of a New York summer, we are even more skeptical. To those who inhabit the hazy, hot and humid portions of the physical world, the Internet will never seem so seminal an invention as the low-tech room air conditioner. Visionaries may claim that the 'net will do nothing less than create new industries, refashion old ones, enhance productivity and rewrite the script of social, economic and political life the world over. Air conditioning has done all that, and more. Yet it has so far created no financial Garden of Eden, and we think we know the reason.

The destination of this essay is the idea that the consequences of technological upheaval are complex and unpredictable. Innovations make the world a more productive place, but also, simultaneously, in ways rarely anticipated, a less productive one. Thus, on the plus side, the Internet has unimaginably expanded the accessible store of human knowledge, up to and including bond analytics. On the minus side, it has brought day trading, e-mail and computer solitaire within the reach of every white-collar employee. It has facilitated the universal dissemination of American nuclear technology. All in all, we submit, the Internet's net contribution to U.S. productivity is considerably smaller than what is represented to be its gross contribution.

Revolutions, once begun, rarely proceed as the revolutionaries intended, and the chief beneficiaries of new inventions are not always the people who dreamt them up, invested in them or promoted them (they are sometimes the children or even the grandchildren of those individuals). Thus, for example, when Willis Haviland Carrier was awarded patent No. 808897 for an "Apparatus for Treating Air," on Jan. 2, 1906, the father of air conditioning almost certainly did not anticipate a future hole in the ozone layer or the political consequences of a 12-month congressional season. "The installation of air conditioning in the 1930s did more, I believe, than cool the Capitol," reminisced Rep. Joseph W. Martin, a Massachusetts Republican, in 1960, "it prolonged the sessions." Would American statism have come full flower in a non-air conditioned capital city? Always, in technology, there are debits and credits.

To leapfrog over 2,500 or so well-chosen words, our top investment conclusions are, first, that innovation constitutes no certain warranty against macroeconomic turmoil and, second, that a margin of safety is just as essential in high-tech investing as it is in the low- and medium-tech kind. Thus, as we will observe, the truly stunning gains in productivity observed in the 1950s and 1960s were followed not by human perfection but by a great inflation. And as for the Internet, we hold it in such high regard that we believe it is fully capable of developing the means to destroy itself in favor of an information technology even more wonderful.

The basic Internet trade has so far been exquisitely simple: Obtain an allocation of an online IPO. Intermediate and advanced Internet trades—those derived from the second- and third-order effects of the 'net—will undoubtedly be subtler and more complex, e.g., sell the shares of the revolutionary businesses that the revolution has begun to devour; buy the shares of the Internet's surprise new beneficiaries; and—just a possibility—sell municipal bonds. An inkling of what the Department of Unintended Consequences might hold in store is the recent alarm expressed by states and municipalities over the loss of sales taxes to e-commerce. Say "Internet" and the first thought that comes to mind is not "public finance." Yet, what is apparently going through the minds of the members of the National Association of Counties and the U.S. Conference of Mayors is a future tax famine (with potential bearish consequences for tax-exempt debt). Knowing what he knows today, would Al Gore invent the Internet all over again?

The story of air conditioning, we think, speaks directly to the risks, opportunities, hopes and delusions of the digital age. Raymond Arsenault, in a brilliant essay entitled "The End of the Long Hot Summer: The Air Conditioner and Southern Culture" (first published in 1984 in *The Journal of Southern History*), observes that the great invention did not catch on at once: "The so-called 'air conditioning revolution'. . . was actually an evolution—a long, slow, uneven process stretching over seven decades." A Brooklyn lithography plant was the first recipient of the Carrier apparatus, in 1902. Sales to a wide variety of industrial customers followed. But the so-called comfort market went uninvaded until the successful commercialization of centrifugal refrigeration, in 1922. When, on Memorial Day in 1925 Carrier successfully cooled the patrons of the Rivoli Theater, New York, a new day dawned. Yet almost 30 years would have to pass before the residential air conditioning market came into its own. Carrier himself wouldn't live to see it.

So unlike the digital revolution—or is it? Very much like it, in fact, with this difference: In 1999, the stock market willingly capitalizes loss-making companies. Through most of Carrier's career, it capitalized only profitable ones (or ones, at least, that started out profitably). "I fish only for edible fish," the inventor was wont to say, "and hunt only for edible game—even in the laboratory."

It may give heart to the speculators in Amazon.com, eBay, Priceline.com and other first-generation Internet businesses to know that Carrier Corp. is today, as it was at the time of Willis Carrier's death in 1950, the undisputed air conditioning leader. York Corp., Frigidaire, Trane Co. and Westinghouse (to name only part of the competitive field) never overtook it.

On the other hand, if you plot the stock price of Carrier in terms of the Dow Jones Industrial Average from 1929 until 1979 (when it was acquired by United Technologies), you find no prolonged outperformance. Many were the bumps on the road to a room-temperature world. In about 1933, according to a biography of the founding genius, Carrier was forced to suspend production of its prototype residential room cooling unit. There was no demand. Yes, the bulls will counter, but that was the Depression. Yes, we reply, but air conditioning did not prevent the Depression. (*Fortune* would call air conditioning "a prime public disappointment of the 1930s.") Innovation alone does not drive the world economy.

Only the most patient and long-lived air conditioning bulls were on hand to be fully vindicated. "In 1945," relates Arsenault, "in a preview of things to come, shipping magnate Henry Kaiser announced plans to build 'complete communities of mass-produced air conditioned homes. . . .' Room air conditioner sales climbed to over 40,000 by 1947, but at that period residential air conditioning still accounted for only 2% of the industry's business. By 1950 the figure had risen to 5%, but in most areas the air conditioned home remained a novelty."

Not long ago on First Call, a brokerage-house analyst pronounced eBay to be cheap at 55 times net income projected for the year 2009. Such an expression of faith—in the permanence of a new technology, in the capacity of a new company to exploit it, in the predictability of the future, in the stability of civilization as we know it—appears on Wall Street only cyclically. It is in the shortest supply when it ought to be most plentiful, i.e., when values are cheap. It was conspicuously not in evidence in 1951, at the start of the home air conditioning age.

What then stood in the way of an air conditioning stock boom was not the future but the past, the memory of bad things and the dread of more. If the market doubts nothing today, it believed nothing then. In the summer of 1951, the Dow had made a 20-year high, at 263. Then, again, it was only back to where it stood in the depression year of 1931.

"In 1951," historian Arsenault proceeds, "the inexpensive, efficient window unit finally hit the market, and sales skyrocketed, especially in the South." "With a growing population," wrote John C. Perham in *Barron's* in August 1951, "a rising standard of living, a slow but diabolical increase in yearly temperatures and more powerful and adaptable air conditioning equipment all converging to rout any obstacles, it is hard to see serious trouble ahead for the industry." What *Barron's* didn't get around to mentioning was that Carrier Corp. traded at 5.2 times trailing net income and 2.4 times the annualized net income of its latest fiscal quarter. Then, too, at a price of 23fl, the stock yielded 4.2% (long-dated Treasurys fetched 2.65%).

What digitally awaits us in the near future, we keep reading, are breakthroughs in "user interfaces" as well as communication and computing technologies. Thus, writes Richard Rowe in the April 9 edition of the *Boston Business Journal*, "In the next decade, we will see electronic ink, heads-up, hands-free displays, smart, personalized and voice-controlled appliances and mind-machine connections that will transform the way knowledge is generated, accessed and used more than any innovation since the advent of print."

Wonderful, certainly, but not clearly so wonderful as a technology that actually changed American migration patterns, that caused the "Sunbelt" to rise up out of sand and scrub and that immeasurably increased human comfort and health from Jakarta to Baltimore. Who could enjoy a life of digital interactivity with sweat pouring into his eyes?

It will be said that the Internet has revolutionized not the world of the body but the life of the mind. However, we feel, the mind is receptive to only so much revolution. Reyner Banham, in *The Architecture of the Well-tempered Environment*, published in 1969, observed that air conditioning, along with electric lighting, had rendered "all environmental constraints on design" obsolete. In the new age, you could live anywhere you wanted to, and in any kind of house (thank you, John Newman).

Yet, Banham went on, "[T]he possibility of absolute variety and infinite choice of building form is now with us—and as so often happens with infinite choices, has led to almost perfect homogenization of what is chosen. In the United States, air conditioning has now made the established lightweight tract-developers' house habitable throughout the nation, and since this is the house that the U.S. building industry is geared to produce above all others, it is now endemic from Maine to California. . . ."

Proponents of the Internet hold out the vision of infinite variety in ideas. To which we say: Not in this life. As in suburbia, so online. On the web, the people's choice in financial information turns out to be a kind of intellectual tract house. A telling case of web-borne homogeneity is the ubiquitous online "company snapshot." You might suppose, reflects Lawrence Sterne, CEO of

Wall Street Research Net, that the Internet would have evolved a corporate financial summary superior to that in the old S&P ring binders. It hasn't. Furthermore, he notes, everybody tends to have the same snapshot: "You've got to have it because everybody else has it." It's not that there is no unique online financial content, Sterne goes on. The problem is that what there is is so narrowly distributed.

We leave it up to the readers of *Grant's* to decide for themselves how much of the experience of managing money is emotional and how much is analytical (the emotional content is not more than 90%, in our experience). And the Internet has become the super-highway of speculative emotion. What a digitally enhanced bear market will look like we may all worry about or pine for. Certainly, the digitally enhanced bull market has been one for the record books. Speaking of his extensive experiences online, William A. Fleckenstein, professional money manager and author, "There is a fundamental belief that information is knowledge. It isn't."

All in all this summer, we'll take air conditioning.

Just in Case

July 16, 1999

Shopping for himself, the man who has everything, Stephen M. Case, founder and chairman of America Online, passed up the sizable gift assortment available in the New Economy and turned instead to the old one. His surprise selection was a 41.2% equity interest in Maui Land & Pineapple, a business so old that its founding preceded the World Wide Web.

Case, 41 years old, was born and raised in Hawaii, so his decision to invest in the 50th state might have been formed in the right-sided, intuitive portion of his capacious brain. Still, he could just as easily have made a logical case for a small reallocation of assets: a shift from that sector of the stock market valued at high multiples of book value (a concept, in fact, deemed to be meaningless in that particular sector) to the one quoted at low multiples of book. Possibly, Case reasoned, the perfect time to invest in Hawaii is when everyone else is investing in the Internet. If so, he's on to something, we think.

It would be hard to imagine an investment less digital and more analogue than Maui Land (MLP on the American Stock Exchange) or, for that matter, Alexander & Baldwin (ALEX), a pair of Old Economy institutions that actually grow things in dirt. MLP raises pineapples; ALEX produces sugarcane and coffee. MLP, in addition, owns the Kapalua Resort, a couple of shopping centers and 28,600 acres of land (including the land under its structures), all on Maui. Besides its agricultural interests, ALEX owns a shipping business and no fewer than 69,000 Maui acres. "From the standpoint of potential value creation," asserts the latest 10-K report of Alexander & Baldwin, striking a marketing tone, "our Maui landholdings. . .could not be located better. Ranked as the number one island travel destination in the world, Maui has a bright future. . . ."*

It is the recent past—approximately a decade—that has left speculators cold. The great disinflationary bull market has passed the islands by. When, in 1986, the late Harry Weinberg was trying to increase his position in Maui Land (he owned 37%), he bid the equivalent of $25 each for a block of shares held by the company's employee stock ownership plan— "a very good price," Weinberg insisted at the time. Just how good a price, he apparently did not begin to imagine. The quote today is less than $18. It was less than $9 as recently as last December 30. The price of Alexander & Baldwin peaked as long ago as 1989.

The story of Hawaiian real estate in the 1980s and 1990s is, of course, in part the story of credit, American and Japanese. It was

---

* Hawaiian real estate proved no world-bearing investment (Maui Land has returned 4.4% a year, Alexander & Baldwin 12.7% a year). But Case was right to hedge. The 2001 merger of AOL and Time Warner created a kind of shareholder-value destruction machine, with annual losses of 13.1%.

the Japanese asset inflation that financed the island bull market of 1988–90 with all its excess (deplorable or delicious, according to personal experience). And it was the contraction of Japanese credit that heavily contributed to the ensuing bear market. Possibly, it seems to us, the stars are coming into alignment for a new bull market, financed this time by the American asset inflation and enhanced by the aging population of boom-blessed moguls and mini-moguls (Case being in the vanguard of the former group).

English-language descriptions of the Hawaiian boom and bust are invariably replete with patronizing references to the poor feckless Japanese. However, as we all know, the American bull market has its own absurd Japanese flavor. When, in April 1998, the shares of Maui Land temporarily soared on the electrifying, yet meaningless news of a four-for-one stock split, the setting might as well have been Tokyo in 1988 as New York a decade later. Then again, zany or well-founded, wealth is wealth for as long as it can be spent. The significance of the Case initiative, it seems to us (and to the reader who kindly pointed it out, William A. Fleckenstein), is that

"Well, I just like bought it, and it kind of, you know, tripled."

an Internet personage has chosen to hedge his paper bets. Maybe others will follow his lead.

Maui Land and Alexander & Baldwin are neither cheap nor exciting, as a value investor and a growth investor, respectively, would use those words. ALEX, it's true, trades at a substantial discount to what might be construed as the fair value of its Maui real estate, but the bullish arguments for the stocks are contingent, and therefore speculative. They depend on the continued growth of that portion of the American population searching for warm and serene surroundings in which to spend its financial wealth. It isn't so much a future price inflation for which the bulls on MLP or ALEX should root (although a little of that perhaps wouldn't hurt). It is rather the perpetuation of the existing asset inflation.

To be sure, the source of the bear market in Hawaiian assets is only partly macroeconomic. Some of the blame rests with the state's growth-stunting politics. (Hawaii is, in that sense, Vermont without the skiing; similarly, Vermont is Hawaii without the surfing.) Thus, Case cannot just buy his block of stock from a consenting shareholder. The Hawaii Control Share Acquisitions Act prescribes an approval process that Case could flaunt only at his cost. Nor are Maui Land's pineapples sold in a free market, but rather in one protected against Thai exports, which have been found to be predatory if tasty.

Then there's the contentious matter of land use. MLP can't freely dispose of its property any more than Case can freely buy his chosen block of stock. There are procedures and policies that have been instituted by the state for the good of the people, if they would only listen and obey. Agricultural land, which constitutes 6,400 acres out of the company's 28,600 acres, is locked into agricultural use for years. "You really do have to understand how the process works here," Paul Meyer, executive vice president, finance, of Maui Land, tells our crack summer intern, Keith Fleischmann. "To take land out of agriculture and to do a subdivision right now from start to finish, assuming that everything went as well as possible, it would take you like 20 years . . . and that's the honest-to-God truth. You've got whole layers of state and county approvals, plus you would have to develop the roads, sewer systems and find the water and develop the water. They've got a 30-year moratorium on water meters in up-country Maui."

Not bullish—except, perhaps, for the owners of established, therefore protected, Hawaiian property. There is, of course, a macroeconomic dimension to the troubles at Maui Land on top of a regulatory one. The long-lived Japanese banking contraction has turned the last cycle's big buyers into forced sellers. "Hawaii has seen a spate of sales of big properties . . . ," *The Wall Street Journal* reported last month. "All were sold for what the Japanese paid for them—sometimes hundreds of millions of dollars less. 'They paid too much for these properties,' said Lowell Kalapa of the nonprofit Tax Foundation of Hawaii."

Is property now too cheap? Maybe not, according to Alexander & Baldwin, which is active on both the buy and the sell side of the local market. "[W]e've been looking fairly aggressively for at least a year for worthwhile properties in Hawaii that we could buy and lease to others as part of our property leasing business," relates John Kelley, the company's investor relations contact, "and prices are sticky for us, too. I mean, we are just not finding many people out there whose price would make it attractive for us to buy."

On the other hand, Maui has never been cheaper in proportion to the off-island paper wealth available to invest in it. Recently, the Yankees uniform that Lou Gehrig wore for his retirement ceremony was hammered down for $451,541 (reportedly, the most ever paid for any piece of Yankees paraphernalia), while an auction of Rothschild family art and antiques at Christie's in London last week fetched $90 million (thereby setting 10 record-high auction prices). If one is bearish on the stock-market valuations that support and finance these extravagant prices, one is necessarily of two minds. On the one mind, paper wealth can be mobilized and spent, as the winning bidders demonstrated. On the other mind, it can also be lost. Possibly, the great American asset inflation will dissolve into a purely conventional price inflation, featuring higher interest rates, higher commodity prices and higher prices for Maui land. As it is, perhaps the most pertinent kind of inflation for the prices on Maui is the inflation in the cost of retiring. Never before has the cost of a dollar of corporate earnings, or of a dollar of corporate dividends, been higher. Alexander & Baldwin might not deem Hawaiian land to be a bargain; Case seems to disagree. In terms of a share of AOL, the cost of Maui has never been cheaper. The ratio of the net worth of the inhabitants of Silicon Valley to the market value of Maui must itself be flirting with record-wide readings. To a wealthy bull facing retirement, an asset that has spent the past decade not appreciating will necessarily seem cheap. Therefore, the appeal of MLP as an investment is that it is not purely an inflation play. It is also a value play (in relative terms) and a play on Asian aggregate demand. One potential boost for Maui Land is a revival of the Japanese economy. As it is, Meyer relates, only 7% to 11% of Kapalua's rooms are filled by eastbound travelers. Then, too, the Case announcement might foretell a replay of the Japanese-driven investment bull market of a decade ago. Maybe, this time around, the Americans will play the part of the spendthrift Japanese.

What about the assets? We begin by noting the humbling facts that Harry Weinberg, a successful and shrewd investor, was a decade-and-a-half early (and counting) in his MLP investment, and that a mistimed entry into the Hawaiian real estate market by JMB Realty Corp. at the peak of the last cycle drove Liberty House, a subsidiary of a company JMB had acquired, into bankruptcy.

By our reckoning, the value of the Kapalua Resort on MLP's balance sheet is worth approximately—very approximately—the stock market capitalization, i.e., $131 million. Under the assumptions described in a 1986 *Barron's* story, the implied value of the current portfolio would have been approximately $486 million. Some of this disparity is owing to different valuation methods. Thus, for example, we have assigned a value of $1,000 an acre to the pineapple fields, not the $20,000 to $30,000 quoted in *Barron's*. Virtually all of the value is concentrated in the 1,650 acres of the Kapalua Resort, which comprises 600 acres of golf course, 500 acres of undeveloped land, 350 acres of residential land and a couple of hundred acres of "other." "You really can't take a simplistic approach to it," Meyer insists. "Kapalua probably has 70 different parcels of land and those range from single-family home sites to a 30-acre site underlying the Ritz Carlton at Kapalua."

The fair market value of the Kapalua Resort? "I'd say somewhere between $100 million and $200 million," Meyer says. Of the 20,000 acres of conservation and pasture land? Nothing, to be conservative. Of the 6,400 acres of pineapple land? Call it nothing, even though pineapple revenues in 1997 and 1998 totaled $91 million and $97.5 million, respectively, and contributed operating profits of $2 million and $5.4 million, respectively. These were the first two back-to-back years of profit from pineapple growing since 1991. (A decade ago, prior to the Thai incursion, according to Meyer, the company's pineapple operations produced 10% pretax operating margins.)

Following the Case announcement effect—not so potent, by the way, as the 1998 stock-split effect—Maui Land is valued at 23 times earnings, 2.0 times book value and 14.8 times operating income. Debt constitutes 41% of common equity. Total enterprise value—$150 million—is within the approximate neighborhood of the company's highly nonspecific estimate of the value of its Kapalua Resort (a second estimate obtained by *Grant's* from another Hawaiian real estate source, incidentally, is comparably nonspecific).

These are not the kind of numbers that caused Benjamin Graham to open his checkbook. Perhaps they are not the most germane numbers. One essential fact about Hawaiian real estate, as Meyer points out, is its extreme cyclicality. "It is almost unbelievable," he tells Fleischmann, "but you'll get a period during which—a year or two years—you'll be able to develop and sell resort property condominiums and homes, and following that period, you will have seven to 10 years when almost no property moves.

"Through most of the '70s," Meyer goes on, "the market was very quiet. From 1978 to 1981, the market was extremely hot. Kapalua sold 528 condominiums during the time period. Then nothing moved for another six years until 1987 and 1988, and things got incredibly hot again. The Japanese were buying everything in sight for twice its value. And then it fell off a cliff in 1990. In the last eight years, nothing has moved. Since 1990, the market has been extremely quiet. Realtors have been starving until about the last six months."

And now? "All of a sudden," Meyer relates, "we have a buyer profile of baby boomer guys, born in 1946 and 1947, who've got some money out of the stock market now and they are starting to retire. . . . It is a very interesting market."

In 1988–90, in the Maui golden age preceding the Japanese-provoked liquidation, eight one-acre building lots in a Kapalua subdivision fetched an average of $4.5 million each; in the same year in another subdivision, 36 two-acre lots were sold for an average of $1.8 million each. Today, Meyer reports, the $1.8 million lots sell for $600,000 to $800,000—and this after a recent rebound. ("The velocity of the real estate market is much higher than it has been for the last six or seven years," says Meyer. "There [are] more properties trading, and average prices are higher.")

What about ALEX? Here, too, valuations are approximate, and once more our analysis ignores the substantial operating businesses in order to focus on the irreplaceable Maui dirt. As in MLP, most of the land under discussion is low-value farming acreage (52,700 acres at $6,500 per) and conservation land (16,000 acres at $750 per). Of the company's 69,040 acres on Maui, in fact, all but 340 fall under those two headings. The precious residual, "fully entitled urban land," commands a value estimated at $700,000 an acre. The approximate value of all the land: $593 million.

Compare this to the company's $1.08 billion stock-market capitalization and its $1.34 billion enterprise value. Do not compare too literally, of course. There is no continuous, liquid or deep market in Maui property. If Alexander & Baldwin wanted to sell 1,000 acres in a hurry, it certainly couldn't. In any case, ALEX is forever trying to move its land from low-value zoning status into the high-value one, and it says that 6,700 acres are, in fact, making their way to the zoning penthouse. Let's assume that half of the 6,700 become fully entitled urban acres over the next five years (not an unreasonable assumption, according to Kelley). If 3,350 acres were upgraded in this fashion, an immense change in the company's value would be achieved: 3,350 times $700,000 equals $2.35 billion. Discount that total by 8% a year to adjust for the time value of money. Still, the number is big: nearly $1.6 billion, a 19% premium over the current enterprise value. The valuation does not reflect the contribution of the assets generating 89% of the company's revenues (the cause of the decline in those revenues is the recent sale of a majority interest in ALEX's sugar refining and marketing business). Nor does it incorporate the value of its property on the other Hawaiian islands or on the U.S. mainland.

It's been a long and—some would say—well-deserved bear market for the kind of assets featured on the balance sheets of resource companies. But no downturn lasts forever. First Warren Buffett buys silver. Now Stephen Case buys MLP. Do two sightings constitute a trend?

Bull-to-Bull

March 17, 2000

The New Economy is about to be augmented by an institution that was created in the days when high technology meant a wall socket. If all goes according to plan, the 102-year-old Chicago Mercantile Exchange will soon become a public company.

Hedging and speculating are as old as the hills, of course. Ditto, the cultivation of those fine arts in a central location within a settled legal and regulatory framework. "B2B," a glittering, multibillion-dollar slogan, refers to a wholesale marketplace, a kind of institution not unlike the one that is sometimes described as a "commodity exchange." It was in 1898 when the spiritual antecedents of the creators of FreeMarkets Inc., Ventro Corp., eBay Inc. et al. walked out of the Chicago Produce Exchange to form the Chicago Butter and Egg Board. And it was the Butter and Egg Board that, in 1919, was reinvented as the Chicago Mercantile Exchange. Now the Merc, which since its inception has been owned by its members, is going to demutualize, if the members (and, of course, the regulators) give their say-so.

Mindful of the speed of Internet time, we will state our conclusion even before we develop our arguments. We are bullish on the Merc. It has a long running start on the complex business of managing counterparty risk in an auction-market setting. It is well positioned to profit from—indeed, to organize—the commodity and derivatives markets of the digital future. And the value currently imputed to the exchange by the combined value of its memberships is a fraction of the capitalized value of the typical upstart Web-based business-to-business exchange, including one—eMerge Interactive Inc.—that solely serves the cattle industry. The star burst of speculative and hedging innovation presents the Merc with risks and opportunities alike. The latter outweigh the former, in our opinion. Hence, we appraise the quoted value of a full Merc membership—last traded at $575,000—as a bargain.* A Boston venture capital firm may think so, too. According to a knowledgeable source, a tech-savvy investment company recently offered to pay approximately that valuation for a minority interest in the CME. (Specifically, we understand, the bid was $335 million for 30%, implying an overall value on the order of $1.1 billion. Also in the rumor department, a consortium of brokerage firms and energy companies is said to have proposed

---

* eMerge Interactive was a wipeout. Before its 2004 merger with Ariba, Freemarkets. com gave up 97% of its value. CME Group, as the Chicago Merc is known today, has returned 53% a year to its owners since it went public.

an investment in the CME's East Coast cousin, the New York Mercantile Exchange. The New York Merc, which is also demutualizing, supposedly has called the proposed terms inadequate.)

"The financial and risk management markets in which we operate are experiencing significant and rapid changes," states the Merc in a new regulatory filing, the pre-going-public S-4 registration statement. "These changes are largely due to advances in technology, a relaxation of regulatory barriers and resultant cost efficiencies. Computer and telecommunications systems today can efficiently and economically bring buyers and sellers together in ways that present new challenges to the traditional exchange model of centralized physical auction markets. The Internet and proprietary networks are changing investor behavior and revolutionizing how investors interface with financial markets. Other technological innovations are reducing the costs and barriers to entry for alternative exchange-type systems."

These are revolutionary times. In the course of a crash program to refashion itself for the New Economy, J.P. Morgan & Co., another financial institution of a certain age, has encouraged the free and open exchange of ideas between management and the rank and file. So free and open have those discussions become, *The Wall Street Journal* reports, that the words "Destroy J.P. Morgan" recently found their way onto one of the bank's own white boards. So it goes in the new era. Zero is the business value commonly assigned to a long-established financial franchise.

Those who, like us, are apt to disagree may weigh an investment in the Merc. A bull could buy a membership today, anticipating the success of the demutualization. Those not inclined to bid for a seat could wait to invest in a future public sale of shares (there will be two classes of stock, the various weightier "B" shares being reserved for seat-holding members). We could not do full justice to the Talmudic details of the exchange offering even if this issue were 16 pages long. One salient detail: The "A" shares will be made available for public purchase only after the expiration of a six-month trading restriction.

Not only has the exchange repeatedly adapted to changing market conditions, but it has also become a significant global clearing and credit institution. Buying or selling on the exchange floor, a member trades without regard for the creditworthiness of his or her counterparty; effectively, the clearinghouse is everybody's counterparty. "The CME Clearing House has a perfect record for performance on its obligations," the Merc's S-4 is able to state, "and no clearing member has ever failed to perform on its obligations to the CME Clearing House." (The corresponding risk factor is that some overextended member could single-handedly bring down the clearinghouse.) To date, the computer-based wholesale exchanges have had no need for a fail-safe clearing system for the simple reason that they have not generated a sufficient volume of activity to force the issue. Then, too, in the current ebullient speculative climate, the stock market is not likely to be much impressed by the depth, strength and integrity of an exchange's credit structure; the lack of such structures in the new Web-based wholesale marts has certainly not resulted in any visible valuation penalty. A CME officer to

"My nephew Andrew and I have decided to close the account and trade the—what do you call them?—tech stocks."

whom we spoke observed that the fledglings face a fundamental choice: Either generate the higher levels of volume and open interest that warrant sophisticated clearing mechanisms, or risk the loss of their lofty stock-market valuations.

Meanwhile, the Merc has been losing its seat-price valuation. The all-time high price for a full membership, $925,000, was recorded in the tumultuous interest-rate year of 1994. The last sale, on February 18, at $575,000, was down by 37.8% from the peak 5½ years ago (but up from the most recent low of $310,000 recorded on Feb. 23, 1999). At the moment, $530,000 is bid for a Merc membership with full trading privileges; $630,000 is asked. At least in relation to the year-earlier transactions, the price of a membership in the CME can be said to be in an uptrend. In contrast, quoted membership prices in both the Chicago Board of Trade and the New York Stock Exchange have been in downtrends, with the recent bid price for a Big Board seat, $1.7 million, lower by almost $1 million than the record-high sale price struck last summer.

As voice power is not always a match for computing power, the Merc's members are fretful about the survival of the open-outcry, or shouting, exchange model. They wonder if, in a virtual age, an exchange can exist anywhere except on a computer screen. And they fear the possibility that a few top member firms will walk out to start their own e-exchange, taking precious liquidity with them. The banks and brokerage houses would love to get their hands on the order flow that now is directed to the floor of the various exchanges; thus, the seat-owning members live in fear of the next advance in software. Globex2, the Merc's automated after-hours trading system, generates just 8% of the exchange's revenues (that, however, is up from 1% in 1996). Then, too, the advent of the euro has caused a drop-off in speculative activity in the displaced Continental currencies.

"The market prices for our shares may fluctuate widely and trade at prices below the recent price of the membership that the shares replace," says the Merc's S-4 in a particularly unnecessary passage from the section on risk factors. However, there are substantive worries, too, including government regulation (the new Web-based exchanges have no Commodity Futures Trading Corp. to worry about), and the unanswerable question of whether the new professional management is up to the task of replacing the ancient self-governing structure. "We derive a significant percentage of our revenue from sales of market data," the exchange says on the subject of technological obsolescence. "[T]he availability of our market data over terminals that access our Globex2 system may diminish the value of our market data and the prices that we can charge for our market data." Then, again, obsolescence has presented a clear and present danger to the exchange since the butter-and-egg men found themselves under siege by oleomargarine on Day One.

Undoubtedly, reflects Jack McHugh, a paid-up subscriber and Chicago futures broker, Bill Gates could, if he wished, set up an e-exchange to compete with the Merc and/or any B2B bazaar under the sun. However, even Gates might find it burdensome to guarantee, as the Merc does, the performance of every member on every trade. "On an average day," the S-4 statement goes on, "we act as custodian for approximately $20 billion in performance bond assets, and we move an average of $990 million of settlement varia-tion funds through our clearing system. . . . [O]ur Clearing House guarantees the performance of our contracts with approximately $64 billion in available assets." Volume of trading at the Merc in all instruments, including index products and options, measured at par, or "notional" volume, totaled no less than $138 trillion last year. "You're guaranteeing part of the U.S. financial system," McHugh reminds Gates and every other potential interloper.

Its butter-and-egg days long past, the Merc does the lion's share of its volume these days in interest rate instruments (60%), equity and index futures contracts (24%) and currency contracts (12%). Agricultural products—including the once-mighty pork belly market, which put the exchange on the map in the early 1960s—account for only 4% of trading volume. Recent product introduc-tions include contracts in personal bankruptcy filings (the CME

Quarterly Bankruptcy Index futures and options) and the weather
(Heating Degree Day and Cooling Degree Day futures and
options). In a recent conversation with Scott Gordon, chairman of
the Merc, and James J. McNulty, president and CEO, we asked
about future product development. Literally hundreds of billions
of dollars of stock- and debt-market capitalization ride on the
prices assigned to high-tech commodities—DRAMs, SRAMs,
telecommunications bandwidth, etc.—we observed. Why shouldn't
there be liquid markets in these things? Why shouldn't the Merc
be the institution to inaugurate them? The executives, as discreet as
their lawyers would want them to be, strongly conveyed the impression that the Merc was all over the case. Indeed, they noted, there
could be a good business for the Merc in servicing the back office
and clearing requirements of the new-age Web marts. As for old-
age innovation, they mentioned the possibility of a water
contract.

The history of the Merc is mainly the history of the membership's adjustments to the rise and fall of markets. For example,
according to Bob Tamarkin's *The Merc*, the butter futures market vanished after the government enacted butter price supports.
The onion contract was abolished by an act of Congress in 1958:
Farmers, blaming a bear market in onion prices on the parasites
in Chicago, prevailed on a Republican administration to suppress
the offending free market (Rep. Gerald Ford of Michigan took the
side of the putatively victimized growers). The onion calamity left
the Merc with exactly one functional contract, the egg contract,
which, at about this time, had become "a constant attraction for
would-be manipulators and attempted corners," in the words of a
Merc chairman. It was innovate or liquidate.

Innovation proceeded apace. The Merc today has exclusive
rights to trade futures and options on futures contracts on speci-
fied S&P stock indices, including the S&P 500 contract until 2008
and the Nasdaq 100 contract until 2005. Miniaturized versions of
both stock index contracts, perfect for today's legions of miniature

speculators, are a hit. Shoring up its principal financial franchise in interest rates, the Merc this week inaugurated a new contract in five- and 10-year federal agency notes.

If, as the Merc estimates, 20% of the American GDP is weather-sensitive, at least 100% is government-sensitive, and the government both helps and hinders. Thus, in the early 1970s, with the abolition of fixed exchange rates, the government gave the gift of exchange-rate volatility and inflation. Seizing the moment, the Merc, led by the visionary Leo Melamed, created the International Monetary Market. About a quarter-century later, European governments created the euro, at a stroke reducing the scope of foreign-exchange futures activity.

Fortunately, the world has created common stocks much faster than it has retired national currencies, and the Merc's S&P 500 and Nasdaq 100 pits are both going strong (so strong that the NDX pit was just enlarged). On the other hand, so were the butter and onion contracts going strong before they came to the end of their useful lives. Galvanized by a bear market, Congress could vote to do what might now seem unthinkable, i.e., implement price supports for the leading equity indices or, alternatively, abolish equity futures and options trading entirely (speculation, at this political juncture, being condemned as a force of destruction and chaos in American life). It is not irrelevant to the discussion that the Clinton administration today faces heavy pressure to suppress a rise in heating oil prices that occurred at the end of an historically mild winter. Then, too, as long as we are conjuring up dire circumstances, there is always the risk of monetary equilibrium. A return to anything like the low and stable interest rates of the onion-futures era would constitute a hammer blow to the Eurodollar-futures contract. "Our existing and future revenues are highly dependent upon maintaining current volume levels in our Eurodollar and S&P 500 futures and options contracts, and in our foreign currency Exchange-for-Physicals ('EFP') market," notes the S-4. What the document might have added is that the value of the CME's hard-won reputation for fair dealing and

"Did I just hear you say, 'I love you, Qualcomm'?"

creditworthiness is highly dependent on the existence of a decent minimum of financial apprehension. In an investment world interpreted by CNBC, "Destroy the CME" makes just as much sense as "Destroy J.P. Morgan."

A disinterested reader would not associate the Merc's historical financial performance with the phrase "growth stock," either—net income has been in a six-year downtrend, at least—but allowances must be made. The foremost mitigating circumstance is that the Merc is a not-for-profit institution. That is, unlike the prototypical B2B start-up, it has not set out to maximize its owners' income. Even so, the Merc is profitable—barely—with roughly two-thirds of its revenue derived from clearing fees. Quotation data fees are the next-biggest revenue generator, followed by communication fees and investment income. In 1999, the CME earned $2.7 million on revenues of $208.5 million. For the second year in a row, investment in high tech swelled the expense line.

In general, it is the rare new futures contract that succeeds in what might be termed the old physical exchange space. To infer from the valuations assigned to some of the largely untried B2B Internet ventures, however, it will be the typical cash cyber-market that succeeds in the new Web space. When U.S. Steel, a division of USX Corp., disclosed last month that it had taken a small stake in a small company that markets steel over the Internet, the *New York Times* (in its dot-com format) speculated that the move "could be aimed at stemming a decline in profits and boosting [USX's] ailing stock." As long ago as 1954, the Merc anticipated the wholesale online steel market with a scrap iron and steel futures contract. The most notable feature of this short-lived experiment was its lack of speculative electricity.

Either the Web has effected a revolution in the structure of American wholesale trade, or it hasn't. Say that it has. Then either the resulting profits will chiefly accrue to the owners of the new exchanges, or they won't. Say that they will. (A leap of faith: an industrialist we know contends that his company has derived more benefit from trading on freemarkets.com than the Web business has produced, or is likely to produce, for itself). Then, either the old exchanges will vanish without a trace, or they won't. They won't, we believe.

So, then, how to value the Merc? Rose Ann Tortora of this staff has conducted an investigation. "First, we start with how the Merc values itself," she leads off. "The inside buying and selling of memberships pegs the Merc's 'market value' at close to $900 million—4.1 times sales and 5.2 times members' equity. Next, consider what the Merc might be likened to. How about freemarkets.com (FMKT), with its $6.9 billion market cap equal to 176 times revenues, or eBay, with its $25 billion market cap at a much more reasonable level of 114 times revenues. Never mind that freemarkets. com shows a loss, or that eBay's earnings per share wouldn't buy a minute of long-distance telephone time."

EMerge Interactive (EMRG), the online cattle brokerage and auction service, is another point of reference. Unlike the Merc, a futures market, eMerge deals entirely in the cash market. And also unlike the

Merc, eMerge has aspirations to create a virtual community of cattle folk, who would deal in livestock in cyber-barns instead of in the fly-blown physical ones. When the Merc unveiled its first live cattle contract in 1964, that was the new thing (the first time any living creature had been commoditized). Now eMerge is the new new thing.

"So what valuation does an online beef trader get from the market?" Tortora goes on. "At the recent price of $63 per share, the market cap is $2 billion, or 50 times book value and 46 times sales (over two-thirds of which is intangible). Using these valuations, the Merc's market cap would be somewhere between $8.4 billion and $9.6 billion, a bit higher than the $900 million or so at which the members value themselves." Then, again, only 2.2% of the Merc's volumes are related to beef. This fact, taken in isolation, would imply a price tag for the CME of between $382 billion and $436 billion (we are rounding).

Grant's itself, always prudent, would stop well short of the higher numbers. However, we believe, the Merc has something to offer that the Web-preoccupied world does not yet fully appreciate. Not the least of that something is credit, the engine room of the ship of enterprise. Just how the Merc will exploit its franchise, we don't know, and can't predict. However, at the quoted seat prices, the old Chicago Butter and Egg Board is cheap at the price.

Chapter Three
New Eras on Parade

Thank Mother Russia

July 30, 1999

W HO PUT THE "New" in the New American Economy? Don't forget to thank the Russians. After the collapse of the resource-squandering command economy of the Former Soviet Union (FSU), Russia has produced more and more even as it has consumed less and less.

There's no gainsaying the contribution made by low commodity prices to the bullish inflation experience of the mid- and late-1990s. And there's no doubting the contribution of the FSU, a top producer of things found in dirt, to the protracted commodity bear market. During the Cold War, Russia was a major raw materials consumer and a minor exporter. Today, it consumes little and exports much. The creditors of the world owe more than they know to this transformation, as a *Grant's* reader has helpfully pointed out. It has helped to bring about the persistent commodity bear market, a phenomenon that has silently contributed to the reputation for genius of the Federal Reserve Board.

Leigh R. Goehring, vice president of Prudential Investments, Newark, N.J., is the reader with the theory. The manager of a pair of high-performing natural resource mutual funds, Goehring is bullish on things that most people aren't—on Stillwater Mining Co., for example, the one and only primary producer of platinum group metals in North America. He's bullish on aluminum, nickel, timber and even on the dog, gold bullion. The gold price, it amuses him to tell the people who don't believe him, will inevitably again approach the level of the Dow Jones Industrial Average (as it actually did in 1980 and had half a mind to do in 1933).

An old-economy devotee, Goehring has stoically borne the stupendous prosperity of the 1990s, and he has made it his business to try to understand (one might use the word "debunk") the principles of the supposed New Economy. He has made a clinical study of the contribution of the FSU to the bear market in things—and therefore, by extension, to the bull market in paper. Except for the surge in Russian supply (and the collapse in Russian demand), he maintains, commodity prices would be higher than they are in this allegedly inflation-proof world. Possibly, by the same force of logic, dollar-denominated interest rates would be higher than they are today, and stock prices would be lower.

Aluminum makes an instructive case study, in Goehring's estimation. In 1988, the year before the Berlin Wall fell, the Soviet Union produced 3,500 tons of aluminum; it consumed 2,900 tons and exported 187 tons. Those exports constituted 1.2% of non-FSU consumption, approximately—Goehring cautions against an over-literal reliance on inexact numbers.

In 1998, the FSU produced 3,307 tons of aluminum. It consumed a mere 454 tons and exported no less than 2,228 tons. Those exports amounted to 10.5% of non-FSU consumption. FSU exports exploded in the early 1990s and have continued unabated.

Dow 36,000 ushers in a better commute.

However, FSU production has not risen. At least, observes Stewart Spector, publisher of the authoritative *Spector Report* on aluminum, the bad news is out: "[T]he Russians are producing and shipping everything they can, just to get cash. . . . Metal supply is tightening, and they can't produce much more."

World aluminum consumption has continued to rise meanwhile, the woes of Japan and the FSU, and the softness of the European economy notwithstanding. "For a virtual world," Goehring dryly notes, "we seem to be still consuming a lot of aluminum."

As with aluminum, so with many other commodity markets, although not with the king of commodities, energy. "FSU nickel supply has gone from 8.1% of Western consumption in 1988 to 18.4% in 1998," Goehring says; "copper from 0.8% to 4.3%. As for steel, the FSU has gone from being an importer to satisfying 5.4% of Western demand in 1998. Numbers like these are repeated in potash, platinum, palladium and uranium. Ironically, the only big commodities not influenced by the FSU collapse are oil and gas."

Mulling these data, Goehring goes on, one might begin to ask if the financial prosperity of the 1990s is based on more than the Federal Reserve and the Internet. Perhaps, he reflects, it is also the result of a commodity bear market caused by a collapse in demand (and a reciprocal gush of supply) from the former Evil Empire. "Remember," comments Spector, "[the Russians] went from consuming three million tonnes per year to 350,000. A country that size should be consuming at least 1½ million tonnes per year, if they had even a reasonably developed economy. It might take 10 years, but they are building can plants and motor plants. So if there were no additional supply in the West, any marginal improvement would make the price go higher."

Of course, adds Goehring, the Japanese authorities, by unwittingly perpetuating the troubles of the world's second largest economy, have also contributed to the well-being of American investors. Ultra-low interest rates in one industrialized country have helped to bring down interest rates in other industrialized countries. All in all, Goehring contends, Americans owe a warm round of applause to the mismanaged foreign economies.

Now what? Goehring likens the world's commodity situation to a thin man in a baggy suit. At first the suit hangs from his bones. However, years pass, and the thin man gains weight. After a decade or so of good eating, lo and behold, the suit does fit. So with the world's commodity markets. Consider, Goehring says, that the world is using significantly more nickel, copper, uranium and zinc than it did in 1988, despite the collapse of Russian industrial demand and the long-slumbering Japanese economy. Who knows what macroeconomic dislocations an outbreak of economic growth might bring about?

"I never believed in the Internet/computer-led productivity paradigm," the man from the Pru winds up. "But after looking at these numbers, I'm more convinced than ever before that the foundation of the present boom is based on 'free' capital from the world's largest savings economy (Japan) and cheap commodities from the world's largest commodity-producing economy (Russia). And both these items—capital and commodities—are about to become more expensive. It will be a rude awakening to people who believe in new paradigms."

Real Estate 36,000

September 10, 1999

❝ Stock prices could double, triple or even quadruple tomorrow and still not be too high. . . ," contend James K. Glassman and Kevin A. Hassett, the authors of the new book, *Dow 36,000* (a lengthy, a very lengthy, excerpt from which appears in this month's *Atlantic Monthly*; it's the cover story). "Stocks are now, we believe, in the midst of a one-time-only rise to much higher ground—to the neighborhood of 36,000 for the Dow Jones Industrial Average."

Even if Dow 36,000 were not "too high" in the judgment of theorists and stockbrokers, might it not seem a trifle rich to the population of potential sellers? Indeed, might not hundreds of thousands of Americans (and foreigners, too) rush to start a new business for the very purpose of issuing common equity at 100 times earnings? Our answer, in advance, is yes, emphatically. The first-order consequences of a sudden tripling in the U.S. stock market capitalization would be thrilling enough (e.g., the mass resignation of 401(k)-plan participants, instant members of the leisure class); the second- and third-order effects, however, might be even more gripping. For instance, trading hours would have to be extended to nights and weekends to accommodate the backlog of IPOs, foreign as well as domestic (especially foreign, if the U.S. were the only country in which the Glassman-Hassett prophecy were fulfilled). Seth Klarman, a Cambridge (Mass.) investor and paid-up subscriber, suggests that the way to think about Dow 36,000 is to try to imagine the effect of a sudden tripling in real estate values. All at once, the developers would start to borrow and build. Presently, they would overborrow and overbuild. Soon

thereafter, landlords would start to cut rents. The ultimate consequence of this feast of real estate value, therefore, Klarman proposes (details to follow), would be a real estate famine.

We turn to the Glassman-Hassett thesis because it captures so
well the pre millennial spirit. The public can see for itself that the
sky's the limit on Wall Street. A best-selling book by serious authors
purporting to prove, mathematically, that the party has just begun
may outsell even the latest eat-all-the-fat-you-want-and-still-lose-
weight self-help guide. Last month's inspiring story of the day-
trading New York taxi driver ("Wheeler Dealer: Cabbie cashing in
on bull market by trading stocks from his taxi"—page one of the
August 19 *Daily News*) is what used to be called a "sign of the top."
Now, perhaps, it is only a sign of another potential hardback buyer
of *Dow 36,000*. We bears don't know much, but what we do know,
we cherish. For instance: Markets can do anything they want, and
will. Also, markets make opinions. And, finally, the pricing of financial assets does not occur in a vacuum but rather in the real economy, which resembles a hall of mirrors. Fact affects perception, and
vice versa. If equity capital were free, people would help themselves
to it. They would create new businesses to compete with existing
businesses, thereby reducing profit margins, their own as well as
other people's. In this way, they would disturb the structure of production, making it more capital-intensive than it would otherwise
be. If capital were free, people would use too much of it, as the Japanese did in the 1980s and—who knows?—as we Americans might
be doing in the 1990s. Redundant investment would lead to excess
productive capacity. These propositions, however, the new super
bulls implicitly reject. The case for instantaneous levitation they
present as revealed truth.

It is not thereby revealed to us, keepers of the flame of Dow
36.000 or thereabouts. Admittedly, looking back, it would have
been better to have bought the S&P 500 so many years ago than to
have carped about its overvaluation. But regret is one thing (and, by
the way, where were Glassman and Hassett in 1991?), the intellectual

and financial embrace of the New Era something else. How should one invest in this most flummoxing of times? "The market" is going up, all right. However, one's painstakingly selected portfolio of low P/E, small-cap value stocks—the ones not featured on CNBC every morning—is very probably not. The Russell 2000 index is not. The rich get richer, the out-of-favor poor get poorer. And now—just in time—comes *Dow 36,000.*

In some walks of human activity, there are indeed new eras, times in which precedent does not apply, or is not supposed to. One thinks of the designated-hitter rule, for example, or, at an earlier time on another continent, the advent of atonal musical composition, so offensive to the orthodox critics. It was true that, to the conventional ear, 12-tone music sounded like noise. Then, again, that is the way it was written.

Is it now the same in finance? If we traditionalists can't hear a melody—"The P/E Sonata" or the "Symphony of Yield"—is it because there isn't one? The answer is "no," we are sure. Aberrations do indeed appear in financial markets, but they must eventually pass the test of supply and demand. New eras are cut short by the financial behavior they reward and condition. And when, as *The Wall Street Journal* reported from San Francisco last week, the shares of Internet start-ups begin to be treated as a kind of improvisational currency, we can suspect that something is wrong.

The Glassman-Hassett argument is not, for the most part, a New Era argument. It isn't the wonders of the microchip or the Greenspan Fed that will cause this brilliant, wealth-conferring liftoff. What is so bullish, the authors claim, is the arithmetic of valuation, which was just as bullish before its discovery as it supposedly is today. Still, it must be a kind of New Era when a stock market that has been allegedly undervalued for 200 years can suddenly become fairly valued thanks to the revelations of one moderately priced book. We ourselves would like to observe that it is a very funny kind of New Era when the United States, the allegedly uniquely favored country, has higher interest rates than Japan and

Europe, and when the prices of smaller American equities continue to lose altitude, relatively and absolutely. When Glassman and Hassett sing the praises of "stocks," they do not mean all stocks, but rather some stocks—the anointed, large-cap ones—and not just any country's stocks, but one country's, this one's.

What is the revolutionary Dow 36,000 insight? That the valuation of U.S. stock prices from the Buttonwood Tree has been based on an epic misunderstanding. Stocks are not riskier than bonds, as the wives' tale has it. On the contrary, over a holding period of more than 20 years, stocks are safer than Treasury bills. They excel unconditionally—or, rather, on condition that the future resembles the past. This is because, unlike bond coupon income, dividends and cash flow tend to grow. The central valuation issue is not the market's multiple to earnings, dividends or book value; fair value is instead defined as a kind of parity. It's the level at which the prospective payout from equities is equal to the contractual payout on bonds. In other words, it's the level at which the traditional equity risk premium is marked to zero.

Really, the authors insist, stocks held over the course of a generation are riskless. The worst average annual return on an S&P 500-type portfolio over a 30-year period since 1802, after accounting for inflation, the book records, was 2.6%. (A quibble: Up until the early 20th century, when industrial companies and retail chains began to issue shares, there was nothing like a diversified portfolio of common stocks available to be purchased.) "Never in American history," writes Team 36,000, "has a diversified basket of stocks failed to double in buying power over a generation. Never."

How high should the stock market go? Raising this basic question, the left-brained authors refer to a "Perfectly Reasonable Price" (a telltale phrase if there ever was one; given the huge disparities persisting between and among various classes of American equity, what does reasonableness have to do with it?). What is this price? Based on the prevailing dividend yield, and on historically observed rates of growth in dividend income, the S&P 500 would have to quadruple to achieve perfect reasonableness. Using cash flow instead of dividends for their calculation, the authors propose that the Dow would have to climb by sixfold. Then and only then should the market stop climbing. (At equilibrium, we can't help but feel, massive borrowing would ensue, as the owners of the new wealth began to monetize it. But we suppose we'll cross that bridge, like so many other Dow 36,000 obstacles, when we come to it.)

"As long as you are a long-term investor with a diversified portfolio, you should not be concerned about warnings of overvaluation or manias or bubbles," the two write, prudently adding one caveat—"provided the P/Es are under 100 [the Nasdaq Composite is already above 100] and the Dow is below 36,000."

If the authors are right about the Perfectly Reasonable Price, then Mr. Market, the know-it-all, is wrong, and has been not just in this glorious decade, but from the start. How an error in valuation so fundamental and glaring could have persisted all this time is a mystery. Maybe (as we happen to think) investors have not been too bearish, but rather alive to the hazards to which all mortal businesses are susceptible. If "the market" flourishes over time, the same can hardly be said for most of the companies that constitute the market. Perhaps, as the authors maintain, investors have become "more rational" (hence more bullish) in recent years. In this one particular, at least, Team 36,000 and the bears do share one speck of common ground. They are both conceited enough to believe that the market is wrong and they are right, although only the super bulls believe that the market has always been wrong. The bears, if we may presume to speak for the five or six still holding day jobs, believe that markets are cyclically inexact, prone to exaggeration at both extremes of valuation. Implicit in the long *Atlantic* essay is that markets do not necessarily over- and undershoot, but, rather, discount a stream of future cash income coolly, if too conservatively. They are as reasonable as the multiplication tables. We wonder about that, as well as about the effect that the disclosure of the greatest and longest-kept secret in the annals of finance will have on the behavior of millions of now-enlightened investors. If Glassman and Hassett are right, "the market" has done so well for so long only because the two of them hadn't gotten around to bringing out their book. Now that the word is out, the market supposedly will leap to its Perfectly Reasonable Price, then just rest there in its glory, like your grandmother's diamond necklace.

Another question comes to mind, at least to the fertile mind of Seth Klarman. If American investors have been systematically error-prone, why, he wonders, wouldn't they revert to error immediately after the market alighted at the point of perfect reasonableness, or when the book finally went out of print? "Let's say that the world adopted your view," says Klarman, directly addressing the authors. "What if it changes back? It is a perception, not reality. I always wonder about that. Why do people think that tomorrow their view of the world will be the same as their view today? Why would they ever think that?"

The more Klarman thought about Dow 36,000, the more he determined to refute it. "Dow 36,000 . . . In Your Dreams," was the title of the essay he sat down to write in rebuttal (and kindly submitted to *Grant's*). "My main point," he leads off, "is that the authors seem to regard the stock market as an entity separate from the rest of the economy rather than as a crucial mechanism for allocating capital to competing projects. . . . The stock market at a given level represents an equilibrium of sorts. Dramatically change the level and you disrupt the equilibrium.

"Were the Dow to trade at 36,000 tomorrow, there would be a gigantic impact on economic behavior," Klarman continues. "Private owners of businesses would rush to come public. Owners of equities would rush to spend some of their incremental wealth. Perhaps most significantly, there would be an entrepreneurial gold rush. Venture capitalists would raise enormous pools to exploit the arbitrage between the costs of starting a business—about $10,000 in office supplies—and the lofty valuations available for that business in the public markets.

"Business school students would pass up conventional opportunities, taking advantage of cheap, plentiful equity capital to start new ventures," Klarman writes. "All of this would unleash an enormous amount of new competition, which, in turn, would have the eventual effect of reducing returns on all capital, in-place as well as newly committed. This self-correcting mechanism is a crucial part of how the market economy works."

In other words, such a financial epiphany as visualized by Glassman and Hassett could happen only in a non-market economic setting—Stalinist Russia, for example.

To gain an instant appreciation of the unintended consequences of Dow 36,000, Klarman suggests, imagine an overnight tripling of American real estate values (real estate, of course, being one kind of equity). Visualize the euphoria. The new valuations would coax out a vast building boom. The demand for credit would erupt; interest rates would rise. Vacancy rates would rise and rents would fall, as landlords pushed prices down to marginal costs, assuming in the short run, as is reasonable, a static population of tenants. (Possibly, the commercial tenant population would be enlarged with $10,000 start-ups, but not many of these corporate seedlings would be in a position to pay much rent.)

"The competitive forces that impact real estate affect other businesses similarly, although perhaps in a less clear-cut way," Klarman goes on. "The stock market boom of the last 12 years has attracted enormous sums of investment into industries of all sorts. While the big stock market averages continue to surge, competitive forces are taking a toll on the profitability of many companies in diverse industries." Sears, Bank One, Office Depot, Dun & Bradstreet and Waste Management constitute a portion of the recent corporate casualty list, which, under the influence of the Internet alone, is sure to lengthen. "Loss-making, fledgling companies with startlingly inexpensive capital (and with shareholders who encourage them to grow faster and lose more) exacerbate the already intensely competitive business environment.

"Bull markets," Klarman winds up, "by influencing business activity, always sow the seeds of their own destruction. The current one is no exception. Were the Dow to surge soon to 36,000, the future would not be one of a permanently high plateau for stock prices but a capitalist free-for-all followed by a market and economic collapse. Many new eras have been proclaimed on Wall Street; few, if any, have withstood the test of time."

Nasdaq's Peak was Greenspan's

August 3, 2001

Sen. Phil Gramm (R., Texas): "If this is the bust, the boom was sure as hell worth it. You agree with that, right?"

Alan Greenspan: "Certainly."

The Wall Street Journal, which last week reported this committee-room exchange, omitted an important detail. The Federal Reserve chairman is no impartial observer of the boom he was asked to appraise. He seeded it, accommodated it, celebrated it and defended it from those who believed they saw it turn into a bubble. He was as uncritically and besottedly bullish as the luckless brokerage-house analysts who have fallen under the gaze of the Washington inquisitor, Rep. Richard H. Baker (R., La.). Not long ago, Greenspan even believed the analysts.

The chairman's analytical record, hazy in most memories (though not in that of the vigilant Bill Fleckenstein), constitutes an important piece of the U.S. interest-rate equation. The structure of forward rates is set by the market in partnership with the Second Most Powerful Man in the World. Insofar as Greenspan leads the market, it is a case of a one-eyed man leading people with two. Perhaps, after they refresh themselves on the chairman's errant judgment—especially off the beam on the eve of the 2000 stock-market peak—the sighted will have more confidence in their own judgment.

As it is, they seem to yield to the chairman. The money-market interest rate and domestic equity markets are priced for a prompt recovery from a downturn neither unusually severe nor protracted. By the shape of the forward Eurodollar curve and the bull-market P/E affixed to the S&P 500 (33 times trailing net income), Mr. Market has thrown in his lot with Greenspan and Gramm. A few quarters of weak GDP growth? A collapse in capital spending offset, in part, by the indomitable leveraged consumer? Is that all there is?

No, it seems to us. In support of this contention, we offer two preliminary propositions. No. 1: Booms not only precede busts; they also cause them. No. 2: Busts are indispensable. At least—behold Japan—no proper boom can be built on the uncleared debris of a preceding boom.

What is this debris? Business and financial error as reflected in misbegotten investment projects, bad debts, impaired balance sheets, wild expectations. The job of the bust is to redress these mistakes—in effect, to mark them to market. Americans, quick to acknowledge their own error and quick to forgive it in others (after the resolution of pending litigation, of course), disposed of the wreckage of the 1980s in short order. As the bubble of the late 1990s dwarfed that of the late 1980s, the cleanup will take longer than the market currently seems to allow for. Thus, we believe, money-market interest rates will continue to fall, the pattern of business activity will describe no letter "V," and the long-awaited recovery in corporate earnings will be pushed well into 2002.

With the telecom and Internet bubbles popped, some would say that the adjustment is nearly complete. In the last cycle, the pace of adjustment was checked by the nature of the problems—overvalued buildings and illiquid banks. Neither was susceptible to an instant cure. In contrast, stock prices, when they get around to falling, fall fast. However, we think, the millennial adjustment is far from over. Telecom and tech were not the whole bubble, only the most visible portion. The bubble was global. It distorted not only the structure of the U.S. economy but also the patterns of world trade. It exaggerated the economic feats of the one and only super-power and enlarged the U.S. current-account deficit. It caused an even greater round trip of dollars—into the hands of overseas cred-itors and back into U.S. securities markets—than might have oth-erwise occurred.

It would be just like Gramm and Greenspan to agree that, with respect to these huge foreign inflows, "no harm, no foul." So con-cluding, however, they would underestimate the risks of investing in highly valued markets in a highly valued currency. The sheer per-sistence of overvaluation in the United States has dulled investors' perceptions of it. News that $10.6 billion had flowed into U.S. equity mutual funds in June did not elicit the logical question: At these val-uations, why was there any? Commentators, instead, wondered why there wasn't more. ("Asset levels for equity mutual funds are much higher now than in 1998 or 1999," writes a dissenting commenta-tor, James Bianco, proprietor of Bianco Research, Barrington, Ill. "Despite the stock market sell-off, only two months have seen out-flows since the market peak in 2000.")

The fundamental cause of the bubble was the mispricing of capital and credit, therefore of risk. In the hottest, most bubble-like sectors of the economy, investment projects were undertaken purely because money or credit was available to finance them. The viability of these ventures depended on the continued availability of ultra-cheap financing. When capital and credit became less cheap, the boom-time ventures became less viable. The massive write-downs of good-will by Nortel Networks and JDS Uniphase begin to suggest how far from viability it is possible to wander. In the case of JDS, $44.8 bil-lion of acquisitions made during "The Fabulous Decade" (to borrow the title of a new book on the 1990s by Clinton Fed appointees Alan Blinder and Janet Yellen) turn out to be worthless.

Money was easy late in the decade, and when the capital mar-kets chose to make it tight, as in the wake of the 1998 Long-Term Capital Management affair, the Fed insisted on making it easy again. The Fed raised the funds rate three times in 2000, at last to 6½% on May 16, two months after the Nasdaq peaked. Was the Fed therefore leaning against the wind? Not the chairman, who contributed to the pro-cyclical gale in a speech on March 6, 2000, before the Boston College Conference on the New Economy. His subject: "The revolution in information technology." As he spoke, orders for high-tech durable goods in the second quarter were on their way to registering a year-over-year gain of 25%. Four quarters later, in April-June 2001, following a sharp rise in the cost of speculative capital, they would register a 31% decline, the steepest on record. John Lonski, Moody's chief economist, aptly describes the surge and plunge as "the picture of a bubble."

It was no bubble to the chairman when he rhapsodized on information technology and productivity growth. Thanks to computer technology, Greenspan declared, business managers were increasingly able to formulate decisions using "real-time" information. Not anticipating how rare a commodity "visibility" would shortly become, he said that this knowledge had reduced uncertainty. "When historians look back at the latter half of the 1990s a decade or two hence," he told his Boston audience, "I suspect they will conclude we are now living through a pivotal period in American economic history. New technologies that evolved from the cumulative innovations of the past half-century have now begun to bring about dramatic changes in the way goods and services are produced and in the way they are distributed to final users. Those innovations, exemplified most recently by the multiplying uses of the Internet, have brought on a flood of start-up firms, many of which claim to offer the chance to revolutionize and dominate large shares of the nation's production and distribution system. And participants in capital markets, not comfortable in dealing with discontinuous shifts in economic structure, are groping for the appropriate valuations of these companies. The exceptional stock price volatility of these newer firms, and, in the view of some, their outsized valuations, indicate the difficulty of divining the particular technologies and business models that will prevail in the decades ahead."

Striking the pose of a benevolently optimistic monetary states-man, Greenspan appeared hopeful, yet heedful of the risks. Heedlessness set in a few paragraphs later. "At a fundamental level," he said, "the essential contribution of information technology is the expansion of knowledge and its obverse, the reduction in uncertainty. Before this quantum jump in information availability, most business decisions were hampered by a fog of uncertainty. Businesses had limited and lagging knowledge of customers' needs and of the location of inventories and materials flowing through complex production systems. In that environment, doubling up on materials and people was essential as a backup to the inevitable misjudgments of the real-time state of play in a company. Decisions were made from information that was hours, days or even weeks old."

Thanks to the clarity afforded by instantaneous communications, Cisco Systems had to write off only $2.25 billion in excess inventories during its third fiscal quarter, in addition to just $1.17 billion in restructuring and other special charges. Using the older technologies—telephone, fax, the mails, citizens' band radio, etc.—the loss would undoubtedly have been greater. Throughout Silicon Valley, makers of PCs, chips, servers, printers and other digital products have admitted to monstrous miscalculations of final demand. Lucent, Corning, Nortel and JDS Uniphase have been devastated by one of the greatest misallocations of investment capital outside the chronicles of the Soviet Gosplan. Who can conceive of the size of this waste had there been no e-mail?

The chairman did not get to where he is in life by forgetting to hedge. He added, "[L]arge voids of information still persist, and forecasts of future events on which all business decisions ultimately depend will always be prone to error." However, he neglected to point out that high-tech revolutions inflame the right portion of the brain even as they enable the left-hand side. They stir up the speculative juices, thereby introducing a new source of potential business error. It is an especially potent source as when, late in the

1990s, the chairman of the world's leading central bank lends his imprimatur to a supposed new age.

Many are the blessings of information technology, Greenspan proceeded. He mentioned the mapping of the human genome, the refinement of financial derivatives and the explosion of big-company mergers: "Without highly sophisticated information technology, it would be nearly impossible to manage firms on the scale of some that have been proposed or actually created of late."

Yet, he noted, "At the end of the day, the benefits of new technologies can be realized only if they are embodied in capital investment, defined to include any outlay that increases the value of the firm. For these investments to be made, the prospective rate of return must exceed the cost of capital. Technological synergies have enlarged the set of productive capital investments, while lofty equity values and declining prices of high-tech equipment have reduced the cost of capital. The result has been a veritable explosion of spending on high-tech equipment and software, which has raised the growth of the capital stock dramatically over the past five years."

Having climbed so far into a logical trap, the chairman pulled the door shut behind him. "The fact that the capital spending boom is still going strong indicates that businesses continue to find a wide array of potential high-rate-of-return, productivity-enhancing investments. And I see nothing to suggest that these opportunities will peter out any time soon." At least, not for the next 96 hours (the Nasdaq peaked on March 10).

Here was a remarkable set of ideas. What drives a capital spending boom, said the central banker, is not—even in part—an excess of bank credit or an artificially low money-market interest rate. Rather, it is the cold and detached analysis of cost and benefit. Here the chairman was being unwontedly modest. Fearful of a Y2K calamity, the Fed stuffed tens of billions of dollars of credit into the banking system late in 1999. Not for the first time in monetary history, excess credit raised speculative spirits, inducing a sense of optimism bordering on invincibility.

Greenspan spoke only 18 months ago, but it was an eternity in speculative time. In March 2000, B2B promotions commanded preposterous valuations, which the chairman proceeded to validate. "Indeed," he said, "many argue that the pace of innovation will continue to quicken in the next few years, as companies exploit the still largely untapped potential for e-commerce, especially in the business-to-business arena, where most observers expect the fastest growth. . . . Already, major efforts have been announced in the auto industry to move purchasing operations to the Internet. Similar developments are planned or in operation in many other industries as well. It appears to be only a matter of time before the Internet becomes the prime venue for the trillions of dollars of business-to-business commerce conducted every year."

The Gartner Group had forecast that business-to-business commerce would generate $7 trillion of volume by 2004. Greenspan, a more experienced forecaster, gave no date and said only "trillions," but even that was wide of the mark. B2B stock prices crashed, and hundreds of Web sites went dark. He was, however, prophetic on one important detail: The potential for e-commerce remains "largely untapped."

The Fed was slow to raise the funds rate in 1999 and early 2000. It was slow to reduce the rate when, in the second half of 2000, boom turned to bust. The Austrian School economists who originated the theory of the investment cycle prescribed aggressive monetary ease in the bust phase, lest a depression feed on itself to become a "secondary depression."

Greenspan, having failed to call a bubble a bubble, was slow to recognize a bust as a bust. In his New Economy talk, he did acknowledge a connection between interest rates and technology investment. However, because information technology was an absolute and unqualified good thing, it followed that it could not be held responsible for a bad thing—for instance, the bottom falling out of capital investment and, therefore, out of the GDP growth rate. Blame for the downturn must lie elsewhere—with inventories or even the weather, as he proposed to the Senate Banking Committee on February 13, 2001. "[A] round of inventory rebalancing appears to be in progress," he told the senators. "Accordingly, the slowdown in the economy that began in the middle of 2000 intensified, perhaps even to the point of stalling out around the turn of the year. As the economy slowed, equity prices fell, especially in the high-tech sector, where previous high valuations and optimistic forecasts were being reevaluated, resulting in significant losses for some investors. . . . The exceptional weakness so evident in a number of economic indicators toward the end of last year (perhaps in part the consequence of adverse weather) apparently did not continue in January." However, he added, the FOMC "retained its sense that the risks are weighted toward conditions that may generate economic weakness in the foreseeable future." What portion of the future was "foreseeable" the chairman did not specify.

He refused to waver from his previously established line, the transforming significance of new technologies. Productivity growth and the availability of real-time information would cut short this inventory and profits slump, he said. Besides, Wall Street wasn't worried: "[A]lthough recent short-term business profits have softened considerably, most corporate managers appear not to have altered to any appreciable extent their longstanding optimism about the future returns from using new technology. . . . Corporate managers more generally, rightly or wrongly, appear to remain remarkably sanguine about the potential for innovations to continue to enhance productivity and profits. At least this is what is gleaned from the projections of equity analysts, who, one must presume, obtain most of their insights from corporate managers. According to one prominent survey, the three- to five-year average earnings projections of more than a thousand analysts, though exhibiting some signs of diminishing in recent months, have generally held firm at a very high level. Such expectations, should they persist, bode well for continued strength in capital accumulation and sustained elevated growth of structural productivity over the long term."

Such expectations, needless to say, have not persisted, and the Wall Street analysts who held them have been scorned and mocked. Not only have earnings plunged, but sales have weakened, undercut by the unforeseen disappearance of demand. "Business sales," observes Moody's Lonski, "are down minus 0.7% in the second quarter of 2001 from the second quarter of 2000. This is the sum of retail sales, manufacturing and wholesale sales. Manufacturing got clobbered—it is down 4.5%. The last time business sales were down year-over-year was the three quarters from the first quarter of 1991 to the third quarter of 1991. Before that was the five quarters from the first quarter of 1982 to the first quarter of 1983. And before that, it was in the 1970s, when inflation made the numbers do funny things, but it was in the first quarter of 1970. All the previous declines occurred in and around recessions."

Alan Greenspan never understood the problem. This defect does not mean he will never hit on the solution. What it does suggest, however, is that he will come to it belatedly, and likely for the wrong reasons.

Meet the New Mary Meeker

April 12, 2002

Last Friday morning, an investor walked into Morgan Stanley's headquarters at Broadway and 50th Street looking for a scheduled seminar on how to read a 10-K form. The firm was offering this tutorial to clients who might never have mastered the art during the long boom. There wasn't time. Reading documents distracted the conscientious portfolio manager from the lucrative business of obtaining IPO allocations.

This investor, who is now enrolled in the *Grant's* source protection program, was directed to the Grand Hyatt, hard by Grand Central Station. Funny, he mused while proceeding downtown, why hold an accounting symposium at a hotel?

The question answered itself as he walked into a cavernous ballroom. It was filled with what he estimated to be 2,000 people. Every seat was taken, and spectators were sitting on the floor. Pulling up a seat on the carpet, he realized that the last time he had seen so many brokerage-house clients in one place was to hear about a tech stock.

The lecturer, Trevor Harris, came to Morgan Stanley in 1997 to devise a system to rationalize international accounting methods—to put the fruit salad of cross-border reporting on an apples-to-apples basis. Today, he serves as the head of the firm's global valuation, accounting and tax policy team.

In fact, he's the bear market version of a celebrity Internet analyst. He is a rising star. *Barron's*, in an April 1 interview, noted that, in the company of Morgan Stanley telecom analyst Simon Flannery, Harris produced a controversial and forehanded report on Qwest. He is knowledgeable about Cisco Systems, too, and has analyzed the nameplate boom-time disasters (some of which other departments of Morgan Stanley might possibly have been bullish on). "Had accountants looked at the big picture, as Harris suggests they should have," *Barron's* reported, "surprises like Enron and Global Crossing might not have occurred."

Apparently, there was a great deal of this at the Grand Hyatt. Harris, a Columbia University professor of accounting who took a leave of absence to join Morgan Stanley, repeatedly helped his students to see how much richer they would be had they only known more (or, in some cases, anything) about the companies in which they invested.

Some people came as an act of penance. Seated on a patch of carpet next to our source was a hedge-fund manager who confessed he was lost. "I don't really understand what he's talking about," the man said, "but I swore I wouldn't leave till it was over." There was chewing gum on the penitent's trousers.

Whom Blodget Displaced

June 21, 2002

In December 1998, while employed as a research analyst by Merrill Lynch, Jonathan Cohen wrote that Amazon.com was "probably the single most expensive publicly traded company in the history of U.S. equity markets." It fell to others, including Henry Blodget, his successor at Merrill, to show how truly expensive an expensive stock could become.

Now Blodget is writing his memoirs and Cohen is managing money, including the Royce Technology Value Fund, just six months old. "Technology stocks have turned into a graveyard and a junkyard," says Chuck Royce, president of Royce & Associates (now owned by Legg Mason) and value investor par excellence. "We're trying to think ahead. . . . I think we have the timing approximately right. We may be a bit early." Cohen's fund has all of $5 million in assets, and its net asset value has fallen by 10.4% since inception. So far, so good, in our opinion. A good investment usually starts small. And often, before ending big, it gets even smaller.

Like Scott Bedford, a San Francisco tech-stock bear who has launched a value fund, Cohen does not believe that "tech stocks" are cheap. On the contrary, he says, briefly putting on (and promptly removing) the hat he wears as the manager of a separate hedge fund, there are plenty of attractive short-sale opportunities left. However, he goes on, lots of small and tiny tech companies are neither dead nor dying, the impression conveyed by the collapse of their share prices notwithstanding.

A friend with long experience in technology investing says that the secret of success isn't the quality of the technology, but the quality of the management. It almost goes without saying that the quantity of the cash is likewise important. Cohen says he begins his analysis with the balance sheet. He attaches more weight to the tangible net worth of an investment candidate than to anyone's guess of its three-to-five-year earnings prospects.

A glance at the accompanying tabulation of Cohen's top-10 holdings will stir old memories of space travel—in the bubble, some of them went to the moon. Now each is back on planet Earth, but not all are as statistically cheap as a non-tech value investor might like them to be. Not one of the 10 companies trades for less than tangible book value, and no P/E is less than 11.5. Half have no "E." We put it to Cohen: Are these absolute values, or merely the kind of stocks that fill out a value portfolio pending the return of value?

"I wish everything we owned was an absolutely hugely compelling value," Cohen replies. "Some of them are merely quite good values. Certainly, I'd hope that some of them, or at least many of them, are absolutely compelling values. . . ."

United Online (UNTD), a $10.73 stock, is the company Cohen mentions first. It has $126 million of cash and short-term securities (net of restricted cash), an amount equal to $3.23 a share. Its tax-loss carryforward, about $250 million, is at least 58% of its $431 million market cap. In the past year, it has purchased one million of its own shares.

United is an Internet service provider, or ISP, and its claim to fame is the low cost of its basic dial-up service ($9.95 a month vs. more than $20 a month for AOL, EarthLink, MSN and AT&T WorldNet). It similarly boasts a low customer-acquisition cost (in the March quarter, $32 per subscriber vs. $195 for EarthLink). As of March 31, it had 1.6 million subscribers, up 9.5% sequentially, and it says it has the capacity to serve 10 million. The company is net-income negative but cash-flow positive.

"There is very little about United that is going to [become] obsolete any time soon," says Cohen in response to the observation that technology companies are forever rendering themselves obsolete. (In bull markets, investors are pleased to pay a premium for this self-destructive behavior. Then they say that the companies are "reinventing" themselves.) "United is largely a dial-up ISP, and there is certainly the perception in the marketplace, and there has been for some time, that dial-up will be replaced by broadband connectivity," Cohen goes on. "That's certainly true. At some point, it will be. But I think that day is relatively long in the future, and I also think that United is in a uniquely strong position to benefit from that migration as opposed to being economically harmed, whereas some of its competitors are in the position of being more likely to be economically harmed."

Register.com, another particular favorite of Cohen's, is a registrar of domain names. This is not to be confused with a registry of domain names. A registrar signs up customers for domain names, charging for the service; a registry is a database of domain names. You may remember the top of the Nasdaq boom in March 2000. It was at that moment that Register.com went public, at $24 a share. It promptly zoomed to $100. Now it's $7.48, with $4.66 per fully diluted share in net cash. "And this is a company that should be able to do a dollar per share in earnings [$0.27 this year] in the not too distant future," says Cohen.

Calculated to deflate enthusiasm are the short average tenure of a Register finance chief (there have been four in little more than two years), the steady stream of insider selling by founder and CEO Richard Forman and the hulking presence of industry leader Veri-Sign, which generated $328 million in first-quarter revenue compared to Register's $27 million.

Cohen contends that the fourth and latest finance officer is a welcome addition to the management team and that, in any case, Register is out-managing VeriSign. "The barriers to entry are very low," Stephanie Marks, of the Register investor relations department, acknowledges to colleague Peter Walmsley. "That's why you've got 149 accredited registrars. I think that the real barrier to success the way we define it is that you have to have enough capital to invest in building a brand—building systems, technology, tools, applications—so that you really have a compelling value-oriented proposition to offer your customers. . . . We have almost 200 people in customer service and even more doing technology and product development. It's big business. I think the way people have tried to enter the business by selling names cheap—it just doesn't work."

Cohen was right in 1998—just early. Our hunch is that he is right, and early, again.

Snoopy Deploys Capital

April 8, 2005

MetLife, once upon a time known as the Metropolitan Life Insurance Co., sold its self-branded, 58-story New York City office tower last week (the one that starred in *Godzilla*) for $1.7 billion. On $83 million in projected annual net operating income, that's a 4.9% yield, or cap rate, a remarkably low number even for this sky-scraping real estate market. It is, in fact, just remarkable enough to inspire a meditation on the risks presented by low interest rates and rampant overvaluation.

Question: How does one invest in an era of low rates? Answer: One invests poorly, because the available investment options are themselves often impoverished. MetLife, the nation's soon-to-be No. 1 life insurance company (pending completion of its acquisition of the Travelers), has survived each and every interest-rate cycle of the past 137 years. Just how remarkable is this achievement becomes apparent when one considers that every investor is a prisoner of the times in which he lives. Yields are what they are. Valuations are what they are. And, belief systems are what they are. A half-century ago, the Met earned rates of return that, adjusted for inflation, taxes and expenses, could not have been much greater than zero. Seeking safety—"security of principal"—it bought bonds yielding 3% or 4%, while disdaining equities yielding more than bonds. It accepted uncritically the ultra-conservative 1950s' investment-belief system.

Looking back on 2005 from the perspective of 2055, what will posterity say about us? Will it shake its know-it-all head over our own errors and omissions? Of course it will. At the top of the list of millennial shortcomings will be: uncritical acceptance of an ultra-progressive and optimistic investment-belief system (e.g., "stocks excel in the long run, because they always have excelled in the long run") and the headlong purchase of low-yielding bonds denominated in the leading unstable currencies. Posterity won't believe that we didn't see the breakdown of the post-1971 monetary system as it was unfolding before our eyes, or that we imputed to the Federal Open Market Committee powers of judgment and pre-knowledge given to no mortal human. "What were they thinking about?" one member of posterity will sadly remark to another.

MetLife has been selling real estate to finance its recent $11.5 billion purchase of Citigroup's insurance assets (besides the MetLife building at 42nd Street, it sold its former New York City headquarters at 1 Madison Ave.). The Citi businesses, valued at 1.54 times book and 12.8 times 2004 earnings, did not come dirt cheap, except in comparison to the valuation of the buildings. "The company is capitalizing on a Manhattan market where top office buildings now sell for more than $700 a square foot after rarely touching $500 before 2002 . . . ," *Bloomberg* News noted. "Think about it," Rob Speyer, a managing director of Tischman Speyer, one of the buyers of the MetLife Building, told the *New York Times*. "It's the opportunity of a lifetime. To buy one of New York City's iconic properties is an opportunity we just leapt at."

Today, at a 4.9% cap rate, one could buy an iconic building or some not-quite-iconic bonds. Which would you prefer? Bonds have no windows to wash, walls to paint, carpets to vacuum, tenants to litigate with or governments to pay property taxes to. On the other hand, the building wouldn't be subject to early call if interest rates fell. Then, again, each stream of income—rentals and coupon payments—is denominated in dollars, of which the world is very long. And if interest rates, and/or the inflation rate, were to climb? Depending on the timing of lease expirations, the building's new management could raise rents. Bondholders could reinvest their coupon income at higher and higher yields. And in the absence of an adverse credit event, they would receive 100 cents on the dollar (whatever a "dollar" happened to be) at maturity.

But neither the building nor the bonds provide the margin of safety that value-seeking investors demand. On the contrary, both asset classes command some of the fanciest valuations in memory. Only last year, MetLife's real estate and real estate joint ventures yielded 11.6%, or more than twice the cap rate to which the buyers of the MetLife Building said "I do" last week. Does overvaluation alone assure a disappointing total return? Emphatically, yes. We consign our judgment in confidence to the *Grant's* time capsule.

It is easier to sift through the past than to speculate about the future—easier and often more remunerative. Economic cycles wax and wane. Ditto, skirt lengths, necktie widths and geopolitical alignments. But low nominal interest rates present the same basic investment challenge to a deployer of capital whether the president be Dwight D. Eisenhower or George W. Bush. Famously, compound interest is the eighth wonder of the world, but some rates of interest are more wondrous than others. Invest $100 at 4% a year for 50 years, compounded twice a year, and you wind up with $724.46. Invest $100 at 8% for 50 years, compounded in the same fashion, and you get $5,050.49. To borrow from Sophie Tucker (1884-1966), the Met has invested at high interest rates, and it has invested at low interest rates, and high interest rates are better. High real interest rates are especially better. Low rates are undesirable not only for what they fail to deliver in investment return, but also for the temptations they present to prudent people to invest imprudently.

The financial hand dealt to the parents and grandparents of present-day *Grant's* readers featured (besides midget bond yields) high marginal tax rates, cheap equities, unleveraged capital structures, regimented investment markets and deep-rooted insecurity. Many Americans feared the resumption of the Great Depression or the onset of World War III, or both. Rare is the individual who can imagine a different set of circumstances than those that surround him. Rarer still is the organization that can imagine them. "Imagination is not a gift usually associated with bureaucracies," wrote the 9/11 Commission. "Insight for the future is . . . not easy to apply in practice," the commission also noted. "It is hardest to mount a major effort while a problem still seems minor. Once the danger has fully materialized, evident to all, mobilizing action is easier— but it then may be too late." Here, though the commission believed it was discussing national security, it could have been ruminating on the art of investing.

Constant readers know that interest-rate markets are long-trending markets; complete cycles, low rates to high rates back to low rates again, can span a generation or more. According to Sidney Homer's *A History of Interest Rates*, a bull bond market began in 1920, with corporate yields at 5¼%, and ended in 1946, with corporate yields at 2½%. The ensuing bear market got off to a slow start. Indeed, so measured was the rise in rates (which were still under the thumb of the Fed and Treasury) that hardly anyone noticed the change in trend. Yields stayed low into the early 1960s. Who expected that this greatest of bond bear markets would culminate in a great inflation and, in 1981, a 15% long Treasury yield? Not the investment committee of the Metropolitan Life Insurance Co.

"As ever," the Met addressed its policyholders in the 1955 annual report, "the prime consideration of the Company's investment policy is safety of principal, combined with a reasonable return, and consideration of regional and national interests." What passed for "reasonable" in 1955 was 3.48% before tax. Last year, the portfolio achieved 6.53% pretax.

In 1955, the Met was a mutual company, meaning the policyholders owned it, even if they couldn't control it. It had $13.9 billion in assets, by which measure it was the biggest company in America (not just the biggest insurance company, but the biggest of any kind). It insured 38.3 million people, one person in five in the 48 states and Canada, and it employed 50,000. It had no mandate to maximize earnings, or, for that matter, anything else. Rather, it sought to protect principal and contribute to the national economic agenda: defense in wartime; prosperity in peacetime. Compare the mandate of the de-mutualized, profit-maximizing, capital-markets savvy MetLife of 2005: "The company's primary investment objective is to optimize, net of income taxes, risk-adjusted investment income and risk-adjusted total return while ensuring that assets and liabilities are managed on a cash flow and duration basis."

Today's MetLife, a holding company, deploys billions of dollars in corporate assets "to build shareholder value"; as it acquires the Travelers Insurance Co., it sells Manhattan real estate. It insures 46 million people worldwide and employs 54,000. In 1955, the Met's surplus amounted to 6.4% of its total liabilities; in 2004, the MetLife insurance subsidiary had surplus in the amount of 3.7% of total liabilities. "We know that people across the globe are under-insured, under-saved and, in the case of the baby-boom generation, in need of retirement solutions that will guarantee income," declares management in the new, approved language of globalization. The Met of yesteryear was in business to serve the policyholders and the country (and, of course, its own officers and employees), not a self-selected core of stockholders. Even if the Eisenhower-era company had decided to change "its methodology of allocating capital to its business segments from Risk-Based Capital ('RBC') to Economic Capital," as the contemporary Met just did, management probably wouldn't have felt the need to disclose the fact in the annual report. The millennial MetLife, with its battalions of quants, CFAs and MBAs, not only hedges its interest-rate and currency risk with derivatives, and spices its bond portfolio with junk, but also discloses these facts in the standard regulatory format.

But despite these epochal changes, asset allocation today is little different than it was in 1955. Now as then, the emphasis is on corporate bonds, an asset class subject to early call, event risk and credit risk. Corporates constitute 43% of the investment portfolio, as compared to 52% in 1955. Mortgages and mortgage-backed securities make up 32% of the portfolio, as opposed to 22.8% in 1955. Today, as in 1955, government securities account for exactly 12.7% of the portfolio. Now as then, equities figure only marginally in the asset mix. Ditto, real estate. And now, as then, "alternative" assets—timber, hedge funds, convertible-bond arbitrage, etc.—seem to figure hardly at all. The millennial MetLife does go in for foreign securities, as the 1955-edition Met may not have (31% of the 2004 corporate portfolio was foreign). But they are only so foreign: the company has no unhedged currency exposure.

In the past half-century, life expectancy in the United States has climbed to 77 years from 68.2 years. "From a demographics standpoint," states the 2004 MetLife annual, "the bulk of the United States population is moving from an asset accumulation phase to an asset distribution phase. People within 10 years of retirement hold significant assets. With continually lengthening life spans and unstructured asset distribution, the company believes many of these people may outlive their retirement savings and/or long-term care. As a result, the company expects that the demand for retirement payout solutions with guarantees will increase dramatically over the next decade."

Fifty years ago, Americans were still briskly accumulating. Certainly, Metropolitan Life was accumulating assets. In 1955, it enjoyed $6.5 billion of new premium income, an astounding 33% jump over 1954. How to invest these massive inflows?

The guiding light of a seven-man investment committee in the early 1950s was an octogenarian. Frederick H. Ecker had been with the company since 1883. Possibly, he was still young at heart. But he had been president during the 1930s, when the delinquency of 58% of the company's agricultural loans resulted in the repossession of two million acres of farmland (the Met had its own "Department of Agriculture"). Reputedly a shrewd investor for his personal account, Ecker tried nothing fancy with the policyholders' savings. "Safety of principal must be the primary consideration of life insurance funds," declared the president, Charles G. Taylor, for emphasis.

Noble words! But what kept principal safe? There was precious little safety to be had in the asset markets in which the Met chose to invest. From the close of World War II through the early 1950s, the company's investment returns barely kept up with (or actually lagged behind) the measured rate of inflation. And that measured rate was flattered by price controls. To earn a return greater than the microscopic prevailing bond yields, the Met, late in the 1930s, stepped up its investments in apartment buildings. It built, among other big projects, the Parkfairfax in Alexandria, Va., the Parkmerced in San Francisco and Peter Cooper Village and Stuyvesant Town in Manhattan. But it could find no economic relief even in bricks and mortar. Inflation pushed up building costs and rent controls capped income. In the 1948 annual report, management wistfully recalled the 5¼% rates it had earned late in the 1920s: "If the interest rate earned last year had been the same as in 1928, it would have meant about $182 million more in income, which would have enabled the company to pay substantially higher dividends to policyholders." That year, the company earned a grand total of 3.03%, which—to look on the bright side, which the Met always tried to do—was up by nine whole basis points from 1947.

Interest rates were flat on their backs—but so, too, were common stocks. Here is a paradox for the modern portfolio theorist to ponder. In 1951, long-dated Treasurys fetched 2.6%—but the S&P 500 threw off a dividend yield of 6.1% and an earnings yield of 10.9%. We mention 1951 because that was the year the New York State Insurance Department revised its draconian investment rules to allow life companies some exposure to common stocks. Did the Met avail itself of this opportunity? "We have no intention of acquiring common stocks," president Taylor told *The Wall Street Journal* in 1952, having taken a year to think it over.

Fast-forward four years, to the press conference at which a new Met president presented the 1955 financial results. A reporter asked if the company had changed its mind about stocks. Frederic W. Ecker, the son of the eminent Ecker, said, "No." For one thing, the law didn't allow the purchase of enough stocks to make a meaningful impact on the investment results. For another, the market really wasn't cheap any more (in 1954, the Dow had finally pushed above the old 1929 highs). As he spoke, the dividend yield on the S&P was a mere 104 basis points higher than the long-term, triple-A-rated corporate bond yield. But even if the company had been allowed to buy enough stock to matter, it wouldn't have. The market might go down.

"Suppose," reported *The National Underwriter*, paraphrasing Ecker, "only 10% were in stocks—and there were a 40% drop in the stock market, as had happened several times in the last half century, it would probably come close to wiping out the company's surplus. Moreover, if at a time when the stock market was falling apart the news should get around that life companies' surpluses were being virtually destroyed it would not be a very good thing for public confidence. These violent fluctuations, Mr. Ecker indicated, are implicit in the nature of common stocks."

And what characteristics were implicit in senior securities? Ecker acknowledged only one: safety. A clairvoyant would have seen that bonds, as then valued, were only apparently safe, because

yields would keep rising until Sept. 30, 1981. But clairvoyants either don't need jobs or can't hold them. Especially are they unsuitable candidates for work in the investment department of the big insurance companies. The "climate of conformity" that the authors of the new Robb-Silberman report on U.S. intelligence bemoaned in the CIA and allied agencies is just as prevalent in the world of institutional investing. Bonds? "Perfectly sound, long-term investments," the investment committees broadly judge. Look at the past quarter-century: Interest rates fell, inflation became quiescent, the dollar achieved worldwide acceptance as a reserve currency. Why must any of that change?

To finance World War II on the cheap, the U.S. Treasury and Federal Reserve suppressed interest rates. Fifty years later, to mitigate the damage from the bursting stock-market bubble, the Fed suppressed interest rates again. The first manipulative episode visited huge losses on bondholders. We expect that the second episode will deal sizable losses to holders of the same kinds of securities. Fifty years ago, refugees from the fixed-income markets found value in equities. Today, there's no such haven (now that every known member of Mensa International is running a hedge fund, investment opportunities are increasingly scarce, both across markets and time zones). The Met deserves a salute for the nimbleness of its real estate sales. And it deserves commiseration on the immensity of its bond portfolio. In filing future complaints about the company's lamentable investment performance (which the present dearth of investment value all but guarantees), policyholders should not forget to copy the Federal Open Market Committee.

Chapter Four

Perils of Tranquility

Parable of Perception

August 17, 2001

A FREEZE-DRIED CORPSE WAS discovered in 1991 poking out of a melting glacier high in the Italian Alps. No identification was found on the body, but that was only to be expected. Death occurred 5,300 years ago.

Teams of forensic doctors performed X-rays and CAT scans on the Copper Age remains. They could see no sign of external injuries. They thought they observed broken ribs, three to be exact, and proposed that the fractures indicated foul play. They called him "Iceman."

However, for all their examining, probing and speculating, the doctors failed to notice a flint arrowhead lodged in Iceman's left shoulder less than an inch from his left lung. The overlooked evidence came to light on June 28 in yet another set of X-rays. "I'm convinced that this injury played an important role in his death," said

Dr. Eduard Egarter Vigi, chief pathologist at General Regional Hospital in Bolzano, Italy.

We turn to Iceman and his doctors as a case study in the perils of perception. Investors, like forensic physicians, must draw conclusions from the facts at hand. The facts, that is, as filtered through fallible human senses. "I had looked at this corpse a hundred times and had never noticed anything there before and then it was clear," said Dr. Egarter Vigi. Probably, most of the readers of *Grant's* have been in the doctor's shoes. Familiar rows of numbers yield the same old message until a new set of eyes fixes on them. The nth look produces a new interpretation. Eureka!

It was Dr. Paul Gostner, chief radiologist at the Bolzano hospital, who furnished the unconventional perception of Iceman, and he did it, as the *New York Times* reported August 7, less than two months before his scheduled retirement. "At least two previous radiological examinations done in Innsbruck, Austria, had failed to turn up the arrowhead," the *Times* account said. "'It's inexcusable that we didn't see it on the CAT scans...,'" said Dr. Dieter zur Nedden, a radiologist at the University Clinic in Innsbruck, who led the radiological investigations.

A collaborator of Dr. zur Nedden's, Dr. William A. Murphy Jr., a radiologist at the M.D. Anderson Cancer Center in Houston, sounded a note of humility that will resonate with every investor, securities analyst and auditor. Press reports of the discovery of the arrowhead struck him, at first, as "crazy," said Dr. Murphy. "He went immediately to his office," the *Times* report continues, "took out his copies of the X-rays and then recognized a 'fluffy density' that had previously not stood out among all the other anomalies in the prehistoric corpse. 'This is just absolutely astounding to me that this little thing is truly there after all the scrutinizing we've done over these images,' Dr. Murphy said. 'We've pulled our hair out and fussed and fretted and tried to drag all these details out, and yet there's probably an arrowhead in there. It makes a person very humble.' "

A layman may speculate that not just any forensic physician was allowed to join the team that studied the prehistoric remains. Presumably, the radiologists who missed the arrowhead were the very doctors you would want to examine your remains, if you had any. Without knowing, we are prepared to venture that Drs. zur Nedden and Murphy had no political biases about flint arrowheads. They were neither bullish nor bearish on them. No stock options hung in the balance of their judgment. They looked at the film and saw what they imagined, which was not at all the same as what was in front of their eyes.

Compare these discrete and measured acts of scientific perception to the innumerable daily acts of financial and economic perception. Investors, unlike the doctors at Innsbruck, pretend to no scientific impartiality. They are long or they are short. They are vested with stock options that can be turned into money if a certain set of numbers can be made to say a particular thing. There is no time, usually, to examine and re-examine a certain specimen in a laboratory setting. It's here and now.

If an arrowhead can be lost in plain sight, so can the truth about a financial statement. Taking one thing with another, we investors should be congratulated. It's a wonder so many of us are solvent.

There Ought to be Deflation

January 14, 2005

Fly now for half price—no restrictions! Take 30% off that top-of-the-line cashmere jacket, which, by the way, looks smashing on you. And may we show you, sir or madam, our special no money-down, zero-percent financing options on any vehicle in stock? Undercoating and rubber floor mats are yours with the compliments of the sales manager.

The world is a cornucopia. Thanks to the infernal machine of American debt finance, the Internet and the economic emergence of China and India, among other millennial economic forces, goods are superabundant. More and more services, too, are globally traded, therefore cheaper than they would be in the absence of international competition. Yet the measured rate of inflation in the United States is positive, not negative, as it was in so many prior eras of free trade and technological progress. Following is a meditation on the meaning of this fact and some thoughts on what to do about it.

From George Washington until the A-bomb, prices alternately rose and fell. They rose in wartime and fell in peacetime. As Alan Greenspan himself has pointed out, the American price level registered little net change between 1800 and 1929. Four years after the Crash, the Roosevelt administration put the gold standard, or what was left of it, out of its misery. In 1946, the Truman administration passed an act to mandate full employment. In effect, inflation became the law of the land. "In the two decades following the abandonment of the gold standard in 1933," Greenspan noted not long ago, "the consumer price index in the United States nearly doubled. And, in the four decades after that, prices quintupled. Monetary policy, unleashed from the constraint of gold convertibility, had allowed a persistent overissuance of money." That is, Greenspan added, until now.

The chairman was holding forth in December 2002, a time when—so his colleagues and he insisted—the U.S. confronted a meaningful risk of falling prices. To forestall this supposed crisis, the Fed pushed down the funds rate to a 46-year low. The object of this policy was to restore the familiar postwar lift to the American price level. Oddly, the public registered no protest, though, as consumers, Americans love a bargain. Economists had drummed it into their heads that falling prices were bad for growth, bad for employment, bad for debtors and, not least, bad for the way the Fed conducts monetary policy. Let the central bank guide the price level gently higher, the call went out.

Which, by appearances, the central bank has done. Supposedly, the great Greenspan has implemented a perfect measure of monetary

*"Whoa—this isn't so bad.
We still own the same number of shares."*

stimulus. He has averted deflation while steering clear of what the bond market might regard as a worrying rate of inflation.

At least, so say the members of the loosely organized Greenspan for Mount Rushmore Committee. *Grant's* has an alternative view, which requires a short definitional preface. What inflation is not, we believe, is "too many dollars chasing too few goods." Pure and simple, it is "too many dollars." What the redundant dollars chase is unpredictable. In recent months, they have chased stocks, commodities, euros, junk bonds, emerging-market debt and houses. On Wall Street, such inflationary episodes take the name "bull markets." They are always welcome. When, on the other hand, the surplus dollars chase skirts (or sweaters or automobiles or medical care), that phenomenon is called "inflation." It is usually unwelcome.

Deflation is not quite the opposite of inflation. We would define deflation as too few dollars chasing too much debt. Dollars extinguish debt; too few dollars in relation to the stock of debt is the precondition for what, these days, is euphemistically called a "credit event." A second-order effect of a credit event is falling prices. Prices fall because, in a big enough credit event, business activity stops cold. In the absence of liquid markets, cash is king. But we would not throw around the term "deflation" to describe every episode of weak or falling prices. If prices fall because the global supply curve has shifted downward and to the right, we would call that circumstance "falling prices." "Deflation," to us, means "debt deflation."

Pending the worldwide acceptance of these ideas (which we have borrowed from economists long dead), we will accommodate our views to the world's. This means we will not pedantically enclose the conventionally employed words inflation and deflation with quotation marks. But the world is doing itself no favors by so narrowly defining inflation and by so carelessly crying deflation.

The Fed is, of course, a prime perpetrator of sloppy thought, loath to acknowledge that inflation is anything other than an unacceptable rate of rise in its favored inflation index. This index is the personal consumption expenditure deflator, excluding such minor and discretionary items as food and energy. It is not that the Maestro has refused to acknowledge that the world's cup of goods and services runneth over. In so many words, he has conceded that the global supply curve has shifted in the direction of plenty. But, as far as we know, he has not followed this observation where it logically leads. If everything else were left the same, the measured inflation rate might, by now, be negative. We emphasize "might," as the cornucopia effect of greater, and cheaper, global supply is offset to a degree by the depreciating dollar exchange rate. However, we are certain that, except for heavy Fed intervention, the measured rate of inflation would be lower than it is now. So, too, the "unmeasured" rate of inflation, by which we mean house prices, credit spreads and other such markers of asset valuation.

We are prepared to wager that the Maestro knows more than he lets on about the true nature of inflation and deflation and about the tendency of the U.S. price level to subside in a world so generously supplied as this one. And we are equally prepared to wager that he has some appreciation of how highly leveraged are American families and businesses. In relation to income, the stock of debt has been rising for decades. If the price level reversed course and declined, uncounted net debtors would struggle to stay solvent. Falling prices, even if they were not caused by a credit event, could easily provoke one (in which, for example, trillion-dollar government-sponsored enterprises just might have to call in their chits to the Treasury).

Small wonder, then, that everything has not been left the same. The Fed, warning about the dire consequences of the "zero bound" (by which it means a federal funds rate stuck at zero percent) and invoking the specter of Japanese stagnation, or worse, assumed a radically easy monetary stance in 2001. It has taken five tightening moves to bring the funds rate back to 2¼%, at which point it is still 75 basis points lower than what passed for an ultra-low funds rate during the 1992–93 easing cycle. The late Daniel Patrick Moynihan spoke of "defining deviancy down." The Fed has been redefining accommodation down. It has been pushing low interest rates lower and lower.

The interest-rate stimulus administered by the Fed in 2001–03 showered wealth on the homeowners who refinanced their mortgages not once but over and over, extracting equity as they went. But as interest rates have stopped falling, the shower is over. So it goes with monetary palliatives. Friedrich von Hayek, winner of the Nobel Prize in economics, touched on the risks of credit creation in a speech as he accepted the prize 20 years ago. Beware the nostrum of printing money to boost aggregate demand, he warned. Such a policy is, of course, inflationary, but the problem goes deeper than that. Money printing distorts prices and wages, the traffic signals of a market economy. Responding to the wrong signals—spending on red and saving on green—people take the wrong jobs and capital flows into the wrong channels. All were misled by the wrong prices, or, in the past couple of years, by the wrong interest rates.

Said Hayek:

> The continuous injection of additional amounts of money
> at points of the economic system where it creates a tem-
> porary demand which must cease when the increase of
> money stops or slows down, together with the expecta-
> tion of a continuing rise in prices, draws labor and other
> resources into employments which can last only so long
> as the increase of the quantity of money continues at the
> same rate—or perhaps even only so long as it continues to
> accelerate at a given rate. What this policy has produced
> is not so much a level of employment that could not have
> been brought about in other ways, as a distribution of
> employment which cannot be indefinitely maintained and
> which after some time can be maintained only by a rate of
> inflation which would rapidly lead to a disorganization of
> all economic activity.

Hayek spoke of injecting money "at points of the economic system," and it is in these favored niches that prosperity temporarily
smiles (until the money printing or the interest-rate slashing
comes to a stop and throws the process into reverse). To an investor, still more to a speculator, "temporarily" is the magic word.
Could the Nobel laureate not be a little more specific? We must
try to fill in the blanks ourselves. One notes, for example, reading
the January 5 *Wall Street Journal*, that "With Market Hot, More
People Now Have Third Homes." Rising interest rates must sooner
or later cause the marginal third-home owner to become a two-
home, or a one-home or even a no-home owner. One would suppose that a similar chain reaction is going to take place in other
highly leveraged sectors of the U.S. economy. Which might they
be? The FOMC itself, in a much-quoted passage in the just-re-
leased minutes of the December 14 meeting, serves up a helpful
list. "Some participants," the text relates, "believed that the prolonged period of policy accommodation had generated a significant degree of liquidity that might be contributing to signs of

potentially excessive risk-taking in financial markets evidenced by quite narrow credit spreads, a pickup in initial public offerings, an upturn in mergers-and-acquisition activity and anecdotal reports that speculative demands were becoming apparent in the markets for single-family homes and condominiums."

In a provocative letter to the editor of the *Financial Times* last weekend, Ann E. Berg, a former director of the Chicago Board of Trade, offered a Hayekian coda to the discussion of the U.S. trade deficit. To correct the huge and growing gap between what this country consumes and what it produces, the market has focused almost entirely on the dollar exchange rate. "I have yet to see a single analyst suggest the trade imbalance could be solved by a general contraction of consumer credit—something that would surely correct the import/export imbalance," Berg writes. "For 25 years, U.S. consumers have enjoyed increasingly easy credit due primarily to a declining interest rate environment."

But, as Berg goes on, in addition to falling interest rates, the American shopper has gained from the growth and resourcefulness of Wall Street in processing, packaging and distributing debt. The advent of futures and options, of swaps and securitizations has facilitated American borrowing "and lined consumer pockets with several hundred billion dollars over the past few years, particularly with the turning of unsecured credit card debt into asset-backed security agreements (home equity loans)." Conveniently for the United States, the "emerging" economies are better at producing and saving than at banking and consuming. Rising U.S. interest rates will likely slow the pace of borrowing, therefore of consumption in this country. However, as Berg notes, for the time being, consumer debt continues to rise faster than consumer incomes. And it is this fact that "will cause some creditors to demand higher risk premiums due to the greater default probabilities of borrowers. Anecdotal evidence suggests that some credit card issuers are demanding significant increases in monthly minimum payments. Further dollar depreciation helping spur export growth is therefore only one solution to the current account deficit. A tighter credit environment forcing a leaner consumer might prove an equally likely resolution, however unwelcome." However un-American.

Deflation a la Eisenhower

February 24, 2006

"Of course, the chief of the Federal Reserve asserted, the board must be alert to the dangers of deflation as well as inflation 'and to counteract either with equal vigor.' "

Ben S. Bernanke could have spoken those words; William McChesney Martin actually did, in a speech to the Pennsylvania Bankers Association 50 years ago (as *The Wall Street Journal* reported at the time). Though the names of Fed chairmen may change, their phrases remain the same.

What Bernanke recently did say is that deflation is a scourge worse than inflation and that the Fed should battle it tooth and claw, even—figuratively speaking—to the point of dropping greenbacks out of helicopter doors. This was in 2002–03, when the 10-year Treasury yield dropped to 3.1%, a mere resting-place (so the propagandized bond bulls hoped) on the road to the pygmy yields of deflationary Japan. Yet there was no deflation. All the while, U.S. price indices continued to inch higher.

Which is not to say that the postwar U.S. economy is deflation-proof. From September 1954 through August 1955, the Consumer Price Index registered 12 consecutive monthly year-over-year declines. The story of this long-ago occurrence is well worth remembering now that the former chairman of the Princeton University economics department has become chairman of the Federal Reserve Board. Besides, to judge by the world's low bond yields, deflation continues to own a big share of the mind of Mr. Market.

We delve into the past to light the way to the future. What can the Eisenhower deflation teach about the Bush inflation? About tomorrow's interest rates and Bernanke's monetary policy? The answers would seem to include, No. 1, that deflation can be purely benign but that, No. 2, modern policy makers will always fear it, although, No. 3, some policy makers have more levers with which to express their fears and forebodings than others. Certainly, Bernanke has many fewer at his disposal than Martin did a half-century earlier. And, No. 4, the 1954–55 experience underscores that, in a deflationary setting, interest rates can go a lot lower than most people would imagine.

Every day's newspaper administers a kind of monetary Rorschach test. Responding to the economic and financial inkblots, a market-minded reader is likely to respond "inflation" or "deflation." We are in the inflation cohort. A fair-minded reader will, of course, weigh the evidence with scientific detachment. But it's a fact that paper currencies have always lost their value, that governments forever spend more than they take in and that modern central bankers actually strive to achieve inflation (not too much, mind you). In reply to the objection that China, India, Wal-Mart and the Internet together constitute an insuperable barrier against

an inflation rate of even 4% or 5%, we reply: Don't underestimate the central bankers.

Yet, equally, as we are well aware, one should not underestimate the power of surprise. Besides, there ought to be deflation. Free trade, globalization and technological advance have pushed the global supply curve downward and to the right. Prices should be falling. However, ultra-low interest rates, lenient borrowing terms and rising asset prices have pushed the U.S. demand curve upward and to the right; they have incited a consumption boom. Prices, therefore, are not falling. Seen from this aspect, they should be—and actually are—rising.

Is everything crystal clear? No, of course it isn't. We therefore proceed with a mind that, we flatter ourselves, is open. If some future recession began with a measured rate of inflation in the neighborhood of 2%, there's no good reason it couldn't wind up at less than zero. What then? What would become of us highly leveraged Americans? What would the deflation-phobic Bernanke do to restart the engines of monetary debasement? Musing in this fashion, we have rummaged through the monetary time capsule.

A little scene setting might be helpful. Immediately preceding the Eisenhower deflation was a 10-month recession, July 1953-May 1954. And immediately preceding the recession was the armistice that ended the war in Korea, June 1950 to July 1953. The war had provoked a run-up in producer and consumer prices. Shortly after the shooting started, the rate of rise in prices peaked. After the peace came the run down.

What did the policy makers think? All of them had lived through the 1930s. The 1946 Employment Act bound them, at a minimum, to try to avert another deflationary collapse. "There's no real worry any more about inflation," the *Journal* quoted a Commerce Department official as saying in October 1953, three months into the post-Korean War recession. "Sharp deflation is the enemy to guard against." Under a gold standard, prices did typically fall in times of peace. And in the 1950s, the United States was on a kind of gold standard (underscore "kind of"). Foreign central banks and governments, though nobody else, had the right to exchange unwanted greenbacks for gold at the statutory rate of $35 per ounce. But the right was not widely exercised. In practice, gold convertibility was no constraint on domestic monetary policy. Anyway, the record shows no fatalistic acceptance of recession and falling prices in the months and years following the armistice. On the contrary, the government pulled out all countercyclical stops.

Many stops were available to it. In the early 1950s, the U.S. had a garrison-state economy. The Great Depression, World War II, the Cold War and the war in Korea had brought forth price controls, wage controls, interest-rate controls, excess-profit controls and other rules and regulations to fill a parade ground. Today, the Fed has one effective instrument of policy, the funds rate; then it had three or four. Today, the Fed has two principal obligations, price stability and full employment; then it had those and one more besides: For a decade up until 1951, the Fed was the Treasury's bond-selling auxiliary. Monetary policy set the interest rates at which the Treasury preferred to borrow. And even when the Fed was liberated from those institutional shackles, the legacy of servitude remained in the form of 2% bond yields and 1% (or less) money market interest rates.

So the Fed, downgrading the risk of inflation, turned accommodative. Early in 1953, it lowered stock-market margin requirements to 50% from 75%. In May, it stepped up the pace of open-market securities purchases. In July, it lowered bank reserve requirements. A year later, as the New York Giants started the move that would end with a four-game sweep of the Cleveland Indians in the 1954 World Series, the Martin Fed administered more of the same open-market and reserve-requirement medicine. The recession—a relatively mild affair, with gross domestic product contracting, at its worst, by 1.6%—was then ending. Deflation was just beginning.

Every deflation should be so benign as the 1954–55 experience. Though consumer prices persistently fell, commodity prices and stock prices zoomed. Only five banks failed. It is a strange deflation in which corporate credit spreads tighten rather than blow open to reflect the distress of income-starved debtors, but that was the deflation of 1954–55 for you. We should all suffer the torments of broadly falling prices in just this way.

We are unlikely to, however, as the U.S. economy is far more leveraged today than it was 50 years ago. Heavy debts work on borrowers in a deflation much as lead weights on a swimmer. Each has trouble staying afloat. Amid falling prices, a debtor's income may shrink, but the nominal value of what he owes remains the same. In 1954, credit-market debt totaled $541 billion, or 145% of GDP; today, it stands at $38.8 trillion, or 320% of GDP. In the early postwar era, the ghosts of the Great Depression still haunted Wall Street. Original-issue junk bonds, option ARMs and chronic, world-beating current account deficits were dreams that, for the most part, were still undreamt (unless as nightmares). The year-end statement of condition of the National City Bank, forerunner to Citigroup, conveyed the tenor of the times. It showed $6.3 billion of assets, of which less than $5 million (that's million) were in real-estate loans, while overall loans and discounts, at $2.3 billion, amounted to just 41% of deposits. In such a setting, falling prices were unlikely to trip off a chain reaction of bankruptcy.

But today? Within the next 12 months, an estimated $200 billion of adjustable-rate mortgages will reset, jolting their obligors with increases in monthly payments as much as 70% greater than the teaser rates originally incurred. Though the U.S. economy is proverbially a mighty fortress, how big an interest-rate shock can it stand?

The Eisenhower deflation is one that the Bernanke Fed might look back on with nostalgia. In April 1955, as consumer prices slid, Allan Sproul, president of the Federal Reserve Bank of New York, declared that his Fed colleagues and he "fear deflation more than inflation, just as do most people, who are aware of the human aspects of economic forces." Fear though they might, however, the money managers tightened in the face of falling prices.

The Fed didn't target interest rates directly but let them go where they would at a given level of reserve provisioning. In the 1953–54 recession, the pace of open market operations was brisk and the demand for credit was slack. Money-market interest rates accordingly tumbled. At the low, reached in November 1954, the fed funds rate was quoted at 0.32%.

But—deflation or no deflation—the rate started working its way higher. Late in the fall of 1954, it was 1%, plus or minus 50 basis points. By August 1955—at which point, just for the record, the Brooklyn Dodgers had the National League race sewn up—it reached 2%. As consumer prices fell, the funds rate effectively doubled.

To not a few observers, a doubling wasn't enough. The purchasing power of the dollar had shrunk by 4.8% from the outbreak of World War II in Europe to the first month of postwar deflation, i.e., from September 1939 to September 1954. By early 1955, credit growth was accelerating, commodity prices were booming and the stock market was looking back on an historic milestone. A full quarter-century after the Crash, the Dow Jones Industrial Average had at last blown through the old 1929 highs. Was monetary growth the source of these animal spirits? The sum of demand deposits, currency in circulation and time deposits had grown by a mere 1.1% in 1953 and 2.6% in 1954 (and would grow by just 2.1% in 1955). Lending and borrowing at ground-hugging interest rates was more likely the stimulus, which the Federal Reserve Board presently took steps to dampen. It ordered a boost in margin requirements to 60% from 50% in January 1955.

We at the millennium will shake our heads in wonder. At the time, the Dow yielded 4.4% as against 3% for high-grade corporate bonds. Brokers' loans totaled $1.45 billion, less than 1% of listed values. Furthermore, the volume of margin debt had risen by only 42% since September 1953, against a 60% jump in the Dow. To be sure, such indebtedness was $372 million greater than the sum in place on the eve of the 1937 break, but listed values were more than $100 billion higher than at that earlier peak. And—to repeat—consumer prices were gently falling.

" 'For poorer?' "

What significance did knowing observers attach to deflation at the time? In a page-one exhortation to the Federal Reserve to keep tightening the screws, the editor of *Barron's* neglected to mention it. A "superabundance of credit," wrote the late Robert M. Bleiberg, "has seeped into the securities markets, where total borrowings against stocks and bonds, though higher than in the twenties, stand at the highest level in many years. It is sparking a new upsurge in consumer credit, on increasingly relaxed terms— the Bank of America, biggest in the country, will finance a new car for a down payment of only 30%, with 30 months left to pay the balance." Your editor feels that, somehow, somewhere, his mentor has his head in his hands contemplating the prevailing terms and conditions of an auto loan in the somewhat generously supplied 2006 market.

The Federal Reserve is, of course, out of the business of manipulating margin requirements—and, for that matter, reserve requirements. It is not so quick as it used to be to exhort the nation's business people to exhibit "business statesmanship" to ward off lurches in the price level to the upside or the down. But, under Bernanke, we believe, the Fed will move fast and hard to reduce the funds rate at the first signs of sagging prices.

In an economy so heavily encumbered as this one, in an economy in which imports contribute (by value) 14% of GDP against only 4% in 1954, and in a world where house prices may well have put in a cyclical, or even long-term, peak—in such a world as this, a bout of falling consumer prices is hardly unthinkable. Ergo, an ultra-low federal funds rate is equally within the realm of possibility. We believe that the purchase of some long-dated Eurodollar futures (or fed funds futures) may pay off handsomely.

Not Too Big to Hit the Wall

March 10, 2006

On the last day of February, a press release announced the founding of a bank without walls, employees, customers or coin-counting machines. This institutional skeleton is called New-Bank, and it will lie dormant until something unthinkable happens. Actually, not unthinkable, because the Federal Reserve has already thought of it. The bank will lie dormant until either J.P. Morgan Chase or the Bank of New York, the two and only clearing banks for the government securities market, becomes financially incapacitated. "Securities dealers need a contingency plan in the event one of the clearing banks is forced to exit the markets," Micah S. Green, president and CEO of the Bond Market Association, tried to explain. "Establishing NewBank is a prudent market-based initiative aimed at mitigating any potential problems caused by the sudden involuntary exit of one of the banks."

Showing a different side of his multifaceted personality, Mr. Market might have read those words and run for the hills. As it was, he smiled and turned the page. The rest of us, however, might profit from a moment's introspection. After all, it isn't every day that a bond market trade group openly speculates on the possible maiming or death of large and—so far as the market is currently aware—perfectly solvent financial institutions. And what are the odds that Morgan Chase will—as the BMA delicately puts it—make a "sudden involuntary exit"? The credit default swap market judges them remote. "Protection" on Morgan Chase is quoted at 20 basis points, about the lowest price on record. In 2002, it almost reached 100.

Four years ago, the Federal Reserve Board decided the government securities market was too important to be left unguarded against a clearing disaster. Operational risk was not the worry—the banks themselves had established redundant processing facilities outside New York after September 11, 2001. What bothered the Fed was the potential for financial failure: "[I]f a credit, legal or other problem caused the market to lose confidence in an existing clearing bank, and no well-qualified bank stepped forward to purchase the existing bank's clearing business," what then?

NewBank was the answer, a kind of preemptive safety net. For now, its paid-in capital will amount to just $2.5 million, but $500 million would be made available from 25 institutional shareholders on the day the market refused to trade with Morgan Chase or the Bank of New York. (We do wonder whether $497.5 million would be so forthcoming on a day when the financial system's heart skipped a beat or two.) Come that interesting day, New-Bank would assume the legal position of the fallen clearing bank and reactivate or perpetuate its operations. In effect, NewBank is the legalistic shell of a government-coordinated guarantee. "It's a great example of the government and the private sector working together," declares Edward C. Forst, chairman of the BMA and chief administrative officer of Goldman Sachs & Co.

It's a great example of something else, too, observes Charles Peabody, founder of Portales Partners, New York. He means the socialization of credit risk or "moral hazard"—another case of the central bank's proclivity to neutralize risk by preempting failure as a consequence of speculative overreaching. People game the Fed, Peabody points out. They take more risk than they otherwise might just because the Bank of Greenspan (now of Bernanke) has reduced the penalties for imprudence. Would activity in the government securities market be just as frenetic—$5.6 trillion a day on average in repurchase and reverse repurchase agreement contracts and $545 billion a day in bills, notes and bonds—except for an interventionist Fed? Would credit protection on Morgan Chase be priced as low as it is except for the doctrine that holds that bubbles cannot be forestalled but can, after the bursting, be "managed"?

We do give the Federal Reserve credit for thinking about risk. In the civilian branch of the financial economy, people would seemingly rather think about anything else. Timothy F. Geithner, the New York Fed's president, observed in a speech last month that innovative financial instruments—credit default swaps, for example—can help to disperse risk, but they can hardly eliminate it. "They have not ended the tendency of markets to occasional periods of mania and panic," he said. "They have not eliminated the possibility of failure of a major financial intermediary."

But the Fed must acknowledge its own contributions to our financial culture of wing walking. The "too big to fail" doctrine emboldened the big New York banks to blaze new trails and absorb more risks; now we have NewBank. The "risk management" and "post-bubble cleanup" policies of Alan Greenspan helped to precipitate the stock market bubble and—after a spell of ultra-low interest rates—the housing bubble. And now the funds rate is apparently going to go up and up—and perhaps up again, on account of the economic strength supposedly revealed in the latest batch of economic data (never mind that monetary policy is acknowledged to work with a "long and variable lag").

Where this all leads, no one can tell, but it can't be tranquility.

Fill in the Suez Canal

March 7, 2008

Many have fingered the lower-than-low federal funds rate of 2002 through 2004 as a cause of today's worldwide financial disturbances. To strike an anticipatory blow against an imagined deflation, Messrs. Greenspan and Bernanke set out to seed a small inflation. It appears they overplanted.

Deflation is the subject under discussion—that and inflation, productivity growth, financial panics, the gold price and the rocks that seem, sometimes, to fill the heads of our central bankers. The rocks, we know about. It's the connection between progress and the price level that needs more attention than it customarily receives. We write to advance the proposition that falling prices are a natural byproduct of human ingenuity. Print money to resist the decline, and the next thing you know, there's a bubble.

Let Fulton harness steam power, Edison the incandescent bulb or Gore the Internet, and more work will be done by fewer hands. In consequence, some prices will fall, some people will lose their jobs and some portion of the world's capital stock will be cast into obsolescence. By intervening to mitigate the sting of these adjustments, on which it fastened the name "deflation," the Fed was instrumental in bringing us to the present state of affairs in credit. It's a funny old world when municipal bonds are priced to outyield Treasurys, when the inflation rate overshadows the 10-year Treasury yield and when the triple-A segments of mortgage derivatives are priced as if for Armageddon. But those are the facts.

Economics, mistaking itself for physics, is wont to turn up its nose at history, but the past has much to teach about price movements. In the last quarter of the 19th century, invention flowered, productivity growth galloped ahead and prices, accordingly, fell—by 1.7% a year between 1875 and 1896, according to Milton Friedman and Anna Schwartz. Missing from the institutional landscape of that day was a Federal Reserve to print the money with which to generate a countervailing inflation. *Recent Economic Changes*, by David A. Wells, was the last word on the subject at the time of its publication in 1889. We had been meaning to catch up on our Wells. A recent 13-hour plane ride afforded just the opportunity.

Wells's conclusion anticipates some of the more incisive treatments of the economic consequences of the Internet. His argument holds that technological progress is disruptive and deflationary. And reading his account of the second-order effects of the opening of the Suez Canal, you believe it. To Wells's generation, progress was creative and destructive at one and the same time. "In the last analysis," Wells quotes a wise contemporary as saying, "it will appear that there is no such thing as fixed capital; there is nothing useful that is very old except the precious metals, and all life consists in the conversion of forces. The only capital which is of permanent value is immaterial—the experience of generations and the development of science."

It was Wells's contention that governments could do nothing to stem the deflationary consequences of such innovative gusts as the one through which he was privileged to live. Then, again, he lived in the age of the gold standard, and he never met Ben Bernanke. "By increasing the number of dollars in circulation, or even by credibly threatening to do so," today's incumbent Federal Reserve chairman famously said in a 2002 speech, "the U.S. government can also reduce the value of a dollar in terms of goods and services, which is equivalent to raising the prices in dollars of those goods and services. We conclude that, under a paper-money system, a determined government can always generate higher spending and hence positive inflation."

Bernanke and Greenspan wanted no part of falling prices. They saw no need to develop the arguments in support of the proposition that "deflation," whatever its cause, was a nonstarter. Japan's so-called lost decade and America's Great Depression were proof enough. To give the devils their due, they might have reasoned that

America's balance sheet was too encumbered to stand up under a sagging price level (though if that was their argument, they made it sotto voce). "As long as you're pumping out money at a faster rate than demand for money is rising, you're going to stimulate spending," the then-president of the Federal Reserve Bank of Dallas, Robert McTeer, gaily said in early 2003. "I think it would be kind of fun to fight deflation, actually." From the perspective of five years and one global debt crisis, one realizes that the Fed stimulated more than spending. It simultaneously uncorked a riot of lending and borrowing.

By Wells's telling, real wages rose in the latter decades of the 19th century, though the growth of an angry populist political movement is testament to the fact that the blessings of productivity growth were, at best, unevenly distributed. Every central banker has the sympathy of every humane monetary critic. For ourselves, we fault the Fed not so much for resisting the so-called deflationary forces of 2002–04 as for failing to anticipate that its reflationary acts would have wide-ranging consequences, not all of them pleasant. Even today, our monetary masters appear blinkered to the unintended second-, third- and Nth-order effects of the plunging funds rate. The soaring dollar gold price might as well be a judgment on the policies of the Department of the Interior for all the attention it seems to be getting at the Marriner S. Eccles Building.

Prices had been falling for 15 years before Wells's book appeared, and the author seemed at peace with bear markets: "[W]hen production increases in excess of current market demand, even to the extent of an inconsiderable fraction, or is cheapened through any agency, prices will decline. . . ." But many of Wells's contemporaries were at their wits' end. The panic and depression of 1873 had not come to a clean cyclical ending point as such slumps had reliably done in the past. Rather, its symptoms persisted. In the 20 years to 1886, Wells reported, the price of a representative basket of globally traded commodities fell by an estimated 31%. Old hands were accustomed to booms and busts. But they had had no experience with what, to some, seemed a perpetual bust. Wells quotes a British economist, Robert Giffen: "The change is more like a revolution in prices than anything which usually happens in an ordinary cycle of prosperity and depression in trade."

Governments on both sides of the Atlantic convened blue-ribbon commissions to get to the bottom of the problem. The experts shone the light of suspicion on "overproduction," "the scarcity and appreciation of gold," war (or, alternatively, peace), speculation, the preceding inflation of the 1860s and/or the inequitable distribution of wealth. "A Dutch committee, in 1886," Wells relates, "found an important cause in 'the low price of German vinegar,'" whereas German researchers cited a bear market in beet sugar and the "immigration of the Polish Jews."

Wells knew that technology held the key to falling prices. Blame the wit of man, he said in so many words. The telegraph and the steam engine, annihilating space and time, had created one worldwide commodity market out of myriad regional ones. The mechanical reaper, the sewing machine, the Bessemer process and the steel rail, the electric light and the telephone had brought unimagined blessings. So doing, they had also pushed the global supply curve downward and to the right. Gold and silver, which constituted the world's monetary base, were in more than ample supply, Wells documents. It was no flaw in the gold standard that delivered up 10-cent-a-pound copper, 67-cent-a-bushel wheat, a two-cent first-class postage stamp (down from three cents in 1883) or rock-bottom seaborne shipping costs. The cause lay rather with the surging rate of productivity growth. It seemed to thrill Wells, if not every other contemporary of his, that the sum total of the world's steam engines at work in 1887 represented the labor of one billion men, or three times the working population of the planet.

Productivity data nowadays are presented with mathematical precision. No such pretended rigor tricked out the reporting of 125 years ago. But there is no mistaking the direction of things. It was onward and upward in a hurry. "In the manufacture of agricultural implements," the U.S. Commissioner of Labor reported in 1886, "specific evidence is submitted, showing that 600 men now do the work that, 15 or 20 years ago, would have required 2,145 men—a displacement of 1,545." The best test of the rate of material progress, writes Wells, a pre-Schumpeter Schumpeterian, is "the rapidity with which that which is old and has been considered wealth is destroyed by the results of new inventions and discoveries."

By which standard the Suez Canal was the final proof of the progress of the age. Before its opening in 1869, Wells relates, "all the trade of the Western hemispheres with the Indies and the East toiled slowly and uncertainly around the Cape, at an expenditure in time of from six to eight months for the round voyage." Now a trip between London and Calcutta took 30 days. It was bliss for the traveler—

and utter ruin for the owners of the not inconsiderable capital that had been tied up in the "vast system of warehousing in and distribution from England, and of British banking and exchange." Sailing ships, sail makers, sailors—all entered bear markets. The canal, rued *The Economist* newspaper, "so altered and so twisted many of the existing modes and channels of business as to create mischief and confusion."

And how might the scales of mischief and confusion have been tipped if the Bank of England had created enough credit to mitigate the disruptions by inflating the price level? We pondered the question at 35,000 feet. Wells relates that, in 1889, the Bank of France produced a new issue of franc notes "in a twentieth part of the time spent on those which are now being withdrawn from circulation." Little did the author anticipate how much more credit could be conjured into being at a computer keyboard—how many mortgages and mortgage-backed securities a digitally equipped lender could create and distribute, or how effortlessly the spreadsheet-empowered ratings analyst could stamp those structures "triple-A."

Rapid technological innovation is always disruptive, and it is usually deflationary. New since Wells's day are Federal Reserve policies intended to alleviate the disruptions. Literally, you pays your money and you takes your choice. By all we can see, the United States government has chosen inflation.

Chapter Five
Mr. Market Buys a House

Hock-a-Home

August 3, 2001

IT WAS THE consumer who painted the second-quarter GDP black, if only a little bit, offsetting a plunge in business investment. Cars and houses continued to find buyers, rising layoffs notwithstanding. At the end of the first quarter, according to the Office of Federal Housing Enterprise Oversight, the average U.S. house price was up by 8.8% from a year earlier.

What could explain a bull market in a nonearning asset in a noninflationary era? Ample credit is the first answer, low interest rates the second. An overly narrow definition of "inflation" is the third.

In the first quarter, Fannie Mae, Freddie Mac and the Federal Home Loan Banks together expanded their book of business by $84.7 billion, or 12.7% annualized. Freddie and Fannie buy mortgages and mortgage-backed securities in the open market. The Home Loan Banks, too, buy mortgage-backed securities, and they lend to member institutions that, in turn, lend to home buyers. The federal leviathan in this way facilitates mortgage lending at interest rates lower than those that would otherwise obtain.

Although fixed-rate mortgage yields have actually risen a bit this year, homeowners have refinanced en masse. So doing, they have extracted tens of billions in mark-to-market equity. They have applied these proceeds both to debt consolidation and—as page one of *The Wall Street Journal* reported last week—spending. Like IBM, they have been running up their debts and running down their equity while presenting a cheerful face to the world.

According to the Mortgage Bankers Association, mortgage originations this year will reach $1.54 trillion, a record, comprising $660 billion of refinancings and $880 billion of home-purchase lending. Fully half of this year's refi transactions have put money in the borrower's pocket, according to *Mortgage Servicing News*. Susan Sterne, the analytical muscle of Economic Analysis Associates, Greenwich, Conn., reports that home-equity mining has become, for some, a kind of career. "There are people [in hot areas] who live on refis of appreciated housing."

In 1945, Americans owed mortgage creditors just 14% of the value of their homes—the rest, 86%, was theirs in equity. In 1985, they owed 32%. As of the first quarter, they owed 45%, leaving 55% in equity.* During the fabulously prosperous 1990s, they ran down their equity by almost 10 percentage points.

If this is the road to ruin, it posts a very slow speed limit. Of what cyclical consequence is such a long-playing secular trend? Consider, first, an appraisal by Franklin Raines, chairman and CEO of Fannie Mae: "[W]e often talk about the values of the stock market and what impact that has on [the average family's] consumption," he said. "But... their own home equity is their largest source of wealth."

---

* At the end of the first quarter of 2008, homeowners owed 53.8% of the value of their homes to mortgage creditors, an all-time high.

Alan Greenspan, in the colloquy following his July 24 testimony before the Senate Banking, Housing and Urban Affairs Committee, seconded Raines. He observed that "so-called home equity wealth" is being mobilized and employed in "all sorts of household decisions." House prices have continued to rise despite the slump in stock prices, and this appreciation, he said, "has created a very substantial buffer of unrealized capital gains, which are being drawn upon through the home equity market, through cash-outs, through the turnover of existing homes, which has been, as you know, quite substantial despite the weakness in the economy. So in that regard, the housing sector . . . has been a very important contributor to the American economy, and I think one of the major reasons why. . .that litany of all the negatives which you can easily line up has not in fact cracked the economy's underlying stability."

Which brings up the question: With inflation moderating and layoffs mounting, why should house prices keep rising? The accompanying graph, created by Fred Sheehan, of John Hancock Asset Management Services, suggests that they may not. On the bottom is housing starts, on the top, existing home sales. The spread between the two, Sheehan proposes, constitutes a measure of speculative real-estate activity. He calls it "day trading of houses." Insofar as high trading volume characterizes a speculative market, the American house market may be described as speculative. If so, it's a thin reed on which to support a bullish GDP forecast.

Rope for the Neck of the Homeowner

October 11, 2002

Interest rates can have unintended consequences. Very low rates often ignite booms, but even ultra-low rates may not fix busts. A case in point is the current federal funds rate.

At 1¾%, the rate seems low and it is low, but it isn't as low as it seems, to borrow from Warren Buffett. Judging by the deceleration in the growth of the credit the Fed creates, the Bank of Alan Greenspan is propping the rate up rather than pushing it down. It is withholding credit from the market to support a rate that, in the absence of Fed open-market operations, would probably be lower than 1¾%. So we expect that the rate soon will be lower—1%, to guess.*

What good a 1% funds rate would do is, of course, debatable. If, by precipitating a new wave of mortgage refinancing, it pushed Fannie Mae into a new prepayment emergency, it might not do any net good at all. Then, too, a 1% funds rate would put the interest-only mortgage on the national map.

Little did the FOMC expect when it pushed the pedal to the metal, that the lowest money-market interest rates in a generation would open a new channel of speculation. But in making possible the popularization of the floating-rate, non-amortizing mortgage loan, they have.

Consumers in growing numbers are choosing interest-only mortgages over the conventional, amortizing kind. Washington Mutual is writing $1 billion worth a month, according to the *Los Angeles Times*. We see no such boom in New York (J.P. Morgan Chase, for example, doesn't offer a non-amortizing mortgage), but Merrill Lynch is showing the way. Its Web site offers interest-only, floating-rate loans at various spreads off Libor. As three-month Libor is quoted at just 1.77%, borrowing costs are quoted in the low 3% range. For the one-month adjustment option, for instance, Merrill quotes 3¼% over 25 years on a $400,000 loan. For the first 10 years, you pay interest only. From years 11 through 25, you pay interest and amortize principal. As the spirit moves, you take a profit and move to Boca Raton.

In answer to the frequently asked question, "Is an interest-only financing solution right for me?" Merrill provided an answer seemingly better suited for a clientele in the Dow 10,000 era. "By paying only the interest on your mortgage," the text explains, "you can reduce your monthly mortgage payment and have more funds avail-

---

* The Fed lowered it funds rate to 1% in June 2003, where it remained until June 2004.

able for investments. Since your home's value is not tied to its equity, its value can grow while your investments do the same. Investing money that would have gone toward paying principal on your mortgage can complement your overall financial plan and help you grow your wealth." The lifetime interest rate cap is a minimum 12%.

E. Everett Puri, of City Capital Inc., was the first to tell us about non-amortizing mortgages, and he says that in his hometown, Atlanta, they're "pervasive." Peter Walmsley of this staff took the temperature of the market in a call to Mark Scott, vice president of marketing for Homebanc Mortgage, licensed lender in Georgia and Florida.

Scott said the sales pitch is that, for the first five to seven years in the life of a mortgage, the borrower mainly pays interest anyway; there is little principal amortization. Besides, most people move out within 10 years of moving in. "So when we tell that to people," Scott said, "they respond to that pretty well. So you put that

"In your case, I'd advise the interest-only mortgage. You'll be traded before it starts to amortize."

with the whole. Not only will you be saving "x" hundred dollars a month on your payment, but you know it is not that scary when you get right down to it."

Walmsley asked what would happen to the person with a Libor mortgage if Libor went back up—say, to 7%?

"Ha-ha-ha-ha," replied Scott. "That's the problem, isn't it? The Libor rate is typically one of our more stable ones. And our data indicate that it hardly ever goes—and I think we have data going back 25 or 30 years—that it is remarkably stable in the face of almost all world events and financial shenanigans that are going on. So that is a good thing and that reassures the customers as well." Never mind about the time Paul Volcker pushed up the funds rate to almost 20%, or when Greenspan inverted the yield curve.

What will the president of the Atlanta Fed say when someone next moves to raise the funds rate? If he dared to vote in favor, they'd hang him on Peachtree Street.

Meet "Mr. I.O.–P.O."

December 19, 2003

In Alpharetta, a northern suburb of Atlanta, a certain financial-services executive is playing the system like a Stradivarius. His car loan requires no interest payments. His mortgage requires no principal payments. Truly, he is Mr. Interest Only–Principal Only, or—as his friends might have it—Mr. I.O.–P.O.

This avatar of resourcefulness is happy to tell his story, though he asks that his name be withheld. The story begins with the house he had always dreamt of owning. One day, while driving his son to school, he noticed a "for sale" sign in front of it. He bought the place on the spot.

Inconveniently, Mr. I.O.–P.O. already owned a house, which he was then renovating and could not easily sell. He was, there-fore, long two houses. It was 2001. The economy was softening and interest rates were falling. How to finance house No. 2 on the most flexible and advantageous terms? He availed himself of an interest-only mortgage.

By now, you have heard of an I.O. mortgage (*Grant's*, Oct. 11, 2002). Usually, the term is 30 years, and the initial rate is floating. The holder is obliged to amortize no principal for a certain number of years—in our man's case, 10. The interest rate is set at a premium to the world's basic wholesale dollar money-market interest rate, i.e., Libor (London interbank offered rate).

On the first business day of 2001, three-month Libor was quoted at 6.37%. One year later, it had a 1% handle. By this point, Mr. I.O.–P.O. thought he "was getting a house for free." His cost of borrowing was pegged to Libor plus 1⅝ percentage points, which, today, works out to 2.8% before tax and even less after tax.

Interest-only mortgages were just coming into vogue when Mr. I.O.–P.O. got one. It will interest the Federal Reserve to know that they are becoming much more popular. "As home prices continue to rise and interest rates inch above their record lows," recently reported Kathleen Pender of the *San Francisco Chronicle*, "more homeowners, especially in high-cost regions like the Bay Area, are choosing interest-only mortgages."

Twenty percent of new mortgages at Wells Fargo Mortgage are I.O.s, according to the *Chronicle*. But "[a]t Quicken Loans, about a third of all home mortgages are interest only, with most of the growth coming in the last five months. . . ."

The year is now 2003, and our inventive consumer is in the market for a car—two cars, actually, as the company car he'd been driving fell victim to a stroke of corporate economy. "It was a time of zero down and zero-percent financing," Mr. I.O.–P.O. explains. Auto debt, of course, is not tax deductible, which makes it a priori undesirable. Not that zero-percent financing is truly and strictly what it seems, either; one accepts the zero rate in lieu of a rebate. "The bet I made," our man goes on, "was that I would own the cars long enough [to make the zero-rate choice worthwhile]."

For the wife, he bought a Silverado pickup truck, for himself, a Corvette—a limited-availability, burgundy Corvette Commemorative Edition, as a matter of fact, with a list price of about $50,000. Mr. I.O.–P.O. denies that his decision had anything to do with a midlife crisis. "Here's the analysis," he says, "very financial. The cost of owning a car is tying up your capital and the depreciation. You've been driving these SUVs like everybody else. You know you buy the hot car, you pay $40,000, and two years later, you sell it for $18,000. And I remember when I was 24 years old, I bought a Corvette, sold it three years later for more than I paid for it, you know a couple-hundred bucks. Why was I so much smarter then than now? Corvette had this zero-down, zero-percent financing, and I said, 'You know what? I'm not going to tie up my capital, and I don't think this thing is going to depreciate much, because I bought the 50th-anniversary one.'"

All-in, after-tax, Mr. I.O.–P.O. figures, it costs him 2½% to live in the house of his dreams and drive the car of his youth. He sees one advantage to his mortgage that many overlook: He can amortize his debt if and when he chooses, and, in fact, did so upon selling his first house in the summer of 2002. He applied the equity to reducing the size of the principal on which he is now paying interest. "Everybody thinks that the appeal is no amortization," says he. "That's part of the appeal, but there's not much amortization on a 30-year mortgage anyway. The real appeal to me was that I could pay it down and get a reduction in my monthly payment. If you pay down a conventional loan, you lower the principal but your payment doesn't reflect that."

Is Mr. I.O.–P.O. not concerned that the funds rate might go up sharply after the lapse of that "considerable period" that the chairman of the Federal Reserve Board keeps alluding to? He is not: "I mean, going up short term isn't a problem if you know you can cover it." And there is one final, overlooked advantage of interest-only mortgage borrowing, our source avers: In the conventional market, jumbo borrowers typically pay a premium interest rate, but there is no such discrimination in the I.O. market.

Though happy as a clam with his own financial decisions,* our man worries a little about the consumers who are doing as he does but without the same cushion of household equity capital. "[T]he discipline of amortization isn't there," he notes of his I.O. mortgage. "Our parents' generation, that generation created their net worth primarily through mortgage amortization. Their biggest asset was their home, and the reason they owned that home was that there was no choice. The bank made them buy that home, paying off that loan. And they didn't realize it, but when they paid that mortgage payment, they were essentially investing in a savings account."

Compare and contrast in the year 2003: "You can finance the sales tax—7% sales tax," he marvels about the institution of consumer auto finance. "You drive this thing 4, 4½ months before you pay the sales tax. Talk about things being upside down! This is my concern for America. You are not amortizing your home loan, people are quick to get second mortgages and other things, they are not putting equity in their house and they have probably negative equity in their vehicle."

Just don't pass this on. The foreign creditors of the United States are skittish enough as it is.

For a Considerable Period

January 16, 2004

The 1% funds rate has changed the borrowing patterns of American home buyers. Certainly, it has transformed the borrowing patterns of the clientele of the Northeast region of Washington Mutual Inc.

WAMU offers an adjustable-rate mortgage with an interest-only feature. It calls this mortgage Option-ARM. In just one

---

* In my situation," said Mr. I.O.–P.O. when reached for comment in June 2008, "it made perfect sense."

year, the percentage of WAMU's customers selecting Option-ARMs has leapt to 40% from 5%, according to Harry Tomlinson, senior vice president for the Northeast region. Today, as many people choose Option-ARMs as choose fixed-rate loans, Tomlinson tells *Grant's*. "Where, before, fixed-rate loans would be kind of nine out of every 10, or seven out of 10, let's say now it's almost on a par with Option-ARM."

The keys are flexibility and the low initial rate, says Tomlinson—just 3½%. The borrower can elect to go interest-only and to make no amortization payment, Tomlinson explains: "If you have a little bit of financial challenges, you can always have the option of deferred amortization, but you don't have to. That's a choice."

"What I see is a shift in the mortgage product, going from a product used to buy one's home . . . to a product where people can leverage their home as a financial asset," Tomlinson advises. "And that's a big shift."

When the Fed lifted the funds rate in 1994, it caught out the hedge funds and interest-rate speculators. When it raises the funds rate next time, it will catch out Mr. and Mrs. America.

Your Home is Your Debt

May 21, 2004

Last month's purchase by the Indian steel magnate, Lakshmi Mittal, of a 12-bedroom house with a 20-car garage in Kensington Palace Gardens, London, for the round sum of $126 million called attention to one of the world's great bull markets. Now comes a report from Smithers & Co., the Cartesian consultant, that quantifies how high is up in U.K. residential real estate. The short answer: Very. The relevance of this insight to the U.S. house market: High.

Smithers plots the trend in the value of the U.K. housing stock relative to GDP over the past half century. The data show a recent deviation from trend—to the upside, of course. In fact, the report says, the only preceding comparable episode in U.K. residential real estate was the boom of 1973, the year of the onset of Britain's own S&L crackup, the "secondary banking crisis." As for the bubble at hand, Smithers finds that a return to trend would mean a drop in prices of 28% from the level of year-end 2003.

Applying the Smithers method, we have calculated the trend in the value of the U.S. housing stock relative to GDP. It, too, is up. And, as in Britain, there is a millennial leap in prices, though one less exaggerated than Britain's. In the U.S., a return to trend would imply a decline in house prices of 15%. We were about to say "only" 15%, but there is nothing insignificant about 15% if the value of one's mortgage, or mortgages, is greater than 85% of the value of one's property.

On average, the Fed calculates, the national loan-to-value ratio is 45%, which happens to be an all-time high. However, 45% is not the contemporary home buyer's idea of getting a good deal. Last year, according to the Federal Housing Finance Board, 29% of new conventional, single-family mortgages had loan-to-value ratios of more than 80%, while 20% had LTVs of more than 90%.

Now then, in the 12 months through September 2003, there were $1.2 trillion of new mortgage originations (separate and distinct from the $3 trillion of refis). If the Housing Finance Board numbers are true, 20% of these originations would have LTVs greater than 90%. Twenty percent of $1.2 trillion in originations works out to $244 billion of mortgages held by approximately one million American families.

Those heavily leveraged homeowners would, in car lingo, be "upside down" if house prices pulled back by 10%. That is, they would owe more on their asset than that asset is worth in the market. A 10% "correction" would mean a retreat to the level of prices seen only 21 months ago.

So it would be better for at least a small, seven-figure subset of American consumers if house prices did not pull back by even so much as 10%. And it would be better for other American consumers if the federal funds rate were left exactly where it is. According to the Housing Finance Board, 18% of the Class of 2003 mortgage originations were adjustable-rate. Here one recalls Alan Greenspan's helpful advice to consumers last February 23. "Indeed," said the Maestro, "recent research within the Federal Reserve suggests that many homeowners might have saved tens of thousands of dollars had they held adjustable-rate mortgages rather than fixed-rate mortgages during the past decade, though this would not have been the case, of course, had interest rates trended sharply higher."

The funds rate, we believe, will not trend sharply higher, but, on the contrary, will creep. Whatever its trajectory, the new rising rate cycle finds record numbers of Americans owning houses, not renting them. No surprise, then, it's cheaper by far to rent.

The 29th Bubble

June 3, 2005

❝We don't perceive that there is a national bubble," Alan Greenspan, speaking about house prices, advised the Economic Club of New York the other day, "but it's hard not to see . . . that there are a lot of local bubbles." For what might be the first time in his life, the Maestro thereby staked out a genuinely contrary investment position. These days, bearishness on house prices has become an Approved Institutional Opinion, much like bullishness on almost everything else.

Following is a new contribution to the negative literature. We do not mean to be repetitive, or—worse yet—banal, and we believe we are not. One proof we offer is the title of an essay by the real-estate authority we are about to quote. It is: "Growth of Dolphins, Coryphaena Hippurus and C. Equiselis, in Hawaiian Waters as Determined by Daily Increments on Otoliths" (*Fishery Bulletin*, U.S. Department of Commerce, Vol. 84, 1986). Which other expert on

U.S. house prices could make an even remotely similar claim? The author's view, and ours, is that, in residential real estate from Miami to Seattle, "bubble" is the word.

It's not a word just to toss around. A bubble market is one that goes way, way up, then comes way, way down. And house prices have gone way, way up—in April, the median existing home price showed a year-over-year gain of 15%. But they have not come way, way down. Indeed, the national average has not registered a broad-based decline in living memory. Since the 1930s, sideways is as bad as a bear market in American residential real estate has gotten (though there have been some ferocious localized declines). "[H]istory is definitive," pronounced the *American Banker* in a May 23 article on interest-only mortgages, "The national average price of a home may remain relatively flat for a number of years, but it doesn't fall." Let's see about that.

If the 2005 U.S. residential real estate market were in a bubble, and if prices did not subsequently fall, that would constitute a first. A bubble is a defined phenomenon; not just any frothy market makes the grade. According to the analysts at GMO, Boston, a bubble is a two standard deviation event, and they have identified only 28 of them since the Coolidge bull stock market.

Physicists rightfully smile at the pretensions of Wall Street's quants. But, in the matter of bubbles, the financial analysts may have discovered an actual law of nature. In 27 of the 28 cases, according to GMO, sky-high prices eventually returned to earth, frequently making a small crater as they landed. The one known outlier is the 28th and current bubble, the S&P 500, which would have to fall to about 750 to revert to the mean (it closed Tuesday at 1,192). "Have to fall," in fact, is not quite accurate. By trading sideways for a decade or so, the S&P might revert to trend with a whimper, not a bang. So, the question that should absorb us all: Are U.S. house prices in that kind of a market?

We base our affirmative reply on many things, including the proliferation of no-money-down and interest-only mortgages;

the soaring growth in the volume of new houses for sale, which houses do not yet happen to exist; and the growing imbalance between rising supply and sated demand. As for the second and third items on the list, students should consult a May 25 report by François Trahan et al. of Bear Stearns, "REIT All About It: A Bubble Looming in Real Estate?" Trahan's thesis is that 2005 is a uniquely risky juncture in real estate. Never before have homeowners been so leveraged; and never before has the residential market been so speculative. And, yes, he's bearish on REITs.

Which brings us to the centerpiece of the investment case against houses. R. King Burch, the originator of the forthcoming analysis, is a paid-up subscriber in Honolulu. As might be inferred from the title of the scientific essay quoted above, he was trained as a marine biologist, but made a career switch to real estate (he was intrigued to discover in business school that investment mathematics resemble the math used to express the dynamics of fish populations). He participated in the Japanese-financed Hawaiian property bubble of 1988–90, worked on hotel deals in Florida in the 1990s and wrote—among other real-estate-relevant works—"The Internal Contradictions of Hotel Real Estate Investment Trusts" (*Real Estate Review*, Fall 1997). Today, he consults and invests for himself in Hawaii. Either house prices are in a bubble, Burch advises, or, if not that, "at least something very different from the usual home buying activity that goes on in the U.S. economy."

We believe that Burch has proven the bubble case, with all it implies for a future slump in the prices of the roofs over our heads. Like many another eureka, this one is calculated to make the reader say, "Now why didn't I think of that?" To draw a bead on U.S. real estate activity, Burch suggests, just take price times volume: Multiply the number of home sales by the average home price. Now divide that value by GDP. The answer expresses the intensity of house fever. Call this measure, as Burch does, the "calculated transaction value," or CTV. Now examine the findings, 1970 to date, plotted nearby. Do you spy a bubble?

For 35 years, 1970 to 2005, the annual CTV—price times volume, both of existing and new houses—averaged just under 9.2% of GDP.* "However," Burch relates, "the data show two periods with remarkable divergences from this mean. The first such period occurred in the inflation-led housing frenzy of the late 1970s, when transactions jumped from early-decade values of around 7% and peaked at nearly 12% in 1978. However, a nudge from Paul Volcker and 16% mortgage rates sent it plummeting back down to 6% of GDP by 1982." Significantly, Burch goes on, the decline was owing not to any fall in average prices, but to a 50% plunge in the number of sales: "Housing transactions then spent the next 15 years ranging from about 8% of GDP to just under 10% of GDP."

The breakout year for the current house-price boom is 1998. Except for a small stumble in 2000, the CTV has made a succession of new highs. It reached 16.2% in 2004, "a proportion," notes Burch, "that is 73%, and 2.95 standard deviations, greater than the average for the last 35 years." Not stopping there, it touched 17.2% at the end of the first quarter of this year, a level 85%, and 3.4 standard deviations, greater than the average for the past 35¼ years. If house prices are not a bubble, house transactions certainly are. Does your brother-in-law, the real estate broker, owe you money? Now is the time to collect.

One might suppose that low mortgage rates are a sufficient condition for bubbling house prices. Burch finds otherwise: "A simple regression shows that average annual interest rates on conventional loans explain only about 30% of housing activity expressed as a percentage of GDP." Only consider 2004: CTV soared as mortgage rates stayed the same. Nor is the driving force behind the real estate bull market elevated income growth. Since 2000, growth in nominal wages and salaries has averaged 2.7%

---

* The CTV peaked at 18.3% in 2005. But by the first quarter of 2008, it had plunged to 9.6%.

"Why the gun?"

a year (5.9 percentage points lower than annual average growth since 2000 in the median price of an existing house).

What has driven the boom is rather the accessibility of dollars. For this monetary superabundance, the revolution in securitized mortgage finance, specifically the post-2000 lift-off in MBS activity, deserves thanks. Comments Burch: "The relatively recent advent and growth of an international market in mortgage-backed securities, whose buyers are neither especially knowledgeable of, nor concerned with, the credit and collateral of the borrower trumps the claim, valid in quaint earlier times when a neighborhood lender made and held local loans, that real estate markets are local." And while you're at it, thank the so-called carry trade (the tactic of borrowing at a low rate and investing at a higher, longer-term rate) and the shape of the yield curve (short rates conveniently below longer ones).

In times past, the home buyer had to apply for a loan. Now, the lenders almost apply to him, whoever he is. Can you fog a mirror?

But wait, Burch cautions. A subprime-grade borrower availing himself of a no-money-down, interest-only mortgage confronts daunting arithmetic. Besides mortgage expense—call it 5% a year—the buyer must bear the cost of property taxes, upkeep and utilities—call that 2½% a year. And say, at the end of year one, he decides to sell. He must pay a sales commission and other closing costs—call that 6.5% of the purchase price. Just to break even, therefore, our buyer-speculator requires 15% in price appreciation (calculated as $[1.00 + 0.05 + 0.025/0.935]$).

"Home prices and financing cannot continuously diverge from the buyer's ability to pay," Burch winds up. "Even the most aggressive MBS investors must eventually balk at funding towering home prices when the buyer has no 'skin' in the game. Since mortgage rates have, generally, stopped declining, I would bet (in fact, I have bet, by purchasing put options on home builders) that the game has already peaked." And the flatter the yield curve becomes, the tighter the lender's margins and the greater his risk.

We led off this article with the concession that bears on houses are thick on the ground. But how many of these doubters have taken bearish action? Your house-owning editor has not. The bearish François Trahan (co-author of the Bear Stearns report) advises against precipitous action: "[T]here's no need to rush for the exits just yet; i.e., real estate, unlike stocks, is a slow-moving asset and none of this will unfold overnight." And from one of the top Wall Street research houses comes this optimistic article of pessimism: "[H]ousing is in a bubble, but [eminent economist's name withheld] places us in the seventh inning with plenty of upside potential." As long as interest rates stay moored, what's the rush?

But maybe the immediate risk to house prices lies not with interest rates but with lending standards, or the shape of the yield curve. Recall, as does Paul Kasriel, director of economic research at Northern Trust Co., the May 16 "guidance" from a brace of federal regulatory agencies to the nation's mortgage makers. The points of risk singled out by the bureaucrats are the very ones that have empowered the marginal home buyer to stretch to buy the marginal home (they include interest-only loans, high loan-to-value loans, low—or no—documentation loans and proliferating home-equity loans). A friend observes that the Fed resisted entreaties late in the 1990s to tighten margin requirements to deflate the stock-market bubble. Not literally deaf to its critics, the Fed—and the other leading federal banking regulators—might just be trying to take some of the helium out of today's bubble in house prices. It's no easy thing to deflate just a little bit. Good luck, federales!

In Kansas We Busted

November 4, 2005

Soaring prices and interest-only loans are the hallmarks of the 2005 real estate market (or were until the recent cooling trend set in). They no less happened to characterize the Great Plains segment of the 1886 real estate market.

Here begins a meditation on whom to blame when there's no Alan Greenspan. The chairman's more vociferous critics—your editor does not forget himself—are prone to blame the Fed for every worm in the financial apple. But other human beings bear their share of responsibility. Humanity is prone to miscalculate. It does not always need a central bank to lead it astray. In the excitement of a fast-moving market, it is capable of grossly miscalculating. Sometimes, as in the late-1990s high-tech frenzy or in the mid-1880s real estate mania, it doesn't even bother to reach for pencil and paper.

In the mid-1880s, excitable people pushed up Western land prices to highs that, in real terms, haven't been seen since. The relevance of this fact to the readers of *Grant's* is the institutional setting in which it occurred. Way back in the first administration of Grover Cleveland, there was no Federal Reserve, no federal deposit insurance and no federally manipulated money-market interest rate. The gold standard was in place: Anybody could push $20.67 through a Treasury Department cashier's window and demand an ounce of gold in exchange. Did such an arrangement not anchor the rate of credit creation and inculcate the Ten Commandments? Whatever it did, Kansas, Nebraska and the Dakota Territory played host to their own debt-financed property bubble.

Who financed it, if not a central bank? Who, if not the Maestro, played Pied Piper? The answers will be found in the unfolding narrative. It begins with a war and ends with a crash. In between come economic growth, entrepreneurial derring-do, wishful thinking, yield groping, technological upheaval and man-made climate change (or a theory to that effect). You'd think it happened yesterday.

As the non-American readers of *Grant's* may not have learned at their mother's knee, the Civil War (1861–65) pitted North and South, free states against slave, nationalists against the proponents of states' rights. In fact, not many states rights' proponents were propounding during these hostilities (they were fighting for the Confederacy). In their absence, Congress voted to get the government into the railroad business. Vast tracts of public land were handed over to the projected transcontinental railroads. Historians have recognized that these transportation companies were, in truth, real-estate companies. Some were bequeathed 20 miles of land on either side of the tracks.

To fill these immense spaces, the railroads advertised for settlers. The Northern Pacific's marketing campaign succeeded in one thing, at least. It inspired a parody. The author of the send-up solemnly described the railroad's holdings as being bigger than the "nine" New England states, the northern part of European Russia, all of France (except for Alsace and Lorraine), Turkey, a portion of New Jersey and Coney Island—all in all, a land mass as big as "the two states of Delaware combined."

Besides enticement, the settlers needed credit, which the railroads also furnished. The Burlington offered not one kind of mortgage but a menu of choices, including a "long credit" 10-year lien priced at 6%; for the first two years, the borrower—would you believe it?—paid interest only. The Union Pacific lent up to 90% of value at 7% over an 11-year term, with interest only due for the first three years. So fertile was the land, so propitious was the climate and so high were prevailing grain prices—as the promoters proclaimed—that a farmer could earn the cost of his farm with a single crop. The bulls did not entirely fabricate this claim: In the early 1880s, it was briefly true.

The weather was a pleasant surprise. Some 18 to 20 inches of rain was necessary to make a good crop, and this quota was annually met. Old-timers scratched their heads; the Kansas, Nebraska and Dakota Territory they knew were dry, especially in their western reaches. What could explain this anomalous succession of wet seasons? Human activity, some reasoned. By breaking sod, irrigating crops and planting trees, the settlers themselves effected a benevolent change in the climate. A professor at the University of Nebraska lent his authority to this pleasing hypothesis.

It was, indeed, a New Era, and not only in climate. With the advent of the railroads, the crops and cattle of the Plains States could reach Eastern markets. And thanks to the march of migration, Western land prices persistently rose. In the decade of the 1870s, the population of Kansas had tripled, to one million. It was as plain as the nose on your face that it would keep on tripling, decade after decade, world without end.

Yield-starved Eastern savers certainly seemed to believe it. Interest rates had climbed with the inflation of the early 1860s (the Lincoln administration had abandoned the gold standard for the printing press in order to wage the Civil War). But rates had been falling since 1866. By the early 1880s, New Englanders were earning just 4% at the bank and slightly less on high-grade railroad bonds. Inasmuch as the cost of living was actually falling (down by an average of 0.7% per annum in the 1880s), a modern-day economist would probably judge that "real" rates of interest were, in fact, generous. But Western mortgages, yielding 6% to 8%, seemed even more generous. So-called chattel mortgages—loans secured by livestock, rolling stock, farm implements, etc.—were quoted at 10% and up.

If the yield pigs of yesteryear were anything like their millennial descendants, no economic pretext was required to induce them to reach for hundreds of basis points of extra yield; the savers' hands grasped almost involuntarily. But if they needed a story, one was ready at hand. The age of free Western land was over or ending, the bulls declared. Waves of pioneers would have to pay increasingly higher prices for what had formerly been theirs for the taking. "Moreover," wrote John D. Hicks in *The Populist Revolt*, first published in 1931, "crop yields in the West over a period of years had averaged high, prices were good and collections were easily made. The mortgage notes themselves, 'gorgeous with gold and green ink,' looked the part of stability, and the idea spread throughout the East that savings placed in this class of investments were as safe as they were remunerative. Small wonder that money descended like a flood upon those who made it their business to place loans in the West!"

Back East, banking regulators urged the smitten depositors to go slow. "Eastern states found it necessary to pass laws for the examining and licensing of western investment companies in order to protect individuals who were being induced to withdraw their deposits from savings banks and invest them in western securities," relates the historian Hallie Farmer (writing, a few years before Hicks, in *The Mississippi Valley Historical Review*). A lot of good it did: "Competition existed not between borrowers but between lenders. 'I found drafts, money orders and currency heaped on my desk every morning,' said the secretary of a western loan company. 'I could not loan the money as fast as it came in.' The manager of another company stated that 'during many months of 1886 and 1887 we were unable to get enough mortgages for the people of the East who wished to invest in that kind of security. My desk was piled high every morning with hundreds of letters each enclosing a draft and asking me to send a farm mortgage from Kansas or Nebraska.'"

There was a nationwide surge in real estate mortgages made in the decade of the 1880s—to $1.4 billion in 1889 from $540 million in 1880. Whereas population rose by 25% and "wealth" by 50%, real estate mortgages climbed by 156%. (For perspective, in 1890, the gross national product totaled $12.5 billion and the population was 63 million.) Writing in 1894 in the *Annals of the American Academy of Political and Social Science*, George K. Holmes ventured that American real estate, considered as an asset class, was fast approaching the point of maximum encumbrance. Whatever that point might be, it still was nowhere in sight a century later.

On the Plains in the 1880s, much as in the cities of the 2000s, conflicts surfaced between principals and agents. The principals, in this case the savers, wanted safety—and an immense pickup in yield. The agents, in this case the lenders, wanted to collect commissions. Not for the first or last time in financial history, the agents fared better than the principals. William Allen White (1868–1944), famed editor of the *Emporia* (Kan.) *Gazette*, told a story about the "agents in Kansas with a plethora of money in their hands [who] drove about the country in buggies, soliciting patronage and freely placing loans on real estate up to its full valuation, pointing in justification to the steadily mounting price of land. The companies tended almost without exception to lend too much on each farm. It was not their own capital that was at stake but the capital of distant investors, and the more they lent the more they made for their own profits."

Pretty clearly, the supply of lendable funds exceeded the demand for lendable funds (as the United States was then intermittently running a trade deficit, some of the surplus was presumably foreign). Promoters reveled in the imbalance. No self-respecting town wanted to be without its streetcar line, school, jail and—especially—railroad connection. "Confidence was high," recounts Farmer, "money was easy to obtain, and the West entered upon such an orgy of railroad building as the world had never seen before. Old companies extended their lines. New companies were organized. Within six weeks in the spring of 1887, the Northwestern Rail-roader recorded the incorporation of 16 new railroad companies and the letting of contracts for work on 13 new branches of old roads. Kansas more than doubled her railroad mileage between 1880 and 1887. That of Nebraska was quadrupled and Dakota had 11 times the mileage in 1890 which she had in 1880."

Frontier due diligence in the 1880s proved no better than the big-city kind 120 years later. "Securities which could not have been sold in ordinary times found a ready market," according to Farmer. "Bonds of Capitola township, Spink county, Dakota, were sold in this period and changed hands many times in eastern markets before it was discovered that no such township existed."

No close and continuous series of real-estate price data is known to exist, but indicative prices can be drawn from newspaper ads. According to the scholar who did so draw them, Kansas farmland appreciated by a factor of between four and six in the years 1881–87. "[I]n rare instances," wrote Raymond C. Miller, a contemporary of Farmer's, "the price of land rose as high as $200 an acre." Wichita was the Las Vegas or Orange County of the Great Plains, and it came to a full boil in the winter of 1886–87. "A clerk who put his $200 savings into a lot sold it two months later for $2,000," according to Hicks. "A barber who dabbled in real estate made $7,000. Real estate agents, many of whom made much larger fortunes, swarmed over the place by the hundreds; they were so numerous that the city derived a considerable revenue from the license fees they had to pay."

Because there was so clearly a bubble, the denials of that fact were expressed with special vehemence. "It is not a sudden impulse in Lincoln or Omaha or Hastings or Atchison or Wichita or Kansas City," protested the editor of the *Nebraska State Journal* in March 1887. "It is simply the effect of the exhaustion of the public lands and the prosperity of the trans-Missouri region." But if the definition of a bubble is a rise in prices so extreme that it blights the affected asset class for not just a few years but a generation or more, Kansas property was a double bubble. A peak price of $200 an acre in 1887 would translate into $4,400 in today's purchasing power. According to the U.S. Department of Agriculture, Kansas farmland today fetches an average price of $800 an acre. Not even the Bernanke Fed will find it easy to return the Jayhawk property market to its Cleveland-era heights.

Our Nebraska editor protested as the bubble was bursting. Some may wonder: As there was no Federal Reserve to raise an interest rate, what was the pin? Historians cite a collapse in speculative-grade bond prices, a bear market in agricultural commodities and a drought. Neither your editor nor his crack researcher, Ben Isaac, have discovered why the bottom fell out of the market in the kind of securities that financed the redundant railroads, streetcar lines, etc. (There had been a financial panic in the East in 1884. Its reverberations might have done some of the damage.) But there's no mystery about the slump in grain prices or the sudden close of the alleged new era in rainfall. Each had devastating effects on the mortgaged settlers. Corn fetched 63 cents a bushel in 1881, 28 cents a bushel nine years later. The drought began in 1887 and lasted for 10 years, in five of which all crops failed.

Lending dried up with the moisture. In the tail end of the boom, 1884-87, 6,000 farm mortgages, in the sum of $5.5 million, were written in Nebraska, Farmer relates. "In the next three years only 500 such mortgages were placed with a total value of $633,889. . . . Eastern investors refused to place more money in the West and much of the money already invested was withdrawn as the lenders became frightened over the agitation of the debtors for relief in the form of stay laws."

To anyone whose point of orientation in consumer finance is 2005 alone, the pioneers will not seem an especially overindebted lot. "There was one mortgage for every two adults," Miller reported, "which means more than one for every family; and the per capita private debt, counting adults alone, was over $347, about four times that of the Union as a whole." On a loan-to-value basis, this burden does not seem especially onerous. Mortgages on land amounted to a quarter or so "of the actual value of all the real estate of Kansas." But any debt is oppressive when there is no income to service it, which was exactly the plight of the Jawhawk farmers.

"Between 1888 and 1892," Miller went on, "one-half of the people of western Kansas trailed eastward out of the state as they had entered it only a few months before, each with his family and his total worldly possessions in a single covered wagon, drawn by two gaunt ponies." Emblazoned on the sides of these wagons were such mottoes as "Going back to the wife's folks," or "In God we trusted, in Kansas we busted."

"Disappointed pioneers handed over their farms to the loan companies by which they had been mortgaged or abandoned them outright," Hicks recorded. "Some of the more courageous may have headed for Oklahoma, where other frontier lands were being opened to settlement, "but doubtless the rank and file had had enough of pioneering."

The voices of the losers in the Great Plains bubble were presently raised to protest against the financial arrangements that had failed them. The Populist Party demanded an end to the gold standard, cheaper and more abundant currency and greater federal control over banks and banking. The more wild-eyed of these radicals actually pushed for a pure paper monetary system—dollar bills whose value owed not to the gold or silver in back of them, but to the government-mandated words, "legal tender." Orthodox financiers cringed or scoffed, but in only a few short years the radicals' ideas began to enter the political mainstream. At last, on Aug. 15, 1971, they were fully realized. The U.S. dollar became a piece of paper, that and no more.

Under this very system, a giant real-estate boom is just beginning to peter out. The Fed's battle against "deflation," with its ultra-low interest rates, must bear a good portion of the blame, or credit, for bringing it into existence in the first place. On the other hand, the lesson of the Great Plains levitation is that, in order to create a really big asset-price bubble, a central bank is neither necessary nor sufficient. A critical mass of human beings is all that's required.

House Prices: Prepare for the Impossible

August 11, 2006

Average U.S. house prices rarely fall from one year to the next. Bankers, brokers, appraisers, loan servicers, mortgage investors, homeowners and the designers and promoters of collateralized debt obligations all attest to the truth of this assertion. What these purely impartial observers usually fail to add, however, is that home values rarely soar, either. According to Yale University economist Robert Shiller, residential real estate prices, in real terms, rose by all of 66% between 1890 and 2004, or by just 0.4% a year. All the more remarkable, then, that between 1997 and 2005 they leapt by 52%, or by 6.2% a year, also in real terms. Many contend that a sustained pullback in house prices is unthinkable. But the unthinkable—or, at least, the highly atypical—has already happened. In 2001–05, prices levitated.

Grant's is now embarked on a series of grand speculations. We ask: What is the likelihood of a coast-to-coast bear market in residential real estate? What effect might such an event have on the U.S. economy? On interest rates? What do history, economic analysis and—yes—theology have to contribute to the penetration of these mysteries? In preview, we conclude that a decline in house prices is already under way. If the house market, like the stock market, were mean-reverting, the sell-off could carry a fair way. A return to the post-1968 trend line would imply a drop of 22%. Which, of course, for these real estate-centric United States, would imply disaster. We do not predict disaster, but we do expect a pullback severe enough to inhibit the leveraged

American consumer and to stunt the growth of the U.S. economy—except for the Treasury-bond-buying branch of the economy, which will likely flourish. Of course, there's more than one way for a mean-reverting price to return to the average. House prices could shuffle sideways for five or 10 years as incomes rose to catch up to them. Such an outcome, however, we judge more convenient than plausible.

Nobody disputes the essential real estate facts. The conclusions to which these facts clearly point would not be controversial if they pertained to any commodity other than the encumbered American castle. Affordability is way down and units offered for sale are way up. The cost of carry is way up and transaction volumes are way down. Price appreciation has all but stopped. "In the year to June," observes Lombard Street Research in a July 25 bulletin, "the median price of existing homes rose by 0.9%. On a six-month annualized basis, it fell by 0.7%. (If the average is used instead of the median, the equivalent numbers are 0.8% and minus 0.4%.) This represents a sharp deceleration from double-digit house-price inflation as recently as January, when prices rose by 11.9% over a 12-month period. The June number was also the lowest annual rise in 11 years. It is no coincidence that this also was a time when the Fed had rapidly raised interest rates. But the deceleration of prices then was much milder than the recent plunge."

The bearish case on house prices may seem unanswerable. But the National Association of Realtors, among others, does try to answer it. Spokesman Walter Molony allowed that while the monthly house price data may soon begin to register year-over-year declines, the declines will be short-lived. The year 2006 will deliver a 5.3% gain in nominal terms, he predicted, in keeping with the post-1968 rule of thumb, namely, a rise equal to the inflation rate plus 1.8 percentage points. *Grant's* asked Molony if the past five years had not brought staggering gains. "It's above normal," he replied. "Absolutely. It's the most rapid rate of price growth relative to inflation in history." Then, isn't some reversion to the mean now in the cards? *Grant's* persisted. Not necessarily, Molony said, referring to post-1968 price history, because, "for much of the '80s and '90s, we had below-trend growth trends with slower-than-historic patterns. [The Shiller data, which stretch all the way back to the 1890s, are in real dollars, while the NAR's are in nominal ones; no surprise, then, that the trend Shiller describes is different than the one the Realtors compute.] There are two things that drive prices. It's inventory and local economic conditions. When you look at both the national data and the metropolitan data, on an annual basis, it's never gone down nationally."*

For "never," we would substitute "infrequently" or "not since the NAR began keeping score." In fact, average national house prices posted modest declines in 1964 and 1959, as well as horrific drops in both the early 1930s and early 1940s. They went flat for 18 months in the early 1980s, prompting the *New York Times* to report, in February 1983: "A House, Once Again, Is Just Shelter: Its Value as an Investment Is Hurt by Demographic and Credit Trends." By "credit trends," the headline alluded to double-digit mortgage rates, never a bullish feature in a real estate market.

Of course, there have been some legendary regional bear markets. Between 1983 and 1988, median house prices in Houston fell by 23%, and between 1990 and 1995, average house prices in Southern California dropped by 21.1% (both according to the 1997 FDIC publication, "An Examination of the Banking Crises of the 1980s and Early 1990s"). Each bear market had a specific local cause, the collapse of oil prices and the post-Cold War shrinkage in defense outlays, respectively. What set of national causes could instigate a coast-to-coast bear house market today?

We submit three: wild and wooly mortgage finance; the propensity of market-determined prices to revert to the mean; and the tendency of flyaway real estate markets to become the drivers of

---

* House prices declined in 43 states during the first quarter of 2008, according to the Office of Housing Enterprise Oversight. Nationwide, house prices were down by 3.1% in 2007. The impossible happened.

economic expansion rather than the mere beneficiaries of growth derived from other sources.

Leverage and interest rates first. The long-running decline in homeowner equity only begins to hint at the growth in the popularity of gimmick-laden mortgages, without which millions of Americans would not have been able to scratch up the means to buy a house. According to UBS, interest-only mortgages, option-ARMs and other so-called affordability loans accounted for 25% of all borrowing by dollar volume in 2004 and 2005. Virtually all of these option mortgages are adjustable-rate, from which it follows that millions of American borrowers, temporary beneficiaries of the Fed's deflation-deflection campaign of 2002–2004, are in for a jolting reset. The Mortgage Bankers Association estimates that, for the holders of $1 trillion of ARMs, the jolt will come next year.

The 2005 Cocktail Party

To support the claim that house prices have radically diverged from trend and are probably headed back to trend, we offer two items of ocular evidence. The first is Shiller's price index, 1890–2004, which appears in his book, *Irrational Exuberance*. The professor himself, noting that his index is, in fact, a number of indices stitched together, cautions against an over-literal reading of the incorporated data, especially the early ones, which, he advises, may betray sampling error. Still, he concludes, the run-up between 1997 and 2004 was "remarkable." No less so is the spike in the dollar value of single-family home sales, a calculation for which we once more thank reader R. King Burch (see *Grant's*, June 3, 2005). Note that, at last report, the value of these residential transactions amounted to 16.4% of GDP, almost double the median reading from 1968 through 2005.

"We know that the behavior of the residential real estate sector tends to lead the behavior of the overall economy," writes Paul Kasriel, the Northern Trust Co. economist. "That's why the folks at the Conference Board stuck housing building permits in the index of Leading Economic Indicators rather than the coincident or lagging indices. Might it be in this cycle that the behavior of the residential real estate sector is even more important than other cycles?" Kasriel answers, "Yes," and so do we. A fast-rising house market is a powerful elixir. What doesn't an optimistic new homeowner want to buy? The Commerce Department's Bureau of Economic Analysis has totted up the contribution of residential fixed investment to GDP going all the way back to 1929. As might be expected, the latest reading, 6.2%, is one of the highest. It is, in fact, the record holder except for the 7% registered in 1950, a year of frantic buying by consumers trying to beat the expected imposition of rationing at the start of the Korean War. Residential fixed investment contributed only 5.2% to GDP in 1964, the previous year in which average national house prices sagged.

A search of the *New York Times* archives turns up no national outcry against that subtraction from household net worth. The absence of publicly expressed anguish might be explained by the modest size of the pullback, just 0.6%. However, a cause to which this complacency could not be plausibly ascribed was the prevailing practices of real estate lending. In October 1964, the Mortgage Bankers Association of America convened in New York to listen to Ehney A. Camp Jr., executive vice president of Liberty National Life Insurance Co., bemoan the ultra-liberal underwriting standards of the Federal Housing Administration, then a principal source of subsidized government mortgage credit. Delinquencies and foreclosures were a growing national problem. But then, demanded Camp, "What can we expect of a borrower who is transferred from his locality or meets with financial reverses when he has an equity of only 3%?" So the FHA was making 97% loan-to-value mortgages. And Camp recalled the day, not so very long before, when "the largest conventional loan was for 66⅔% with a term of 20 years," and only better credit risks, borrowing against selected properties, need have applied. "But," the *Times* reported, "as the F.H.A. gradually expanded its terms, Mr. Camp said, so have the conventional lenders, and 'on occasion it appears to be a race to see which can outdo the other.'"

Possibly, Camp's memory played tricks on him. Maybe a certain segment of the population has always been able to find accommodation on LTV terms approaching 100%. Historical data on mortgage finance are, to say the least, incomplete. But such numbers as do exist clearly point to the present day as being the most openhanded in the long history of lending and borrowing. At no time prior to the present was home-equity extraction so temptingly easy as it is now. Since 2002, according to Goldman Sachs, American homeowners have withdrawn funds enough to add 2.5% of growth a year to real GDP (assuming, as Goldman does, that two-thirds of this money has wound up in the nation's cash registers). And at no time prior to the present was the machinery of the global capital markets so accommodating to American mortgage borrowers. An incomplete inventory of federal agency securities held by foreign central banks foots to $532 billion. The great bulk of these notes and bonds are mortgage-backed or mortgage–related. And, of course, a tally of foreign official holdings of MBS does not capture the billions more held by nonofficial, non-U.S. financial institutions. However, an American would be tempting the fates to assume that the appetite of foreign investors for dollar-denominated MBS is insatiable. Let the dollar exchange rate fall out of bed, and the cost of buying the already unaffordable average American house could jump even further out of range.

What sustains and supports the value of residential real estate is, among other things, unblinking faith. "House prices don't fall" is not so much an economic assertion as a theological one. Our grandparents, or great-grandparents, would be astonished to hear it. Their own experience taught them that house prices, on average, don't rise. It will surprise nobody to learn that prices plunged in the Great Depression—down by 4.3% in 1930, 8.2% in 1931, 10.5% in 1932 and 3.8% in 1933, according to Shiller's data. But did you know that the bear market was already under way in 1926 (down 4%) or that it persisted through the late 1930s and ended in what seems a kind of selling climax only in 1941?

Of course, that distant time—with its primitive mortgage industry, its diminutive federal mortgage subsidy effort and its highly cyclical economy—bears only the faintest resemblance to our own. But it shares with the present day one characteristic, at least, besides the suggestible human mind, and that is a new and disruptive technology. In the 1920s and 1930s, this technology was the automobile, and it seemed to spell the end of the life of cities. Today, there are many such technologies, not the least of which is the financial engineering by which subprime mortgages and second-lien mortgages are refashioned into collateralized debt obligations and distributed the world over.

"For the past 11 years," John C. Kiley, a professional real estate man, wrote in the June 1941 edition of *The Bulletin of the Business Historical Society*, "we have witnessed real estate values receding in Boston as well as in all the other older cities. This span of time, although short in the history of a city, represents a fairly large portion of the life of a real estate owner. The buying and selling of real estate since 1936 has been quite as extensive as in the normal years previous to the first World War. Real estate prices, however, in some of the older business and residential sections of the city of Boston have returned to levels below those of the pre-Civil War years."

For Kiley, long gone were the days when "the chief argument for buying a residential lot was the fact that it could be sold at a fancy profit before the next tax and interest payments became due" (as another real estate writer, Stanley L. McMichael, characterized the carefree portion of the 1920s). Up until 1920, Kiley related, it seemed that the sky was the limit for property in a growing American city. But then came the automobile, the suburbs, the 1929 Crash, the ensuing Depression and, in the train of the Depression, a falloff in immigration and a rising and ruinous burden of local real estate taxation. There had been 11 years of "receding real estate values," Kiley related in the year when Ted Williams batted .406, "and yet there is no sign of an upward curve. Even a stabilized base has not been established." Stock and bond prices had snapped back from their Depression lows. Real estate prices had only kept falling.

Kiley cited some very particular details from Boston, including the example of 45 Beacon St., an immense old pile opposite Boston Common that was built about 1808 for the Federalist politician and moneymaker, Harrison Gray Otis. In 1940, the house had been sold for $3.25 a square foot, or $55,231, following a "thorough" modernization. Not only was this price steeply discounted from the previous sale in 1929 for $403,608; it was also substantially lower than transactions recorded in 1859, for $135,952, and in 1853, for $91,768. (All such prices assume a constant square footage, the dimensions being the ones currently on the Boston tax rolls.)

The property, which today houses the American Meteorological Society, is appraised at $6.2 million, a sum undreamt of in 1940, let alone 1853. More to the point, it is a sum possibly unimagined even in 2000, when the city of Boston valued the house at $2.9 million, or less than half its present appraisal. If 45 Beacon St. could suffer an 86% markdown between 1929 and 1940, only to enjoy a 114% markup between 2000 and 2006, we judge that many things are possible in residential real estate. Not least among them is one today regarded as impossible, namely, the long-provoked national bear market already under way.

Chapter Six
Mortgage Science Projects

Find That Risk

May 20, 2005

THE POINT IS carried—again: There's risk in the U.S. residential mortgage market. Is it properly priced? Who owns it? Answers—or, at least, suppositions and inferences—to follow. Our most important findings we offer in preview: No. 1, while corporate credit spreads have widened this spring, mortgage spreads have actually tightened—in fact, have been tightening (or holding steady) for years. No. 2, the riskiest pieces of the riskiest mortgages are held not in the United States, but in Asia and Europe.

A very worrisome situation, indeed. But you may wonder, as one subscriber does, how to pace yourself. Should you worry this year, next or the year after? "I agree the increasing amount of innovative mortgages is scary," reader Dave Folz, of Dallas, e-mails. "However," he asks, "is not the real question, 'When do these adjustable rate mortgages roll over and readjust to what must be significantly higher rates?' If the answer is, 'On average, five years,' I am much less concerned than if it is two years." Answer: Adjustable-rate mortgages representing 11% to 13% of all single-family mortgages outstanding will reset within the next three years. Only about 5% of all single-family mortgages will reset within the next 12 months. For context, at par value, there are $7 trillion of single-family mortgages outstanding, of which approximately $1.7 trillion, or 24%, are ARMs.

It helps to remember that ARMs were not invented yesterday, and that—in the nature of things—mortgages are always resetting. In 1994, the year the funds rate was hoisted to 6% from 3%, about 12% of all U.S. mortgages were adjustable in one year or less. Yet, no interest-rate-reset bomb was detonated, and no recession ensued. Then, too, it's a fact that a mortgage usually resets when an American homeowner sells one dwelling to buy another. In 2003, 14% of the population pulled up stakes, according to the Census Bureau.

So worry is wasted? No, we believe, it is timely. What, then, to worry about? The mispricing of credit risk in a huge market, a market that, to the nonspecialist, is literally invisible. We exempt from concern the huge swath of MBS guaranteed by Fannie, Freddie or Ginnie (yes, we know, the first two agencies have no explicit federal support, but we can't worry about everything). Rather, we focus on the so-called private label, or niche, mortgages produced by the sweat of private enterprise. Some niche. In the fourth quarter, interest-only mortgages, negative-amortization mortgages and similar variable-rate paper totaled some $800 billion, Lehman Brothers estimates. For perspective, the junk-bond market foots to $726 billion, according to Moody's.

The very acme of a selective and focused worrier is, in our opinion, Scott Simon, head of the Pimco mortgage and asset-backed group. "It's not that we think the sky is falling," he tells *Grant's*, "but if there's a chance that it is, you're supposed to get paid for it. . . . Our central forecast isn't that triple-A subprime floaters are going to explode and take losses; but, at the spreads they trade at, you better be darn sure your risk is close to zero. Our only gripe is that you

"I understand we own $1 billion of CDOs.
Question: What's a CDO?"

aren't getting paid enough for it. We don't want to get paid nothing for the possibility. It doesn't matter what your central forecast is. If you're selling lottery tickets, somebody might hit one."

In the same vein, Simon insists there is nothing intrinsically wrong with the newfangled, interest-only ARMs, "no matter how strange they look." When they were truly a niche product, offered mainly to rich people with cash-flow or tax issues, who could object? "But," Simon adds, "when people use them to buy houses that they should not be able to afford legitimately, and drive up prices in doing so—and then the next person has to take out an even crazier loan—then it's a problem."

We came across Simon's name and thought processes in an article in the May 11 *American Banker* (our daily must-read on the coming mortgage crack-up). "Where's Mortgage Risk? New Answers Emerging," said the headline over what proved an excellent survey of the subject to which we now turn. In this piece, Simon was

quoted as saying that the recent favorable default experience in residential mortgages is a consequence of the refi wave and the real-
estate bull market. Homeowners haven't defaulted because their
lenders won't let them. And he complained that the rating agencies
haven't adjusted their credit models to discount this glow of fake
financial health. The upshot is that triple-A-rated mortgages are
sometimes not as sound as advertised. But, he added, the cost of
incremental credit insurance is a pittance. A prudent investor can,
in effect, build himself a quadruple-A asset.

To *Grant's*, he elaborates: "The bulk of these crazy loans are in
the subprime market, that is, between 550 and 640 FICO borrowers [the median FICO score is 723]. They all typically get issued
in asset-backed structures. This market they call 'home equities' or
'subprime floaters'—that's where these bonds mostly go."

Some of the mortgages are originated by banks, and some of the
banks hold on to them. Others are run through the investment-
banking Veg-o-matic to produce "a senior-subordinated structure
where you go from unrated pieces through low-rated pieces, up
through triple-B, single-A, double-A, triple-A," Simon goes on.
"The bulk of the subordinated pieces end up in CDOs [collater-
alized debt obligations] and asset-backed CDOs." And then, he
said, they are exported. "Probably 95% of the loss pieces are going
to Asia and Europe—financial institutions, insurance companies,
relatively unsophisticated banks."

We checked with other sources. A man who works for a mortgage hedge fund speculates that foreign central banks are among the
buyers of these mortgage slices (now that Fannie is actually shrinking its balance sheet, the supply of triple-A-rated federal agency
assets, long a favorite of foreign central banks, is much reduced).
And this same source adds that subprime mortgage derivatives
are an asset calculated to appeal to the hedge funds that "mark to
model." In the absence of deep and liquid public markets, such a
fund can value its mortgage derivatives according to what a Ph.D.
infers they ought to be worth.

You won't find mortgage CDOs quoted on *Bloomberg*, much less on Trace or the New York Stock Exchange. It helps to have a cousin in the business, or know David Liu, a UBS mortgage analyst, or Eric Szabo, of Annaly Mortgage Management. What the outsider can know, courtesy of his friends or relatives, is that the collateral supporting mortgage derivatives is not what it was—interest-only loans loom larger than they did, and loan-to-value ratios are higher. How much higher is not easy to determine, however, because of the growing prevalence of undisclosed junior liens ("silent seconds").

Do the yields fairly compensate an investor for the risks? "Yes," the market insists. ARMs float, of course; that's the point. Their yield is quoted at a spread off investment-grade money-market interest rates, and bond rates—"swaps," as they say, plus 30 or 40 basis points, for the high-rated slices. So if rates go up? Mr. Market insists no harm would come. The ARMs would eventually reset. But they would not reset all at once.

The gentleman might be right, but we are with Simon. Investors in mortgage CDOs go uncompensated for the risk of a bear market in houses, or of a breakdown in mortgage credit. How great is the risk? Clear and present, we judge. Bulls counter that the much greater prevalence of interest-only mortgages in the collateral pools (as well as the rising ratios of loan-to-value) is amply reflected in the subordination structure of the mortgage pools. They had better be right. The fact is that nobody knows what the default and prepayment characteristics of the subprime, private-label mortgages may prove to be. Since the riskiest kinds have hit the market, bond yields have done nothing but fall, house prices have done nothing but rise and loan officers have said nothing but "Yes!" The CDO machine resembles some giant monetary snowblower, scattering dollar bills into the open hands of underwriters, investment banks, investment managers and rating agencies.

As of last fall, Simon reports, Pimco decided to stop participating: "We said at that point, if things look like they do right now, we're not going to manage any new asset-backed CDOs. It's one of the most profitable things we can do as a money manager. But in the asset-backed area, you've got, simultaneously, underwriting standards going down significantly, credit quality will be going down, and spreads have narrowed. Finance 101 doesn't say that is supposed to happen."

Simon quotes the line that Fed tightenings work by bankrupting the marginal borrower. And the marginal borrower in today's mortgage market, he goes on, "is taking relatively short resets, below-market loans on expensive houses." Simon holds up as typical a new mortgage from New Century Financial: interest-only available to a borrower with a relatively weak credit profile and no income verification required. According to Simon, you can borrow up to 95% of the value of your house, up to $1 million, and you can pledge half of your income for debt service. (A call to New Century to check the terms of the mortgage went unreturned.) Simon scratches his head: What happens if, come the time the interest rate on the loan resets higher by 40% or 50%, the borrower can't find a way to refinance? Might not the householder slip the keys into an envelope and mail them to the lender (whoever and wherever he is)?

"The subprime market didn't exist 10 years ago," Simon winds up. "The main reason that home ownership has gone from 64% of the population to 69% in the past seven or eight years, which is a massive increase, is because the bulk of the people that are the subprime market literally could not get home loans ever before. Their mortgage? They called it rent. They could not get a home mortgage. Once somebody said, 'I'll take the credit risk,' you can lend money to them. But currently, that's not us. Mostly, the real end users are the people on the back side of these CDOs who are funding this market."*And, we would add, not getting paid very well for their trouble.

---

* Some $256 billion of CDOs backed by residential mortgages were issued in 2006, but Mr. Market presently reconsidered. In the first three months of 2008, just $1.5 billion's worth came into the world.

Inside ACE Securities' HEL Trust, Series 2005–HE5

September 8, 2006

The nation is running out of magazine covers on which to announce the coming collapse of house prices. From which fact it could be inferred that Mr. Market is running out of sellers of the statistically cheap housing stocks. Is there even one surviving bull on Toll Brothers or Countrywide Financial or New Century Financial Corp. who doesn't know that the house-price bubble has burst?

Maybe not. But the news has strangely failed to register in the mortgage-backed securities market. For the buyers of CDOs, HEL trusts, RMBS and every other alphabetic variation on the words "mortgage debt," the year might as well be 2004, not 2006. As far as the bond bulls seem to know, house prices are still climbing, homeowners are still painlessly extracting cash from their bricks and granite countertops, and foreclosures are just a tiny cloud in an otherwise clear blue sky. The worse the news from the home front, the closer mortgage yields seem to hug the Treasury yield curve—and the more determined the bidding by Wall Street's asset-backed securities mills for First Franklin, Saxon Capital and the other mortgage originators lately put on the auction block. (The world returned to its desk after the Labor Day weekend to discover that Merrill Lynch had agreed to buy National City Corp.'s home-mortgage subsidiary for $1.3 billion.)

This paradox is the subject at hand. Our approach is at once bottom-up and top-down: a clinical examination of the mortgage security named in the headline as well as a review of the micro and macro forces that have contributed to its stunning overvaluation. Now the cat's out of the bag. "Overvalued," we, in fact, judge trillions of dollars of asset-backed securities and collateralized debt obligations to be, and we are bearish on them. Housing-related stocks may or may not be prospectively cheap; they at least look historically cheap. But housing-related debt is cheap by no standard of value. For institutional investors equipped to deal in credit default swaps, there's an opportunity to lay down a low-cost bearish bet.

The sheer volume of issuance of non-Fannie and non-Freddie residential mortgage-backed securities may surprise you. In the first six months of this year, $303 billion was minted vs. $490 billion in all of 2005. As recently as 2000, such issuance totaled a mere $58.5 billion. If you've guessed that there's money to be made in the creation and distribution of these mortgage conflations, you're well on your way to penetrating the mystery of why the Bloomberg/ Bear Stearns Home Equity HELOC Index is trading at the tightest spread to the Treasury curve in the past 10 years.

A Moody's managing director, John Kriz, helped to sort things out in a recent article in the *American Banker*. Why, he was asked, is the value of M&A activity in mortgage-origination businesses on its way to hitting a decade high? Why are Wall Street's best and brightest so keen to own the companies that lend against the no-longer gold-plated collateral of residential real estate?

"If you have a significant distribution platform," replied Kriz, "there are many things you can do to move those assets—through securitizations and outright resale, among other things. What you need is product to feed the machine." This machine is one of Wall Street's most treasured. It processes mortgages into asset-backed securities and ABS tranches into collateralized debt obligations and CDO tranches into CDOs squared (a CDO squared is, of course, a CDO of a CDO). It is a wondrous kind of machine that spits out fees for its owners at every step of the manufacturing process.

Last month, Reuters took note of the burgeoning sale of home equity loans packaged as asset-backed securities. The story quoted a practitioner who ascribed the surge to a parallel boom in the issuance of a kind of mortgage insurance. The insurance in question is the credit default swap, a common enough item in the corporate and sovereign debt markets but a late arrival in the mortgage market. Nowadays, a qualified investor can buy a CDS on a particular mortgage-backed bond and even a specific particular tranche of that security. In the language of Wall Street, the CDS buyer is a "buyer of protection." The cost he pays is an interest rate, and the party to which he pays it is the seller of protection. "With the advent of the synthetic market," observed the Reuters expert, "there are tremendous amounts of home equity risks being traded, much of which is driven by the CDO desire to sell protection in their structures."

This last comment explains more than it might seem. To see it for the revelation that it is, a layman may need to pause to catch his breath and review some basic nomenclature. Recall, to start with, that a CDO is a pile of debts refashioned into a security. It is structured in slices, or tranches, from supposedly bulletproof (triple-A) to admittedly perilous (speculative-grade or not-rated). It is highly leveraged, with a single dollar of equity supporting as much as $100 in debt.

There are at least two kinds of CDOs. The first is the cash variety, which is stocked with bonds or tranches of asset-backed securities. The second is the synthetic kind, which is created by selling protection on the bonds or ABS. How can a CDO be built from credit options? Consider that the seller of protection has the same credit exposure as does the buyer of bonds—in case of a credit event, he is on the hook. The rage to create synthetic CDOs is, on balance, a good thing for the prudent readers of *Grant's*. The booming supply of CDS lowers the cost of protection they buy, or can (and should) buy. Synthetic CDOs are believed to be widely marketed to the trusting financial institutions of Europe and Asia.

In this essay about derivatives, our view is itself partially a derivative. The entity from which it is derived is Pennant Capital Management, a New Jersey long-short equity hedge fund. Alan Fournier, a paid-up subscriber to *Grant's*, is the managing member. Fournier says that Pennant is expressing a bearish view on housing in the CDS market by buying protection on the weaker tranches of at-risk mortgage structures. At the cost of $14.25 million a year, the fund has exposure to $750 million face amount of mortgage debt.

"I come to this as a student of subprime lending and the housing sector," Fournier tells colleague Dan Gertner. "We were actually long the subprime lending stocks until four or five months ago. We have been short the housing stocks since last summer. The dynamics of those two industries are sort of colliding here in what I think will be a very significant home-price decline. That is the backdrop."

As a buyer of protection, Fournier writes checks to the sellers of protection. The prices he's paying are remarkably low, both he and we judge. They range from 190 basis points a year for the so-called better loans to 220 basis points a year for the riskier ones. He keeps writing checks to the sellers unless and until there is a "credit event," an interruption in the payment of principal and interest by the home buyers to the lenders. If and when trouble strikes, it's the sellers of protection who start writing checks to the buyers.

The odds of a credit event heavily depend on the structure of the mortgage security, or tranches of mortgage security, on which one is buying protection. As a rule in an asset-backed deal, principal and interest come in at the top of the credit ladder and cascade down, while losses come in at the bottom of the credit ladder and infiltrate up. At the penthouse are triple-A assets; at the ground floor, triple-B-minus-rated ones; in the basement are the unrated assets, including what is called an "overcollateralization" tranche. "What has happened over the last four or five years," Fournier observes, "is that home prices have been rising so rapidly that not only did you have the shock absorber of overcollateralization in the loan, but you also have the 10% accretion in values of homes per year that created additional equity to create very solid credit performance for these securities historically."

Yet, even in the best of times, subprime mortgages suffered losses of 4% to 5% a year. In what are no longer the best of times, the damage is bound to be greater. Overcollateralization today runs to about 5% per CDO, Fournier says. Is it so hard to imagine losses equal to, or in excess of, 5% in a national housing bear market? Losses over and above the overcollateralization shock absorber would eat first into the lowest-rated investment-grade tranche, i.e., the triple-B-minus layer, which typically accounts for 2% or 3% of assets. They would next undercut the triple-B-rated tranche, which accounts for another 2% or 3% of assets. If the losses kept coming, the higher-rated tranches would follow the lower-rated ones to the mark-to-market chopping block.

But it would require no national catastrophe to deliver outsize returns to the discriminating CDS buyer. The sharp corrections already under way in the boomier real estate markets might suffice to wreak havoc in a geographically concentrated CDO. Fournier says he invests security by security. He likes "high Florida exposure, high California exposure, high second-lien exposure. You look for equity take-out loans, because those appraisals tend to be over-stated, a high percentage of stated-income loans (a.k.a. liars' loans), and you build yourself a portfolio of credits from weak underwriters that are ultimately likely to be impaired.

"Most people start with the assumption that house prices don't go down," Fournier goes on. "I think they will. I think if they only went down 2% or 3%, it would be remarkable. This paper has been experiencing 4% to 5% cumulative losses during a home price environment where we've seen 10% annual increases. In theory, if we just went flat, you would see 14% to 15% losses in these same portfolios, all else being equal. All else isn't equal, obviously. We have oil prices up, we have $400 billion of ARMs adjusting up this year, another $1 trillion reset next year, and the whole idea that people will simply refi their way out of trouble is no longer going to be an option. The guys that write this paper—the subprime lenders—view these guys that are having these resets as future business, 'because we will just write them a new loan.' It is not going to work if home prices are not going up, and the fed funds rate is not back to 1%."

Prompted by Fournier, Gertner delved into one of the myriad of mortgage-backed structures on which a professional investor can buy or sell protection (administrative complexities bar the amateur, even a rich and sophisticated one, from doing the same for his or her own account). The ACE Securities Corp. Home Equity Loan Trust, Series 2005-HE5, is the specimen under examination. The trust, which came into the world in August 2005, is no outlier but a fairly standard item of the hundreds of billions of dollars' worth in the market today. It was created from a pool of first and second liens of varying credit characteristics (4,666 of the loans conformed to Freddie Mac loan limits, which earned them the imprimatur, "Group I"; the balance of the loans may or may not so conform and are designated "Group II"). At inception, the trust had a par value of a little more than $1.4 billion; 17.8% of the loans were fixed-rate, the balance adjustable.

Simplicity is not the trust's outstanding design feature. It holds 20 tranches, with the bulk of the dollar value in triple-A loans but—as the diagram points up—tens of millions of dollars in loans in the lower realms of investment-grade and an equity pool in the sum of $11.5 million. These tranches are the cannon fodder of a hypothetical real-estate bear market. Realized losses on the mortgages held in the portfolio would be absorbed, first, by that net monthly excess cash-flow account; second, by the CE certificates (for "credit enhancement"); third, by the class B-3 certificates, and so forth, until housing Armageddon, when not even the A-1 tranche would be left undamaged.

Studying the architecture of this edifice of home equity loans, Gertner notes a striking lack of diversification. At the time of creation, no less than 34.5% of the principal balance of the mortgages was exposed to California, 11% to Florida and 10.4% to New York. Interest-rate reset dates were bunched in May-June 2007, when more than 90% of the ARMs in the portfolio are expected to be adjusted. Forty-odd percent could be adjusted by two percentage points, while 59% could be adjusted by as many as three percentage points. Subsequently, the loans can be adjusted between one and two percentage points every six months.

"Of course," notes Gertner, "the rate could be adjusted down as well as up, but looking at the reference rate—for the most part, six-month Libor—an upward reset seems much more likely. First payments for the loans in the trusts occurred between September 2004 and August 2005, between which dates six-month Libor climbed to 4.1% from 2.2%. Today, with Libor at 5.4%, a three-percentage-point reset is possible, and a reset of more than one percentage point is probable. Naturally, interest rates could fall by the middle of next year. But a weak economy—if that were the reason for the drop—would add another hurdle to the already obstacle-littered real-estate playing field."

At the time of closing, 29% of the loans were of the interest-only kind (70% had the traditional principal amortization feature and 1% were balloon loans). As to the purpose of the loans, almost half were earmarked for cash-out refinancing. As to documentation, 58% had the works, with most of the balance showing only "stated documentation" (cross your heart, Mr. or Ms. Mortgage Applicant, please, not your fingers).

To date, the trust has given a good account of itself, with not one credit event blackening the record of the first year. In the 13 months since launch, the natural churn of the U.S. housing market has reduced the outstanding principal balance of the trust by $414 million, to $1.023 billion, and the number of loans by 1,935, to 5,277. Because the junior tranches are supporting a lower dollar value of senior debt, effective credit support for the high-rated debt has ratcheted up. All of which is to the good.

But termites are busily gnawing at the mortgage foundations. At last report, which was August's, 8.8% of the principal was delinquent and 4.2% was in foreclosure—$90 million and $43 million, respectively. For perspective, just $66 million of principal buffer stands between the two lowest-rated mezzanine tranches, M-9 and M-10 on the diagram, and some future loss.*

Yet, according to Fournier, credit protection on those very two tranches is available for only 220 basis points a year. Is it so hard

---

* By May 2008, the outstanding balance had been reduced to $455.7 million. Of the remaining loans, 16.1% were delinquent, 24.7% were in foreclosure, and 17.5% were owned by the lender—$74 million, $112 million and $80 million, respectively.

to envision the circumstances in which delinquencies and foreclosures on the California and Florida segments of the trust's portfolio would move drastically higher? We can hardly imagine circumstances in which they wouldn't.

"What I have done," Fournier tells Gertner, "is put together a
portfolio of this stuff. I have $750 million of this stuff shorted.
My cost is 1.9% [the previously cited $14.25 million a year]. My
return could be $750 million." As risks and rewards go, we judge,
not bad.

Age of Aquarius

September 22, 2006

A CA Aquarius 2006-1 is the subject under discussion. Are you
still with us? Good! A short catechism will serve to introduce
the fine points.

To start with, what is it? ACA Aquarius 2006-1 is a $2 billion,
mezzanine-structured, hybrid collateralized debt obligation, or
CDO. What is a CDO? A CDO is a kind of bond, the collateral
of which is debt. In the case at hand, the underlying, or reference,
collateral is residential mortgage debt. What does it mean to call
this contraption a "hybrid?" It means that Aquarius holds not only
mortgages, and structures packed with mortgages, but also options
on mortgages.

Here is another question: Why should anyone care about something so very much unlike a good, cheap value stock—anyone,
that is, not directly involved as a basis-point-grubbing bond investor, collateral manager, mortgage scientist, rating-agency quant or
member of the immediate families of such as the foregoing? One
should care because (a) complexity in financial instruments sometimes obscures risk for which an investor may or may not be ade-
quately compensated; (b) the issuance of complex mortgage structures is booming when house prices are not; and (c) the visible

and looming difficulties in residential real estate have not yet depressed the prices of such instruments as these mezzanine-structured hybrid CDOs. Investors in the senior tranches of ACA Aquarius 2006-1 earn a few dozen basis points over Libor. Holders of the junior tranches earn 300 basis points, more or less, over Libor. Equity holders have come to expect 15% to 20% (of which more below). Expressing a personal preference, we would feel undercompensated holding any portion of the ACA Aquarius 2006-1 capital structure, in view of the risks and rewards, as we understand them.

Others have a different understanding. The progenitor and collateral manager of this transaction, ACA Management LLC, manages 19 CDOs with a cumulative par value of $12.75 billion. Not once, says ACA, has any rated note in any ACA-managed CDO been downgraded or placed on negative credit watch.* Standing by its merchandise, ACA has invested $200 million in the equity portions of the CDOs it manages. And some smart money has invested in ACA, including Bear Stearns Merchant Banking, Stephens Group and Third Avenue Value Fund.

The deal at hand caught our eye not because its genus is so rare—this year, through September 15, $126 billion of asset-backed securities in CDOs have come to market, vs. $118 billion in all of 2005, according to Thomson Financial. Rather, what piqued our interest was the species. The new Aquarius offering is a hybrid CDO. Its assets consist chiefly of credit default swaps. Actual slices of cash mortgages furnish only 10% of the portfolio.

It takes a little doing to visualize a derivative of a derivative, but that's what this hybrid CDO is. The CDO itself is a derivative—and so are its assets. Credit default swaps are credit derivatives. They resemble insurance policies. The underwriter of CDS sells protection against a default or other defined credit event with reference

---

* Late in the spring of 2008, an Aquarius-managed CDO did default. As for ACA Aquarius 2006-1, its formerly triple-A rated tranches have been downgraded to the lowest depths of junk.

*"Thought I owned the good stuff—triple-A. Incorrect.
It seems I owned the other stuff—'triple-A.' "*

to a stipulated security, index or portfolio of securities. The buyer of protection writes checks to the seller—unless, and until, such credit event occurs, at which time the seller of protection writes checks to the buyer. In the case at hand, the underwriter is ACA Aquarius 2006-1, and the referenced credit items are clumps, or tranches, of residential mortgages. Thus, for as long as the mortgages pay on time, Aquarius receives money from the buyers of protection, and these funds it distributes to its investors. Money cascades down the totem pole of credit, with the highest-rated securities (the Class A1S notes, in this case) receiving first priority—after payment of fees and expenses to the managers and trustee, of course. If enough homeowners stop paying on time, Aquarius must make whole the buyers of protection, at which point the Aquarius investors (starting with the lowest-rated tranches) stand in line for a haircut.

There are plenty of loans in the Aquarius constellation—loans held outright or only referenced. The structure is, as noted, only

90% synthetic; 10% of its assets are invested in actual mortgages, or, more exactly, in actual tranches of mortgage-backed securities. Do you wonder if, by investing 90% in CDS and only 10% in cash CDOs, you bear any additional credit risk—not only the risk of the mortgages going bad but also the risk of a counterparty keeling over? Bulls insist not.

Anyway, the Aquarius structure has 51 issues behind the cash CDO component of the structure and another 129 issues that serve as reference entities for $1.4 billion in CDS contracts, for a grand total of 180. Colleague Dan Gertner sampled 40 of them. California dominated, he relates; one issue was 50% exposed to the Golden State. The 40 had an average of 6,500 loans at origination, he says. Projecting that number to all 180 issues suggests that Aquarius has exposure to about 1.2 million loans.

Performing due diligence on 1.2 million loans sounds like just the thing that nobody would do, not even in this age of "liars' loans," and interest-only and negative-amortization loans. Bulls would reply that structures like Aquarius' are stress-tested for changes in mortgage prepayment speed as well as for the timing and incidence of defaults. "We have a default probability generator model that runs a Monte Carlo multi-step simulation default probability model. . . ," a man from Fitch advises Gertner. What we wonder is whether the stress tests take full account of the unprecedentedly open-handed lending practices of recent years. Possibly not.

Demand for the junior-most tranches of these mortgage structures is reported to be red hot. "Magnetar Financial, an Evanston, Ill.-based multi-strategy hedge fund, is dominating the market for asset-backed securities collateralized debt obligations by buying bespoke deals in massive sizes," discloses the August 11 *Derivatives Week*. "The fund has enlisted a clutch of Wall Street firms to structure full-capital structure deals in which it buys the equity slice. . . . The deals are being pushed through in such size that spreads are tightening and structurers gripe it is becoming difficult to ramp. It is also becoming difficult to place the rest of the capital structure."

Reports have it that Magnestar hedges its equity exposure by buying protection on the BBB-rated tranches in the deals in which it invests. (The fund did not respond to Gertner's requests for comment.) If so, its management may reason that the world is not coming to an end and the equity tranches will likely pay 20%, but that, if worse came to worse, the BBB tranches, too, would get wiped out. Even absent such a calamity, the cost of the hedge is hardly onerous compared to the hoped-for equity return; the BBB slice yields Libor plus 300 points or so.

Of course, timing is critical. Bulls observe that the equity gets paid in relatively short order, after the so-called step-down, or trigger date, which typically falls three years after the issue date. "Everyone is playing the same game," a non-bullish practitioner tells Gertner, "which is: 'As long as the problems don't occur too soon, we are all okay.' This is a very important thing to understand."

We do understand that, at least.

Inside the Mortgage Machine

October 6, 2006

Through mysterious alchemical processes, Wall Street transforms BBB-minus-rated mortgages into AAA-rated tranches of mortgage securities. So often and so profitably is this miracle performed that most investors have suspended their disbelief about it. One who hasn't is Paul Singer, general partner of Elliott Associates, and he shared his doubts at the conference.

Singer shared more than his doubts. He also laid out the arguments for avoiding lower-rated mortgages—or better still, for those with the institutional capability to put on the trade, selling them short via the purchase of credit default swaps. He set the scene with a few facts. Thus, as recently as 2000, just 25% of subprime mortgage issuance was characterized by limited documentation—information submitted, in effect, on the honor system. Only 1% of the market consisted of piggyback loans junior to the first mortgage, and exactly no percent was represented by the interest-only payment option. At last report, 44% was characterized by limited documentation, 31% by piggyback loans and 22% by the interest-only alternative.

The outpouring of so-called affordability products has effectively turned homeowners into renters, Singer pointed out. What they substantively own is not the house in which they live, but rather an option to buy it. Yet, he added, jarring even the worldly *Grant's* crowd, only the first lien is typically disclosed to the mortgage-securities investor. Even if the combination of an 80% first mortgage and a 20% junior lien pushed the home buyer's effective loan-to-value ratio to 100%, the buyer of a typical CDO wouldn't know it. He would see only the 80% senior claim.

How are these mortgage contraptions created? The mortgage collateral is assembled and aggregated, Singer said, and then it is rated. On form, the agencies confer a double-A or triple-A rating on as much as 87% of the CDO, though each of the component mortgage pieces is rated no higher than triple-B.

Here is a miracle of faith. Rating agencies and investors share a belief in the risk-attenuating powers of diversification. They assume, noted Singer, "some diversity of underlying mortgage collateral characteristics, therefore low correlation in mortgage credit performance." They assume too much, our speaker contended. For example, California looms large in most of these structures—it's next to impossible to have less than 30% exposure to the nation's No. 1 mortgage market. Then, too, the incidence of piggyback loans and limited-documentation loans is "actually very similar across subprime mortgage pools." Besides, the mortgage engineers implicitly bet that abundant liquidity, indulgent regulation and satisfactory default experience will persist—and that the ability to refinance will continue to be, as it long has been, the market's great safety valve.

So it is that a CDO consisting of BBB-rated and BBB-minus-rated mortgage material can be blessed with ratings roughly as follows: AAA, 75%; AA, 12%; A, 4%; BBB, 4%; equity, 5%. All the while, noted Singer, home sales are plunging, home inventories are climbing and subprime mortgage delinquencies are beginning to accelerate—yet the yields on lower-rated mortgage tranches continue to trade close to the Treasury yield curve.

Which brought Singer to his grand finale. "It is not a precise blueprint," he said, as the accompanying table flashed on the PowerPoint screen, "but it roughly shows what happens given the leverage and structure of the mortgage-backed securities in the CDOs. There are timing and structural issues that delay the transmission of pain from the homeowner to the CDO tranche buyer and other subtleties, because some of the loans are originated at earlier stages in the bull market. However, if the housing boom turns down and if the downturn results in losses in the mortgage pools, the CDO tranche losses in this slide are inevitable."

The table requires a word or two of explanation. The second column, "mortgage pool cumulative loss," describes losses borne in the

Mortgage Schematic*

House -prices, mortgage defaults, and CDO loss transmission mechanism

Home price** appreciation	Mortgage pool cumulative loss	Most senior MBS class written off	Loss to CDO	Most senior CDO class written off
+7% to +10%	2%	None	0%	None
+4% to +7%	4	BB	3	None
0% to +4%	6	BBB–	39	AA
0% to –4%	10	BBB+	84	AAA (partial)
–4% to –7%	12	A	100	AAA
–7% to –10%	16	AA–	100	AAA

* assumes CDO constructed from BBB-rated tranches of subprime mortgage-backed securities; rough approximation of estimated collateral losses and tranche write-downs
** cumulative appreciation over two years
Source: Paul Singer

mortgage pools from which the CDO is fabricated.* The fourth column, "loss to CDO," translates that damage into likely losses in the CDO. The numbers are estimates, Singer emphasized, sensitive to many factors, including the timing of losses on the underlying mortgage loans.

Run your eye across the fourth line, Singer invited the audience: "This scenario is not extreme. A flat to minus 4% house-price performance over two years—this results in a 10% mortgage pool cumulative loss. This creates a wipeout of the CDO AA tranche and a partial loss on the AAA tranche. Eighty-four percent of the principal of the CDO—not just the BBBs—84% of the whole principal is wiped out." All this from a minor perturbation in the real estate market.

Singer closed with three observations:

1. "The primary drivers of housing securities and home prices are the ratings agencies," he said, "whose models and calculations of correlations, diversity and default probabilities are currently based only on bull-market experience. . . ."

2. "These subprime loans, increasingly gamey in their terms and the quality of the borrower, provide returns that do not compensate for the risks."

3. "It is said in poker that the more complicated the game, the greater the advantage of the expert. Well, in mortgage securities, the job of many of the experts is to sell this stuff to people and hope for the best."

In housing finance, the best is far behind us. That the cost of credit default protection on lower-rated mortgage tranches has only begun to reflect this fact constitutes, depending on how one is positioned, either a great peril or a shining opportunity.

---

* In January 2008, Moody's Investor Service projected that cumulative losses for the 2006 first-lien subprime mortgage backed securities would reach as high as 18%.

Up the Capital Structure

December 15, 2006

The not very shocking news that low-rated tranches of poorly underwritten mortgages on depreciating houses are susceptible to loss has nonetheless managed to shock. The cost of insuring the lowliest such slice on the standard subprime reference index has climbed by 25% in seven short days, according to the guardians of the untransparent mortgage derivatives market. *Grant's* has had much to say about mortgage credit this year. Following is a speculation on 2007, if we have our timing right. In preview, we find that, under some not very adverse assumptions, even higher-rated mortgage structures are vulnerable to infestation by credit termites. Insurance on these supposedly safe and sound mortgage derivatives is available for a song.

We write not only for the well-staffed professional investor who could actually buy protection on the penthouse levels of an arcane mortgage index. Our intended audience is, equally, the curious investment amateur who ordinarily has no truck with tranches and derivatives but is always prepared to make an exception for a $1 trillion market. Our hypothetical layman should know that the experts, so-called, are almost as confused as he is. Certainly, they are of many minds. A few—a minority—believe that the troubles now unfolding at the margins of subprime are the leading edge of much deeper problems. We are in that camp. The majority contend that the derangement of the BBB-minus-rated tranches is a fluke. The broad market, they say, even the broad subprime market, is hale and hearty. Bear Stearns, the top mortgage-backed securities underwriter, is an exponent of this idea, as is Triad Guaranty. Both are expanding their businesses as if the bear markets in mortgage debt and residential real estate were already over and done with—if, indeed, they ever really got underway.

The subprime arena is the Wal-Mart Nation of American leveraged finance. Like the Wal-Mart customer, it is a bellwether of financial disturbance. Perhaps, it's no accident that the giant retailer's sales have weakened as the cost of insuring low-rated subprime mortgage tranches against default has risen. But there is something about the sudden blight of delinquencies and foreclosures in the bottom of the 2006 mortgage barrel that doesn't quite add up. Yes, the median house price has fallen by 3.5%. But the jobless rate stands at only 4.5%. Nominal interest rates—even following 17 quarter-point jumps in the fed funds rate—remain low. The Russell 2000 Index the other day hit an all-time high. Blame for the distress at the fringes of subprime, we judge, cannot be laid at the feet of the U.S. economy. It should, rather, attach to the lenders and borrowers who piled debt on debt until the edifice sways even in a dead calm.

A common reaction to our descriptions of the elaborate design, and not especially generous yields, of asset-backed securities (ABS) is amazement: "Who buys this stuff?" *Grant's* readers want to know. Yield pigs the world over, is the answer. "Who creates and promotes it—and what would cause them to stop?" is another oft-heard question. The answer to that is Wall Street. Its mortgage mills create asset-backed securities like the previously mentioned ACE Securities' HEL Trust, Series 2005-HE5. And the same mills issue collateralized debt obligations, a.k.a. CDOs. It's the CDOs that dependably buy the lower-rated ABS tranches.

Constant readers will recall that CDOs are highly leveraged debt-acquisition machines. So it is all important to the subprime market that new mortgage-packed CDOs continue to come tumbling down the Wall Street production lines as, indeed, they have been: According to the latest data, year-to-date CDO issuance totals $223.7 billion, no less than 89% higher than in the like period a year ago.

To sustain this pell-mell growth, the Street needs buyers, specifically buyers of CDO equity. The equity tranche is like the understander in a human pyramid. Without him, there can be no show. Upon a CDO's equity is loaded tranches of lower-rated ABS at a ratio of as much as 20:1.

Mortgage traders speak lovingly of "the CDO bid." It is mother's milk to the ABS market. Without it, fewer asset-backed structures could be built, and those that were would have to meet a much more conservative standard of design. The resulting pangs of credit withdrawal would certainly be felt in the residential real-estate market. So the musing of a knowledgeable salesman to whom colleague Dan Gertner spoke the other day is worth considering. "The CDO managers have certainly stepped back," said our source (so knowledgeable is he that he asks to go nameless). He explained that what is worrying the CDO managers has nothing to do with the macroeconomy. It is all about microeconomics, particularly a sudden paucity of buyers. "Clearly," our source went on, "the end buyer of this rubbish— whether it be the Middle East or, more likely, the Far East—has had second thoughts about home-equity loans and subprime in general. I think that is key. If you follow the money trail, it has implications for other asset markets as well." Perhaps, the flies on the wall at the upcoming talks between Chinese finance officials and Treasury Secretary Paulson will have the consideration to leak the gist of any concerns Chinese analysts harbor about the subprime market.

The $1 trillion size of the market should push it to the top of any international financial agenda. Through September 30, overall U.S. mortgage issuance totaled a little more than $1.5 trillion, according to UBS. Of this grand total, no less than 22.2%, or $342.4 billion, was subprime, i.e., speculative grade (meaning, generally, a FICO score of less than 620, 100 points lower than the national median). Another 17.5%, or $269.5 billion, was Alt-A, the class between speculative and prime. At 39.7% of year-to-date issuance, the sum total of subprime and Alt-A emissions thus begins to approach the 43.9% of the higher-quality mortgages that Fannie Mae and Freddie Mac are allowed to buy.

Credit quality in the U.S. residential mortgage market has been in a long-term downtrend, which is another way of saying that house prices and homeownership rates have been on a long-term uptrend. As recently as 1994, again according to UBS, subprime issuance amounted to just 5.6% of total mortgage issuance, with Alt-A amounting to only 0.2%. Fannie, Freddie, Ginnie et al. had the mortgage-securitization field virtually to themselves—and because they stamped their issuance with a federal guarantee (implied or actual), credit risk, from the investor's standpoint, was virtually nonexistent. "Since 1994," observes Gertner, the *Grant's* special vice president in charge of mortgage complexities, "agency-eligible mortgage issuance has grown by a factor of 2.5, subprime issuance by a factor of more than 19 times and Alt-A by a factor of more than 500 times."

The long vigil of the mortgage bears for signs that they have not been imagining things has ended with a succession of confidence-rattling news items. The first was the shuttering of Texas-based Sebring Capital Partners, a subprime and Alt-A originator, on December 1. Sebring, with 325 employees and 10 years of operating experience, was forced to turn off the lights after rising defaults left it without a banker. Ownit Mortgage Solutions, a California subprime lender founded in 2003, followed Sebring into the darkness on December 5. The *Los Angeles Times* quoted a valedictory Ownit press release that blamed Merrill Lynch for pulling the plug; Merrill held about 20% of Ownit's equity. Two days later, Fitch Ratings placed a subsidiary of AMC Mortgage Services under surveillance for possible downgrade, citing a plunge in origination volume, rising credit problems and a consequent knock to the profitability of the firm's servicing business. In remarks that bear on all subprime originators, the *L.A. Times* quoted John Bancroft, managing editor of *Inside Mortgage Finance*, as follows: "These are companies that depend almost exclusively on new loans for their earnings. That market grew rapidly in the last 10 years, but it couldn't last forever. Eventually, you reach just about every marginally qualified borrower you can."

That not one borrower was left behind is increasingly evident in the market for lower-rated subprime mortgage tranches. An index that references a particular subspecies of mortgage slices—the ABX.HE 06-2 BBB-minus—is the one that suddenly costs 25% more to insure against loss than it did at the end of November. Informants say that it is nearly impossible to buy credit protection on poorly performing tranches of the mortgage stack. Mr. Market, though sometimes slow on the uptake, does not have to be told twice that the fat's in the fire.

We will proceed to identify a few slices of fat that have not yet fallen off the griddle—colleague Gertner has spotted some excellent candidates for sale. First, though, a few helpful words of background.

"ABX" is the basic index designation, and that is simple enough. ABX.HE is a fuller designation, and it is wholly misleading. "HE" signifies home equity, but you may put that out of your mind. This is an index overwhelmingly of first liens; home-equity-type seconds may constitute no more than 10% of a given tranche. The basic index consists of an equal-weighted static pool of 20 credit default swaps, or CDS, that reference U.S. subprime mortgage securities. Have you tripped over the words "credit default swaps"? Pick yourself up and dust yourself off. In effect, CDS are insurance policies on credit risks. They may, therefore, be viewed as mirrors to the credit risk against which they offer protection.

The basic ABX.HE index contains five subindices, each of which tracks a different grade of mortgage credit quality. Which may lead you to wonder: "If all the mortgages are subprime, how can there be more than one rating category?" Yes, the mortgages that pack the various tranches are all subprime. But derivatives architects convert subprime into investment-grade by armoring the higher tranches with extra collateral. A triple-A-rated subprime tranche is one reinforced with enough mortgages to make it impervious—supposedly—to loss. Remember that, in all such structures, income cascades down from the top while losses infiltrate up from the bottom. The higher-rated tranches get paid first; the lower-rated ones bear the first loss.

The ABX.HE index series is a joint production of CDS IndexCo and Markit Group Ltd. CDS IndexCo is a consortium of 16 brokerage-house-cum-market-makers; Markit, which was founded in 2001, is a pricing, asset-valuation and risk-management data vendor. On the occasion of the launch of the first index series last January, Bradford S. Levy, a Goldman Sachs managing director and acting chairman of CDS IndexCo, explained what it was all about: "The CDS of [the] ABS market has grown at a rapid pace over the past six months, and we have seen increasing appetite among clients for a way to take a synthetic view on ABS. ABX is a direct response to that demand, and gives clients an efficient, standardized tool with which to quickly gain exposure to this asset class."

In short, here was a new derivative index to fill the supposedly crying need for a way to speculate on the value of stacks of subprime mortgage tranches. The first index series to be launched was the ABX.HE 06-1, and the mortgages from which it derives its value were originated in the second half of 2005. The next index made its appearance in July. This was the ABX.HE 06-2; the mortgages to which it refers were originated in the first half of 2006. The promoters say they intend to introduce a new series every six months.

The index that keeps getting its name in the paper is the July edition. What makes it notorious is the shockingly weak credit quality of the early-2006 subprime mortgage cohort. Not surprisingly, the weakest of the five constituent subindices is the lowest-rated one, the BBB-minus tranche. The aforementioned plunge of confidence in its creditworthiness translated into a spike in the cost of insuring it against loss to 380 basis points per annum from 300, all in the space of a week. No doubt the move was exaggerated by the usual depopulation of year-end trading desks.

The bad news is oddly uncontagious so far. Nothing like that loss has been registered in the higher-rated subindices of the same ABX. HE 06-2; the AA-rated tranche is little changed. Neither has the ABX.HE 06-1 index—which, to repeat, references the late-2005 subprime cohort—been dragged down. The BBB-minus tranche of the 06-1 index trades around par. The annual cost of insuring it against loss amounts to just 270 basis points, 110 fewer basis points of risk premium than assigned to the same tranche in the 06-2 subindex.

Is the subprime mortgage class of 2006 uniquely blighted? Were the underwriting standards prevailing during the first six months of the year uniquely slapdash? Or, are the remarkable losses borne on the unseasoned 2006 vintage simply the consequence of a bear market in house prices (and the preceding riot in easy credit) that sooner or later will corrupt the 2005 subprime mortgage crop as well? Our replies are, respectively, "no," "no," and "yes."

For evidence to support our affirmative response to question No. 3, we invoke the September 28 Merrill Lynch *Review of the ABS Markets*. In it, the Thundering Herd's ABS research group posits that losses on recent subprime ABS issues could be big enough to eat well into the structures' mezzanine levels, i.e., a principal loss on the order of 6% to 8%. This could occur if house prices do no worse next year than move sideways. But the Merrill economics squad has forecast a house-price decline of up to 5%. In which case, the ABS researchers warn, losses in subprime asset-backed structures would spike into the double digits. Losses could infiltrate all the way up to the A-rated mortgage stack, the researchers speculate. Just as rising house prices tended to cover up affordability and solvency problems, so falling house prices would unmask them.

It goes without saying that these excellent analysts are groping in the dark. We all are. None of us, for example, can be sure how long it might take for delinquencies and foreclosures to translate into money losses. But some things are certain. With only a glance at the tote board, for example, we can know today's odds on tomorrow's possible outcomes. Specifically, the probability of a default on the AA tranche of the ABX.HE 06-2 subindex is reckoned to be close to zero. You can buy credit protection on the AA slice of subprime mortgage exposure for a mere 13.8 basis points. That is, the cost of insuring $10 million in notional value of the AA index will set you back a mere $13,800 a year. "Pretty cheap insurance," Gertner notes. "But is there any chance of getting paid?"

Gertner has made a study of the 20 ABS deals that constitute the ABX.HE 06-2 index. He pronounces their performance to be lamentable. After just eight months of seasoning on average, 10.3% of the constituent mortgages are delinquent, in foreclosure or classified as real estate owned. (The runt of the ABS litter, the Long Beach Mortgage Loan Trust 2006-1, shows 16% of the loans in one state of distress or another.) Now, credit support for the AA-rated tranches, at 17%, provides 6.7 percentage points of insulation against loss—and, of course, there's no telling when, or if, the loans now troubled would go irretrievably bad. But given the wretched performance of the collateral to date, the cost of insurance seems strikingly cheap. "Nor is a cash loss the only way to get paid," Gertner points out. "Spreads could widen—as the spreads on lower-rated tranches have already begun to do."*

For the time being, the bear market in subprime credit is tightly focused on the lowest tranche of the 2006 index. It would, to repeat, cost you 380 basis points a year to insure it against credit loss. Better value, as Gertner points out, is protection on the BBB-minus tranche of the earlier index, the ABX.HE BBB-06-1. "If deterioration in subprime mortgage quality finds its way into the loans originated late in 2005, and I believe it will," Gertner winds up, "then the cost of insurance will only steepen."

As bull markets are said to climb a wall of worry, bear markets grow on a trellis of complacency. Is Mr. Market yawning? A good sign—for the mortgage bears.

---

* Early in June 2008, the AA-rated tranche of the ABX.HE 06-02 traded at just 30 cents on the dollar.

Wheezing CDO Machine

March 9, 2007

First came the mortgage, then the mortgage-backed security and finally—what's this about America in decline?—the collateralized debt obligation. Individual mortgages are hard enough to value. Mortgage-backed securities are that much more difficult. And securities collateralized by mortgage-backed securities—i.e., CDOs—are the very devil. But the devil got his due in 2006, when, according to J.P. Morgan, $769 billion of CDOs came into the world. By the looks of things, the world could have done with less.

The world will have to do with less as the famous CDO machine goes into the shop for cyclical repairs. So will the U.S. economy. The securitization, and re-securitization, of residential mortgages was the motive force behind the house-price boom and all that boomed along with it, home-equity extraction not least. You may remember the phrase "banking system." Today, in residential mortgage finance, there is a CDO system.

Are you in the dark? So, for the most part, are the federal banking regulators. But we laymen know a few things. We can see by the dust and debris that mortgage investors have had an encounter with credit. We know it by the plunge in the now-notorious ABX index (a conflation of 20 securities backed by slices of less-than-stellar mortgages), by the telltale weakness in a brand-new CDO index and, of course, by the collapse in the stocks of the subprime lenders. Mortgage aficionados speak of the "CDO bid." They mean that, within the fast-growing subprime mortgage market, CDOs have been the buyers of first, middle and last resort. The thesis of this essay is that the CDO machine is sputtering.

Pure and simple, CDOs are stacks of debts: debts on the asset side of the balance sheet, debts on the liabilities side. They resemble banks without walls—or depositors or regulators. At a glance, the structures are indistinguishable from those of everyday asset-backed securities. So are the protocols. The highest-rated lenders have first call on income and principal payments; the lowest-rated lenders absorb the first losses. So income trickles down from the top, losses infiltrate up from the bottom.

CDO alchemy is also very much like the kind employed in conventional asset-backed securities (of which mortgage-backed securities are the main type). In a CDO, as in an ABS, mortgage scientists and rating agencies perform a miracle of distillation. They boil down a clump of speculative-grade loans into an unrecognizable glory of investment-grade liabilities—as many as 80% are rated double-A and triple-A. How do they do it? By augmenting the high-rated tranches with extra junk, enough—so they scientifically determine—to insulate against any reasonable losses.

CDOs are better than a bank, the promoters insist, because (among other advantages) their assets are match-funded. And, they are permanently funded. Holders of CDO tranches, unlike bank depositors, can't make a run for their money. It is locked up. Indeed, in certain cases, the money is not even paid in. It is only pledged.

To understand today's CDOs, it helps to recall their predecessors. Today, CDOs invest heavily in mortgages, including lower-rated ones, or derivatives thereof. More than half of the collateral filling the $197 billion in "cash-flow" CDOs of ABS that Standard & Poor's rated last year consisted of subprime and Alt-A mortgages, the agency estimates. Perhaps 40% of the collateral that stocked the shelves of the $450 billion in "synthetic" CDOs issued worldwide last year was linked to subprime mortgage loans.

At the turn of the 21st century, mortgages held no such pride of place. CDOs invested in a ragtag bunch of claims, from junk bonds to trailer loans to securitized mutual-fund fees. That superb new paper by Mason and Rosner tells the story of how the CDOs of the early 2000s stocked up with such oddments, only to turn sellers "when collateral underperformance and fraud revealed heavy losses in the pools and, subsequently, a great many defaults. . . ."

That once-favored assets lost their popularity and never regained it is a lesson to ponder, Mason, a finance professor at Drexel University, and Rosner, managing director at the Graham Fisher & Co. financial research firm, point out. "The manufactured housing, aircraft lease, franchise business loan, and 12-b1 mutual fund fee ABS sectors are significantly smaller than they were when CDOs were pouring in during 1999–2001," the two write. "We argue that the shrinkage in those sectors arose from decreased funding by the CDO markets."

Which introduces the risk that the residential mortgage market could undergo the same type of shrinkage. Lenders, recoiling from defaults and delinquencies, might walk away. "Decreased funding for RMBS [residential mortgage-backed securities] could set off a downward spiral in credit availability that can deprive individuals of home ownership and substantially hurt the U.S. economy," the authors go on. Of course, Congress would have something to say about a derivatives-induced mortgage drought. Besides, Fannie Mae and Freddie Mac, which bought 20% of last year's crop of subprime securitizations (according to *Inside Mortgage Finance*, as quoted in *The Wall Street Journal*), would likely lean against the wind of a credit gale. Or would they? The other day, to the accompaniment of the crashing ABX index, Freddie announced it was tightening standards for subprime acquisitions, thereby showing not its face, but its back, to the winds of contraction.

CDOs come in two basic models, cash-flow and synthetic. Cash-flow CDOs acquire mortgage-backed securities, among other assets, and issue liabilities. The cheaper the cost of the liabilities in relation to the yield on the assets, of course, the better. Therefore, the more triple-A-rated liabilities, the better. Recall, please, that most of the mortgage assets are not inherently triple-A. Anything but, they owe their top-drawer rating to the art of over-collateralization and to the various assumptions—concerning prepayment speeds, correlations and so forth—that the architects and rating agencies agree to use.

Synthetic CDOs are different. They don't buy actual mortgages, or mortgage slices, as their cash-flow cousins do. Rather, they sell credit protection against such loans and slices. That is, they gain exposure to the subprime market by writing credit-default swaps on it. Only to a degree do they resemble insurers. True, synthetic CDOs earn premium income from the insurance, or protection, they sell. But a regulated property and casualty company must set aside reserves against loss. No such statutory requirement bears on CDOs. Their reserving policy is a matter between themselves, their counterparties and their liability holders.

What instigated this article was this publication's curiosity about the CDO crisis that, as of March 6 at 7 p.m. EST, hadn't happened. It should have happened, and will yet happen, in our opinion. We say this as nonbelievers in the magic by which a collection of subprime assets can be reconstituted into triple- and double-A-rated liabilities. And we say it as lifelong students of the tendency of something to go wrong when a sudden price drop occurs in an index against which hundreds of billions of dollars in notional value are traded ($300 billion is reportedly linked to the ABX index).

We are the first to admit our shortcomings in knowledge about structured mortgage finance. But, then, we have found—colleague Dan Gertner, our man on the case, can attest to it—that ignorance about CDOs and ABS is far-reaching. In fact, it reaches far into the population of CDO investors. A subscriber who has made a study of the subprime market—he is a long-short equity investor by trade—e-mails to share his observation that "somewhere in the neighborhood of 70% of CDO buyers rely almost entirely on the ratings because they don't have the time or expertise to evaluate the underlying collateral and structure." It follows, our reader points out, that "once the rating agency integrity is gone, so is the CDO market, it would seem."

What could undermine the market's confidence in CDO ratings? Well, the market itself could—and, in a sense, already has. The

Securities analyst to security analyst

sky-high cost of protecting slices of ostensibly BBB or BBB-minus-rated mortgage securities against default rather cuts the ground from under the agencies' imprimatur. So, too, does the quoted cost of protecting a portfolio of BBB and BBB-minus-rated CDO liabilities against default. The TABX is a brand-new tranched index of low-rated subprime mortgages. Immediately upon its February 14 debut, it headed down to levels strongly suggesting that the market is more worried about subprime mortgages, and mortgage derivatives, than Moody's, S&P or Fitch is.

Either the agencies are right and the market is wrong, or the structures are flawed and the ratings are misconceived. One likely point of vulnerability is that synthetic CDOs are mostly "unfunded." That is, the senior lenders put up no money unless and until an outright loss forces a capital call. "Loss" is the critical word. Falling index levels do not, in themselves, trigger adverse action under most CDO debt indentures, as we understand it. But the falling index levels, unless they are wholly detached from economic reality, point to actual or prospective impairment in the value of the collateral. Someone must be meeting a margin call.

The outpouring of new synthetic CDOs was not merely an underwriting sensation. It was also a credit event. With more CDOs came—of course—more CDS; in other words, more sub-prime mortgage insurance policies. The greater the supply of this protection on offer, the more its price tended to fall. The drop in the perceived risk of lending to people who had next to no money of their own in the house of their dreams could not have been lost on the nation's basis-point-hungry lenders.

But the CDO machine is wheezing, in part for a lack of finan-cial fuel. Wall Street furnished the so-called warehouse lines that financed the assembly of CDOs. Thus, *Bloomberg* reports that, as of September 30, New Century had credit lines to Morgan Stan-ley (for $3 billion, of which $1.5 billion was outstanding) and UBS (for $2 billion, of which $1.5 billion was outstanding). All in all, New Century—now the object of a criminal investigation, on top of everything else—had 16 warehouse lines, which, together with other credit facilities, footed to $17.4 billion.

Now much of this warehouse money is withdrawn. "We've heard about it for the past five months," an anonymity-seeking subprime investor tells Gertner. "That is, about people being really afraid and really worried about 'how long are we going to have to maintain this warehouse stuff that is completely on our books?' And what they have tended to do is to say, 'The mark will probably get better in the next three to six months. So I'm going to go out and use the ABX to hedge this.' So that's one of the reasons that there's been a massive buying of protection." In other words, the brokers them-selves have contributed to the plunge in the ABX by buying credit protection on it. So doing, they have contributed to the state of panic in which new CDOs are unmarketable.

Last week brought news of a warehouse liquidation—the auc-tion of a variety of collateral that had been earmarked for a new CDO but which, instead, was thrown on the market piecemeal.

The auctioned items of the CDO-that-is-never-to-be included commercial mortgage-backed securities, Alt-A residential loans, other grades of residential loans and CDOs. The sale went well, a spy reports, but the withdrawal of a warehouse bodes ill for a number of things. "The reality here is that without active warehouses there are no CDOs, no natural buyers of risk, no support bids for credit . . . ," Morgan Stanley wrote in its daily subprime bulletin on the last day of February. "What has been a credit concern seems to be morphing into a liquidity crunch for all parties involved (HEL [home-equity loan] borrower, HEL originator—and finally—HEL trader/investor)." According to the March 2 edition of *Asset-Backed Alert*, mortgage-securitization volumes dropped by 26% in January and February from year-ago levels. "While most of the top investment banks say they are still hiring mid-level staff," the Alert added, "'it looks like some people don't think they'll have any work to do,' one headhunter said."

Knowledgeable buyers of broken mortgage credit may materialize in their own good time. For now, the market confronts the contradiction long obscured by rising prices. In the words of the aforementioned Mason and Rosner, the mortgage market "is built upon the statistical predictability of mortgage performance." Such supposed predictability is the intellectual foundation of the CDO boom. However, the two authors add, "As the performance of mortgages shifts due to fundamental changes in origination and servicing practices, investors may be surprised to find the mortgage claim they purchased is based on a pool of loans with very different statistical performance properties than previously experienced or expected." Or even imagined.

Chapter Seven

Mr. Market in the Dock

Carter Glass, R.I.P.

November 5, 1999

NEW REPORT ON Amazon.com from the securities affiliate of Bank of America is notable not only for the fact
that the analyst's 12-month price target looks like a typo-
graphical error; the redeeming value of this work lies also in the
timing of its publication. By chance, it appeared within days of the
political deal that would expunge the last remains of the Glass-
Steagall Act of 1933 from the federal law books.

Years ago, by the letter of the law, no such opinion could have
been rendered, as the drug of speculation was expressly forbidden
to deposit-taking institutions. Commercial banking and investment banking were put asunder on the grounds that the safety and
soundness of the former would always be compromised by the latter. Then, again, long before repeal seemed to be imminent, the law
was made practically moot: Nationsbank acquired Montgomery

Securities in 1997, and the Bank of America merged with Nations-bank in 1998 (it was the Montgomery division of Banc of America Securities that produced the tour de force on Amazon).

The essay you hold in your hands was provoked by the outpouring of glee over the news about Glass-Steagall. To us, there is nothing to be gleeful about. Great booms produce large abuses, which usually do not seem abusive until after the up cycle ends. What chiefly separates *Grant's* from our New Era sparring partners in this matter is our conviction that abuses are not always legislated by Congress. People in markets periodically overdo it themselves, especially when (as now) the government has planted the seed of the idea that some of the very biggest financial institutions are too big to fail. It is a useful exercise for these seemingly perfect, cloudless days to try to imagine what some future U.S. Senator might seek to regulate, rein in, suppress or outlaw after the close of this fabulous upturn. Many possibilities come to mind, e.g., the government-sponsored enterprises, financial debt in general (and asset-backed securities in particular; thank you, John Lonski), junk bonds, stock options and Wall Street "research," the integrity of corporate "full disclosure" or the $10 million launch party (the kind recently thrown, according to *The Wall Street Journal*, by Pixelon.com).

Sympathetic toward Glass, we hold no brief today for the law he was instrumental in writing long ago. But we do understand the cyclical reasons for its enactment. What ought to interest a present-day investor, we think, is not the undeniable fact that the law was misbegotten, but that it was enacted despite its defects, obvious as they were even in 1933. The history of Glass-Steagall teaches many lessons, one of which is that the law of the land is cyclically variable; there is one set of rules for bull markets, another for bear markets.

In the Great Depression, the government tried to legislate absolute financial safety; it was an impossibility. Today, at what may be the middle or maybe the end, but certainly not the beginning, of a span of stupendous prosperity, the government is seeking to promote enlightened risk taking. This is a fine and laudable goal, although there is one small blemish. The computation of risk and reward has been permanently distorted by the partial socialization of credit risk, another legacy of the era of Glass and Steagall. On the clear understanding that the structure of leveraged finance will be protected against what is described as "systemic risk," people take greater risks than they would otherwise take. The upshot is that there is never a dull moment in credit, with new accidents and upheavals all the time, even in business expansions like this one. Perennially, therefore, the question before the house is where the next eruption might occur.

The B of A analysis of Amazon.com, to begin at the beginning, suggests the obvious thought, that the greatest risk in American finance lies with the stock market. Although the analyst professed to be bullish, the price of the stock on the date of the report's publication (almost $76 a share) was higher than the projected 12-month price target ($65 a share). On the page, it looks a little like Andruw Jones's name on a scorecard, improbable but authentic (for the benefit of foreign readers, Jones was the starting left fielder for the other team in the 1999 World Series).

Not just anyone could sound persuasive about the bullish potential of an implied minus 14% annual return, but the B of A's man, Tom Courtney, did his duty as he seemed to see that duty. "We are maintaining our rating of Strong Buy, based on our belief in the channel and Amazon's number one market position," wrote Courtney. "We maintain our 12-month price target of $65, which the stock recently ran through, and we would encourage long-term investors to be opportunistic in establishing a position."

It is not hard to imagine Glass, a crusty Virginia conservative Democrat, tearing his white hair over that one, and, more generally, over the diversion of Federal Reserve Bank credit into the unholy channels of Wall Street, which he regarded as a gambling hell. Glass was a founding father of the Fed, and it broke his heart when his own creation seemed to facilitate the boom that preceded the 1929 bust. "Speculation, then, caused the depression, and bankers had been responsible for the speculation," relates the superb official history of Citibank, by Harold van B. Cleveland and Thomas F. Huertas. "So read the indictment as it unfolded in 1931 and 1932 in the course of a series of congressional investigations."

It was to prevent a recurrence of this wanton speculative episode that Glass, along with his colleague in the House of Representatives, Henry Steagall, Democrat of Alabama, pushed through the Banking Act of 1933.

The title of the bill helps to explain its reason for being. It was an act "to provide for the safer and more effective use of the assets of Federal Reserve Banks and of national banking associations [i.e., nationally chartered commercial banks], to regulate interbank control, to prevent the undue diversion of funds into speculative operations and for other purposes." Besides separating commercial banking from the Wall Street kind of banking, the bill established ceilings on deposit interest rates (none was allowed to be paid on demand deposits). By the time the act was presented to President Franklin D. Roosevelt for his signature in June 1933, another essential provision had been added: the guarantee of bank deposits by a new Federal Deposit Insurance Corp.

The legislation offended every orthodox sensibility, financial, political and constitutional. All the big commercial banks owned securities and investment banking affiliates, just as Citicorp, Morgan and BankAmerica et al. do again today. They would have to be sold off or closed down, resulting in a significant loss of income and diversification. As for deposit insurance, Roosevelt himself was a late convert to the cause, and Glass had his own reservations. The case against it was forcefully argued by, among others, the American Bankers Association, *The Wall Street Journal* and National City Bank, forerunner to Citigroup. National City's critique is worth recalling, especially in view of the modern Citi's acute troubles in the early 1990s: "The element of character in the choice of bank is eliminated, and the competitive appeal is shifted to other and lower standards, such as liberality in making loans. The natural result is

"Lucky we don't work for Enron."

that the standards of management are lowered, bankers may take greater risks for the sake of larger profits and the economic loss which accompanies bad bank management increases."

If the benefit of deposit insurance is obvious, the cost is hardly less so. So, too, with a range of other Depression-era reforms and institutions, the Federal Home Loan Banks, to name one. The Home Loan Banking System, created by the Hoover administration to rejuvenate a moribund housing industry, has become almost a parallel American central bank, dispensing subsidized credit to thrift institutions and commercial banks for a variety of purposes (some having to do with replacing deposits lost to the stock market). Notably absent in the celebration of the fall of Glass-Steagall has been the demand for the abrogation of the rest of the key laws and institutions of the welfare state of credit. (For the record, in the June quarter, the consolidated assets of the Home Loan Banks showed year-over-year growth of 31%, brisk for a supposedly non-inflationary environment.)

Like the purchase of Conoco by DuPont in 1981, which signaled a top in oil and inflation, or the sale of Conoco by DuPont beginning in 1999, which seems to point to the opposite, the imminent federal action to erase portions of Glass-Steagall constitutes a cyclical milestone. Just the other day, an e-pundit proposed that Murphy's Law had been superseded: Everything that could go right, would. It would be an exaggeration to claim that Americans in 1999 can only imagine the upside. After all, even though the Nasdaq Composite Index is making new highs, scores of junk bonds and hundreds of small-cap common stocks are selling at bear-market valuations. But risk is what CNBC doesn't talk about.

In these circumstances, few editorial tears were shed for the loss of Glass-Steagall. Commentators noted that the congressional action was forced by the 1998 Citicorp-Travelers amalgamation. "The law prohibited money-saving combinations," said a *Wall Street Journal* editorial, "entrenched monopolies and created a complex skein of regulatory issues that impeded change. The splintering spirit of the 1930s also produced disasters-in-waiting, such as the Savings & Loan and Farm Credit systems; the heart of financial security, we repeatedly and painfully learned, is diversification."

Is it? In 1998, to the best of the knowledge and belief of the Mensa-caliber executives of Long-Term Capital Management, the portfolio of that hedge fund was not only well diversified but also thoroughly hedged. Ten years earlier, the great New York City clearing banks were busy digging themselves into the hole of real estate, not considering that this apparently lucrative asset would cause them the kind of acute financial embarrassment that they had managed to avoid even in the Great Depression. The truth is that leveraged financial institutions are inherently prone to crisis, especially when, as John Reed, co-chairman of Citigroup, admitted in a confessional speech to an audience of bank examiners recently, bank presidents are susceptible to the power of suggestion (or "group thinking," as he put it). Alas, the true and permanent legacy of Glass-Steagall is one that *The Wall Street Journal* did not get around to deploring in last week's editorial. It is the idea—insidious or constructive, according to taste—that the U.S. government will always prevent a general breakdown. Carter Glass, no socialist, was instrumental in putting the government in the financial guaranty business.

Not the least ironic feature of Glass-Steagall was its impeccably bad timing. On the date of its signing, June 16, 1933, a little less than four years had elapsed since the 1929 stock market peak; margin debt had almost disappeared. Almost all the terrible things that were going to happen had happened. It was at this fearful time that the federal government got around to guarding against speculative excess, which the nation would not have the heart to perpetrate for another financial generation, at least. It was not pure coincidence that the federal tax-evasion trial of Charles E. Mitchell, pilloried chairman of National City Bank, was winding up as President Roosevelt signed the Glass-Steagall bill, handing the pen to Glass as he finished. Having celebrated bankers during the boom, the public reviled them (now they were "banksters") in the bust. Mitchell, incidentally, was acquitted.

Speculative sentiment was just as much in need of legislative restraint in 1933 as it is today in need of legislative stimulus; Congress never seems to fail to make the grand counterproductive gesture. In 1933, risk taking had almost been conditioned out of lending. In a statement it issued upon Mitchell's resignation in February 1933, National City pledged to confine the activities of its securities affiliate to "government, state, municipal and corporate bonds of the highest character." The *New York Times*, far less liberal in editorial policy than it is now, commended this undertaking as follows: "This should mean an end to the mad speculation of banks in the years when nearly everybody was mad."

Everybody was not mad, according to the consensus of modern financial historians; what sunk the economy was not speculation but the Great Depression. We put the question to the readers of *Grant's*, however: In a great boom, absent federal securities laws, would there not have been a roaring good time? Would the securities affiliates of commercial banks not have been tempted to deploy their funds for the benefit of their parent companies, even if that meant cutting an occasional corner? What cannot be proven is that risk was systematically underpriced during the Coolidge boom. However, we think, it is easy to show that it was systematically overpriced in the aftermath. Thus, in May 1933, the *American Banker* polled its readers on the advisability of a bank investing in Baa-rated corporates at the prevailing rate of 7¾%, compared with the average bank lending rate of 4½% (it being understood that the President of the United States had personally pledged to try to reflate the economy). "[W]ould it be wise to speculate a little now consciously in the investment account with which bankers were speculating so unconsciously and unwisely in 1929?" the paper asked. The response was a thunderous "No!" Many of the respondents were frankly shocked to be asked. "The questionnaire showed clearly," the *Banker* concluded, "that the last four years [have] strengthened the real basis of conservative banking thought."

Yet, we think, it had done no such thing. The "real basis of conservative banking thought" is enlightened risk taking, not a safe deposit box. But there is no need to try to put ourselves in the position of our shell-shocked grandfathers, or great-grandfathers. Only recall the shortage of real-estate finance at the bottom of the property bear market in the early 1990s. It was, in fact, an ideal time to get involved in real estate speculation.

Just as the *Journal* and *The Economist* contend, therefore, Glass-Steagall was punitive and ill-conceived. However, it was an essential element of the dawning new age. As the Banking Act was passed, so was legislation to create the National Recovery Administration, an agency devoted to the regimentation of the formerly free U.S. economy, Gen. Hugh Johnson presiding. More than six decades later, of course, the politico-speculative mind-set has been reversed, with regulation and taxation rolled back, and even the communists paying lip service to enterprise. However, we are sure, that does not mean it will stay reversed. It was to protect against the possibility of an adverse change that Benjamin Graham prescribed investments that offered a margin of safety.

What could be safer than big diversified financial supermarkets, big liquid bond issues and big indexed equities? Nothing, according to received opinion.

It was, in fact, Leon Trotsky, exiled Russian revolutionary, who predicted this state of affairs at the very low ebb of American banking fortunes. The ultimate outcome of the crisis would be a great American expansion, he told the Associated Press in March 1933, "a grandiose centralization of the banking system, ultimately merely reinforcing United States financial hegemony." (Buy the dollar and sell sterling, Trotsky also strongly suggested. Here, too, was a splendid, money-making forecast, available for the price of the *New York Times*.)

To the best of our knowledge, however, not even Trotsky anticipated that the rise of the megabank would take place concurrently with the proliferation of derivative financial instruments. Nor did he predict (perhaps he was not asked to predict) that the U.S. junk-bond market would generate startlingly high default numbers in what would be described as the best of all possible economic worlds. Put these things together, and it's no mystery that credit crises have become a recurring element of American finance.

In 1933, the Glass-Steagall Act figuratively closed the barn door behind the Great Depression. The expected repeal of this ill-suited legislation may or may not mark the close of the most speculative chapter of the Great Boom. However, some such outcome would not surprise a poet.

The Miscreants We Deserve

February 15, 2002

In the New Economy, even the scandals are unimaginably stu-pendous. Nothing bigger than Enron came to light in the inqui-sitions following the 1929 stock market crash. No breach of trust uncovered by the Senate Banking Committee in 1933–34 was more condemning than that laid at the feet of the mute and forgetful executives from Houston. "I think the market was a God-given market," famously said Albert H. Wiggin, long-ago chairman of the Chase National Bank, when asked about a certain price-rigging scheme in the Coolidge era. Jeffrey K. Skilling, the ex-president of Enron, has so far failed to measure up to Wiggin's standard of public speaking. However, so important and thoroughgoing is the change in the country's political and regulatory mood that Skilling will certainly have an opportunity to refine his delivery.

As a rule, investors see what they want to see. In the boom, they saw it was good that the cost of executive stock options was nowhere reflected in the reported profits of the company dispens-ing them. They were happy to participate in the fictions allowed under generally accepted accounting principles in the matter of the consolidation (or nonconsolidation) of corporate subsidiaries. They thought none the worse of CEOs who sold their shares but didn't immediately disclose the fact. However, the bear market has raised a hue and cry for truth telling and fair dealing. Wall Street, understandably, is on edge.

To prepare for the big change, we have been reading *Wall Street Under Oath: The Story of Our Modern Money Changers*, by Ferdi-nand Pecora, first published in 1939. Pecora led the famous Sen-ate hearings into the banking and stock market practices of the late 1920s and early 1930s. Out of these immense proceedings came the Securities and Exchange Commission and the rules and regulations of full disclosure, reforms intended to prevent the likes of Enron.

Pecora-inspired legislation caused commercial banking and investment banking to be torn asunder (they were recently reattached), and public utility holding companies to be brought to heel. It was thanks to Pecora that the public was introduced to the baffling details of Samuel Insull's public-utility empire, the rampant use of pools to manipulate stock prices and the brazen (or so it appeared after the fact) use of tax-avoidance schemes by the bankers, Tories and economic royalists. The Pecora proceedings were instrumental in rewriting the rule book of American finance. Now it is on the verge of being re-rewritten.

All of which is preface to a comparison of Enron with Insull, of Arthur Andersen with itself, of the National City Bank with Citigroup and of the New Era (the latter 1920s) with the New Economy (the latter 1990s). We find that we prefer the old capitalist miscreants to the new. And if, as we believe, the millennial money changers will come out looking worse than their ancestors, the financial markets will be in for adjustment. The safeguards put in place in reaction to the Great Depression have spared the country another Great Depression. However, far from sparing us another Insull, they helped to incubate Enron.

Pecora, peering down from cloud nine, would hardly recognize the millennial financial system. It is significantly more leveraged than its Depression-era predecessor. Derivatives-laden, it is more sophisticated. Computer-powered, it is more efficient. No more a gentlemen's club, it is more competitive. It is substantially more integrated into the world financial system and—in consequence of the piling up of chronic U.S. current-account deficits—infinitely more dependent on the choices of foreign creditors.

By design, the U.S. economy c. 2002 is resistant to panics, crashes and depressions. Many are its built-in stabilizers. However, "stability" does not come for free. To forestall crisis, the Federal Reserve creates credit. Seeing that this elixir heals the sick and causes the lame to walk, investors lower their guards. They trust absolutely in equities and in the U.S. dollar ("a strong dollar is in the U.S. interest," intoned Robert E. Rubin over and over during the Clinton boom). And when, at what is supposed to be a bear-market bottom, the S&P 500 is quoted at 22 times forecast earnings, *The Wall Street Journal* can authoritatively explain a given day's rally in terms of "bargain hunting."

Since antiquity, the Fastows and Skillings and Lays of the world have been able to find each other. Only rarely, however, have they been able to run up multibillion-dollar debts and achieve multi-billion-dollar stock market capitalizations. Epic feats of bubble building presuppose artificially low interest rates. Artificially low interest rates induce extraordinary levels of borrowing. Overborrowing stimulates overinvestment. Overinvestment elicits the kind of inflation we call "a wonderful bull market."

Excessive credit creation is a fair description of the impersonal force that helped to raise Insull's personal net worth to $150 million at the 1929 peak from $5 million in 1926. And it was, indeed, the delayed effects of this same excessive credit creation that, at the bottom in 1932, caused Insull to be "too broke to be bankrupt," as a banker put it. An explosion of financial leverage equally helped to make Enron what it is today. However, after a week's immersion in the subject of comparative scandals, we have come to see the truth of a remark casually tossed off by *Grant's* reader Paul Isaac the other day. "The 1930s are starting to look pretty good," he said.

Pecora judged the Wall Street of his day to be a moral sinkhole, and in the defalcation of Richard Whitney, chairman of the New York Stock Exchange, and in the short selling of Albert Wiggin, he seemed to prove the point. However, he assigned too much blame to the lightly regulated financial system and too little to the boom. It wasn't the lack of rules and regulations that raised the depravity index in American finance. It was the conditioned belief in a new era.

The millennial investigations into Enron and related subjects may yet reveal an alleged perpetrator whom history will judge to be tragic. Guessing, we think that that man will not be Dennis Kozlowski, the well-compensated CEO of Tyco International.

Pecora pilloried Charles E. Mitchell, chairman of National City Bank, as the living symbol of the failure of unbridled capitalism. However, Mitchell lost his fortune by trying to support his bank's post-Crash share price. Tried for income-tax fraud, he was acquitted, and he went back to work to repay his debts, saying that to file for personal bankruptcy wouldn't be "square." Neither was Insull dishonorable. In rejecting a potentially lucrative scheme to manipulate lower the price of an Insull holding company's stock, he gave as his reason: "That would be immoral."

So when *The Wall Street Journal* the other day suggested that Enron was a lineal descendant of the Insull empire, it was hard on Insull's memory and unduly flattering to the ethical and financial standards of the post-Pecora age. Insull's affairs, like Enron's, were tangled and complex. And Insull himself seemed not entirely to understand them. However, Insull's downfall was hubris, not subterfuge, and his hubris was enflamed by the temptations presented in every boom.

"[B]etween 1924 and 1927," writes Forrest McDonald in *Insull*, his fine and sympathetic biography of the Midwest utilities titan, "virtually every old pro in the Chicago banking community died, leaving the banks in the hands of persons whose lack of seasoning prepared them ill for the financial storms ahead. Assuming command during the expansionist fever of the late 1920s, they began throwing money at everyone who seemed prosperous; Insull they deluged with easy credit, begging him to accept it, for any purpose. At a party, the new president of the Continental Bank sidled up to Junior [Insull's son] and, with the manner of a French postcard peddler, said, 'Say, I just want you to know that if you fellows ever want to borrow more than the legal limit, all you have to do is organize a new corporation and we'll be happy to lend you another $21 million.' . . .[T]o an organization that had always been kept in check by the difficulty of raising capital for expansion, this new situation had the impact of three stiff drinks on an empty stomach."

Insull was a utilities pioneer: inventor, builder, visionary, manager. At their peak in 1930, his companies constituted the nation's third-largest power-and-light enterprise, behind Electric Bond & Share and the United Corp. Busy readers not enrolled in a graduate history program should not be afraid: Only the bare minimum of detail about the structure of Insull's companies will be recited here. Without it, however, there can be no proper savoring of the irony of Arthur Andersen or appreciation of the role of Enron in the evolution of modern American finance.

The biggest of five Insull holding companies was Middle West Utilities Co., with assets of $1.2 billion and 111 subsidiaries. Commonwealth Edison, with $450 million of assets and six subsidiaries, was No. 2, followed by Midland United Co. ($352 million in assets and 30 subsidiaries), People's Gas, Light & Coke Co. ($211 million in assets and eight subsidiaries) and Public Service Co. of Northern Illinois ($210 million of assets, one subsidiary). Insull's collection of operating businesses generated more than one-eighth of the country's electrical power and served 4.5 million customers.

The titan himself, writes McDonald, "wasn't interested in the money. All he really wanted was to run things—and, after a fashion, to continue to run them after he was dead." It was to fend off a threat to his control that Insull made two fatal strategic errors. He got into the financial engineering business, and he borrowed heavily in 1930, a year that (contrary to expectations) would not prove to be the end of the Depression but only the beginning.

In testimony concerning Enron before the Senate Committee on Governmental Affairs on January 24, Frank Partnoy, professor of law at the University of San Diego School of Law (and the author of *F.I.A.S.C.O.: The Inside Story of a Wall Street Trader*, 1999), observed that the former energy company was, in fact, a derivatives mill. Whereas Long-Term Capital Management lost a mere $4.6 billion, Enron wiped out $70 billion of equity market capitalization and impaired billions more of debt. Enron, said Partnoy, made LTCM "look like a lemonade stand." It earned more in derivatives trading in 2000—a single year—than LTCM did in its existence.

Insull had no more access to derivatives than he had to an executive jet. Neither was he imbued with the gospel of shareholder value. So when the Cleveland financier Cyrus S. Eaton started to accumulate shares in the Insull companies, Sam Insull took countermeasures. A December 1928 press release disclosing the formation of an investment company designed to block Eaton was commendably forthright. The reason stated was "to perpetuate the existing management of the Insull group of public utilities." This entity was called Insull Utility Investments, or IUI.

"What no one anticipated," writes McDonald, "was that the stock market was about to go mad. On the first day of trading in the IUI common, on Jan. 17, 1929, the stock opened at 25 and closed at 30. As winter turned into spring, IUI common soared . . . to 60, 70, 80, and beyond; and when spring turned into summer, it shot beyond 100 and then to 150 a share. Commonwealth Edison went from 202 in January to 450 in August; Middle West rocketed from 169 to 529 in the same period."

McDonald records that Insull saw the bubble for what it was and dreaded its bursting. He saw, too, how the flyaway market was complicating the business of accumulating shares in the five Insull holding companies, which was the reason for the incorporation of IUI in the first place. Insull's solution to this problem was to form a second investment trust, Corporation Securities Co. of Chicago, "on essentially the same lines as IUI," McDonald writes, "except that Corp. and IUI partially owned one another and control of Corp. was assured through a voting trust. The net effect was that after September 1929, these twin investment trusts emerged as the throne room to the Insull empire."

Like the 1990s, the 1920s were prolific in financial innovation. Banks prohibited under the National Banking Act from engaging in investment activities conducted that business through securities affiliates. The 1933 Banking Act outlawed them. Forced to choose between commercial banking and the investment kind, J.P. Morgan, for example, selected the former. The investment affiliate it hived off was called Morgan Stanley. Years passed and memories faded. Under the Gramm-Leach-Billey Financial Services Modernization Act of 1998, investment banking and commercial banking were formally reunited. And in the person of Robert Rubin, chairman of the executive committee of Citigroup, investment banking, commercial banking and string pulling at the highest governmental level have been consolidated.

Whether or not, in Pecora's day, the big New York banks were too big to fail, they were managed in such a fashion as to make the question academic. At year-end 1929, National City Bank, forerunner to Citibank, showed a ratio of equity to assets of no less than 11.4%. On that equity it coincidentally earned 11.4%; in 2000, a more aggressively leveraged Citibank earned 16.9% on its equity, which represented 8.7% of assets. The very strength of the leading banks lulled historically minded Americans into errors of complacency, observes Barrie Wigmore in *The Crash and Its After-*

"He called me a CEO first."

math. Never before had an economic crisis not been preceded by a banking crisis: ". . . the stability of the banking system in 1929 augured a mild recession."

Insull expressed his confidence by borrowing. Interest rates had plunged along with stock prices. As his credit was deemed to be superb, the titan availed himself of bank credit and the corporate bond market. "Insull's 1930 financing set Chicago observers gaping," McDonald writes. "And if Chicagoans were impressed by a man willing to take on more than $200 million of new debts in the wake of the great crash, the New York investment bankers must have ached with envy. Insull's credit was so good that buyers snapped up and oversubscribed almost every issue; for the most part Halsey, Stuart did not have to sell the securities, it had to ration them, and though no one knew what the house profit was, at typical New York spreads it would have been $10 million to $20 million."

It was more than enough to finance a series of radio programs extolling the merits of Halsey, Stuart securities, the Insull bonds not least. The shows, recorded Pecora, were "presided over by a professor of the University of Chicago, who came in the course of time to be known to the public as 'The Old Counselor.'"

The Insull operating businesses showed no immediate ill effects of the Depression. They invested heavily in plant and equipment in 1930 (redeeming a promise Insull had made to President Hoover at a post-Crash meeting of business leaders to promote the cause of business-as-usual), and showed record earnings through the middle of 1931. But the stock advanced by Insull as collateral against bank borrowings suffered a sharp loss of value. McDonald gives two reasons for this decline. One had to do with force majeure (Britain going off the gold standard, in September 1931), the other did not (a bear raid by hostile creditors). Insull "borrowed to the limit of his personal credit in behalf of his companies, shifted money around from one of the companies to another so as to use the strongest to shore up the weakest, and effected drastic reorganizations to reduce expenses," McDonald relates. "The effort was pathetically futile: Its only effect was to enmesh him deeper, and to leave a confused, disorderly record that would soon be used against him."

The impetus to reform is only latent in bull markets; it's during bear markets that the rules are changed. The rules were changed for Insull in March 1932. It had been customary at the Insull companies to write up the book value of securities and subsidiaries based on a determination of the value of improvements and interconnections (a determination made, conveniently enough, in-house). The earnings thereby caused to materialize were certainly dubious, but they were not so great that, if disallowed, Insull would be plunged into crisis.

Insull's greater vulnerability lay in his depreciation schedules, or lack thereof. Instead of assigning to an asset an estimated useful life and depreciating it over that life, Insull employed a "retirement reserve." Into this fund would go the sums that Insull himself (famous in his younger days as a micromanager) deemed adequate to write off the complete value of an asset at the end of its useful life. So rapidly was electrical technology evolving, Insull reasoned, that to guess how long a piece of equipment would last was futile. Wisconsin regulators, as skeptical of business as any, endorsed the reserve method, according to McDonald, and it was generally employed in the utilities industry.

Colleague Peter Walmsley, having examined the Insull postmortem compiled by the Federal Trade Commission, finds heavy criticism of the retirement reserves. By systematically understating depreciation expense, the indictment went, the Insull companies systematically inflated profits. The only critics who mattered to Insull in his highly leveraged position were his creditors. As Middle West weakened, they installed their own accountants.

"Under the circumstances," McDonald writes, "it was necessary that the new auditors be a firm with high professional standing and one with no extensive connection with Insull and his companies." Quickly, they imposed straight-line depreciation and threw out the value step-up calculations: "By a stroke of a pen," McDonald continues, "Middle West became insolvent; and when the system was extended backward, Middle West became retroactively insolvent, never having earned any money and thus nothing but a worthless pile of paper that had been kept alive only by continuous impairment of capital, disguised by improper bookkeeping." The prestigious auditors who wielded the axe were none other than Arthur Andersen & Co. "Markets make opinions," as the Old Counselor might have said: Bear markets demand conservatism. Then, as now, Andersen was a mirror to the times.

Owen D. Young, chairman of General Electric Co., was called on to mediate between Insull and his creditors, and what he saw and heard was wholly outside the realm of his own business experience. A purely industrial business, GE was conservatively capitalized, indeed, almost debt-free. In 1929, at the peak, it covered fixed charges out of cash flow (that's EBIT, not EBITDA, an invention of the 1980s) 109.6 times over. In 1932, at the bottom, it covered by 11.5 times. In 1929, GE generated a return on equity of 18.8%. In 2001, a thoroughly up-to-date GE produced an ROE of 26.3% while employing vastly more debt (it had, of course, long before entered the financial services line).

"Great numbers of operating utilities," Young told Pecora, in trying to describe the Insull edifice, "with holding companies superimposed on the utilities, and holding companies superimposed on those holding companies, investment companies and affiliates. . . ."

"And all overcapitalized?" a senator prompted.

"I express no opinion on that," Young replied, "because I do not know. But I say it is impossible for any man to grasp the situation of that vast structure. And if I may add: I should like to say here that I believe Mr. Samuel Insull was very largely the victim of that complicated structure, which got even beyond his power, competent as he was, to understand it."

Pecora was indignant that certain great financiers had enriched themselves at the expense of their employees and stockholders. He heaped contempt on the City Bank for creating a so-called morale fund with which to extend a helping hand to senior officers. No such succor was made available to the clerks. The worst offender under the general heading of predatory executive behavior was Albert Wiggin, "the most popular banker in Wall Street," who earned $4 million after the Crash by selling short the shares of the bank he knew best, his own.

"You did sell it short beginning in September [1929]?" Pecora demanded.

"Yes," said Wiggin, not taking the Fifth, "and I did think that the bank stock market was high, and I did want a buying power for that bank stock." The "buying power" referred to was the expected purchase of the short seller. By closing out his transaction, Wiggin would actually be doing the other shareholders a favor. Pecora seemed unmollified.

Offenders against the new political sensibilities were also called to justify themselves. A Morgan partner named William Ewing was roughly handled for choosing to defer a federal tax liability. He had, in fact, engaged in two forms of antisocial behavior, Pecora pointed out, conducting a profitable short sale and then refusing to cover it (by not closing the transaction, he postponed the taxable event). Was this a crime? It was a crime against the people who "could not see the justice or equity of financial giants paying nothing, while Tom, Dick and Harry scraped the bottoms of their modest purses to meet their tax obligations to the Government," as Pecora put it. The inquisitor contrasted the avoidance of taxes, however "lawful," with the "public-spirited gesture of a Stanley Baldwin gratuitously contributing 20% of his entire fortune to the British Government after the war. The country, in 1933, was in no mood for nice distinctions between tax 'evasion' and tax 'avoidance.'" In so many words, the country was in no mood for the law.

No fair comparison is possible between an historical event and the breaking news. Assessing the life and works of Samuel Insull, we have the scholarship of Forrest McDonald. Trying to make sense of Kenneth Lay, we have *The Wall Street Journal*. However, we think, it would be an unwarrantable expression of optimism to expect that the financial practices of the millennial boom would look any better under the prosecutorial spotlight than those of the 1920s did. Latter-day Pecoras have a whole new field of monkey business to explore in the comedy of the "analysts" (in the 1920s, they had no analysts, only "statisticians," and not many of them). In place of Arthur Cutten and the great pool operators of the Coolidge era, a modern-day investigator could probe the end-of-quarter markups of the mutual-fund portfolio managers. As for the shame of Albert Wiggin, the derivatives and options markets provide a most efficient way to lay down a bet against the house without obviously doing so. The nation would sit riveted in front of the TV as "Pecora: The Next Generation," went about its interrogations.

It set Pecora's hair on fire that the Morgan bank distributed shares of hot IPOs, virtually free of cost, to roughly 500 of the nation's rich and famous citizens. The names of these lucky recipients filled the Morgan "'preferred lists,' whose publication stirred the nation, and opened the eyes of millions to the hidden ways of Wall Street," Pecora wrote. In his book is quoted a laconic letter from the Morgan bank to one of the beneficiaries of the coveted stock. It said in part:

> There are no strings tied to this stock, so you can sell it whenever you wish. . . . We just want you to know that we were thinking of you in this connection and thought you might like to have a little of the stock at the same price we are paying for it. . . .

At the 1929 top, the capitalization of the U.S. equity markets amounted to just 81.4% of U.S. GDP. By the March 2000 peak, the reading was 183% of GDP. The democratization of finance in the generations following the Senate hearings would have gratified Pecora, but the new abuses might have shocked him. The insouciance of the public to those abuses might have amazed him. In the hot IPO market of the 1990s, Credit Suisse First Boston reprised the Morgan preferred list but without the subtlety (and without, to date, a subsequent public backlash). Shares went not to the beautiful people, necessarily, but to the responsive ones. A CSFB e-mail, subsequently divulged to regulators, left nothing to the imagination. "Okay," a brokerage-house minion addressed a preferred client, "we got another screaming deal and I weaseled you guys some stock . . . we've yet to see any leverage out of you guys for the free dough-re-me . . . does it make sense for me . . . to continue to feed you guys with deal stock or should I take the stock to someone who will pay us direct for the allocation." No furor remotely comparable to the scandal over the preferred lists ensued. CSFB paid a fine and settled the charges, admitting to nothing.

Pecora put his faith in laws and sunshine. "[H]ad there been full disclosure of what was being done in furtherance of these schemes," he wrote concerning a banker's transgressions, "they could not long have survived the fierce light of publicity and criticism."

In the second half of the 1990s, the "fierce light of publicity and criticism" was a flickering candle. So dim was the light that professional investors complained they could hardly read by it. Footnotes to the financial statements of companies seemed particularly hard to make out. Disclosure, of course, was not the problem. A clean breast of the risks of LBO-related junk bonds was made in the 1980s to no particular effect. Full disclosure was made of the odds-on failure of the Internet companies of the 1990s. Besotted investors paid no attention (the market was going up).

Many are the senior executives who, in recent years, chose to do what Mitchell and Insull abstained from doing. Their businesses weakening, they sold shares, sometimes lots of them (as disclosed in 144 filings with the SEC). Among them: Joseph Nacchio of Qwest, Catherine Hapka of Rhythms Netconnections, Ellen Hancock of Exodus Communications, Peter Cartwright of Calpine, John Schofield of Advanced Fibre Communications, Robert

Knowling of Covad Communications Group; Coppy Holzman of Webvan (never mind Gary Winnick, founder of Global Crossing, and assorted members of the Enron brain trust).

Ferdinand Pecora harnessed financial revulsion to a political agenda. The revulsion was a long time coming. The stock market peaked in September 1929 and bottomed in July 1932, from top to bottom losing 88% of its value. There had been a depression, a bank holiday and a renunciation of the monetary standard.

So far from revulsion is the American public at this writing that CNBC is still broadcasting. The stock market is discounting a strong earnings recovery, the Eurodollar futures market is discounting an imminent reversal in the Fed's ultra-easy monetary policy and the Treasury inflation-protected securities market is discounting a decade or more of negligible price inflation. And when the new director of the corporate finance division of the SEC recently held his first staff meeting, he issued no ultimatum but instead sought to console. Don't blame yourselves for failing to detect Enron's lapses, Alan Beller told his 331-member team, "when hundreds of experts with much more information than the SEC has, including analysts, were unable to detect them."

No depression, bank holiday or renunciation of the monetary standard is likely in 2002 (there is no monetary standard, except for the freedom to choose one's own stores of value). Nonetheless, Americans seem to be fed up. Think how much market capitalization and foreign-exchange value is supported by confidence. Now imagine that confidence eroding. It should erode. It was a wild and crazy boom.

Mr. Market's Shiner

May 24, 2002

Capitalism began a major uptrend in the Carter term, when people were least expecting it. And it has begun a major downtrend in the administration of George W. Bush, again taking the country by surprise.

For most of the past quarter-century in the United States, certain propositions were held to be self-evident. For instance: Markets are the fairest and most efficient means of allocating scarce resources; government intervention is usually counterproductive; free trade and the international division of labor are essential to world prosperity; and, more controversially, a reduction of marginal tax rates is equivalent to a release of social energy. Each tenet has lately come in for reappraisal, especially the belief that markets are fair and efficient. The financial consequences of this ideological reversal are unlikely to be bullish for dollar-denominated stocks and bonds.

We write in an impartial, scientific spirit. A Grover Cleveland Democrat who favors free markets and traditional business attire, your editor votes the straight capitalist ticket, when available. However, it's an investor's bounden duty to take the world as it is, not as it should be or could be. In the world in which we live, the politicians are gaining on the capitalists.

Our headline-hogging captains of industry—Messrs. Rigas, Kozlowski, Winnick, Ebbers, Lay, Skilling, Nacchio, etc.—are the kind of capitalists the Soviet propagandists would have invented if they did not exist in the flesh. Sadly for the Reds, the Soviet state perished before the great American boom ended. It's at the end of such cycles that full-blooded corporate excess usually comes to light. A quarter-century of blooming prosperity breaks down the defenses of skepticism. It facilitates corner-cutting, tape-painting, number-fudging and sheep-shearing. It inculcates the notion that the value-enhancing head of a public corporation can be underpaid at the annual rate of $100 million a year.

All things are cyclical, not least the political standing of the marketplace in a social democracy. Throughout the administrations of Ronald Reagan, George H. W. Bush and Bill Clinton, the marketplace made higher highs and higher lows. Now, we think, it has broken support and begun a move to the downside. Poised for a cyclical rebound are recrimination, reflation and reform. What shape the three R's might assume in the millennial post-bubble environment is the question under examination.

The form of capitalism that found bipartisan favor in the 1980s and 1990s was not Ayn Rand's "unknown ideal." Republicans and Democrats found nothing objectionable in a subsidy-level federal funds rate, or in government interventions to relieve the suffering of speculators trapped in the Mexican peso (1994) or in Long-Term Capital Management (1998). All cheered rising stock prices. Few noticed when the interventions became habit-forming. Tacitly committing itself to preserving and protecting U.S. financial markets, the Federal Reserve created more credit than it would otherwise have had to do. So today, in a business setting that is no longer commonly described as recessionary, the Bank of Alan Greenspan continues to define a 1.75% funds rate as "neutral."

Possibly, the chairman believes he has no choice; the stock market, richly valued, requires liquidity in lieu of earnings growth. In the meantime, federal outlays are soaring, a trade war is brewing, credit quality is fraying and the dirty linen of Corporate America is showing. Is it so far-fetched to think that America's foreign creditors will wake up one morning and decide they own more than enough dollars? If not, the 1990s' era story line of American finance is coming in for substantial revision.

In his just-published book, *Wealth and Democracy*, Kevin Phillips traces the recurrent migration of democratic societies between populism and the "money power." To read him, the author would not vote for Cleveland even if that 19th-century, gold-standard president were still alive and running for office. Phillips condemns the "financialization" of America and the subordination of economic policy to speculation. Of the end result of the 1990s, he writes, "The Fed and the Treasury in a sense become joint, proactive managers of the multi-trillion-dollar 'USA Fund.' Market economics might be the claim, but globalized U.S. government economic management was the game." He predicts a revolt against a plutocracy that has bought the government for the convenience of having it on call to reduce tax rates and raise P/E multiples. Come the inevitable reaction, Phillips suggests, the gap between rich and poor will close in a way the rich will regret: the poor will receive more of what the rich used to have.

The author of *The Politics of Rich and Poor* (1990) and *Arrogant Capital* (1994), Phillips is vague on the timing of this coming upheaval; he has anticipated a revolt against "market utopianism" before. Common sense suggests that the degree of popular resentment should be proportional to the electorate's sense of loss. However, according to the front page of Tuesday's *New York Times*, the electorate is bullish. Though it has lost jobs, stock market wealth and a sense of the unique physical security of the United States, it is undaunted. Reports the *Times*:

> In place of the economic malaise that generally plagued the public in the 1970s and from the late 1980s through the early 1990s, polls show that by wide margins Americans now say that the coming years will be prosperous and that today's children will live better than their parents.

American capitalists admonish never to be bearish on America. Nor are we. America is a great country at 25 times "core" earnings on the S&P 500, as calculated by none other than S&P (in the rigorous new definition of earnings the ratings agency disclosed last week). It has been, and will be once more, a great country at much lower valuations. As capitalism could make a cyclical bottom about the time equities were pronounced dead, so—as we believe—it can make a cyclical top in the aftermath of a generation-long equity cult.

The "public mood" is a somewhat ethereal question, but the consequences of a change in mood are as tangible as a P&L. We have been watching four bellwether financial dramas, i.e., the apparent political rehabilitation of the governor of California; a rare work stoppage at Hershey Foods; the looming battle over repeal of the inheritance tax; and the rechartering of Stanley Works, the Connecticut tool company, in the tax paradise of Bermuda.

Only last summer, Gov. Gray Davis seemed a beaten man for his signal misreading of California's partially deregulated energy market. However, following sensational disclosures of the manipulation of that very market, Davis seems to have gained a new lease on life. When he called last week for the jailing of the "robber barons" of the Enron executive suite, the governor conjured up a sight both old and new. Baiting the rich is as old as envy, but it long ago went missing from mainstream Democratic politics. Under the capital gains-producing partnership of Bill Clinton and Robert Rubin, the "bloated bondholder" of yesteryear was transformed into the "Millionaire Next Door." Anybody with a 401(k) account could get rich. Davis is running for reelection against Republican Bill Simon Jr., son of the former Salomon Brothers partner, Treasury secretary and LBO pioneer. If the idea of capitalism has truly entered a bear market, Davis ought to defeat Simon, a capitalist. He should win despite the seemingly self-destructive pledge he has made to raise taxes to close the state's big budget deficit. Burdensome tax rates are an essential part of a post-bubble zeitgeist.

Another sign of the times (as we understand the times) is a month-old strike by 2,700 unionized workers against Hershey Foods. Superficially at issue is a demand that the employees bear a bigger share of health costs. Substantively at issue is labor's resentment against an imported CEO who would shift a portion of the rising cost of health care to the workers in order to boost the profitability at an already profitable corporation. "Milton Hershey worried about the workers," the *New York Times* quoted machine operator Yvonne McNaughton as saying about the paternalistic corporate founder. "The new guy here is nothing but corporate greed."

McNaughton refers to Richard H. Lenny, brought in 14 months ago to run the nation's top candy company, which had never before had an outsider at the helm. According to the paper, "Workers . . .

complain that Mr. Lenny himself made $4.7 million last year, not including stock options that could someday be worth more than $10 million." The article quoted an employee's idea that Lenny should write a personal check for the incremental health-care expense; it was suggested that $1 million would do the trick. Closing the story was a quote by Stephen P. Schappe, a professor at the Pennsylvania State University School of Business at Harrisburg. The CEO "underestimated the resolve of the workers," said Schappe. "The workers have lost more money from the strike than they would lose from these [proposed] changes. That shows they're on strike more for principle than for money." It's the first strike at Hershey in 22 years.

The lament of the Hershey machine operator recalls a chilling remark attributed earlier this year by *The Wall Street Journal* to Amy Ghazle, a 30-year-old former project manager at Global Crossing: "Here these people who are making millions and millions of dollars do well and they come and make middle class and hard-working people suffer so."

It can't be said of William Gates Sr., whose son has done so well in life, that he wants to do the middle class dirt. On the contrary, he has devoted himself to good works, including a controversial stance over the federal inheritance tax. He wants it retained. Last year, the elder Gates—in alliance with Warren Buffett, George Soros and other capitalists not always in accord with the editorial policy of *The Wall Street Journal*—led an unsuccessful fight to prevent the tax's phaseout. They lost, but Gates is spoiling for a rematch. As the tax cuts engineered by George Bush last year are slated to expire in 2010, Congress must act to preserve them. The Senate is expected to take up legislation next month.

"I find it astounding that we have come to this point in this country," Gates told the *Financial Times* the other day. "It seems a huge anomaly to me that we are talking about the need to increase the federal debt limit, we are uncertain about how to finance the war on terrorism, nobody has quite figured out how airport security will be paid for and in the midst of this very severe set of critical demands on the national treasury, we are talking about permanently repealing a very significant tax." Is America in the mood to soak the rich, even allowing that some of the rich want to be soaked? A vote to reinstate the tax would fortify the case that the idea of capitalism has reached a cyclical peak.

Upcoming shareholder votes over proposed corporate recharterings are similarly fraught with political and ideological meaning. The Stanley Works CEO, John M. Trani, is a former GE executive who went to New Britain, Conn., with the goal of creating value for the Stanley stockholders, period. To advance the owners' interests, he proposed a renunciation of U.S. corporate citizenship. The matter was put to a vote on May 9. The motion passed—yet, owing to botched shareholder communications and the intervention of the Connecticut attorney general, the vote was canceled. What, in Florida politics, is called a "revote" is pending.

"When companies are fleeing the U.S. tax code to stay competitive abroad," *The Wall Street Journal* editorial page opined recently,

*"You mean that Daddy liked Enron
just because everybody else did?"*

"there's something wrong with the tax code, not with the companies." "All those guys walking around with missing fingers and hunchbacks made Stanley," the mayor of New Britain, Lucian J. Pawlak, told the *New York Times*, "but Trani doesn't want to hear that." The revote will tell.

As deceit in the deregulated energy markets has presented Gray Davis with a political club, so widespread abuse of the rules of corporate governance has made a gift to Davis's ideological helpmeets in the other 49 states. The top four business and finance stories in the page-one news summary of Monday's *Wall Street Journal* concerned alleged corporate law-breaking. It will be said by some that this is the kind of news that makes stock market bottoms. It will be said right back again that stock market bottoms are usually not made at nosebleed valuations. We endorse the latter argument. And we therefore view the black eye worn by Mr. Market as a leading indicator of social and political change.

It's not impossible that a cyclical bull market in capitalism would end during a Republican administration. It started in a Democratic one. In 1978, under cover of high inflation, national "malaise" and a bear market in equities, a little-known Wisconsin congressman pushed through a bill to slash the tax rate on capital gains to 28% from 49%. Michael Blumenthal, the Treasury secretary under Jimmy Carter, disparaged Rep. William Steiger's supply-side legislation as the "Millionaires' Relief Act." The stock market, at first, seemed almost oblivious to it (just as the bond market did to the appointment, in August 1979, of Paul A. Volcker to the chairmanship of the Federal Reserve Board). Investors caught on later.

Most of the credit for the prosperity of the 1980s rightfully belongs to the Reagan administration. However, if Ronald Reagan caused the sun to rise in what the GOP described as "morning in America," the first rosy glimmers in the eastern sky belonged to Jimmy Carter.

Today, under cover of low inflation, global hegemony and booming "productivity growth," bearish political events are unfolding.

Government outlays are soaring, protectionism is menacing and the excesses of the bubble years are casting long ideological shadows. Mr. Market's embarrassment would not matter so much except that his image has almost supplanted that of Uncle Sam as the American figurehead. Trusting in American markets and American standards of disclosure and accounting, foreigners have willingly exchanged their merchandise for our securities. Recent developments foretell a change in the terms of trade in favor of the foreigners.

Some of these developments are mainly symbolic, as in the financial crisis of Edison Schools. Edison, the No.1 private operator of public schools, set out to teach a lesson to the nation's educational bureaucracy. Teach it has, but not the lesson it set out to do. It has taught by example that the best time to promote a loss-making company is near the peak of a market bubble. It has similarly taught that a company should never pick a fight with the Securities and Exchange Commission unless it is innocent, or at least sure it can win. (Edison last week settled charges leveled by the SEC, including that "a substantial portion of its reported revenues consist of payments that never reach Edison.") What it has not taught is that private enterprise can lick even such a tomato can as the public school establishment. It's as if the New York Yankees had lost a multiyear series to the Staten Island Yankees.

In *Wealth and Democracy*, Phillips contends that populism and plutocracy are forever contending. In effect, down through history, it's been Jack Welch vs. Erin Brockovich. When the money power is riding high, Phillips goes on, it seems as if it were irresistible. However, as human affairs are cyclical, the rich periodically are made to become a little less rich. "Few upper-class Britons of 1906 would have dreamt that within two decades a Socialist prime minister would head a party of labor unions, committed to a considerable program of income and wealth redistribution," he writes. By the same token, few American creditors, watching the 1932 election returns, anticipated that the victor would adopt a program of state planning, income redistribution and monetary experimentation. Yet that is what FDR did.

World War I transformed Britain's politics as the Great Depression did America's. Optimists, we see nothing on the horizon even remotely comparable to those cataclysms. In the absence of social or military catastrophe, what form might a bear market in capitalism take?

We anticipate more of what the 1990s were short of, including federal budget difficulties, conflicts over trade and tariffs, a comeuppance for the dollar, rising price inflation, a steepening of the yield curve and falling P/E multiples. A legacy of the serial interventions of the 1990s is that the Federal Reserve will probably continue to intervene. It will pin the funds rate lower than would otherwise be necessary in order to try to sustain the fancy equity valuations in place. It will create enough credit to nurse the post-bubble economy back to health. So doing, it seems to us, it must face the heightened risk of a chain of events involving a rising inflation rate and a weakened dollar exchange rate.

According to *The Wall Street Journal*, domestic non-military spending is set to rise by 15% this congressional session, "which means President Bush will have presided over the largest two-year spending boost since the Great Society." The star at the top of the fiscal Christmas tree is the new $190 billion farm bill, a subsidy that the 18-member Cairns Group of food-producing countries, employing diplomatic language, last week called "immoral."

The sole remaining superpower has come in for even sharper criticism over President Bush's decision to slap punitive tariffs on imported steel. Japan, Norway and the European Union have notified the World Trade Organization of plans to retaliate; the World Bank, the IMF and the WTO have likewise protested. Japan's opposition is especially noteworthy. Never before has it retaliated against a U.S. trade measure, the *Journal* observes.

For many years, the U.S. merchandise trade deficit was widely discounted as an accounting convention. Treasury Secretary O'Neill continues to regard it as meaningless. We will meet the secretary halfway. We will concede that the deficit is "meaningless" for as long as it can be advantageously financed. However, there is growing evidence that foreign creditors are restive. Possibly, they have become wary of a capital market in which the investment-grade debt of AT&T can fall (as it did on May 1) by eight points intraday, before recovering. Perhaps, for whatever conceivable reason, they have come to trust the integrity of audited U.S. financials a little less. Or maybe, the contingent of overseas *Grant's* readers judges the stock market rich.

Americans, as noted, seem less concerned with these problems. In 1975, only 10 million Americans participated in direct-contribution pension plans, according to John Bogle, founder and former chairman of the Vanguard Group. Today, there are 60 million. No doubt, many of these 401(k) investors have made heavy weather of it. Bogle told the New York Society of Security Analysts on Valentine's Day that, "in a fairly valued stock market when the decade began, the average participant had . . . 70% in fixed-income investments and 30% in equities. But in the highly valued market as 2001 began, the ratio averaged 19% in fixed-income and 81% in equities. Not only has risk risen, but even more risky options are being introduced. Funds with hot past performances are demanded by many plan sponsors, and a self-directed brokerage-account option is the newest gimmick. Just imagine the likelihood of success of an employee who engages in day-trading to build a comfortable retirement nest egg!"

Imagine millions of these plan participants pulling the curtains behind them in the voting booth next fall. Imagine the voters weighing a choice between candidates we will call the "capitalists" and the "reformers." Now imagine the battered investors yanking the capitalist lever. It is easy enough to do assuming that the stock market is poised for recovery. However, if lower lows are in the offing, the reformers may show to advantage. As always, "the rich" should closely read the papers.

Houses of Ill Repute

May 9, 2003

Even hardened sinners blushed for Wall Street following news that five financial institutions had paid others to publish research reports on stocks of companies the five had underwritten during the great bull market. According to Gretchen Morgenson, writing in the Sunday *New York Times*, Morgan Stanley was the most openhanded of the perpetrators, passing around $2.7 million in "research guarantees" to some two dozen "competing" firms.

The revelations shattered myths and dislodged perceptions concerning the good old businesses of stock brokerage, investment banking and investment research. It was always true, we believe, that some Wall Street firms would do anything for money. However, as we also believe, it was equally true that some Wall Street firms would not do anything for money. What seems to have changed is that very nearly all Wall Street firms will do anything for money—or would do anything, when the money was big enough and the coast was clear.

Much has been said about these sorry facts, but no one has answered an analytical question: How should an investor think about these businesses now? They are not exactly investment businesses, as we knew investment businesses. But they aren't exactly not investment businesses, either. Then what are they? Just in time, the Australian IPO market has provided a benchmark for comparison. Daily Planet Ltd. is a Melbourne brothel. It went public on May 1 in what a spokesman for the stock exchange in Sydney described as "among the best first-day performers on the exchange since at least the tech-stock boom."

If the officers, directors and employees of the five research transgressors bridle at being compared to the Daily Planet, imagine how the officers, directors and employees of the Daily Planet feel about being compared to Wall Street.

The Peoples' Wrath—Delayed

March 22, 2008

"We are going to take it out of the hides of Wall Street," William Poole, president of the Federal Reserve Bank of St. Louis, said into an open microphone at a monetary conference in St. Louis on October 19. Just who "we" might be Poole didn't say, but he could have spoken for the 2008 presidential contenders. The political chill of this election season is enough to drive Steven A. Cohen himself into the safe harbor of tax-exempt municipal bonds.

"Wall Street," charged the president of Notre Dame University, the Rev. John Cavanaugh, almost a century ago, "is our national bad example simply because it is so successful." Watching Bernard M. Baruch or E.H. Harriman get rich, ordinary Americans caught "the contagion of the money craze" and were never heard from again.

The Street is hard enough to love in a bull market. In a bear market, it virtually wears a "kick me" sign. Following the "biggest failure of ratings and risk management ever," as the analysts at UBS justly characterize the post-millennial mortgage scandal, and in the wake of the first recorded year-over-year decline in the median American house price, the bankers and the brokers would seem to have put themselves, and the markets in which they operate, in the way of popular vengeance.

Grover Cleveland is the one and only candidate that *Grant's* has ever endorsed for president, and we support him again in 2008. It's true he's unavailable, having already served two full terms in the White House (1884–88, 1892–96) and being dead besides. But he has the compensating virtue of a proven record in support of a sound dollar, which, in his day, was a dollar collateralized by gold. Paper money and credit are in crisis together today, and Cleveland's ghost is the candidate for us.

We keep waiting for someone to lower the boom on Wall Street, that metaphor for wealth and financial enterprise. Somebody will, but, as yet, nobody has. The candidates—all of them— have taken their oblique swipes at "greed" and at the tax system (for one failing or another), but none has made anything like full use of the incriminating material the titans of finance have handed over to them. Is it not remarkable, a politician of no special gifts might demand of a national television audience, that Robert Rubin, the former Goldman Sachs partner and Treasury Secretary and the ever-so-richly compensated ex-chairman of the executive committee of Citigroup, has admitted to *Fortune* magazine that, until the structured-finance crisis burst out into the open, he had "no familiarity at all with CDOs"? And is it not still more remarkable that Rubin is now the Citigroup chairman of the board?

Huey Long must be gnashing his teeth on that heavenly cloud reserved for demagogues. "We have a home-loan problem because we have too many houses," said Long in his 1934 speech, "Every Man a King," "and yet nobody can buy them and live in them." The excess of debt and shortage of money he blamed on the bloated bondholders. "[T]heir pleasure," he said of Morgan and the Astors and the rest, "consists in the starvation of the masses, and in their possessing things they cannot use, and their children cannot use, but who bask in the splendor of sunlight and wealth, casting darkness and despair and impressing it on everyone else." John D. Rockefeller, said Long on another occasion, was like the fat guy who ruins a good barbeque by taking too much.

Andrew Jackson, too, must be wondering what happened to the fine art of banker baiting. In his famous veto of an 1832 act to renew the charter of the Bank of the United States, a forerunner of the Federal Reserve, Old Hickory seemed to anticipate the objections that some of us have raised against the Greenspan put and the low and lower Bernanke funds rate, which is bad for the savers but good—in theory, at least—for the speculative interests.

"It is to be regretted that the rich and the powerful too often bend the acts of government to their selfish purposes," Jackson wrote. "Distinctions in society will always exist under every just government. Equality of talents, of education, or of wealth cannot be produced by human institutions. In the full enjoyment of the gifts of Heaven and the fruits of superior industry, economy and virtue, every man is equally entitled to protection by law; but when the laws undertake to add to these natural and just advantages artificial distinctions, to grant titles, gratuities and exclusive privileges, to make the rich richer and the potent more powerful, the humble members of society—the farmers, mechanics and laborers—who have neither the time nor the means of securing like favors to themselves, have a right to complain of the injustice of their government. There are no necessary evils in government. Its evils exist only in its abuses."

To listen to Barack Obama lash Wall Street with his supposed silver tongue, you wouldn't even know he was mad. "That's why we need a president who will listen to Main Street, not just to Wall Street, a president who will stand with workers not just when it's easy, but when it's hard," he forgettably said the other day in Madison, Wis. With Mary Elizabeth Lease, a populist in the age of Cleveland, the audience didn't have to guess. "We want money, land and transportation," she harangued them. "We want the abolition of the National Banks, and we want the power to make loans direct from the government. We want the accursed foreclosure system wiped out. . . . We will stand by our homes and stay by our firesides by force if necessary, and we will not pay our debts to the loan-shark companies until the Government pays its debts to us. The people are at bay; let the bloodhounds of money who have dogged us this far beware."

The Wall Street Journal characterized Obama's remarks as part of an escalation of the Democratic candidates' "antitrade, anticorporate rhetoric." By the standards of populist eras past, however, the politicians have hardly taken off their coats. Obama and Hillary Clinton have spoken as if their speechwriters, too, had been out on strike.

It's a sad day for American populism when the heaviest punch of the primary-election season is landed by the president of a regional Federal Reserve bank and when the second heaviest, arguably, belongs to a former Republican governor of Arkansas. "I'm not against the hedge-fund manager," Mike Huckabee was quoted as saying, or, rather, insincerely protesting, by the *Washington Post* at the end of the year (this in the context of Huckabee contrasting the poor working stiff with the rich hedge-fund guy). Not even John Edwards, when he was in the race, began to match the rage of the ancient populist diatribes. Then, again, Mrs. Lease did no paid consulting for the Morgan bank (the Fortress Investment Group not then being in business to engage her services).

Possibly, the candidates are pulling their punches because "Wall Street," in this age of defined-contribution plans, is no distant citadel of privilege but rather the place where everyman invests. We doubt it, however—everyman thought he was invest-

"Who are you calling an analyst?"

ing in his house—just as we doubt that the candidates' forbearance is owing to some sophisticated 21st-century understanding about the true causes of booms and busts and of contagious financial malfeasance. Nor do we accept that the voters, knowing how many people brought on their own financial pain by cheating on their no-doc mortgage applications, are unreceptive to appeals for populist vengeance because they themselves feel guilty. Rather, we believe, the principal reason the candidates have scored so few telling hits against Wall Street so far in this election season is because they're still warming up. Besides, the voters are not so receptive to populist agitation as they would be if the unemployment rate were climbing.

Charles E. Mitchell, chairman of the National City Bank (from which Citigroup evolved), became the leading scapegoat for Wall Street's sins, real and trumped up, during America's Great Depression. But his martyrdom came late. The stock market crashed in the fall of 1929. The averages hit bottom in the summer of 1932. Mitchell was forced to resign from the bank in February 1933, only a month before Franklin D. Roosevelt would declare, in his first inaugural, that the money changers had fled the temple.

"The title of banker, formerly regarded as a mark of esteem in the United States, is almost a mark of opprobrium," Clifford Reeves wrote in H.L. Mencken's *American Mercury* magazine in September 1932. "There seems some danger, in fact, that in forthcoming editions of the dictionary it may be necessary to define the word as a peculiar American colloquialism, synonymous with rascal . . . and we may even see the day when to be called a son-of-a-banker will be regarded as justifiable ground for the commission of assault and mayhem."

It would hardly take Depression-era levels of privation to effect a similar transformation of American attitudes today. In 1932, Roosevelt ran on a platform of fiscal and monetary orthodoxy; the tax and regulatory policies he immediately proceeded to implement sprang not from some grand, pre-inaugural design, but rather from an impulse to "do something" in the face of a coast-to-coast bank run. This publication supports a program of free and unhindered price discovery in the financial markets. We favor non-intrusive and constitutionally limited government. We like our dollars hard, our taxes low and our foreign enemies on the run. We note, however, that these preferences, taken together, are shared by none of the mainstream candidates. The presumptive Republican nominee, John McCain, was recently quoted by *The Wall Street Journal* as saying that "unfettered capitalism is not something that I support," and that, "from time to time throughout our history, there are excesses and we [had] to fix them as quickly as possible. . .we have to take measures to make sure they never happen again." It figures. McCain was a big Greenspan fan.

So our politicians are as data-dependent as our central bank. Public policy is a hostage to the news. The grimmer the headlines, the more activist the government. As it is—in an economy that is not only not in depression but which may or may not even be in recession—the incumbent Republicans are implementing a mortgage forbearance scheme that, in its principles, is as radical as anything that sprang from the New Deal. And all this has happened without a meaningful ratcheting up in the jobless rate.

Let the labor market take a turn for the worse, and one could imagine the autumn debates between the Republican and Democratic presidential nominees featuring a broadly shared agreement over the necessity of re-regulating the banking system ("Bring back Glass-Steagall!") and of restoring the "fairness" to free trade ("Down with Nafta!"). Cleveland would have no part of such a consensus, and neither would Ron Paul or New York City Mayor Michael Bloomberg, who recently condemned the Bush administration's "economic stimulus" plan as tantamount to buying a drink for a drunk. But none of those three worthies is likely to be on the 2008 national ticket.

At this writing, 10-year, double-A-rated municipal bonds trade at a yield of 3.55%, only a slight discount to the taxable 10-year Treasury note (taxable, that is, at the federal level, though not by the states). At 35%, the top federal tax rate, a 3.55% return is equivalent to a taxable yield of 5.5%. But the top federal rate is unlikely to go down and may very well go up. Both leading Democrats want to raise taxes on the kinds of people who are wealthy enough to need tax exemption. Only twice before in the past 20 years have tax-exempt yields traded virtually on top of the Treasury curve (those occasions were the fall of 1998 and the spring of 2003).

The municipal market is the dullest backwater in capitalism. But the troubles of the bond insurers and the rhetoric of the politicians are pushing it out into the limelight. In a time when much of the Treasury yield curve is quoted at yields below the measured rise in the cost of living, every bond is deservedly under suspicion. Creditworthy tax-exempts may just be the least-bad bonds available.

Chapter Eight

Federalized Interest Rates

Monetary Regime Change

September 13, 2002

O N AUGUST 30, at the annual monetary jamboree of the
Kansas City Federal Reserve Bank in Jackson Hole,
Wyo., Alan Greenspan washed his hands of responsibility for the bubble he said he could not have pricked even if he
had noticed it floating above his desk on a string. "The struggle to
understand developments in the economy and financial markets
since the mid-1990s has been particularly challenging for monetary policy makers," declared the Maestro. "We were confronted
with forces that none of us had personally experienced. Aside from
the then recent experience of Japan, only history books and musty
archives gave us clues to the appropriate stance for policy."

The chairman's Jackson Hole speech has been, will be and should be
deplored as the worst kind of self-exculpating revisionism. However, it

was a letter to the editor in Sunday's *New York Times* that hit the critical nail on the head.

"Mr. Greenspan is a human being," writes Victor A. Altshul, of New Haven, Conn., "subject to the same frailties as anyone else. Why should we expect him to be exempt from the universal tendency to rationalize one's errors and to distort the record to protect one's self-esteem? Shouldn't we instead be looking at our own complicity in investing so much power in one man?"

CEOs are celebrated not for who they are but for what they do. Until he presided over the great bull market, Greenspan did not give many outward signs of genius. But the higher stock prices went, the smarter he seemed to become. By late in the 1990s, he was heralded as a miracle worker. Indisputably, he was the only federal employee whose reputation for financial sagacity rivaled that of Jack Welch. Miracles being few and far between these past two years, Greenspan's reputation has begun to be marked down, if only by eighths and quarters. Welch's, last week, entered what looked like a secular bear market.

Following is a speculation on the outlines of a post-Greenspan monetary system. It is supported by some of the historical works that the chairman can read in the well-deserved retirement he should have taken starting in about 1996. We say "post-Greenspan" because, we believe, the Jackson Hole speech will raise the odds against his reappointment (his current term expires in 2004), speed the day of his departure and reduce his policy-making influence for as long as he remains in office. It would be no small thing if the chairman's myriad admirers decided that their idol had lost his touch. Although the Federal Reserve System employs 485 Ph.D. economists, only one is a living symbol of the dynamic U.S. economy. And now this one man says that he didn't know about the stock-market bubble, couldn't have known and, even if he had known, wouldn't have been able to make a move against it. It isn't a great advertisement for a monetary dictatorship.

Monetary policy under Greenspan consists of fixing an optimal funds rate. In better times, Greenspan's mysterious rate-setting

"Next time, I'm joinin' the <u>Federal</u> Reserve."

method was deemed as great an American secret as the Coca-Cola formula. As recently as Aug. 2, 2001, David Wessel of *The Wall Street Journal* entered a page-one plea that the chairman share his secret lest the country suffer irreparable harm when nature finally called him to rest. To enforce this most perfect interest rate, the Fed creates the needed volume of credit. It "prints" money, as every trainee knows, by acquiring earning assets, mainly Treasury securities; it buys them with dollars that it creates for the very purpose.

Grant's monitors the growth of these assets to see how many dollars it takes to set and maintain the desired rate. To set an artificially low rate, the Fed pumps money into the market. To impose an artificially high rate, it withholds money from the market. (A rate that is neither artificially low nor artificially high is the rate that would balance the demand for savings with the supply of savings without central bank intervention.) The current, 1¾% funds rate has been maintained by prodigies of credit creation. As recently as July 17, growth in Fed credit was running on the order of 11.27%, measured year-over-year. Today, it's clocked at just 9.28%. It's noteworthy that the Fed is able to continue to impose a generationally low funds rate without deploying more and more credit (indeed, by deploying less). If the slower growth in credit supply reflects a faltering growth in credit demand, it may presage still lower money-market rates.

Only one of the troubles with bubbles is that, after they pop, ultra-low interest rates and extraordinary rates of credit expansion lose their stimulative potency. The rate of creation of new yen by the Bank of Japan stands at 26.1%, year-over-year, but this outpouring has yielded no appreciable reflationary results. It interests relatively few investors that the central bank of the world's second-largest economy is engaged in a monetary expansion of a scale suitable to one of the minor United Nations members. It would interest a great many more if the Fed were forced into the same exigencies. No one can know whether it will be or won't be. However, in January, the Federal Open Market Committee did discuss "unconventional policy measures" to deploy if "the economy were to deteriorate substantially in a period when nominal short-term interest rates were already at very low levels," according to the minutes of a meeting held on January 25–26.

The Founding Fathers, well remembering King George III, held the exercise of arbitrary authority in abhorrence. Their contemporary, stock-minded political descendants, however, have gladly tolerated the kind of arbitrary authority exercised by the Fed chairman. Willingly did this government of the people, by the people and for the people cede monetary power virtually to a committee of one. However, the more the economy labors and the lower stock prices fall, the worse this remarkable act of delegation will come to appear. The bear market will bring the question posed by letter-writer Altshul—why was so much power given to one man?—into the political mainstream.

A survey of the dead authors not much read at the Federal Reserve supports an observation familiar to the readers of *Grant's*. This observation is that monetary systems are impermanent—one has succeeded another at intervals since the late 19th century. To their originators, each method of monetary organization was fit for the ages. But none lasted much longer than a generation. The system in place since 1971 is the worldwide paper-dollar system. In part, it's an "information standard," to borrow from retired Citibanker Walter Wriston, with interest rates and exchange rates mainly set by the market. But the federal funds rate, anchor rate of the dollar-denominated yield curve, is a government-issue rate, and the latent power to create massive amounts of credit (as at year-end 1999 and in September 2001) is a governmental power. As much as it might be an information standard, the current dollar system is just as much, or even more, a faith-in-government standard.

It wasn't faith in an impersonal government, or in the rules laid down by government, that brought CNBC into American homes and taverns in the late 1990s. Rather, it was faith in the capacities of government masterminds. At the peak of their renown, Alan Greenspan and Robert Rubin seemed to work with tomorrow's edition of *The Wall Street Journal* always open before them. And now, instead of Rubin at Treasury, there is Paul O'Neill, a man who seems not to have read yesterday's paper. And there is Greenspan, who in Jackson Hole revealed a faulty memory and a guilty conscience.

The text of his speech is available on the Federal Reserve Board's Web site (http://federalreserve.gov/boarddocs/speeches/2002/) and it deserves a careful reading—or, rather, repeated careful readings, as the student will hardly believe it the first time through. Here is the history of the 1990s according to Greenspan, a decade in which "greater economic stability" fostered risk taking, and in which earnings prospects improved as the pace of innovation accelerated. Responding to these stimuli, stock prices rose. "The associated decline in the cost of equity capital spurred a pronounced rise in capital investment and productivity growth that broadened impressively in the latter years of the 1990s," the Jackson Hole audience heard him say. "Stock prices rose further, responding to the growing optimism about greater stability, strengthening investment, and faster productivity growth." Regrettably, they rose too far, but there was no way, except in retrospect, to have known that. Indeed, even the March 2000 highs might not have been too high "if all of the drop in equity premiums had resulted from a permanent reduction in cyclical volatility. . . ." And, of course, "productivity growth" was a gift almost beyond measure.

Greenspan disputed that a rise in margin requirements would have deflated the bloated market, forgetting that he himself had acknowledged the need to address the "stock market bubble problem" in the Sept. 24, 1996, meeting of the FOMC: "I guarantee you that if you want to get rid of the bubble, whatever it is, that will do it," the transcript of the meeting quotes him as saying (http://federalreserve.gov/fomc/#calendars). "My concern is that I am not sure what else it will do."

Greenspan's shortcomings as a memoirist in his Jackson Hole address are matched by his failings as an economic theorist. He perpetuates popular nostrums about productivity growth, "price stability" and interest-rate policy. For example, he offers no insight into the unintended consequences of suppressing market interest rates. He implies (though it is possible to infer from Bob Woodward's *Maestro* that he doesn't really believe it) that gains in productivity are registered automatically in profits, rather than in wages or prices, or in a combination of the three. He fails to mention that "price stability" can, and on many occasions in the past has, led to bull stock markets that elicited enough redundant capital investment to distort the economy in which they spread their joy. And he declines to address the risk that the very prestige of a popular central banker tends to cause investors to forget themselves and push up asset prices to the heights that all come to regret. The propensity to regret is especially keen if the prestigious central banker in question blesses the bubble both in word and deed.

A month before the Jackson Hole festivities, the BIS published a working paper by Claudio Borio and Philip Lowe that anticipated the subjects Greenspan discussed on August 30. The BIS, of course, is the Bank for International Settlements, the central bankers' central bank, and an unlikely source of criticism of the only central banker up for knighthood this fall. Yet the BIS authors come down hard on the side of doing what Greenspan didn't do, incidentally anticipating (and refuting) the reasons Greenspan presents for not doing it. The more successful a central bank in smiting the conventional kind of inflation, write Borio and Lowe, the greater the risk of an outbreak of the unconventional kind (i.e., a bubble). "Failure to respond to these imbalances," the two contend, "either using monetary policy or another policy instrument, may ultimately increase the risk of both financial instability and subsequently deflation (during the period in which the imbalances are unwound)."

Not once in his Jackson Hole recitation did Greenspan concede that his repeated interventions to prolong the up cycle had misdirected capital and hurt the owners of it (not to mention the people who work for the owners of it and the children of all the foregoing). The BIS authors clinically refer to the risks presented by "asymmetric" policies, i.e., cutting rates to rescue the market but never raising them to slow it down. It will speed the close of the Greenspan era when the public reflects on how lopsided was this asymmetry. Grant the chairman, for argument's sake, the prudence of intervening in the wake of the Long-Term Capital Management explosion in October 1998. Give him the benefit of the doubt about the stupendous infusion of credit with which the Fed prepared the nation to meet the crisis of the computer clocks at year-end 1999. And allow him the justice of the argument that in a deregulated world, the manipulation of margin requirements is a gesture certain to fail. Grant every point, and still it is not possible to explain away the fact that Greenspan sounded more like a broker than a central banker in his speeches and congressional testimony in the mid- and late 1990s. He was a greater seducer than any big-money analyst, in fact, because the public could see that he spoke from the heart. He wasn't in the bonus pool.

A week or so after the Jackson Hole speech found Stephen Cecchetti on the op-ed page of the *Financial Times* with a most becoming mea culpa. Cecchetti, currently professor of economics at Ohio State University, was director of research at the Federal Reserve Bank of New York in Wall Street's all-you-can-eat years, 1997–99. He reviews the damage inflicted by the bubble, from underfunded pension funds to distorted GDP statistics to the slight over-ordering of telecommunications equipment and computers. "Add all of this together," writes Cecchetti, "and the cost is several percent of U.S. GDP and still counting. When faced with the potential for output losses of this size, central bankers usually work fast to try to minimize the damage. So why, when faced with strong evidence of a bubble, do they react so differently, claiming that there is nothing they can do? The response is surprising." Having acknowledged that a move to withdraw the punch bowl was in order, the economist admirably closes, "I cannot claim this would have worked and did not push for it at the time—but I certainly should have."

The BIS essay almost diffidently makes the case for a "paradigm shift" in central banking. It urges an acceptance of the fact that asset inflation is a source of economic distortion, therefore a problem suitable for central bankers. Years ago in the pages of *Grant's*, colleague Gert von der Linde recalled Greenspan's own very neat definition of inflation. It was approximately this: Inflation is a rate of rise in prices sufficient to cause a change in human behavior. And von der Linde pointed out that the stock market bubble had caused millions of people to do things they had never thought of doing before it happened—for example, not working for a living.

We predict that the reaction against Greenspan will take the form of a rejection of policy making through intuition. In times past, many believed that the chairman could look into the future and improve it before it happened. How he did this was never clear, but it was not for the layman to understand. Proof that it was possible to do was that he was doing it (or so his acolytes insisted).

How far the reaction against the Greenspan intuition will go will depend on how much post-bubble suffering is left to endure. If more than a little, as we expect, the Fed might be obliged to introduce a set of more or less explicit operating rules. It has done so before—for example, from interest-rate targeting to money-supply targeting in 1979 and back to interest-rate targeting from money-supply targeting in 1982. The Fed could shoot at an inflation target—higher than zero, probably, if the post-bubble adjustment proves long, drawn-out and deflationary. The chairman's successor might announce the setting of a watch against the next distorting episode of asset price inflation. The history of monetary policy is an everlasting tale of the frying pan and the fire. The search for price stability has oftentimes led to financial instability (e.g., in the United States in the 1920s and 1990s and in Japan in the 1980s). And though we cannot now recall a central bank that directly targeted asset prices, we have every confidence that such a policy would eventually lead to price inflation. Why? Because money turned away from stocks or real estate would bid up the prices of the items measured in cost-of-living indices.

As dress on Wall Street has become more casual, so have the monetary arrangements. In less than a century, the gold standard and swallowtail coats have given way to Greenspan and open-neck shirts. Possibly, in both money and clothes, a reaction against the long-running trend is today in place. If so, before long analysts in neckties will be trying to decipher the intentions of a new, but-toned-up and rule-bound FOMC.

In the meantime, there will be monetary-policy separation anxiety to bear. Greenspan is a Washington fixture and his mumbles about the mysteries of finance have brought comfort to many, especially to those who don't quite follow him. Since he first reported for government duty in 1974, the nation has had many more successes than failures. He himself has been hailed as a saint and a clairvoyant. Now it develops that he is neither, but only a fellow in a business suit trying to hold his job and not look bad. The chairman is revealed to be a government worker who, perhaps, unlike some of his lay colleagues, did not think it odd that companies with no revenues commanded multibillion-dollar stock-market capitalizations or that bicycle messengers made their rounds with beepers to alert them to the news of publicly announced stock splits (in the bubble, stock splits were regarded as very bullish). Possibly, the up-creeping gold price is nothing more than a war tocsin. However, to us, it is more plausibly a measure of the market's unease over approaching changes in the personnel and operating methods of the Federal Reserve. Even we, bearish on the chairman though we are, must admit that his successor might be worse. In any case, changes are in store for the institution of the dollar.

Many will doubt that any wrenching discontinuity is possible, much less probable. But the financial history of the past 100 years is the story of just such jarring change. To the skeptics, we commend a few lines of reminiscence about the 1920s by the wonderful German economist Wilhelm Röpke, taken from his *Crises and Cycles,* which appeared in 1936. "With production and trade increasing month by month throughout the world, the moment actually seemed in sight when social problems would be solved by prosperity for all...," Röpke wrote. "Thinking back to those 'gay twenties,' we cannot help but be inclined to regard them as one of the most remarkable and astonishing periods in modern history. Probably economic history has never before beheld such a speed, or such a scale of material progress and improvement in the technique of production and organization. It is a curious token of human fickleness that ten years later men are simply wallowing in abuse of that period and are decrying its spirit almost as a strange abomination, an attitude which is all the more curious and even tragic as this total reversal of atmosphere is one of the main reasons for the persistence of the present depression."

The trouble with not knowing history is not that one is condemned to repeat it. As history is cyclical, the only alternative to not repeating it is not being around for the privilege. The trouble is rather that the history-deprived person meets a surprise at every cyclical bend in the road. He or she lives in a childlike state of wonderment. It was thus that the chairman seems to have confronted the computer revolution (astounding!), the attendant gains in measured productivity growth (unprecedented!) and the persistence of stable consumer prices (most gratifying!). He could see the dawn of the New Economy.

And he did, too, as others have seen before him, because the economy is always new and always old. In 1902, R.E. May, a German theorist, was warning about the blessings and risks of productivity growth—"to enable producers to sell their growing output promptly prices must be reduced and wages must be raised in proportion as the supply of goods increases," said May. What he wanted was what the 20th century partially delivered, namely an equitable division of the spoils of productivity growth between wages and profits.

May is quoted in the summa of the dean of American business cycle theorists, Wesley Clair Mitchell. *Business Cycles*, published in the very year the Federal Reserve was founded, 1913, reveal Mitchell to be an optimist, but for a set of reasons that will make posterity smile. Nothing like the tulip mania or the South Sea bubble would likely be seen again, Mitchell concluded, because speculative excess was being wrung out of Wall Street. The agent of this progress was enlightened regulation. "By a combination of various agencies such as public regulation of the prospectuses of new companies," the economist asserted 20 years before the creation of the SEC, "legislation supported by efficient administration against fraudulent promotion, more rigid requirements on the part of stock exchanges regarding the securities admitted to official lists, more efficient agencies for giving investors information, and more conservative policy on the part of the banks toward speculative booms, we have learned to avoid certain of the rashest errors committed by earlier generations." This particular section Mitchell entitled "Man's Mastery over the Workings of the Money Economy."

Not one to read history or even to hire someone to do it for him (not one Ph.D. in history draws a Fed paycheck), Greenspan may not be familiar with a masterly 1937 work by C.A. Phillips, T.F. McManus and R.W. Nelson, *Banking and the Business Cycle.*

In it, Phillips et al. produce a thorough monetary postmortem of the boom and bust of the 1920s and 1930s. And in so doing, they provide a detailed preview of the ups and downs of the millennial New Economy. In the earlier period, as in the later, the source of the bust was the boom. ("The only cause of depression is prosperity," wrote Clement Juglar, a French theorist, many years before.) Then, as now, the Fed achieved stable goods prices only to foment flyaway asset prices. And then, as now, credit expanded at a rate "vastly in excess of the needs of trade and industry."

"The new excess credit," wrote the Phillips team, "was in considerable measure directed into channels divorced from the normal nonspeculative operations of production and commerce, and found expression in the rise of prices in the stock market, in the real estate market and in wage rates. Federal Reserve control activities, primarily directed at stabilization of the price level, produced the speculative and investment booms, with the attendant disequilibrium between investment and saving, and thereby may be considered a generating cause of our recent plight. Investment inflation ended in depression."

Nowadays, investment inflation doesn't end in depression. With the chairman, it ends in confusion. There's some progress in that, we have to admit.

So It's the Government's Yield Curve

April 11, 2003

Federal Reserve officials insist that the risk of deflation is "remote," but it's the only low-probability event they seem to talk about. A new global monetary standard centered on the Iraqi dinar? A 50% federal funds rate? A congressional investigation into the statistical validity of the productivity data so dear to the heart of Chairman Greenspan? Not a word on these potential monetary-policy dislocations.

Last week, Vincent Reinhart, secretary to the Federal Open Market Committee and director of the board's Division of Monetary Affairs, became the latest ranking Federal Reserve official to discuss the ostensibly unlikely event of a sagging price level. Like Alan Greenspan and governor Ben S. Bernanke, Reinhart characterized the odds of deflation as "remote" (actually, he called them "quite remote"). And, like his superiors, Reinhart asserted that the Fed, if pressed, could respond with a measure that ought to shock the global financial markets but which, to date, has seemed not to register on them: the re-regulation of the Treasury yield curve.

"If asset prices don't adjust sufficiently to stimulate spending," Reinhart was quoted as saying by *Bloomberg*, "then open market purchases of long-term Treasurys in sizable quantities can move term premiums lower." Which we take to mean that if stock prices (or house prices, or other prices yet to be named) don't do what they're supposed to do, the Fed will cap the yields of longer-dated Treasurys in a bid to depreciate the value of the dollar.

The Internet chat rooms are buzzing with new speculation that the federal government is secretly manipulating the stock market. Because we contend that a Wall Street secret is a contradiction in terms, we don't believe it. However, we do believe the Fed when it says it's prepared to try to control the longer-dated regions of the Treasury yield curve. If a conspiracy to manipulate the government bond market is openly divulged by the conspirators, is it any less a conspiracy? It is not. It is more than a conspiracy, in fact. It is an opportunity, if—as seems now to be the case—investors refuse to take the conspirators at their word.

As it is, the Fed manipulates only the funds rate. It buys and sells Treasurys to hit the Federal Open Market Committee's target (the great bulk of its holdings are concentrated in maturities of five years and under; in the past year, holdings of securities of less than 15 days' maturity have shown the fastest growth, up 90%, of any segment in the portfolio). It has not gone unnoticed that, at a funds rate of 1¼%, there is only so much room to cut, so the Fed is forming contingency plans. It wants the market to know that it could cheapen the purchasing power of the dollar—i.e., mount a successful campaign of reflation—even with the funds rate at zero. Bernanke (on November 21), Greenspan (on December 19) and now Reinhart (on March 25) have all held out the possibility of a transformation of policy to the end of suppressing government bond yields. Said Greenspan: "Such actions have precedent. Between 1942 and 1951, the Federal Reserve put a ceiling on longer-term Treasury yields at 21/2%."

Because modern central banks date from the 17th century, there is almost bound to be a precedent. Virtually every monetary policy has been tried before, many more than once. Inflation has been given an especially thorough test run. In the decade mentioned by Alan Greenspan, the Fed obediently enforced the yields that the Treasury mandated. Reinhart, according to *Bloomberg*, said that he "doesn't consider the notes purchases [idea] to be unconventional, because the Fed capped rates during the 1940s and used a quantity-of-money target from 1979–82." The mandarin himself was quoted as saying:

"Funny, I don't remember a recession either."

"What is usual, orthodox and conventional is the Federal Reserve's willingness to adapt its policy to the circumstances."

Even when the circumstances are of its own making. Booms and busts are always with us, and the Fed is not solely responsible for the millennial cycle. However, it was complicit in its excesses. And now the very people who erred in the '90s are prescribing for the '00s. The notions being prescribed are exactly the ones you would not have expected. It's the shock of the down cycle that Greenspan, the former Ayn Rand disciple, is weighing a de facto nationalization of the Treasury yield curve.

Evidently, the chairman tosses and turns at night. A dozen funds-rate reductions have failed to recharge the New Economy, about which he had so much to say on the eve of the peak in the Nasdaq Stock Market. There is no deflation at present (on the contrary, the CPI is registering 3% year-over-year growth), the junk-bond market has rallied and the banking system is functional. Yet, he and his staff are holding out the promise of radical action to depreciate the currency.

We should try to imagine ourselves in the shoes of a foreign holder of the 10-year Treasury. We, too, have read the Fed's pronouncements. We have rubbed our eyes and performed a calculation. If the Fed did peg the yield at 2.5%, the implied 150 basis-point rally from the now-prevailing 4% would deliver a 13-point price rise in our holdings. We are, provisionally, delighted. But the dollar is not our native currency. We decide it is the part of prudence to sell some dollars to hedge our exposure. And we are not alone. Many other people reach the same decision. The selling snowballs and the dollar exchange rate slips. The gold price shoots up. Interest rates not under the thumb of the Fed begin to lift (as do prices of imported merchandise, reflecting, after a short lag, the weakened dollar exchange rate). All at once, a latent deflationary crisis becomes an actual inflationary crisis.

On March 30, the *New York Times* quoted an ex-Fed governor on the potentially inflationary implications of the contingency plans now under discussion. "They would have to be ready to stand by and buy every 10-year Treasury security that anybody wants to sell them at that rate," said Lyle Gramley, now an economist with Schwab Capital Markets, "and they would have to persist until they have long-term success. We're talking about massive increases of liquidity into the system."

The immediate precedent for such a policy, the 1942–51 episode, occurred in wartime, in a setting of capital controls and in the context of current account surpluses. The U.S. economy was thoroughly mobilized. Wages, prices and profits were under government control. Industrial production was regimented. The Fed's job was to facilitate low-cost government borrowing and, after the war was won, to defend against a postwar depression. It pegged the three-month bill rate at 0.375% and the long-dated bond yield at 21/2%, buying all securities offered at those levels. Presented with the opportunity to borrow short (at a low rate) and lend long (at a higher rate), the nation's investors seized the chance. "With all rates expected to remain fixed," writes Allan H. Meltzer in his new *History of the Federal Reserve* (Vol. I), "banks, financial institutions, and the public increased profits by buying higher-yielding long-term bonds and selling short-term bills in the market, where they were acquired by the System."

In his talk of March 25, Reinhart seemed to offer up a world of arbitrage profits to a new generation of fixed-income sharpshooters. "Of course," *Bloomberg* quoted him as saying, "such a promise to put a ceiling on parts of the yield curve would be reinforced with a credible promise to keep the short rate along a path consistent with long-term rates." In other words, the shape of the yield curve would be determined by the FOMC instead of by the market.

When, in November, Bernanke famously reminded the creditors of the United States that it cost almost nothing to print a dollar bill, it appeared as though the newest Fed governor were speaking out of school. Then, a month later, the chairman himself vowed to slay deflation, if necessary, by reverting to the practice of yield pegging. In mid-February, Robert McTeer, president of the Dallas Fed, lightened the deflationary mood with his own special joie de vivre: "As long as you're pumping out money at a faster rate than demand for money is rising, you're going to stimulate spending. I think it would be kind of fun to fight deflation, actually."

These open threats against market-clearing interest rates have been met mainly with silence in the capital markets. No outcry, either of outrage or incredulity, has greeted the Federal Reserve's brainstorming. In 1942–51, the central bank became a most reluctant rubber stamp of the Truman administration's war finance. Now, in a wholly different set of circumstances, it is leading the reflationary charge—with the understanding, of course, that the chances of any such seismic change are "remote."

It isn't every day that the central bank of the world's premier capitalist economy openly weighs the advisability of unplugging a market mechanism. In the end, it may not happen, but this much has already come to light: The Fed has revealed a depth of institutional arrogance that even its friendly critics had never imagined.

Mission Creeps
November 7, 2003

On December 23, at 6:02 p.m. on the basis point, the Federal Reserve System will turn 90 years old. It may dance a jig. For ourselves, we have composed an essay on money and bureaucracy, which we publish preemptively, in the same way the Fed attacks recessions. We have decided that Fannie Mae and Freddie Mac have too long absorbed congressional heat for operating in a manner and on a scale unimagined by the lawmakers who chartered them. In the matter of "mission creep," they are the flintiest pikers.

The Federal Reserve would be unrecognizable to the men who conceived it. If, indeed, the founders could be brought back to earth to inspect their evolved creation, the shock might kill them all over again. The meaning of these changes for the dollar and for interest rates is the subject under discussion. In preview, we predict many more dollars will be printed. In consequence—eventually—we expect that there will be much higher interest rates.

We leave it to the readers of *Grant's* to identify the operative words in the Federal Reserve's enabling legislation. The act projected an institution "to provide for the establishment of the Federal Reserve banks, to furnish an elastic currency, to afford means of rediscounting commercial paper and to establish a more effective supervision of banking in the United States, and for other purposes." Have you picked them out? Right: "for other purposes."

Among these purposes are four enumerated on the Federal Reserve's Internet home page and a fifth that we will have to supply. No. 1, to conduct "the nation's monetary policy." In 1913, there was no such policy. No. 2, to supervise and regulate banks and "[protect] the credit rights of consumers." In Woodrow Wilson's day, there were no such rights. No. 3, to maintain "the stability of the financial system." This, at least, would have rung a bell with the founders: In the 30 years before the law's enactment, there were four American banking panics. No. 4, to clear checks, administer FedWire, serve as a kind of sales window for the Treasury and operate a custody business on behalf of the Treasury for foreign central banks and international financial institutions. In 1913, clearing was performed privately, the public debt was insignificant and the prompt settlement of international payments deficits was a sine qua non of the gold standard (ergo, no mountain of Treasury holdings could have arisen on the balance sheets of foreign central banks). No. 5, to serve as national economic oracle. Of all the changes, this one, from the vantage point of the first Wilson administration, would seem least explicable. In a free market, of what use is a government seer?

The deviations of present function from original intent are almost too numerous to count, and some may hope they will stay uncounted, if the point of adding them up is to charge the Fed with the heinous crime of evolving. Institutions either adapt or fall by the wayside, it will be correctly observed. The United States Navy, to pick a bureaucracy out of the hat, has adapted by deploying aircraft and guided missiles, even though John Paul Jones knew nothing about them. Open-market operations and econometric modeling would similarly have drawn a blank from Sen. Carter Glass (D.–Va.), one of the central bank's legislative fathers. The argument goes that the Fed, like the Navy, has only kept up with modern improvements.

Or maybe not, for here we encounter the difference between physics and economics. Both use quantitative methods to build predictive models, but physics deals with matter; economics confronts human beings. And because matter doesn't talk back or change its mind in the middle of a controlled experiment or buy high with the hope of selling even higher, economists can never match the predictive success of the scientists who wear lab coats. If you believe that human action is unpredictable, you will not be overly impressed by econometric forecasts of next year's GDP. Still less will you share the confidence of some Federal Reserve officials in the ability of interest-rate manipulations to herd human beings in a desired direction. Gov. Ben S. Bernanke is one of these true believers, as he reiterated last month in a lecture at the London School of Economics. "If all goes as planned," said Bernanke, getting off on the wrong foot, "the changes in financial asset prices and returns induced by the actions of monetary policymakers lead to changes in economic behavior that the policy was trying to achieve." If all went according to plan, the LSE would be teaching case studies in the triumphs of the Soviet economy.

The institution envisioned by the founders was intended to function passively. It was designed to forestall panics by centralizing the nation's gold reserve and serving as a lender of last resort. It would develop a market in bankers' acceptances, bills of exchange and other commercial paper. It would lend against acceptable collateral. Improving the future before it happened was not one of its legacy lines of business.

The Fed would not, in fact, be a central bank, as Allan Meltzer explains in the first volume of his projected two-volume work, *A History of the Federal Reserve, 1913–1951*, but rather a hybrid: a "partly public, partly private institution, intended to be independent of political influence with principal officers of the government on its supervisory board, endowed with central banking functions, but not a central bank." The founders were conventional thinkers, Meltzer observes (as they would almost have to had been: if visionaries write legislation, they rarely get it enacted). They believed that the gold standard was a superior form of monetary organization. They believed that the quality of credit, much more than the quantity of credit, was a controlling factor in central-banking policy—if the Fed lent against the right kind of collateral, specifically, commercial paper, it would not go far wrong. And if it lent only against the volume of commercial paper brought to the discount window, it would create neither too much credit nor too little. There was one behavior-modifying intention embedded in these propositions. Credit channeled into commerce was credit denied to the New York broker-loan market. "Speculation" was, to the founders, a national fever that the Fed should starve by nurturing commerce and agriculture. As for "monetary policy," there was really nothing to do except abide by the rules of the international gold standard. No economic research apparatus was either created or envisioned.

Almost immediately, events thwarted the founders' intentions. The international gold standard perished in World War I, which began just eight months after the Federal Reserve was signed into existence. With America's entry into the war, in April 1917, the Federal Reserve began to facilitate deficit finance with credit creation—a preview of the modern age.

Modernization marched double-time during the war and afterward. Open-market operations got their start in the early 1920s, and "stabilization" of international finance began in the mid-1920s. As clinching proof that nothing is new under the sun, economists and congressmen in the 1920s periodically called on the Fed to stabilize the price level through monetary operations. They invoked many of the same arguments brought forward today on behalf of inflation targeting. And the Fed resisted these pleas with many of the same objections produced today on behalf of central-bank discretion. Benjamin Strong, head of the Federal Reserve Bank of New York, was the miracle-working central banker of his day. Irving Fisher, a leading proponent of price stabilization, was the star economist. In about 1928, Fisher said to Strong: "I would trust you to do [stabilize the price level] without a legislative mandate, but you will not live forever, and when you die I fear that this will die with you." Roughly 75 years later, Greg Ip wrote in *The Wall Street Journal*: "How will the Federal Reserve operate once Alan Greenspan is gone? The question has increasing urgency."

The prewar gold standard was never put back together again; in the 1920s, the New York Fed used monetary statistics more than monetary gold movements as a guide to policy. So much for one of the pillars of the Federal Reserve. The Depression knocked down the others. In 1932, the first Glass-Steagall Act authorized the Fed to lend against formerly proscribed collateral, including unholy government securities. In 1933–34, the nation's gold reserve, "centralized" in the Federal Reserve System, was scooped up by the Treasury and marked up in value, to $35 an ounce from $20.67; the gain seeded what became the Exchange Stabilization Fund, the Treasury's own cookie jar. (In exchange for its bullion, the Federal Reserve received "gold certificates," which on the balance sheet today are assigned a carrying value of $11 billion.)

The Fed was presented with a broad variety of behavior-altering policy tools, including, in 1933, the power to set ceiling interest rates on time deposits and the power to regulate margin requirements; in 1935, it was given the power to set reserve requirements. It presently doubled reserve requirements, thereby entering a strong claim of paternity for the nasty 1937–38 recession, an early preemptive stroke.

The system celebrated its 30th birthday in a world wholly unlike the one in which it was founded. The gold standard was "as dead as mutton," to quote Keynes, and the discount window was dysfunctional. With the entry of the United States into World War II, the Fed was once more conscripted into deficit finance. It purchased every 90-day Treasury bill it was offered at 0.375%; it purchased all one-year bills at 0.875% and all maturities longer than 25 years at 2.5%. In this way it socialized the yield curve. Lest this piece of history seem musty and irrelevant, Greenspan speculated on reviving just these methods during the springtime deflation scare.

Not every vestige of the founders' intentions was scrubbed from the central bank's operations (for the Fed had, during the New Deal, become a conventionally centralized central bank, no more a federal one). The really bad ideas were retained. In 1946, to deal a preemptive blow against postwar stock-market speculation, the Fed lifted margin requirements all the way to 100% from 40%. Speculation staggered under the blow, as did the Dow Jones Industrial Average, down by 13% for the year.

But the big news of 1946 was the Employment Act, which committed the federal government to the goals of "maximum employment, production and purchasing power." The declaration brought about no immediate change in monetary policy: The Federal Reserve was still wearing the Treasury's chains of servitude. However, it made it clearer than ever that the burden of future adjustments to international imbalances would be borne by the value of the dollar, not by the economy. If it could, Congress would burden the voters neither with joblessness nor a depreciated currency. However, the Employment Act cleared up any remaining questions about which blight was the less acceptable. The spirit of the Employment Act shines through even in the directives of the Federal Open Market Committee. "The committee judges that, on balance, the risk of inflation becoming undesirably low remains the predominant concern for the foreseeable future," said the October 28 directive. "In these

circumstances, the committee believes that policy accommodations can be maintained for a considerable period."

Fast-forward now past the attack of the Great Inflation and past Chairman Paul A. Volcker's brave and successful counterattack. Stop at the October 19, 1987, panic, and the Fed's morning-after policy declaration: "The Federal Reserve, consistent with its responsibilities as the nation's central bank, affirmed today its readiness to serve as a source of liquidity to support the economic and financial system." Beyond this deceptively bland statement, as Martin Mayer relates in *The Fed*, his must-read 2001 study, the central bank employed its powers of persuasion to force Wall Street banks to do their duty by extending succor to the then-illiquid market makers. Bankers Trust, for one, was leaned upon by E. Gerald Corrigan, president of the Federal Reserve Bank of New York, according to Mayer, and BT obediently lent. "Corrigan was also in touch with others, vigorously."

A succession of market-stabilizing, panic-subduing and chestnut-yanking Federal Reserve measures ensued: in 1991–93, a monetary expansion to shore up the American banking system, laid low by improvident real-estate lending; in 1995, a coordinated intervention with the Treasury Department to contain the damage brought about by the devaluation of the peso (an intervention financed, on the American end, by the aforementioned Exchange Stabilization Fund, bad seed of the 1934 gold confiscation); and in 1998, the pièce de résistance, a surprise 25 basis-point cut in the federal funds rate during the Long-Term Capital Management distress, a gesture so ingeniously timed that, on October 15–16, it set in motion an options-fueled buying panic in the stock market. "Both the fixed-income markets and the stock markets have come to rely to an unprecedented degree on a safety net from the Federal Reserve," as Mayer observes.

We now enter into evidence a fragment of a review of a book on oracles, Michael Wood's *The Road to Delphi*, published this year. The critic, Christopher Mayer, is a banker, and he picks up on a reference in the book to the oracular role of the Fed chairman. "Wood's book," he writes, "reveals that our attachment to oracles is as much a coping mechanism as anything else. It helps us deal with the unknown future and fear and hope that accompanies such a state. Wood writes, 'The balancing of hopes and fears is a human constant, and oracles are an important part of that balancing act.' Greenspan lacquers a slate of ignorance with a thin coating of knowledge. His existence satisfies a contradiction in human thought that longs for, in Wood's words, 'certainty and infallibility in those areas of human life where they are characteristically least available.'"

Viewed clinically, Greenspan should be losing power, not gaining it. He presides over an institution that was built for a bank-centered world, but this is the age of securities markets. He figuratively controls the printing press in a phase of our finance in which printing more dollars (i.e., creating more credit) has lost some of its macroeconomic potency. Yet, he remains oracle-in-chief, suggesting that the world does indeed long for "certainty and infallibility." Good luck!

Under Greenspan, the Fed has evolved into a kind of national financial fire department. It is not merely the lender of last resort but also the damage-control coordinator of first resort. No act of Congress has made it so. But so reliably has the Fed appeared at the scene of speculative accidents that it probably couldn't stay away from the next one even if it wanted to. It must keep trying to fix what's broken even when, as in October 1998, almost nobody realized what was broken (Martin Mayer relates that the proximate cause for Greenspan's funds-rate reduction was the seizing-up of the Treasury market, an event that went unreported in the news pages of either the *New York Times* or the *Washington Post*).

Repeated and predictable acts of intervention can't help but change behavior. The more dependably the Fed fends off disaster, the bolder and more leveraged investors become. The bolder investors become, the higher the markets go. And the higher the prices and the greater the leverage, the more likely does a financial accident become. In response to which, of course, the Fed would intervene.

The 1% funds rate is the interest-rate legacy of these interventions. And while it is not true that the rate can go no lower, it can't go much lower. Arriving at the scene of the next financial blaze, what will the monetary fire department do for water? Peg the 10-year yield? Drop money from aircraft? Because we believe that there will be another financial conflagration (timing uncertain), we are bearish on the dollar for the long run. Likewise, we are bearish on bonds for the long run.

In 1991, the Truth in Savings Act was passed to enlist the Fed to protect thrifty Americans against deceitful advertising. However, after a dozen years' worth of timely financial-market interventions, savers earn interest rates that are hardly worth being deceitful about. The unintended consequence of bailing out the investors has therefore been the immiserization of the savers. Missions don't creep, they gallop, and in unplanned directions.

Bonds: The Next Generation

June 4, 2004

Cycles in the bond market are monumental, literally epochal. In the United States, yields fell in the last 40 years of the 19th century. They rose in the first 20 years of the 20th. They fell between 1920 and 1946, and rose between 1946 and 1981. They fell between 1981 and 2003. Now, we believe, they are going back up again. If past is prologue, they might go up for a very long time. Following is a sneak preview of the unfolding generational bond bear market, which, if our cyclical clock is keeping the correct time, began on June 13, 2003, as the 10-year Treasury touched 3.11%.

Great cycles in bond yields are delineated by great events— events, at least, that were revealed as decisive after they occurred. Yields fell in the last four decades of the 19th century because the Civil War gave way to peace and deflation. Around 1899, men struck gold in Alaska and South Africa—which, given the monetary arrangements of the time, was tantamount to striking money—and yields turned back up again. Rates kept on rising through the war-induced inflation of 1914–20. They peaked in 1920 and fell for the next quarter-century, even during World War II, when the Fed controlled, or "pegged," them. They didn't bottom until 1946, the year of the passage of the Employment Act, by which the federal government undertook to stamp out depression and joblessness for all time. For the next 35 years, yields pushed higher, at each new peak level shocking anyone who knew anything about the history of interest rates. No single transforming bullish event occurred in 1981, the year they finally peaked: The bond market, with its then-prevailing alpine yields (and a prime rate averaging almost 19%) was its own bullish catalyst. Yields proceeded to fall, in hand with the inflation rate, for the next 22 years. The new bear market is about to have its first birthday.

At the Berkshire Hathaway meeting last month, Warren Buffett admitted that if someone had told him steel prices would rise "several hundred percent" in the context of a 1% funds rate, he wouldn't have believed it. Now he believes it. However, true to form, no bunting was hung to mark the occasion. In the scheme of things, long cycles end, and begin, unceremoniously. The significance of the great events that punctuate them is revealed mainly in retrospect. Perception depends critically not only on what one sees, but also on what one expects to see. For fixed-income investors, the experience of the past 23 years has been overwhelmingly bullish, and their perception has been filtered accordingly. It would be a first in human nature if the market, alarmed at the trend in commodity prices, or the return of "pricing power," suddenly turned generationally bearish. (On the other hand, ISI notes, expectations for a rise in interest rates found their greatest support among consumers in at least 14 years, according to a poll conducted last month by the University of Michigan.)

Interest-rate markets are long-trending markets. In the United States, they have risen and fallen at generational intervals for more than 150 years. No one theory can explain why. Cycles in inflation and deflation are also long-trending, and systems of monetary organization have risen and fallen at multidecade intervals since the late 19th century. Possibly, technology and innovation—derivatives, activist central-bank management, electronically enhanced trading and funds transfers, etc.—have sped up the cyclical rhythms. There is no way to know. We guess not, and on that guess hangs the thesis.

By scholarly standards, we are rushing it into print. Sidney Homer and Richard Sylla, in the third edition of *A History of Interest Rates*, published in 1991, refused to speculate whether the bull market that had begun 10 years before was a secular bull market "or something else." It was a secular bull market, all right, and now we're reading last rites over it.

How do we know that one cycle has ended and another has begun? How does the prophesied bear market square with common sense—i.e., with the visible and plausible facts? Answers, where available, to be furnished presently. However, one question deserves to be asked, and answered, immediately. *Grant's*, for most of its 20 years of existence, has refused to try to predict short- and medium-term swings in interest rates. It can't be done, we've protested. Therefore, inquiring minds will ask: What makes us think we can call the next 20 years? Our reply is that a 20-year forecast is defensible if the bond market is still long-trending and if the bull bond market is over. Believing those things to be true, we expect that yields will go on rising for as far as the eye can see—in fact, farther. As for the next four weeks, months or fiscal quarters, don't ask.

We say that great cycles are punctuated by great events. We could as easily say that they are bracketed with absurdities. The late bull bond market began following a 1981 spike in yields to close to 15% almost two years after the then-chairman of the Federal Reserve Board, Paul A. Volcker, implemented the monetary policy that doomed inflation. Far more remarkably, yields topped 13% in 1984, almost five years after Volcker lowered the boom. Fixed-income investors didn't close their eyes to these developments. It's just that they didn't see them. What they saw was the past, in 3-D.

As the fear of inflation pulled yields to their 1981 highs, so the fear of deflation pushed them to their 2003 lows. However, the two cycles were not quite symmetrical. The difference was that inflation, in the early 1980s, was an established fact, whereas deflation, in the early 'oos, was only a theory. In fairness, it was a theory draped with the prestige of the world's leading central bankers.

On the eve of the first anniversary of the peak in bond prices, it's useful to recall that the market soared on governmental wings. From late 2002, senior Fed officials reiterated their determination to manipulate interest rates down to push the inflation rate up. "If asset prices don't adjust sufficiently to stimulate spending," Vincent Reinhart, secretary to the Federal Open Market Committee, was quoted by *Bloomberg* on March 25, 2003, "then open market purchases of long-term Treasurys in sizeable quantities can move term premiums lower." Alan Greenspan broadly hinted that, should the U.S. price level begin to sag, the Fed would not scruple to peg bond yields again, as it did in World War II (thereby effectively socializing the capital markets, the supposed pride and joy of American capitalism). Central bankers, although they are professionally disingenuous, are not professionally stupid. It wasn't everyday low prices they feared, but the financial consequences of falling prices in a heavily leveraged economy.

The Bank for International Settlements, the central bankers' central bank, lent its authority to the campaign to restore inflation to its rightful place in a typical modern economy—one, that is, with rigid labor markets and encumbered balance sheets. "It may be desirable, at the extreme," said the 2003 BIS annual report, "to attempt to peg certain prices, such as the exchange rate. In fact, many countries escaped deflation during the interwar period through currency devaluations."

By definition, in the bond market, reversals in trend occur only once or twice in an investment lifetime. Also by definition, the trend in place is most powerful—i.e., most socially contagious—in its last push to the extreme heights or depths. It should therefore not surprise if most investors are caught looking back when they ought to be looking ahead. "When [World War II] ended," write Homer and Sylla in their interest-rate history, "some people thought that the Treasury would not always be offering as much as 2½%. Perhaps rates as high as 2½% would vanish forever. Therefore, in 1945, after the war ended, purchases of the last issues of 2½s approached $20 billion. The Treasury indeed stopped issuing new bonds altogether." So it was that one issue of wartime 2½s was bid to a price to yield 2.12%, another to an even grander price to yield 1.93%. "This was the great crest of a 26-year bull bond market."

What were the corresponding signs of delusion at the top of the 2003 market? To name three: the absolute low level of interest rates, the low level of interest rates relative to inflation (and, in the corporate market, to credit risk) and the almost irresistible urge to invest in bonds despite the numbers. "They just can't stay short anymore," a bond investor was quoted as saying in *The Wall Street Journal* one year ago. "It's too painful. The cost of staying in cash is too great." We lay particular emphasis on this compulsion to buy bonds because it was the Fed that yelled "Buy!" in the crowded theater. By dangling a 2½% yield in front of the market, we believe, Greenspan et al. were responsible for the last 50 or so basis points of levitation. To push the 10-year yield back to 3.11%, the Fed will need an even more persuasive stable of speech writers or an actual deflationary crisis.

At a bull-market peak, the verities of the preceding bear market are turned inside out and upside down. Thus, in the early 1980s, it seemed the sensible course of action to position oneself for continued rises in interest rates. In the early ʻoos, it seemed—to many, still seems—prudence itself to prepare oneself for continued declines in interest rates. Financial historians will rub their eyes when they come across the text of Chairman Greenspan's heavy hint to homeowners to go out and get an adjustable-rate mortgage (which he delivered on February 23). And they are taking the hint. In the week of May 21, ARMs made up 34.6% of mortgage applications, one of the largest shares of ARMs in any week on record.

The bond bear market of 1946–81 was the longest and most severe—top to bottom, the holder of a 2½%, constant maturity, 30-year security would have lost 83% of his principal—but it may or may not point the way to the future. Hear Homer and Sylla on the first bear market of the 20th century: "The first price decline, 1899–1907, was very large, accounting for almost half of the gross decline, but it was spread over a period of nine years," they write. "From 1907 to 1917, the fluctuations in price were smaller. Finally, the three years from January 1917, through May 1920, contained more than half of the 21-year aggregate bear market. This three-year decline amounted to 23.6% in price; such a drop in the market had not been experienced for 56 years, or since the first year of the Civil War. It approximated the demoralized decline of the market for government bonds that occurred late in the War of 1812." And do you know how far this 21-year ordeal carried in price and yield? In yield, to 5.56% from 3.20%; in price—on a 3¼%, constant maturity, 30-year bond—to a grand total of 34½ points. This was what passed for volatility in a world with a gold standard but without hedge funds.

We say that a protracted bond bear market is beginning because a protracted bond bull market has ended. Does this contention square with common sense? With the evident facts? Many will roll their eyes. It is mysticism, they will say. Whatever caused interest rates to do what they did in the past, there is something new at the millennium. The new thing is the finely tuned mechanism of global capital markets. If bond yields trend with the rate of inflation, they will continue to trend down, the argument goes. Central banks will police the inflation rate, and the capital markets will police the central banks.

We commend to these rationalists a new report by the Board of Trustees of the Federal Hospital Insurance and Federal Supplementary Medical Insurance Trust Funds. The prognosis for federal finances, none too sound this year, starts to worsen materially after the baby boomers begin to make their generational call on Medicare, starting about 2010. A taste of the looming fiscal disaster is provided by the fact that, in the space of just one year, the trustees have moved up the expected date of "asset exhaustion" of the Hospital Insurance Trust Fund (also known as Medicare Part A, financier of care for the aged and disabled) to 2019 from 2026. In political circles, the impending lack of money is called the "entitlement gap," and it can be closed by raising taxes, reducing benefits or cranking the monetary printing press a little faster. We know which alternative is the easiest.

The persistent shortening of the average maturity of the public debt, questionable on its face at a time of low nominal interest rates, may prove a blessing for the nation's bond buyers. "[L]ost in the coverage of [the Medicare] report," writes Sen. Joseph

Liebermann (D., Conn.) in the May 25 *Financial Times*, "was an even more startling revelation: the entire U.S. government is going broke." Let us say, instead, that the government's credit is at risk and that the prospective downgrade points to higher Treasury yields, other things being the same.

So in the game of imagining the cause of a future bear market, one candidate, at least, presents itself. For a comprehensive catalog of other reasons, pretexts and catalysts, there's a May 6 speech by Alan Greenspan. The Maestro observes that the U.S. economy has "been pressing a number of historic limits in recent years," yet appears none the worse for the liberties taken. "We in the United States," Greenspan continues, "have been incurring ever larger trade deficits, with the broader current account measure having reached 5% of our gross domestic product (GDP). Yet the dollar's real exchange value, despite its recent decline, remains close to its average of the past two decades. Meanwhile, we have lurched from a budget surplus in 2000 to a deficit that is projected by the Congressional Budget Office to be 4¼% of GDP this year. In addition, we have legislated commitments to our senior citizens that, given the inevitable retirement by our baby-boom generation, will create significant fiscal challenges in the years ahead. Yet the yield on Treasury notes maturing a decade from now remains at low levels."

Reading between the lines, we think we detect acquiescence by the chairman to a future dollar bear market. It's a testament to "international flexibility," he says, that so large a portion of the world's savings can be whisked to this country "in response to relative rates of return." So the foreigners send us their merchandise, and we send them our dollars, and everyone—approximately—is happy. But not forever. "At some point, however," the chairman goes on, "international investors, private and official, faced with a concentration of dollar assets in their portfolios, will seek diversification, irrespective of the competitive returns on dollar assets. That shift, over time, would likely induce contractions in both the U.S. current account deficit and the corresponding current account surpluses of other nations." So add another possible cause of a future dollar bear market to the list: Portfolio-balancing sales of dollars and dollar-denominated securities by America's now-faithful foreign creditors.

No catalog of potential bear-market catalysts would be complete without a speculation on monetary-policy error. We have it on the authority of Gov. Ben S. Bernanke, as quoted in the May 21 *Wall Street Journal*, that the so-called neutral funds rate—"one which would neither stimulate nor restrict economic activity"—is as high as 3.7% to 4.7%, a long way from the prevailing 1%. And how does the Fed intend to return to neutrality? It says it wants to take its time.

"Gradualism," in fact, was the title of a talk delivered by Bernanke on May 20, and in it he lays out the reasons for moving in little, measured, unhurried baby steps, which, of course, is what the Fed has done before, notably in the more than 24 actions between June 1989 and September 1992 in which it whittled the funds rate by 675 basis points. In support of gradualism, Bernanke invokes both economic scholarship and golfing metaphor, the latter involving a comparison between funds rate fixing and putting.

But wait, a physician friend wonders: What if the relevant metaphor isn't golf? Think of the Fed as a doctor administering narcotics. What is accepted best practice in modern pain management? The answer is not gradualism, but the opposite. The rationale for aggressive use of opiates rests on several principles, our doctor explains: "Certain pain pathways are thought to be two-way, that is, they carry painful stimuli to and from the brain. In support of this hypothesis, the fear of pain has been experimentally shown to produce pain. Also, this explains the oft-demonstrated powerful effect of a placebo on pain."

"Pain pathways" fairly honeycomb Wall Street, and they are certainly two-way. And the fear of pain—of a new Fed tightening cycle—has, indeed, produced some pain in the bond market already. Bernanke, in his speech, professes to be pleased about that—"a significant portion of the financial adjustment associated with the tightening cycle may already be behind us."

We doubt that this self-administered tightening cycle is almost ended, however. And as the Fed lifts the funds rate, it will rediscover a truth that our doctor expresses as follows: "Studies have shown that pain nerves develop a kind of auto-stimulation; that is, after prolonged application of a painful stimulus, the nerves become refractory to analgesia."

Wall Street's nerves, too, can become deadened to treatment, and it wouldn't be surprising if, come the next easing cycle, the opiate of an ultra-low funds rate lost some of its punch. "Morphine and its derivatives are hands down the most effective drugs for acute pain relief," our medical source counsels. But there are two problems: No. 1, addiction; No. 2, diminishing potency. "Almost everyone who uses opioids will develop tolerance, or decreasing benefit. Tolerance has been shown within 12 to 24 hours of administration in mice."

As for the rats who race around the bond market, we believe that their pain is being badly managed, and that they face many years of adversity. However, on the bright side, it is within their power to mitigate their own discomfort. In the unfolding bear cycle, they are advised to shorten maturities, sell rallies—and only cautiously swallow the pills prescribed by central bankers.

Our medical consultant has a final metaphorical thought. Central bankers, unlike doctors, have no way to know if they are killing the patient. For an overdose of morphine, a doctor can administer Narcan. For an overdose of super-stimulative monetary policy, the Federal Reserve can only administer a higher funds rate—and as much soothing oratory as the market can bear.

Chapter Nine
Bonfire of the Currencies

Paper Tigers

May 21, 1999

A NEW HIGH IN the prestige of modern central banks was recorded two Fridays ago when Britain waylaid the gold market. Without warning, Her Majesty's government announced the sale of more than half of the U.K. gold reserve, formerly called "treasure." Instead of selling the currency, however, Mr. Market chose to sell the collateral behind it. The Bank of England, protector and defender of the pound, should have blushed: The plunge in the bullion price was the most extravagantly undeserved compliment it has ever received.

The world's oldest currency, sterling has, in this century, also been among the most perishable. It has depreciated in terms of both gold and British domestic prices, without let or hindrance, to borrow from Kipling. That the world should now be prepared to forgive the

Bank of England is testament not only to the strength of the global bull bond market, but also to the blessed forgetfulness of the human species, even the monied portion of the species. It is testament, too, to deflation, or more exactly, we think, to the fear of it. In Japan, where the action in bank stocks suggests that a death-dealing financial collapse has been avoided, the two-year note today yields seven basis points (repeat: seven).

To accommodate those readers who have threatened to cancel their subscriptions over the continued unprofitable subtext of gold-bugism in these pages, we will not ourselves make the obvious and necessary point about the relative constancy of the value of bullion, or about the cycles of fashion in monetary assets, or about the tendency of managed currencies down through time to self-immolate. Rather, we will quote other noted authorities on these matters (any complaints, address to them). Thus, Christopher Fildes in the May 15 issue of *The Spectator*: "As late as 1931, a pound note was as good as a gold sovereign. Today's price for a sovereign is £41, so what was a dead heat is now a race won by a distance."

And Harry Bingham, of Van Eck Institutional Advisors in New York, in a recent concise history of the currency that is not called "sterling" for nothing:

> Britain's Isaac Newton defined the British pound in terms of gold and silver almost 300 years ago. At the time, the pound was stated to be worth one-fourth of an ounce of gold and a pound of sterling silver. . . . Except for an interruption during the wars with Napoleon [and a century later, the war against the kaiser], the pound maintained its parity with gold and silver until 1931, when Britain formally refused to redeem pound notes for gold. Today, the pound is worth 1/170th of an ounce of gold and less than one-third of an ounce, not a pound, of silver, and this for the only paper currency that has survived for as long as 300 years.

Gold has borne its share of abuse during the almost 20-year bear market, but few indignities can match the market's demonstrated preference today for currencies of no particular pedigree, which includes nearly all of them. Either British social democracy has turned over a new leaf, or Mr. Market—having for so long pushed paper assets in one direction and gold in the opposite direction—is preparing to change his mind. We cling to the latter hypothesis, although we have taken to heart the observation of a reader who said that gold will move when it is good and ready to, not when we tell it to.

Still, we can't help but comment on the poor quality of the competition for gold that the central banks are fielding. As for the pound, nobody who has read its history will be able to take it seriously in 1999, a year that happens to mark the 50th anniversary of its epic devaluation in 1949 and the 35th anniversary of the British payments crisis of 1964. The latter episode, which anticipated the sterling devaluation of 1967 (which is not to be confused with the float-cum-devaluation of 1972 or the float-cum-devaluation of 1992), was the one that inspired an economics minister in the first government of Harold Wilson to fasten the blame for Britain's currency troubles on the "gnomes of Zurich." Putting the nation's gold where their mouth was, the Laborites in 1966 proceeded to sell gold at the then-prevailing $35-per-ounce price. By 1972, Britain had ditched 1,356 tons, more than half of its stash.

Now, not only do the Laborites, or rather the New Laborites, hate gold, but so do the gnomes and, indeed, the non-gnomes (these days, we do not exclude most gold bulls from the gold-hating majority—even we have our limits). The outer darkness into which the ancient monetary metal has been cast is illuminating, nevertheless. New lows in bullion are as much a sign of the times as are new highs in Japanese government debt instruments (last week's one-year bill auction was more than 13 times oversubscribed; priced at 0.049%, the securities rallied all the way to 0.035%, thereby demonstrating momentum if not what is known as "value"). Bullion and

"OK, fine. So you look like a <u>billion</u> bucks."

bonds, we think, together constitute a grade-A historical anomaly. The juxtaposition should force people in markets to confront the cyclically recurring question: "Is it really different this time?" This much, at least, is different: With the marginalization of the euro (not predicted here) and the weakness of the yen, the dollar has become the world's only universally acceptable monetary asset. It's Coke without Pepsi, a position never before obtained by a currency that can be duplicated at next to no cost on a high-speed printing press. (Arguably, sterling was just as important in its heyday as gold is today. Then, again, look what happened to sterling.)

It is hardly out of character for the Bank of England to show gold the gate. Our older readers may remember when, late in the Napoleonic era, the bank dragged its feet on the resumption of a gold-backed pound (was it really only 190 years ago?!). Down through the centuries, central banks have struggled with the dual mission of running a sound monetary policy and earning their keep. In formal gold-based monetary systems, of which none survive, gold not only collateralized the currency but also tempered the growth in bank credit. Both functions have been sorely missed on occasion in the post-gold era, although the lack of a regulator on bank-credit expansion has proven an excellent facilitator of bull markets. Still, the ingots yielded no income (by definition, they couldn't, any more than a $10 bill can; they were money, i.e., "cash"). Even central bankers who believed in the gold standard sometimes wished their vaults held fewer ingots and more interest-bearing securities.

What's new about the present day, therefore, is not that the official stewards of the golden ingots would like to sell, but that their plans for doing so elicit so little opposition. Essentially, the preference for currencies over bullion in 1999 is unconditional; interest rates no longer seem to figure into the monetary-asset demand calculation very much. It is, of course, the mirror image of 1980, when the panicked demand for gold was itself unconditional. Then, as you may remember, no interest rate was deemed high enough to turn back the tide of inflation. (Is any Japanese interest rate deemed low enough to check deflation? Not to judge by the yen-denominated yield curve.)

If central bankers were scorned 20 years ago, they are lionized today, even when a particular government makes no secret of its determination to cause its currency to depreciate (as the British and the Swiss have done) or when the modern history of a particular currency is really the history of debasement (as is the post-1931 history of sterling). It's true that the Bank of Japan has come in for concerted criticism, and perhaps the reason for the collapse of Japanese interest rates is not so much trust in the BoJ as it is doubt that the bank will ever be able to effect an economic recovery. Still, someone must have faith in the integrity of the currency—enough, at least, to accept a 1¼% yield over the next 10 years.

The first of what is promised to be a series of British gold auctions is set for July. Barring a U.S.-led collapse in bond prices, the interest rates at which the Bank of England will reinvest the proceeds of the sale will be among the lowest of the past half-century. The Japanese two-year note, as mentioned, yields all of seven one-hundredths of one percentage point, before tax. For ourselves, bearing in mind that the doubling time of money invested at seven basis points is only slightly less than a millennium (990.5 years), we can't see the appeal. Safety? Not very likely in the event the Bank of Japan ever considers a rise in the overnight call rate. As a point of perspective, a gold ingot lent for three months yields just under 1.25%; indeed, as of Monday every gold lease rate out to 12 months was greater than every Japanese government bond yield out to 10 years.

By comparison, it's true, the German 10-year bond yield is almost full-bodied, at 4.11%, and the U.S. rate is positively towering, at 5.66%. Yet, over the sweep of the past quarter century, these yields, too, must be reckoned low. As for gold, the only thing one can say is that there is really nothing to say. Having made new lows, it's been written down and written off. (An investor friend relates that he recently bought 250,000 gold calls struck at $500 for five years at a cost of $2 each. Given that the forward gold price is approximately $370, he observed, the calls are essentially free. Oil can go up 80% or so in less than a year, he reflects, but to take the options market at face value, no way can gold go up 30% in five years.)

Following a debasement of the pound by Edward VI in 1549, there was a peasant revolt in Norfolk, Devon and Cornwall. After years of inflationary war finance, in 1810 there were parliamentary hearings into the cause of the alarming loss of the paper pound's purchasing power. And when, at the turn of the 20th century, cheap silver was offered up in competition to the gold-based pound, there was a Gold Standard Defence Association to stand up for the British creditor class.

No such resistance to the course of action announced by the British Treasury is evident today when, to many observers, the clear and present monetary danger is deflation rather than the opposite. Even a little currency appreciation is deemed to be too much (from the time last fall that the Bank of England began to cut its base rate, the trade-weighted sterling index has appreciated by 4.6%). Or, perhaps, the market is looking through immediate events to future British membership in the European Monetary Union, at which point the pound would cease to exist and Britain would share in the European Central Bank's monetary reserves. Certainly, to judge by the shape of the British government yield curve, some such story is making the rounds. Every market rate on the sterling curve is lower than the 5¼% short-term lending rate. The global bond markets are beginning to meld the British curve into Europe's.

But, for now, Britain is still Britain, and sterling is still sterling, and the pound's strength against the puny euro has set off alarm bells within the British commercial and monetary establishments. These concerns came to light in a remarkable report on the day of the gold sale bombshell. "The Bank of England, the U.K. central bank," the *Financial Times* story led off, "yesterday signalled growing concern over the pound's continued resilience, saying it would cut interest rates again if the currency remained strong."

The fourth paragraph got to the essential monetary issue:

> The Bank said that if the pound did not fall, inflation could undershoot the targeted annual rate of 2.5%. 'Depending on other developments in the economy, there might, therefore, need to be further easing of interest rates in order to keep inflation on track,' it said.

Certainly, this is not the one and only official view of British monetary policy. The deputy governor of the Bank of England, Mervyn King, made hawkish sounds on Monday. However, the main fact, we think, is that sterling's depreciation is predestined; the only issue is the rate of decay.

In the wake of the British gold sale announcement, Haruko Fukuda, chief executive of the World Gold Council, a not disinterested party in the transaction, charged, "We at the World Gold Council have been told by HM Treasury that it was emphatically a political decision." Then, again, most monetary policy decisions are. In the circumstances, the choice of holding low-yielding currencies and selling $275 gold is more than trust. It is an act of faith.

Money Less Bad

May 11, 2001

Suddenly, the federal funds rate is lower than the euro-denominated fulcrum interest rate, and the two-year Treasury yields less than the two-year German bund. The Federal Reserve is easing policy in the face of a rising inflation rate. The European Central Bank is holding policy steady in the teeth of a weakening economy. Which is the lesser evil?

We say "lesser evil" because we are reluctant to accept any central bank, or any managed currency, as a greater good. To us, long-term success in the management of a paper monetary asset is so improbable as to be effectively impossible. Stamp a chit with the words "legal tender." Balance an immeasurable demand for that currency against a finite, but only approximately measurable, supply. Omit the golden anchor; let the exchange rate float instead. Supply a prudent fiscal policy and a growing economy. It is a tall order. The deutschemark, the great postwar monetary success story, excelled in the context of the Bretton Woods system, in which the dollar was convertible into gold and the other currencies were convertible into dollars. The dollar has been a brilliant success since 1995, anchored not to gold but to the most stupendous stock market of all time. Now that the stock market is less stupendous, maybe the currency will be brought down a peg.

A proposition: The soundness of a central bank varies inversely with the breadth of its mandate. The more it's expected to do, the longer the odds against its success. The Fed's mandate is all-encompassing. Roughly speaking, it is expected to deliver the earth ("price stability"), the moon (full employment) and the sky (a solvent financial system, at the center of which is a rising stock market).

Lately, of course, the moon and the sky have been at the top of the policy agenda. To the argument that the Fed has somehow managed to succeed at this impossible work, we reply: Wait till all the cyclical returns are in.

We hereby embark on a comparative analysis of the risks and rewards of four principal monetary assets. Besides the dollar and the euro, we include the yen and gold. From an American perspective, the question we pose effectively reduces to the following: What are the risks to a natural owner of dollars of choosing to own nothing but dollars? They are counterintuitively high. Though the U.S. economy is still the envy of the world, and though the dollar still outyields two out of the three competing assets on our list, the monetary fundamentals are changing. For reasons only dimly apparent, the euro and the yen may be poised to gain monetary market share. The basic reason for this shift is one already identified: The Fed is overreaching.

Grant's ventures this view with what is known in the currency-trading world as a cold hand. Non-believers in the New Economy and other putative miracles of the mid- and late 1990s, we campaigned against the great dollar bull market. We thought we saw in the euro a viable competitor to the dollar as an international reserve asset. And we thought we saw in gold bullion an attractive alternative to any currency, the dollar not least. To put the most charitable face on this constellation of misjudgments, we seem to have been early.

But, we insist, the international monetary system is too important to be left to market timers. Besides, a clarifying new debate is raging across the Atlantic. Bulls and bears on the euro are arguing the respective merits and demerits of the Fed and the ECB: Which monetary authority is more stiff-necked, obdurate, irresponsible and uncomprehending? It is a close-run contest, but the ECB can claim one important advantage: Its mandate is simpler than the Fed's; its paramount responsibility is to guard against inflation. The Fed, nowadays, is mainly concerned with suppressing and beating back bear markets and recessions.

Famously, money is a store of value as well as a medium of exchange. As managed currencies are prone to inflation, the expected rate of inflation weighs heavily in the determination of exchange rates. However, it weighs more heavily in risk-averse times than in speculative ones. In the late 1970s, the Swiss franc owed its preeminence to the arch-conservatism of the Swiss bankers. Today, after a decade of unmatched dollar-denominated equity returns, the value that a currency stores is more and more defined in terms of anticipated growth. Comparative interest rates and inflation rates are regarded merely as the means to an end. The end in view is total return. The currency that offers the highest prospective total return (bull-market assumptions being liberally applied in the calculation thereof) is the one with the high and rising exchange rate.

The dollar is the Swiss franc of the growth era. (We say "is" because the era, officially, is still intact.) A quarter-century ago, the Swissie offered protection against the ravages of price inflation. Today, the dollar provides exposure to the sweets of asset inflation. A quarter-century ago, the mythology of the Swiss gnomes lent value to the franc. Today, the vaunted reputation of Alan Greenspan enhances the value of the dollar. In the early 1970s, the Swiss government charged negative interest rates to dissuade nonresident speculators from holding francs. In 2001, the Federal Reserve is chopping away at the funds rate but not with the object of discouraging monetary inflows; on the contrary, the current account deficit (and the world's willingness to finance it) is at the heart of the American system.

The dollar is, of course, more than a cult currency. It is the international invoicing money par excellence, and it passes hand to hand the world over, supported by the prestige of the one and only superpower. There is something else to be said for the dollar: Of all the bulge-bracket central banks, the Fed is the one with the lowest tolerance for price deflation. The risk that the weight of debts will sink the global economy, driving down prices and bringing about an appreciation in the value of the dollar against the things in a shopping cart, is not, to us, the paramount risk. However, it is not a trivial one, either (it is frequently discussed by Greg Weldon on GrantsInvestor.com). The Fed cries at the drop of a stock market. It would commandeer every printing press to combat a depression.

This is a uniquely American attitude. The ECB seems not even to acknowledge the risk that a too vigilant fight against rising prices might result in falling ones. The Bank of Japan has been slow to move against the very real symptoms of Japanese debt deflation. A principal, if not the final, arbiter of the wisdom of monetary policy is the bond market, and here the judgment is mixed. Following the third of the Fed's four 50 basis-point easings, the U.S. Treasury yield curve started to steepen—i.e., long-term yields rose as short rates fell. In so many words, the nation's creditors cried, "Enough!" Yet, others—holders of the Treasury's inflation-protected securities, or TIPS—remained sanguine. In fact, the pricing of TIPS implies that the CPI will rise by no more than 2% or so for years to come. To appreciate the optimism of this imputed forecast, you should know that the CPI has risen by less than 2% in only two intervals in the past 20 years: April 1986–January 1987, and November 1997 to March 1999.

Holders of inflation-linked government securities in Australia, Britain, Canada and on the Continent are similarly complacent. In none of these markets is anxiety about a future inflationary flare-up on display, even to so modest a flaring height of 3% or 4%. If, however, the TIPS holders are actually discounting the onset of deflation, the worry is only selectively shared. Not only has the U.S. yield curve steepened, but a bull market remains in force in the stocks of aggressive credit-card lenders (not obvious beneficiaries of a deflationary debt spiral). Capital One, for instance, is quoted at 27 times earnings and 6 1/2 times book value.

For so long has the U.S. inflation experience been benign that investors have forgotten that it was ever intractable. The Fed aided and abetted this amnesia by refocusing its attention (and inviting investors to redirect theirs) to the real economy. Thus, observes

Martin Wolf in the *Financial Times*, Greenspan talks less and less about the things that central bankers have customarily addressed. In his three latest semiannual appearances before Congress, the chairman "mentioned productivity 42 times, inflation 13 times and money and credit not even once."

As Greenspanism is the prevailing American monetary doctrine, one must look outside the 50 states for an alternative operating method. Classical central-banking doctrine holds that the bank of issue stands aloof from workaday business activity, and even from the business cycle itself. Keep the money sound and the rest will take care of itself. Ernst Welteke, president of the Bundesbank, recently drew a sharp distinction between the Fed's operating philosophy and that of the ECB: "Monetary policy is not an instrument of cyclical policy-making. The ECB differs fundamentally from the U.S. central bank, in terms of its task and strategy. . . . Price stability is the primary goal for the ECB. The ECB could never argue in the way the Fed did in justifying its most recent rate cuts, by citing markets and the economy." Echoing Welteke, Otmar Issing, the ECB's chief economist, declared that the bank "has little room for fine-tuning the economy and controlling the economic cycle."

Rarely do the monetary lodge brothers talk about one another in this tone, but it isn't every day that such a clear delineation is apparent between classical methods and interventionist ones. Probably, too, the Europeans' backs are up over the very generous shipments of free advice that have come their way from Washington. Treasury Secretary Paul O'Neill has made no secret of his preference for lower European interest rates, and the chief economist of the IMF, Michael Mussa, has described the case for ECB ease as "unambiguous." The *Financial Times*, which has been on a page-one crusade to bring Greenspanism to Europe, reported the context in which Mussa vouchsafed this coaching. He said that the ECB must ease "to help boost the international economy." What the international economy has to do with a 2.9% German inflation rate must, to the ECB's management, be a mystery.

Since time out of mind, observes Gert von der Linde, chief economist among all retired Wall Street economists, each of the G-3 countries has had its own characteristic preoccupation. The Japanese worried about their dependence on imports (and hence their ability to export), the Germans about inflation and the U.S. about unemployment. The concerns haven't changed. What's new, von der Linde proposes, is that the Europeans and Japanese may each, for their own reasons, be prepared to defend the external value of their respective currencies. Thus, the ECB clings to its 4¾% intervention rate, and the Bank of Japan resists persistent demands for the wholesale depreciation of the yen.

Remember, though, von der Linde adds: It isn't central banks that set exchange rate policy, but finance ministers and secretaries of the Treasury. The author of the strong dollar policy of the 1990s was Robert Rubin. The euro is at a chronic disadvantage in this regard. As there are many finance ministers to stand behind it, there are effectively none.

The dollar exchange rate has been going up since early 1995. It has appreciated in conjunction with the greatest bull market and the greatest credit expansion. It has risen in tandem with an historic widening of the U.S. current account deficit (by which the economists mean that Americans have been privileged to consume more than they produced). Last year, the deficit reached $461 billion, or 4.6% of GDP. For perspective, the deficit peaked at 3.5% of GDP in the mid-1980s, a foreign-exchange era best remembered for the dollar bear market that preceded a famous stock-market panic. "And it's growing at an unsustainably rapid rate in a global context," writes Neal Soss et al, of Credit Suisse First Boston; "we are already using more than 80% of the globe's freely available savings." The counterpart to which, as Soss points out, is that Americans are doing almost no saving of their own.

"Unsustainable" is frequently used to describe a trend that the speaker or writer did not anticipate, and that he or she wishes would go into reverse. We ourselves have applied the word to the

U.S. dollar exchange rate and to the belief system by which the widening deficit is financed. Once upon a time, it was supposed that circumstances would force a deficit country to raise its bank rate, deflate its cost structure and thereby balance its external accounts. Little did the theorists anticipate a method by which a deficit country could reduce its bank rate, expand its borrowing and— either because of those steps or despite them—become the world's investment mecca. In effect, the No. 1 export of the United States has become the dollar.

Why do foreign producers so readily exchange their merchandise for American stocks and bonds? The recent surprise ejection of the United States from the U.N. Human Rights Commission affirms that the reason isn't a universal love of baseball and apple pie. Rather, the demand for dollars is sustained by the high returns on U.S. assets and by confidence in high future returns. Furthermore, the world has conceived a deep appreciation of the resiliency of the U.S. economy. It may run into trouble, but because of the willingness of Americans to mark their problems to market, it doesn't stay down for long. Dollar bulls proclaim that the U.S. will be exiting from its downturn before the Japanese and Europeans realize they're in one. Last but not least, the world continues to harbor faith in the existence of a new era of American productivity growth. "The favorable performance of U.S. productivity," comments the April 30 edition of J.P. Morgan's *World Financial Markets*, "which has helped to boost the share of corporate profits as a percent of GDP to 40-year highs, even allowing for recent softness, has been instrumental in attracting the large-scale capital inflows that underpin the currency." Even granting the validity of the hedonically enlarged U.S. productivity data—not advised, we said, even before Tuesday's news of a first-quarter productivity downturn—we sense a crowd forming at the top.

The Statue-of-Liberty effect is particularly prevalent in M&A activity. Thus, in the last three months of 2000, foreigners acquired U.S. corporate assets worth $86.3 billion, while U.S. investors bought foreign assets valued at only $2.8 billion. In the first three months of 2001, the totals were not quite so lopsided: Foreigners acquired $16.1 billion of U.S. assets, while Americans bought $5.3 billion in overseas claims. However, according to the dollar bulls, not even the downshifting in foreign acquisitions of U.S. assets will weaken the dollar exchange rate. This is because the American recipients of foreign securities (wampum used in payment for U.S. assets) are doing what any trend-following patriot would do: selling them for dollars.

The gnomes of Zurich were prized for mystery. Greenspan is heralded for a quality of foresight bordering on clairvoyance. Yet—it must be said—there were no gnomes, and Greenspan is only human. However, the Fed is conducting a monetary policy that presupposes the gift of prophecy. It presumes to regulate the GDP, not merely the inflation rate, by raising or lowering a money rate. In the press release it issued to explain its last half-point easing, the FOMC sounded like a composite of the economic planning agencies of unredeemed socialist Britain and communist Poland. "[C]apital investment has continued to soften," stated the committee, "and the persistent erosion in current and expected profitability, in combination with rising uncertainty about the business outlook, seems poised to dampen capital spending going forward. This potential restraint, together with the possible effects of earlier reductions in equity wealth on consumption and the risk of slower growth abroad, threatens to keep the pace of economic activity unacceptably weak."

The Fed caught the market napping—a good thing, Chairman Greenspan seems to believe, as speculative sentiment is there to be managed, like the funds rate—and Stephen Cecchetti, a one-time director of research at the New York Fed, duly expressed his amazement. "The speed of the monetary easing this winter and spring—four interest rate reductions in just over three months—has taken everyone's breath away," he wrote in the *Financial Times*. "The clear sense of urgency is without precedent."

The clear and present danger is that the chairman, being mortal, will miscalculate. It has happened before. Perhaps, he (and for that matter, the predictive consensus on Wall Street) has underestimated the strength and persistence of domestic inflation. Perhaps, by over-stimulating, the Fed will push bond yields and mortgage rates higher. Possibly, by perpetuating a belief in the Federal Reserve's capacity to control essentially uncontrollable events, Greenspan will embolden American investors and precipitate even greater market losses. These are the risks that may be inferred by reading between the lines of the Europeans' critique of American policy.

Many are the pitfalls of international currency selection. We ourselves are mortally certain that the Fed's operating techniques are unsound—they represent what the late, great Friedrich von Hayek described as the "pretense of knowledge." We are also painfully aware that currency markets do not always respond to the most penetrating central banking critique (even if we have managed to produce one). Furthermore, we know, the forces bearing on exchange rates are almost beyond counting. The dollar is in a bull market to match the great, finally absurd ascension of the early 1980s. It will end on nobody's cue. So we repeat the threshold question: What is the risk to a natural holder of dollars of holding only dollars?

"The risk," replies Albert Friedberg, director and general partner of the Friedberg Mercantile Group, Toronto, to whom our Jay Diamond put the question, "is that external and internal inflation will begin eating away money, savings. There is an attack on both sides: the internal attack is already on, with the inflation rate in the U.S. creeping upwards and upwards, and the U.S. has been lucky because the dollar was strong and the dollar held down imported inflation. When the dollar now begins to weaken, I think that we will begin to see inflation get a little worse because external inflation will come in. You won't want to sit through the dollar declining 15% or 20%, which is likely to happen in our view."

Diamond proposed that being long the dollar was the great trade of the past five years. "No," said Friedberg, "the great trade was not dollars; the great trade was Nasdaq. And because of that, the dollar was strong. Let's call a spade a spade. So you could've been in yen and long Nasdaq and still made a fortune, or been in euro and long Nasdaq and made a fortune. Now that the Nasdaq has deflated, and the stock market is receding as a factor, the dollar is no longer the play."

What is? Friedberg, like us, is more certain of what he doesn't like than of what he does. He says that he is buying the euro, but mainly as a play against the dollar. Lately, he adds, he's been buying the yen, "which we think will do better in the very, very, very short term."

The euro, considered by itself? "Is getting a little bit better," Friedberg goes on. "Clearly, it is a better currency today if I compare central banks. I would be a lot happier if behind that central bank, behind that hard-money central bank, there was a faster-growing economy and a more coherent fiscal policy all around. Those things are important when looking at a currency."

The yen has behind it neither a growing economy nor a coherent fiscal policy. It offers no visible interest rate. The dollar's merits are obvious, but not so the yen's. The potential rewards available to the holders of Japanese assets under the new reformist government of Junichiro Koizumi are purely speculative. However, we observe, the Bank of Japan has resisted the demands of its critics to implement a "radical" monetary reform (i.e., to debase the currency). Furthermore, notes Kathy Matsui, strategist at Goldman Sachs, professional investors are functionally short the world's No. 2 economy: "People are buying Japan because they fear being underweight. Everyone's overweight Europe and underweight Japan." To which we would add that the world is not underweight the United States.

"Every year I go to France for vacation for two weeks," says Jean-Marie Eveillard, fund manager at Arnhold & S. Bleichroeder and portfolio manager of First Eagle Sogen Funds. "Last year was the first time that daily life was cheap. Before, it was always expensive." It has been a six-year bull market in the dollar, Eveillard proceeds. "It can keep going on, but it already has gone on for a long time.

And now, since the beginning of the year, we see the Fed printing more and more money. Maybe the consumer price index is stirring, the American economy is weakening, the Nasdaq (up to a month ago) is declining. Are they worried about something, or are they ignoring the lessons of the 1970s, which is that you should not accommodate an increase in energy prices? Also, whenever I see comments made by currency analysts or traders, it seems to me that they are up on the dollar because the dollar is up!

"We try to be as much bottom-up as we can in the fund," Eveillard goes on. In what we perceive to be normal times, we are 50% hedged [with respect to euro exposure—inasmuch as the fund's shareholders are American, they count their returns in dollars]. Only if we perceive that something is really odd, or bizarre, or vaguely threatening will we change. Currently, I think we are 15% hedged in our exposure to the euro. We think the euro is undervalued and maybe it is about to change. If the dollar were to strengthen further, it would be painful to us."

As for gold, it has a 21-year bear market to answer for, but it's been spared worse humiliations. Unlike the Fed, the ECB or the Bank of Japan, it is not a government bureaucracy. It employs no economists and makes no forecasts. It manipulates no interest rates. It is owned—reluctantly, in many cases—by central banks, and it can be sold or leased at their whim. However, it cannot be materialized by an act of monetary policy. Gold is inherently scarce. Its value is the reciprocal of the perceived competence of central bankers and finance ministers. It has its place.

Broadside of the Barn

December 2, 2005

Before it became synonymous with deflation fighting and "helicopter money," the name of the new Federal Reserve chairman-designate was identified with "inflation targeting." Ben S. Bernanke

helped to write a book on the subject. And although he vows to follow in the footsteps of Alan Greenspan, an archopponent of any
check on the policy-making discretion of the Federal Open Market
Committee, inflation targeting is bound to figure increasingly in the
councils of central bankers and investors alike.

We are against it, as, indeed, we are against the system it's
intended to modify. Both the system in place and the one advo-
cated by the Maestro-to-be require someone—necessarily, a fallible human being—to venture a forecast. We must all deal with the
future, but the Fed goes one step over the line. It fixes an interest
rate to try to improve the future before it can even come to pass. By
"improve," the central bankers mean a policy to bring about gently
rising prices. Inflation targeting would, in fact, be no great departure from the methods the Fed already employs. However, by instituting a target, the FOMC would make even more explicit the
faith it shares with every other modern monetary policy-making
agency. The central banks believe they can control future events.
We say that events control the central banks.

The logic of our case would lead an investor to seek less exposure to bonds and the dollar (indeed, to all currencies) and more
to non-government-issued stores of value. We proceed from a pair
of homely truths. No.1, central bankers hold no greater claim to
clairvoyance than the rest of us. No. 2, the currencies they manage
are accident-prone and combustible. Paper currencies inevitably
lose their value, and gold-backed currencies have always been trans-
muted into paper. In the United States, as for most other nations,
the history of money since 1900 is the story of debasement.

So low are the world's monetary expectations that "price stability" is today defined as a positive rate of inflation. A 2% or 3%
inflation rate is, in fact, what many of the inflation targeting central banks strive for. Hitting the bull's eye—as some do some of
the time—they bask in the kudos of investors and governments.
One hand clapping would be kudo enough. Over a decade, a 2.5%
rate of currency depreciation results in a 20.3% destruction of

purchasing power. When investment returns are booming, it is easy to overlook the loss. But the boom went out of the S&P 500 in 2000. From 1998 to date, the total return of the index is flat when calculated in inflation-adjusted dollars (for the purpose, we use the "core" CPI).

Money is a social contrivance. It is imperfect, as is every other social contrivance: Laws cause a proliferation of lawyers. The language gets twisted by politicians and securities analysts. A certain number of marriages end in divorce. A 2% or 3% rate of price inflation is also imperfect, of course, but no more so than the indices that purport to measure the price changes themselves. The past hundred years have encompassed great inflations, suppressed inflations and debt deflations. Rated against these horrors, the argument goes, the monetary record of the industrialized countries over the past 10 or 15 years is more than creditable.

Could it not be better? Enter—pending Senate confirmation—Bernanke and his new ideas. In a 2003 speech, the then Fed governor compared inflation targeting to the metric system—in wide use outside the United States, but regarded inside it as "foreign, impenetrable, and possibly subversive." He noted that, since the early 1990s, such pioneering central banks as those of New Zealand, Australia, Canada, Britain and Sweden, among others, had nailed an inflation target to the wall and, as often as not, come close to hitting it. "Central banks that have switched to inflation targeting have generally been pleased with the results they have obtained," Bernanke said. "The strongest evidence on that score is that, thus far at least, none of the several dozen adopters of inflation targeting has abandoned the approach."

The strongest evidence that something besides inflation targeting is responsible for the results obtained by inflation-targeting central banks is suggested by the pictures produced by colleague Ian McCulley. Two of the three central banks here portrayed were early adopters of inflation targeting. The third is the one that Bernanke hopes to lead into inflation-targeting enlightenment. If the graphs were unlabeled, could you identify the central bank that tacked no inflation target to the wall?

Since inflation is a lagging indicator, a would-be monetary marksman must take aim at the future. To do so raises practical questions. Which inflation index to use? By what means to attempt to exert control? In the case of the Fed, how to juggle the triple mandate of "price stability," "financial stability" and "full employment"? What do these phrases mean? What is a "stable" price level? Is stability invariably desirable? Is it desirable at a time when China and India have pushed the global supply curve downward and to the right (implying falling prices for tradable goods and services)? To the last we say no; in those circumstances, "stability" is a fabrication of the central banks that over-crank the printing presses to make the price level rise. Perhaps, the excess money has financed the global bull markets in bonds and houses. What is the difference, in monetary terms, between a bull real estate market and "inflation"? Answer: Bull real-estate markets

"Say, I'll pay you ten thousand bucks for that gold inlay."

go unregistered in the indices that central banks target (or, in the case of the Fed, don't explicitly target but certainly watch).

Former Fed governor Laurence H. Meyer, in a 2003 talk at the Federal Reserve Bank of St. Louis, described a telltale exchange on the subject of how to define "stability." The scene was Meyer's first FOMC meeting, in July 1996, and governor Janet Yellen was making the case for inflation targeting; she said she would aim at 2%. Greenspan replied that the Federal Reserve had a mandate to foster stable prices, not rising ones. To which Yellen rejoined that the Fed also has a mandate to promote full employment. To hear her tell it, a small positive rate of currency depreciation is a necessary lubricant for economic growth (not so, according to a survey of 133 economies over 50 years, produced in 2002 by Stanley Fischer et al.).

"Janet then seized the initiative," Meyer related, "asking the chairman to indicate how he would define price stability. Greenspan tried to get away with his vague definition: 'Price stability is the state in which expected changes in the general price level do not effectively alter business or household decisions.' But Yellen pressed him and asked him if he could put a number on that. Remarkably, the chairman agreed, and said he preferred zero inflation, correctly measured. Janet asked him if he could settle for 2% incorrectly measured."

Meyer finished his story:

> During a go-around on the topic, only a few Committee members preferred a target of zero, and the consensus was very strong for a 2% inflation target. The chairman ended up summarizing the discussion as 'an agreement for 2%,' but he cautioned committee members not to reveal that such a discussion ever took place.

Eavesdropping from wherever dead politicians spend eternity, the founders of the Fed might have been confused. The original 1913 legislation made no reference to "price stability," that item of business having been disposed of for all time (or so the legislators might have believed) by the 1900 law that wrote the gold standard into the federal statute books. The Federal Reserve Act merely directed the new institution to "furnish an elastic currency [and] to afford means of rediscounting commercial paper." The legislative authors sought to prevent panics (the 1907 collapse being fresh in mind) and to apportion the nation's banking resources more equitably between the city banks and their country cousins.

"Financial stability" has proven as susceptible to varying interpretations as "price stability." William McChesney Martin Jr., Fed chairman from 1951 to 1970, assumed a symmetrical obligation: to guard against panics but also, approximately, to "take away the punch bowl just when the party's getting good." The Greenspan Fed, in contrast, has operated in a manner that economists at the Bank for International Settlements neatly criticized a few years ago: "Lowering [interest] rates or providing ample liquidity when problems materialize, but not raising them as imbalances build up, can be rather insidious in the longer run," wrote Claudio Borio and Philip Lowe in BIS Working Paper No. 114. "They promote a form of moral hazard that can sow the seeds of instability and of costly fluctuations in the real economy."

Of course, under Greenspan, the Fed has had a free hand in this regard (and most others). In the absence of a published operational benchmark, it can hit anything it cares to aim for, its marksmanship being materially enhanced by its ability to keep the identity of its targets secret until after it nails them. "I think that the U.S. economy has benefited from the flexibility that the Federal Reserve has derived by eschewing a formal inflation target," governor Donald Kohn, Greenspan's disciple on the FOMC and a disappointed runner-up in the contest to succeed him, said in 2003. "By flexibility, I mean not frequent changes in long-term objectives, but rather the freedom to deviate from long-term price stability, perhaps for a while."

Kohn here describes every bureaucrat's kingdom of heaven. Unconstrained, the Fed sets its overnight interest rate to steer the economy and the level of prices toward a set of destinations it does not have to disclose. Companies can measure their success by earnings per share, baseball players by batting averages and students by grade-point averages. Success for the Fed is undefined, both as to immediate result and to that result's distant consequences.

The tendency of the Greenspan Fed to make it up as it goes along could be criticized on principle. "Ours is a government of laws, not of men," New York City Mayor William Jay Gaynor was fond of repeating at around the time the Fed came into existence. But that objection is rarely heard. "If it ain't broke, don't fix it," is the more commonly voiced sentiment; Kohn himself took that approach in the aforementioned 2003 speech. The United States had "achieved price stability," he declared. "[I]nflation expectations are low and stable, and we have done this with two relatively shallow recessions in 20 years. Many factors have contributed to this economic performance, but monetary policy has been an important element. So for me, the default option is to keep doing what we have been doing—however hard it might be to model or explain."

Model, no; explain, yes. Under Greenspan, "stability" has come to mean "not going down." The decade-long sag in the Japanese economy and Japanese price level badly frightened him. To ward off a similar occurrence, the Fed points for a rate of inflation on the order of what the Bank of England and the European Central Bank call their reference points (2% or so). The difference between Greenspan and Bernanke is that the left-brained former spelling champion and chairman of the Princeton University economics department would announce what rate of dollar depreciation the central bank actually hopes to achieve. Announce it as a "framework" of policy, not a straitjacket, Bernanke says.

Why not spell it out? Maybe Greenspan is mindful of the fate of statistical relationships that fall under the official gaze. Goodhart's Law, propounded by the English economist and central banker C.A.E. Goodhart, holds that "any observed statistical regularity will tend to collapse once pressure is placed upon it for control purposes." Christopher Fildes, the unique English financial journalist, reformulates Goodhart thus: "It's all very well when the anthropologists observe the savages, but all bets are off when the savages start observing the anthropologists."

You wouldn't suppose that the money supply data would be corrupted through the workings of Goodhart's Law—undergoing a statistical personality change just by returning the stare of the world's central bankers. But that is exactly what happened in the early 1980s. The story of how this came to pass holds lessons today for all who espouse targeting interest rates or inflation rates, or for anyone who buys bonds in the belief that "the authorities" control the future.

By the early- to mid-1970s, worldwide inflation rates were tripping along in the high single digits (or, in the cases of Japan, the U.K. and Italy, the not-so-low double digits). Arthur Burns, as eminent a scholar as Bernanke himself, was Fed chairman. A synchronous global boom was under way. Commodity prices and money supply were booming. Currencies floated (or, in value, sank) after the Nixon administration put what remained of the gold standard out of its misery in 1971. (Foreign governments and central banks had had the privilege of exchanging unwanted dollars for gold at the fixed rate of $35 to the ounce; on Aug. 15 of that year, Nixon said: No more.) To beat back inflation, one central bank after another "adopted publicly announced, qualified targets for a key monetary aggregate," as Goodhart relates in his excellent textbook, *Money, Information and Uncertainty* (the MIT Press, 1991). Silver-haired readers may recall some of the national preferences: for West Germany, "central bank money"; for Japan and France, M-2; for the United States and Canada, M-1. The target was expressed in different ways by different countries—the United States used upper and lower bounds of percentage growth from the announcement date. Hence the cone-shaped growth targets that featured in the financial press of the day.

Money-supply targeting came to the United States in 1976, but the Fed's heart wasn't in it. The funds rate remained the beacon of monetary policy. It's a fact of life that a regulatory authority can control the supply or the price of the thing it regulates, but not both at once. But that fact was glossed over until the Volcker reform of Oct. 6, 1979. On that day, the Fed picked its poison. It decided to target non-borrowed reserves and let the funds rate go where it might. Where the rate went was up—and up and up.

The experiment lasted for three years. In the way of the world, it lacked scientific purity (the Fed did not entirely let go of the funds rate, a fact about which the monetarists bitterly complained). But the back of an especially virulent inflation was eventually broken. Not that the bond market believed what it was seeing. You would have supposed, Goodhart points out, that so determined an anti-inflation initiative as Paul Volcker's would have given the long end of the yield curve a little backbone. But no: "In the event, the correlation between movements in short and long rates actually increased." As the funds rate climbed and dove, so did bond yields, a fact to bear in mind the next time someone speculates on the macroeconomic significance of persistently low long-term interest rates in the year 2005. Maybe creditors are just a little slow on the uptake.

The Volcker Fed abandoned its monetarist experiment in October 1982. The U.S. economy was in recession, and the less developed nations, a.k.a. the Third World, were in financial crisis. High and volatile interest rates had inspired a wave of banking innovation—money supply, never easily tabulated, had become much harder to count. And the tried-and-true relationship between money supply and nominal incomes had broken down; the very meaning of monetary growth had become problematical, as Goodhart's Law preordained. The new-new idea in monetary policy was judgment, or "discretion."

Today, the monetary policy watchwords are "constrained discretion." Inflation targeting is the thing. Dozens of central banks set their interest rates with reference to a specific inflation target. As inflation targeting is inherently forward-looking, this means that these dozens of central banks have gotten themselves into the star-gazing business.

One of the inflation-targeting banks is the Bank of England. In 1992, the year George Soros helped to speed the pound's exit from the Exchange Rate Mechanism, the bank started aiming at an explicit inflation target. Now the bull's eye reads "2% per annum." In 1997, the government reassigned responsibility for decisions on interest rates to a new Monetary Policy Committee (read: brainiac economists) from the Chancellor of the Exchequer (read: politician). Since 1992, and even more so from 1997, the measured rate of inflation in Britain has been lower and less volatile than the rates preceding the inflation-targeting reforms.

Mervyn King, governor of the Bank of England, and Rachel Lomax, deputy governor, have explained how they do what they do in a pair of speeches accessible on the bank's Web site: "The Inflation Target Ten Years On," by King in November 2002, and "Inflation Targeting—Achievement and Challenges," by Lomax in February 2004. Neither makes extravagant claims for inflation targeting. But neither do they acknowledge the full implications of Goodhart's Law. Lomax, addressing an audience of nonspecialists in Bristol, served up a "Short History of Twentieth Century Monetary Policy" in just one sentence: "For the first time since the collapse of Bretton Woods—arguably since the Gold Standard—after decades of unhappy experiments with fine-tuning, incomes policies and monetary targets, buffeted by the explosive growth of financial markets and often misled by economic dogma, governments have finally found an approach to monetary policy that seems to work." That policy, of course, is inflation targeting.

Yes, the gold standard did work. Over long cycles it anchored the price level to a fixed point of value. But even this most efficient and elegant of monetary structures was unable to deliver "price stability" in the short or medium haul. Prices sagged in the late 19th century, and they rose in the early 20th century (in general, they rose in wartime and sank in peacetime). In the 13 years leading up to the creation of the Fed, as a matter of fact, the dollar lost more than 21% of its value against an index of wholesale prices. Bond prices fell from 1900 to 1920.

Does inflation targeting work? Is the evident statistical relationship between short-term interest rates and next year's inflation rate really immutable? It is not, we are wagering. What ruined the early 1980s' experiment in money-supply targeting was, in part, the constant reinvention of the "money supply" by enterprising bankers and their depositors. So, too, we believe, with "inflation." Let the world's central banks define inflation as "core CPI"—no food, no energy, no house prices—and that arbitrary inflation measure will inevitably lose some of its economic significance. As a central bank is congratulating itself on a brilliant job of inflation containment, house prices (let us say) go through the roof. It's not that Greenspan, King et al. can't hit the target. The problem is that they don't hit the new target that pops up unannounced outside their field of macroeconomic vision.

We wonder if the "conundrum" of low bond yields and a flat yield curve is not another manifestation of the tendencies observed by Goodhart and Fildes. The Fed targets the funds rate. Knowing this—and knowing that the Fed is, above all things these days, "transparent"—opportunistic traders borrow at the funds rate and buy an assortment of longer-dated, and higher-yielding, coupons. The yield curve thereby flattens and bond prices rally. Central bankers shake their heads at the mystery of it all. But, like Fildes's anthropologists, they have carelessly failed to notice that the statistical relationships in which they put their trust are—so to speak—staring back at them. By targeting the putative relationship between short-term interest rates and price inflation, central banks are targeting themselves, and us, into error.

Error comes with the territory in central banking (as it does in commentary about central banking). Investors can be sure of nothing so much as the need to find a margin of safety. The problem is that, at this writing, in the bond market none is available. The 50-year, inflation-linked British gilt is priced to yield less than 1%. An unindexed 50-year French government bond is quoted at less than 4%. The 10-year Japanese government bond fetches 1.45% and the 10-year U.S. Treasury, 4.45%. If the idea of central banking had a CUSIP number or a ticker symbol, it would be trading near its all-time high. It would make an excellent short sale.

Though there is $45 trillion of debt in the world and only $2 trillion of gold, we wonder if the smaller of the two markets hasn't figured something out.

End of the Honor System

December 14, 2007

If the U.S. economy is "fundamentally sound," as Treasury Secretary Henry Paulson patriotically insisted before a Washington, D.C., housing conference last week, it's a new kind of soundness. Today, a credit crisis is overlaid on a dollar bear market in a time of moderate GDP growth and rising, but still subdued, inflation. Incongruously, the Bush administration is promoting a mortgage-forbearance scheme as philosophically radical as any dreamed up by Franklin D. Roosevelt in the wake of the Great Depression. UBS does not exaggerate when it characterizes the debacle in mortgage-backed-securities structures as "the biggest failure of ratings and risk management ever."

It speaks volumes about this statistically prosperous time that the words "Great Depression" are on the tip of the American tongue. Query Factiva, the Dow Jones search engine, for the conjunction of the words "mortgages," "housing" and "Great Depression," and you will find that they appeared together in 168 news stories in the past month alone—more than were published in any 12 months up until the mortgage-blighted year of 2007. Something, somewhere, is fundamentally unsound. The question before the house is what.

We surmise that that something lies in our system of money and credit. We don't mean the mistakes that precipitated the mortgage pileup, as gross as some were. After all, mistakes are what come from getting out of bed in the morning. The question we raise is why error continued to be piled on error long after it was obvious that the subprime math was fuzzy. In market economies, absent collusion or government intervention, mistakes tend to be rectified expeditiously. They tend not to be perpetuated until, say, the fall of the Berlin Wall (as in the old Soviet Union) or until the 70-year-old bankers can push the 80-year-old bankers out of the chairman's seat (as in the Japan of the 1990s). Yesteryear's errors in mortgage underwriting are, at this moment, being marked to market, but not before immense, unnecessary losses were dealt. By February of this year, if not before, the crisis in subprime was out in the open. In that month, HSBC and New Century Financial Corp. confessed to shockingly big write-downs, and the low-rated segment of the tradable mortgage index (the 06-1 ABX) took a 16.6% tumble. But lenders and borrowers continued to do business together on the same discredited terms. From March through November, according to *Bloomberg* data, $161 billion of subprime liens were originated and securitized. Never was there such a swarm of lemmings, each packing a personal computer.

Many today worry about a run on the institutions of structured finance. We worry about the absence of a run. Why did confidence remain unshattered for so long? Where were the knowledgeable runners in, say, 2006? Something put them to sleep.

In this season of gift giving and finger pointing, we lay blame on the system of monetary organization that has not, up until this moment, been given its proper name. This faulty construct is the honor system. In monetary and credit terms, it's tennis without the net—currencies unsecured by gold and loans unsupported by the customary collateral or documentation or both. The spirit and protocols of the honor system have been overspreading America since the early 1930s. Behind it was the noble ideal of human progress.

Humanity is better than it used to be—more principled, more knowing, more capable, or so the logic ran. Alternatively, many argued, humanity should have been better but Wall Street kept it down. To raise it up, governments had to build banking systems at once safer and more openhanded than the free-market models allowed. And they should crank the monetary printing presses faster. Yes, the early exponents of the new system allowed, money backed by nothing but the hearty promises of the issuing government had had a checkered past. It was, indeed, a flop in revolutionary France and Civil War-era America, and almost everywhere else it had been put to the test. But a better kind of paper could be, and would be, devised. Some of it would be backed, in part or indirectly, by gold. Some of it would be uncollateralized. In any case, starting at about the time of the Great Depression, the world edged away from monetary orthodoxy and into the misty fields of monetary experimentation. It has continued to experiment to this day. Results have been mixed, but a common theme has persisted. In a word, it is "more."

The push toward more can be easily seen in the international monetary system, such as it is. It's an arrangement tailor-made to perpetuate such errors as the misrating, mismodeling and mispricing of American subprime mortgages. Only compare the discipline imposed by foreign creditors on the free-spending United States in the late 1960s to the relative lack of discipline imposed on an even-freer-spending United States in 2007. In the 1960s, the Bretton Woods monetary system was still in force. Under it, currencies were exchangeable into the dollar at fixed rates, and the dollar was exchangeable into gold. The dollar was defined as one-thirty-fifth of an ounce of gold. From this definition arose a fact. The fact was that the Federal Reserve was not a free agent. Its ability to print money was constrained. Let it overstep the mark, and it would hear from suspicious foreigners choosing to exercise their right to exchange dollars for gold at the stipulated rate. And in the late 1960s, a properly suspicious France so chose.

A glance at the accompanying pictures vindicates the French attitude, so nettlesome to the Johnson and Nixon administrations. The decades preceding and following the closing of the American gold window could hardly be more different. In the 10 years preceding that defining event, interest rates, and the pace of monetary expansion, were relatively low. In the following 10 years, they were relatively high.

And now? The dollar is undefined. It is what the market—and the meddling central banks and their governments—say it is. Its value today ostensibly floats or rises or sinks. As it has lately sunk, the United States' trade deficit has narrowed—since August, by 16.4%, thanks to the delayed effects of the weaker dollar. But, of course, the dollar floats freely only against currencies that themselves are permitted to float, a community from which the scrip of America's leading creditors is notably absent. Are China, Russia and the Gulf States as constructively suspicious today as France was in the 1960s about the dollar and America's persistently outsize current-account deficit? Do they voice their disapproval of America's fundamentally unsound mortgage market and off-balance-sheet banking liabilities? Are they critical of the reserve-currency system itself, that "exorbitant privilege" so roundly condemned by France? There is some expressed disapproval. And there is some shuffling of reserve assets out of dollars and into alternative stores of value. But, mostly, there is the continued high-speed printing of renminbi and rubles and dinars and riyals with which to buy more dollars. In this way, the creditor nations suppress the rise in the value of their currencies. In China, especially, a relatively undervalued currency is prized for the lift it gives to export earnings and thus to employment and so to the stature of the Communist Party.

But none of this muttering and shuffling induces the United States to tighten its monetary policy in acknowledgment of the dollar's declining value. On the contrary, the Federal Reserve is easing. Under the orthodox gold standard, imbalances between countries in payments deficit and surplus tended to be self-correcting.

"The perception that national currencies would maintain their values and convertibility into the future," writes Giulio M. Gallarotti in his splendid volume, *The Anatomy of an International Monetary Regime*, "essentially created a set of circumstances in which the exchange rates and convertibility came to defend themselves through a process characterized by elements of self-fulfilling prophecy." No gold-club member, whether operating (with respect to the balance of payments) in the red or in the black, conducted its domestic monetary affairs as if the outside world didn't exist. Today, the monetary hegemon permits itself the luxury of formulating its interest rate policy for the 50 states alone. Thus do imbalances become institutionalized.

Institutionalized, too, is that crowd-pleasing elixir, liquidity. It is what the world needs more and more of and what the world sorely misses when, as at present, it is temporarily gone. It can be no accident that asset markets are in orbit. What today's system lacks—an anchor—is what sent the prices of houses, office buildings, soybeans and equities higher and higher across many time zones. And so, we believe, did the absence of an anchor help to foster a decline in the quality of debt obligations and the collapse of credit spreads, conditions that directly led to the mortgage debacle. Gold-anchored monetary systems were grounded in a view of humanity that was at once philosophically skeptical and philosophically liberal. The ancients believed that free markets were best but that some check on the tendencies to over-print, overborrow and overspeculate might be useful. Compare and contrast that view to the print-money-with-which-to-buy-dollars regime. It fairly dares the United States, issuer of the world's top monetary brand, to overindulge.

It would take a nation of saints to resist exploiting the privileges accorded to the owner of the reserve-currency franchise. Imagine if this priceless gift were one day settled, out of the blue, on an unsuspecting country. Imagine if this lucky people were presented with a proposition along the following lines: "You may now consume much more than you produce while financing the deficit with the currency only you can print. Emit as much of this scrip as you think advisable. The world treasures it." Would not the citizens of this lucky nation spend a little more freely, eat a little bit better and speculate a little more readily than they had before their currency passed for good money the world over? Might they not take it upon themselves to wage a small war, if financial limitations had previously constrained them? Such is the unique position of a reserve-currency franchise holder in a paper-money system.

We are not trying to glorify the past, only to illuminate the present and peer into the future. Financial man in the time of Bretton Woods (1944–71) was no better than his 2007 descendant. The gold-backed dollar notwithstanding, we Americans contrived to engineer a tempest in the Treasury bond market in 1958 (a case of speculating on interest rates with heavy leverage) and a "credit crunch" in the banking system in1966 (when the Fed tightened policy to check inflationary tendencies). And when the Bretton Woods system started falling apart—as every monetary system eventually does—the United States resorted to various big-power expedients to postpone the reckoning. It threw around its strategic weight, manipulated (or tried to manipulate) the free-market gold price, imposed capital controls on the American people and generally busied itself with addressing the symptoms of the gold drain rather than the underlying causes. It had no time for the simple truth that there were too many dollars issued in relation to the collateral supporting them. And when that truth became undeniable, the Nixon administration declared the dollar to be unconvertible at any rate. Henceforth, the greenback's value would float. So, at a stroke, was removed what economist Robert Triffin called "harsh, but healthy, balance-of-payments disciplines."

In the absence of anything resembling those salutary checks, lenders and borrowers have flung off their inhibitions (before recently retrieving them). Dollars pile sky-high in foreign central banks, an American-generated credit crisis resists the usual monetary ministrations and rising "headline" prices compete for the attention of central banks with the unmistakable symptoms of debt deflation. Every credit cycle, by definition, ends in crisis, or at least embarrassment, and so has the 2007 edition. We leave it to the scholars in the field of comparative financial crack-ups to test our hypothesis, namely: Lenders and borrowers and ratings-agency analysts and market makers kept making the same errors long after they should have seen the light. Do we not live in the Information Age? Is this not a time of constant connectivity? Why, then, the achingly slow response time of lenders and borrowers to the unmistakable signs of trouble in mortgage finance? Why, in the midst of these trumpeted subprime problems, has the credit quality of new commercial mortgage-backed securities taken a turn for the worse? (Moody's reports that the third quarter marked a new low.) Does no one read the papers?

A while back, the designers of banking offices decided to abandon the customary steel grillwork that long separated the depositors from the money. The bars and gates and bulletproof plastic were unwelcoming and obsolete, the new thinking had it. So down came the bars and bandit barriers—and up went bank robberies (notably in the New Jersey branches of Commerce Bank, America's "Most Convenient Bank"). The police have asked the architects to reconsider.

So, too, in the field of monetary and credit design. Central bankers, mortgage lenders and financial engineers have continued to push out the frontiers of the honor system. They lend against ever more liberally defined collateral (if any at all); appraise credit risk in actuarial fashion, rather than case by case; and fire up the governmental printing presses. Such, in a nutshell, has been the late-20th and early-21st century credit and monetary program. It's not now the detectives who are pushing back against these initiatives, but the investors, the gold bulls not least. To be long gold is, in a grand thematic way, to be short the socialization of risk.

We don't claim that the print-money-with-which-to-buy-dollars system is the only cause of the global credit crisis, just that it must

"In what way, precisely, Mr. Leffingwell, do bonds 'suck'?"

have made a signal contribution. So, we would guess, have changes in banking and financial-markets regulation. The Bretton Woods era was heavily policed. Not only were exchange rates fixed; so, too, were domestic bank deposit rates and New York Stock Exchange commission rates. By lifting the funds rate above the maximum permissible bank deposit rates, the Fed could "disintermediate" the banking system and stop mortgage lending in its tracks. The "harsh but healthy balance-of-payments disciplines" in place as recently as 36 years ago were complemented by many another kind of discipline, none of it encouraging of the forms of innovation and risk taking that characterize the present day.

Technology, deregulation, a faith in mankind and really big bonuses have brought us to where we are. Before the advent of cheap computing power, it is inconceivable that a lender would have made a mortgage to a perfect stranger and sold that lien to an investment bank for packaging in a residential mortgage-backed security. Or that still another investment bank would fashion a collateralized debt obligation of that and other RMBS, the sum total referencing more, perhaps, than a million separate mortgages. Or that the creditworthiness of the unseen borrowers would be modeled in such a fashion that $100 million of subprime liens could assay, in the form of an RMBS, $80 million of double- or triple-A mortgage obligations. To the lenders of only a generation or two ago, it would have seemed fantastic. Indeed, to not a few observers today, it is beginning to seem like a bit of a stretch.

Fitch Ratings last month, in a report entitled "The Impact of Poor Underwriting Practices and Fraud in Subprime RMBS Performance," described its hunt for an answer to the question of why so many statistically creditworthy borrowers in the class of 2006 had defaulted on their mortgages virtually out of the gate. The proliferation of so-called affordability products—interest-only loans, option-rate ARMs, etc.—played a part, but so, too, did old-fashioned lying. A Fitch-commissioned study of more than three million loans originated between 1997 and 2006 (most of 2005–06 vintage) "found that as much as 70% of early payment default loans contained fraud misrepresentations on the application," the agency said. Still curious, Fitch directed its analysts to pull the full origination and servicing files on 45 loans that had gone into early-payment default. It seemed passing strange, Fitch noted, that these failed borrowers had checked the right boxes: They were buying the houses to occupy, not to invest in, and their FICO scores, at an average of 686, were high enough to give a lender comfort. "The result of the analysis was disconcerting at best," the Fitch report sorrowfully related, "as there was the appearance of fraud or misrepresentation in almost every file." But not every defaulting borrower fibbed. One forthrightly disclosed on his application that he was the "straw buyer" in a property-flipping fandango.

In finance, language and symbols are not far from substance. The collateral that stood behind the pound sterling in the heyday of the international gold standard was little more than filigree, scholars tell us. Arthur I. Bloomfield, in a 1959 study for the Federal Reserve

Bank of New York, found that the ratio of gold to the demand liabilities of the British banking system was less than 5%. "Yet," adds
Bloomfield, "at no time during the period, as far as I am aware, were
the continuing stability and convertibility of sterling, or indeed
the currencies of other leading gold standard countries, ever seriously questioned." It wasn't the number of ingots in the basement
that counted, but, rather, the demonstrated ability of central banks
to materialize enough bullion to satisfy any taker. A suitably high
discount rate would fetch gold from across the seas.

So the market trusted the Old Lady of Threadneedle Street
implicitly, and that trust, from 1880 to 1914, was duly repaid. But the
market did not trust the Bank of England to manage paper money.
That would only come later, and at odd intervals. It happens, even
under the honor system, that the market loses faith in the bank's
miracle-working abilities. At those not-infrequent moments, sterling depreciates against better stores of value. Twenty-first century
central bankers go on and on about their "credibility." Hearing that
word, we are inclined to substitute "incredibility," for, to us, the
notion that the stewards of paper money can pick the right interest
rate out of the air and successfully impose it on the economies they
pretend to manage is literally unbelievable.

In the United States, the honor system in credit was effectively
launched with the Banking Act of 1935. It institutionalized federal
deposit insurance, centralized power within the Federal Reserve
System in Washington, D.C., and eliminated the double liability on
bank stocks. Erasing this double liability excited no great opposition, but it set the philosophical tone of financial regulation for the
next 75 years and counting. Up until the 1935 act, the stockholders
of a nationally chartered bank bore a particular kind of risk. If the
bank in which they invested went broke, they were on the hook for
the depositors' losses up to the par value of the shares they owned.
In practice, bank-stock owners found ways to circumvent the rule,
which, in any case, hardly prevented the runs and failures that did so
much to galvanize public opinion in support of modern financial

reforms—deposit insurance, the Federal Reserve System and the hundred and one other kinds of governmental initiatives that have gone so far in socializing the risk of loss in American finance. Double liability on the par value of bank shares was a symbol of individual responsibility in an earlier day. The "too big to fail" doctrine is a symbol of collective responsibility in the present time.

In a speech before the Cato Institute in Washington a couple of weeks ago, William Poole, president of the Federal Reserve Bank of St. Louis, made the usual case for the honor system, contrasting it favorably with arrangements in place before the New Deal. Recall, he prodded his audience, the exploded doctrines of one of Paulson's predecessors, Secretary of the Treasury Andrew Mellon. Mellon's formula, so Poole recounted, was to let the market alone, to "liquidate labor, liquidate stocks, liquidate the farmers, liquidate real estate."

"That view," Poole went on, "is long gone. Macroeconomists today do not believe that policies to stabilize the price level and aggregate economic activity create a hazard. Federal Reserve policy that yields greater stability has not and will not protect from loss those who invest in failed strategies, financial or otherwise. Investors and entrepreneurs have as much incentive as they ever had to manage risk appropriately. What they do not have to deal with is macroeconomic risk of the magnitude experienced all too often in the past."

About a century and a half before Poole held forth, a French economist, Frederic Bastiat, put down his thoughts on the often unseen consequences of well-intended actions. He entitled his essay, "That Which Is Seen, and That Which Is Not Seen." "In the economy," wrote Bastiat, "an act, a habit, an institution, a law, gives birth not only to an effect, but to a series of effects. Of these effects, the first one only is immediate; it manifests itself simultaneously with its cause—it is seen. The others unfold in succession—they are not seen: it is well for us if they are foreseen." So it happens, Bastiat explained, that lawmakers and policy makers, in pursuit of a "small present good," bring down on society "a great evil to come."

In the early 1930s, in the aftermath of the Great Depression and a national banking holiday, there seemed no such thing as a "small present good." Anything answering that description was welcome. And if the question had been put to the voters, "Would you exchange today's relief—assuming it, in fact, does any good—for a worldwide mortgage and credit disturbance seven and a half decades down the road?" not many, probably, would have voted it down.

Now that seven and a half decades have come and gone, a Republican administration is sponsoring an anti-foreclosure initiative featuring the not-quite-voluntary revision of certain contracted rates of interest. In the preceding decade, the Federal Reserve has intervened to contain the damage of a collapsed hedge fund (Long-Term Capital Management in 1998), the threatened mass stoppage of the computer clocks (the Y2K affair in 1999) and the threat of everyday low, and lower, prices (a.k.a. "deflation" in 2003–04). At every turn, non-readers of Bastiat overestimated the value of the "present good" and underestimated the cost of the "great evil to come."

Inflation is one such evil, debt deflation another. The present-day monetary system has managed to induce the symptoms of both. It's established central-bank doctrine that, to heal the damage inflicted by a prior gust of monetary stimulus, a new blast is necessary. It's what leads us to expect lower short-term interest rates and, eventually, higher long-term bond yields—in any case, more positively sloped yield curves in the United States and Europe. Paper money and the socialization of credit risk may not, ultimately, be good for the world economy. But they are God's gift to financial journalism.

Chapter Ten

Lenders Don Lampshades

———— ✤ ————

"[There are] capital flows around the market from what feels like
limitless sources—from CDOs, CLOs, hedge funds, private equity
and recycled foreign trade surpluses."

—Victor Consoli, head of corporate credit strategy at Bear Stearns,
quoted in the May 11 *Financial Times.*

Missing Bankruptcies

July 14, 2006

GOING BROKE TAKES some determination in 2006. Low
interest rates and intrepid lenders give many a failing company a stay of execution. The readiest sources of such dis-
pensation are not necessarily banks (which still bear scars from the
crack-ups of the early 1990s), nor thrifts (which came a cropper in
the late 1980s), nor junk-bond mutual funds (which splattered with
the banks). They are, rather, this cycle's composite of those most
aggressive lenders of yesteryear, namely, the hedge funds. Which
fact affords thoughtful members of the bankruptcy bar the leisure
in which to contemplate the sources of their reduced incomes—

and gives the readers of *Grant's* the opportunity to prepare for the coming shambles in credit.

Fewer public companies filed for Chapter 11 protection in 2005 than in any year since 1994, according to PricewaterhouseCoopers, and no reacceleration is yet in evidence in 2006. Strong cash flow is the wholesome reason for this bankruptcy famine. Debtor companies tracked by the analysts at Standard & Poor's Leveraged Commentary & Data show 20% year-over-year growth in EBITDA (earnings before interest, taxes, depreciation and amortization). Changes in the bankruptcy law that took effect in October may also have contributed to the relative paucity of filings. But the elixir called "liquidity" is the most powerful bankruptcy deferral force of all.

Liquidity is a state of mind and a state of finance, commingled. To say that liquidity is abundant means that interest rates are manageable and lenders are compliant. Both have been true, until almost the present day. Tuesday's *Wall Street Journal* reports on the 72% jump in investment-grade bond issuance in the first half of this year, on the rising preponderance of bond-rating downgrades to upgrades, and on the increased application of borrowing proceeds to the payment of dividends and fees to promoters and equity holders of the leveraged business (never mind actually investing in said business—we don't seem to do that anymore). Lloyd Greif, a Los Angeles investment banker, writing in the July 7 *American Banker*, chided lenders for pushing more and more debt on less and less cash flow. "The greed factor has kicked in," he writes, "as lenders see that they can collect fees not just once or twice, but sometimes several times from refinancing leveraged buyout deals over and over again."

No surprise, then, that the "breakout loan product of 2006" is one called "covenant-lite," according to Steven Miller, managing director at S&P's LCD. The name derives from the near absence of the contractual language that reduces a borrower's flexibility to take on additional debt or otherwise weaken the position of its

"How are we quoting bail bonds?"

secured creditors. So far this year, says Miller, 28 covenant-lite loans have come to market in the grand total of $13 billion. In the nine previous years, 1997 to 2005, the market absorbed only $8.4 billion of them. The frisson of fear that rippled through world markets last month did not entirely bypass the credit markets. And lenders have resumed demanding some basic minimum of covenant protection, Miller adds. You may be wondering, what happens to the borrower who violates one of these interest-coverage or leverage tests? Why, on 14 occasions through the first five months of 2006, also according to LCD, borrowers prevailed on their forbearing lenders to grant them a waiver. In a less-forgiving credit market, some number of these covenant violators would have wound up in bankruptcy court.

No two credit cycles are the same, of course. A distinguishing feature of this one, according to Robert J. Rosenberg, global head of the insolvency practice at Latham & Watkins, is the loan-dispensing hedge funds, "and their willingness to refinance almost anything, frequently with a 'loan-to-own' strategy." Loan-to-own?

A stratagem, Rosenberg explains, in which the creditors actually expect a default. In fact, they hope for one, after which their debt will be transformed into equity. It is a sign of these still hopeful times that the loan-to-own practitioners assume their new equity will be worth significantly more than the pre-bankruptcy debt.

In separate developments last month, Goldman Sachs hired a star bankruptcy lawyer, and the federal bankruptcy court in Wilmington, Del., added four new judges, raising the size of that judiciary staff to six. Both actions were anticipatory. As it is, there is scarcely a cloud in the sky of corporate finance. "It's as if you were a trusts and estates lawyer and they declared a moratorium on death," muses William J. Rochelle III, a partner in the New York office of Fulbright & Jaworski, where he specializes in bankruptcies and corporate reorganizations. "As soon as a company catches cold, somebody throws money at them. So they don't wind up in bankruptcy—just with more leverage."

A credit market so unruffled as this one is naturally open to innovation. Of particular concern to the underbilling bankruptcy bar is the "second lien." In days of yore, banks supplied the senior debt, junk-bond buyers the subordinated kind. The second lien, a junior kind of secured loan, made its appearance a couple of years ago. It pays more than senior secured debt (Libor plus 625 basis points vs. Libor plus 279, according to the latest tally by S&P's LCD). But acquisitive hedge funds like it for another reason: Second-lien holders command a better place at the restructuring table than subordinated lenders do. Hence the melodious phrase, "loan to own." Some control-seeking lenders regard second liens as equity-in-waiting, pure and simple. They buy it in hopes of a bankruptcy (as a number of hedge funds did in the case of J.L. French, the failed auto-parts supplier). Never mind that, by definition, those companies are on the road to Chapter 11—or, rather, would be except for the openhandedness of a liquidity-soaked market. Last year, $16 billion of such debt came into the world, and $13 billion has followed in 2006 already.

Once upon a time, of course, banks did the credit work, made the loans and—when the credit work left a little something to be desired—performed the workout. Now, increasingly, says Rosenberg, hedge funds are front and center. If they don't actually originate loans, they participate in loan syndications. "And they continue to buy and take out the other, more traditional lenders at the first sign of trouble," he adds. "They continue to trade among themselves, refinance and frequently end up owning."

"In a few cases last year," reported an article in the January 5 *New York Law Journal*, "second-lien holders have successfully held the restructuring process ransom, demanding to be paid in full or compensated with supersized interest rates. Even so-called 'silent seconds,' who agree in intercreditor agreements to defer to senior debt, are challenging the notion that first-lien holders can dictate strategy and terms. Some judges have rendered rulings sympathetic to those challenges."

Rosenberg demurs: At this point in the cycle, Mr. Market is judge and jury. "I don't want to overstate it," he says, "but it is almost a case that the up-front negotiation, and what you agree to in terms of rights or non-rights in terms of the second lien, almost becomes irrelevant.... [T]here is so much liquidity that, if the seconds don't like it at the end of the day, they just go into the marketplace and buy up the first."

Yes, Rosenberg acknowledges, the airline and auto-parts industries have done their bit for the bankruptcy bar. Calpine, Adelphia and Refco have filed, providing billable hours to himself and his colleagues. But the so-called middle market, "the bread and butter of your insolvency professionals," has been eerily underrepresented in bankruptcy proceedings. The super-accommodative lending environment has borrowed time for innumerable bankrupts of the future.

But this cycle, too, will end, Rosenberg predicts. "And it will end with some spectacular hedge-fund failures. That will be the turning point."

Value at Risk

November 5, 2006

An address by James Grant before the Third Avenue Management Value Conference:

Once you've heard the voice of Martin J. Whitman, you are very likely to keep on hearing it. I mean the terse authorial voice as much as the basso conversational one. Passages from *The Aggressive Conservative Investor*, to name only one of Marty's books (and one that he wrote with Martin Shubik), are fixed in my memory. They jostle me as I try to settle down with the morning newspapers. Marty starts arguing with *The Wall Street Journal* and the *Financial Times* before I can even open them up to read. Sometimes, I can't seem to get a thought in edgewise.

The progenitor of the Third Avenue Funds is a man of settled views. On investment topics, he brooks no airy-fairy speculation. Once I made the mistake of asking him where he thought the stock market was going. His reply was silence. It was a forbidding, sub-freezing silence, and the seconds it lasted seemed like hours. Something told me not to ask the follow-up question I had prepared about the likely course of interest rates.

The precepts of "safe and cheap" investing, of which Marty is no doubt the master theorist-practitioner, sound deceptively simple. Insist on financial strength and honest management (Marty, no utopian, actually gives you some slack on this count; he stipulates "reasonably" honest management). Look for high-quality assets and non-burdensome liabilities. Seek out free cash flows from operations. Look for safety in the price you pay. Put not your trust in forecasts. Invest in what's in front of you. Don't shrink from investing in complex securities. Think twice or three times before selling. Strive to understand the financial data under which an investor is fairly buried these days—that is, what the numbers mean, not just what they say. Marty doesn't claim that this is the one and only true church of investment. But it's the approach to investing that has worked for him, and, of course, for his fortunate investors.

It follows that the safe and cheap investor is a selective consumer of the news. He can afford to give the "A" section of *The Wall Street Journal* short shrift, he believes, because he is armored against macroeconomic or geopolitical disappointment. "Macro data such as predictions about general stock market averages, interest rates, the economy, consumer spending and so on are unimportant for safe and cheap investors, as long as the environment is characterized by relative political stability and an absence of violence in the streets," Marty has written. The Whitmanian investor is protected by a margin of safety. The lower his cost basis in relation to the net asset value of the company in which he invests, the less he stands to be buffeted by adverse news from Iraq, Iran, North Korea or even from Washington, D.C.

I am going to suggest a slight modification in the reading habits of value-seeking people. My strong advice is not to pass too quickly by the credit news. Low nominal interest rates, tight credit spreads and unprecedentedly easy access to mortgage debt and private-equity financing are critical supports under today's valuations. Kick away those props and the world would be a very different place—worse for a leveraged holder of stocks and bonds, better, certainly in the long run, for a liquid and opportunistic value investor. In post-millennial America, Calvin Coolidge's proposition no longer applies. The business of America isn't so much business as it is lending and borrowing. So, I submit, the Whitmanian investor may enjoy less protection against the assaults of the macroeconomic world than he believes.

Today, remarkably, American households are huge net debtors. The United States itself is a net debtor. Neither fact has generated political instability, much less violence or anarchy. Rather, they have produced a huge, yawning complacency.

Great debt expansions carry two kinds of investment risk. The first is that, when the expansion ends and the contraction begins, valuations supported by borrowed money will be put at risk. Though we value tribesmen—heeding Marty's admonitions— invest in soundly financed businesses, we, too, will find ourselves in harm's way. Lots of the unsoundly financed kind will be coming out for the bid, deepening what the market technicians call a downturn, or a "widespread loss of bonuses." Then, too, when lenders retreat, so will the private equity funds that have done such a good job bidding up share prices: Through the first nine months of this year, acquisitions made by financial sponsors totaled $462 billion, or 18% of overall M&A volume, double the private-equity deal volume over the like period a year ago.

The second kind of risk associated with promiscuous credit formation is subtler but also potentially hazardous to one's portfolio. I mean the risk easy money presents to profit margins. When just about anybody can get a loan, companies that ought to go out of business don't. They stay and stay, as they did in Japan through the 1990s. Ultra-easy credit not only facilitates the creation of efficient new competitors but also delays the essential exit of the old, obsolete ones.

A Third Avenue audience is unlikely to be overly sympathetic to the idea that excessive indebtedness is bad for your net worth. The Whitmanian kind of investor, steeped as he is in the art of bankruptcies and workouts, has seemed to thrive on it. In 1990, the year Third Avenue Value Fund opened for business, the banking system creaked and groaned under the weight of insupportable real estate loans. In 1994, an unanticipated Federal Reserve tightening campaign devastated the bond market. In 1998, Long-Term Capital Management came a cropper and seemed to threaten the financial system—certainly, the Fed believed it did. And in 2002, the bid went out of the junk-bond market. Yet, over the sweep of those years, safe and cheap investors prospered. Since the autumn of 1990, the Third Avenue Value Fund has generated annualized returns of 16.7%.

So why worry about credit disturbances this year or any other? One might almost root for them. Sweet were the post-crisis buying opportunities—bank stocks in 1991, Treasurys in 1995, junk bonds in 2003. On form, the current expansion in lending and borrowing will ultimately give way to a contraction, with the usual attendant bear market in whatever has gone up the most and dealers' counters stacked high with cast-off and marked-down merchandise. Martin Fridson, the excellent independent high-yield bond analyst, has calculated that, based on the current ratings mix, a recession even as relatively mild as that of 1990–91 could produce junk-bond defaults on a scale not seen since the mid-1930s. But nobody knows when the next slump will start. "It seems as if most predictions of the future turn out to be wrong most of the time," as Marty has written. "Most of the time"? He was being charitable.

You will notice that I still haven't answered my own question: What's to fear from a credit crack-up, the nature of which is that it will come out of the blue? Why take evasive or preventive action if you—as a member of the company of value investors—stand to profit by the event? My first reason is monetary.

No matter how cheap and safe an American investment, it is denominated in U.S. dollars. Now the dollar is the world's greatest monetary achievement; it passes for money the world over. Yet nothing stands behind it; it is uncollateralized. When sterling ruled the global roost, you could slip a £10 note through the teller's window at the Bank of England and get the lawfully stipulated gold value in return. The dollar is faith-based.

Admittedly, this is not exactly front-page news, but not everyone seems aware of it, or of how to interpret it. Marty himself acknowledges, and I quote, "A characteristic of safe and cheap is that such investors are usually the last to know." So if you haven't heard, it's true: Nixon closed the gold window in 1971.

The significance of this fact is that the United States can borrow until its creditors get tired of lending. Not for a generation has a finite stock of monetary gold checked the rate of American con-

HB07

sumption. In consequence, the United States has racked up enormous debts. I ask you to imagine a highly leveraged corporation—
its debt grows and grows. You, as an analyst and prospective investor
in this enterprise, would want to know something about the use to
which the proceeds were being put. What kind of assets did they
buy? In the case of the United States, the proceeds are overwhelmingly earmarked for consumption. Only consider that the corporate sector is today in surplus—a net provider of funds to the economy—while the household sector is massively in deficit. In a
well-tempered economy, it is usually the other way around. Families save and corporations invest. By investing, they boost their
own productivity and therefore the economy's. Today, on balance,
corporations are saving and families are spending.

The net U.S. international investment position, measured
at market value as of year-end 2005, was minus $2.5 trillion. Of
course, not every economist believes that this number means much
of anything. But, it is not the only number that invites scrutiny of
the U.S. financial position. For instance, in the June quarter, for
the third quarter in a row, income payments to foreigners exceeded

income receipts from foreigners. Here is a fact to ponder. Since 1960, one sees that the income account was usually in the black. It went negative for the first time at the turn of the new century. But never, prior to the past three quarters, did a deficit persist for nine months. If this nation must now begin to borrow from, say, Japan to pay, for instance, China, we have embarked on a new and interesting financial voyage.

The United States is a great and good nation and J.P. Morgan was well advised when his father urged him not to sell it short. But, as far as I know, the elder Morgan did not refer to the pure paper dollar. A country that chronically consumes much more than it produces, that emits its uncollateralized IOUs into the world's payment stream at a rate equivalent to more than 6% of its GDP each year, and that is engaged in a protracted war seems an unlikely candidate for long-term monetary stability. "The long run," admittedly, is not the time frame in which most people manage their investments. Performance is measured in weeks, months or fiscal quarters. But, to misquote Keynes, the long run eventually happens. Things that can't go on forever, won't. Nobody had the courtesy to ring a bell in the City of London in 1914 to announce the end of British financial hegemony.

An underwriter of "super cat" insurance must assign a price to an unlikely, but potentially devastating, event. A dollar crisis would be costly for any who hold the greenback. Yet most of us are unhedged against the risk. Some of us, perhaps, have reasoned through the risks and concluded that the dollar will never be toppled. What would replace it? Most of us, however, haven't given the matter the thought it deserves, or, perhaps—and this applies especially to the readers of *Grant's*—had worried for years on end before deciding that their worries, or hedges, were in vain. But the uneventful passage of time does not necessarily diminish the odds of a chronic debtor being called to account. On the contrary, every passing year of cumulating dollar indebtedness only raises the odds that, one fine day, the marginal offshore bidder for dollars will decide that he owns quite enough of them and would prefer another monetary asset. If, therefore, you happen to encounter safe and cheap securities denominated in a nondollar currency, they might deserve an extra close look. As a hedge against all currencies, and the central bankers who print them, I prefer gold. Yes, yes, I know: Gold earns nothing, yields nothing and therefore defies analysis. I say the world monetary system defies comprehension.

That the U.S. economy is highly leveraged is old news—even for the non-newspaper-reading, stock-by-stock value investor. The new news is that the credit risk associated with this leverage resides on remote balance sheets. In the old days, banks did the lending— and kept the loans they made. They performed the due diligence and, if necessary, the subsequent workouts. Nowadays, everyone seems to be lending—hedge funds and brokerage houses, among others. But the lenders no longer own the loans. In large part, the investors in asset-backed securities do.

This breakthrough in financial technique has far-reaching consequences. More and more, credit analysis is subordinated to financial engineering. You know the difference between the two, don't you? I am now going to quote *Grant's Interest Rate Observer* instead of *The Aggressive Conservative Investor*. "Financial engineering is the science of structuring cash flows," we have written; "credit analysis is the art of getting paid." In this, the expansion phase of the credit cycle, few worry much about getting paid. One can infer as much from the low level of nominal interest rates, the still-tight spreads of risk rates over Treasury rates and the booming issuance of structured debt instruments. Not since the alchemists has so much triple-B-rated dross been transformed into so much triple-A gold as that which is remodeled in the busy workrooms of today's investment banks and rating agencies.

If it seems that the actuarial approach to lending has triumphed over the pre-digital, case-by-case method, it has. And if it seems that indebtedness, in proportion to the nation's output of goods and services, is about as high as it's ever been, it is. Contemplating these things, a man could bite his nails. But wait: There are no bread lines and no bank runs. There is no Great Depression. It is a slightly inconvenient fact for us debt bears that the triumph of the actuarial approach to underwriting and the acceleration in national leverage have been accompanied by soaring securities markets and a pretty fair run of prosperity. At year-end 1975, the ratio of debt to GDP was 1.6:1 and the Dow was at 852. At this writing, the ratio of debt to GDP is 3.2:1 and the Dow is at 12,000.

Of course, this triumph of leveraged wealth did not occur without interruption. It couldn't have. The question before the house is whether the next cyclical interruption will be any more damaging than the ones that, since 1990, have only spelled opportunity for the Whitmanian investor.

I expect that it will. Well, let me come right out and say it—I predict that it will. I'll apologize later to Marty for this no doubt doomed forecast. But first I want to quote him (again, from *The Aggressive Conservative Investor*): "In looking at a transaction, the single most important question seems to be, What have I got to lose? Only when it seems that risks can be controlled or minimized does the second question come up: How much can I make?" I'm here to tell you that, in today's credit markets, the second question comes first.

Sometimes, the first question seems not to come up at all. Investors in the lower-rated tranches of subprime mortgage securities, for example, stand to make a couple of hundred basis points over the Treasury curve if all goes according to plan. If not, they stand to lose their principal. The downside is, in fact, looming larger these days, as house prices weaken and foreclosures rise. In the past, a careful lender could sleep a little better with the knowledge that, come what may, he knew his credits. No such source of strength is available to most mortgage investors today. They didn't make the loans and they didn't rate the loans. They didn't devise the econometric model that clears the way for the reengineering of more than 80% of a pool of triple-B-rated mortgages into double-A or triple-A-rated status. In their ignorance of what is inside their portfolios, mortgage investors resemble the research-deprived equity investor who sells because the market is going down.

As in mortgage loans, so in corporate loans. Standard & Poor's last week called attention to the risks presented by syndicated lending. Banks do still lend, of course, but they don't hold all of the loans they create. Rather, they sell them off to investors. S&P finds—you may not be astonished—that due diligence is a little less exacting when the lender knows that the loan he makes will come to rest on somebody else's balance sheet. "We see a risk that syndication has been so quick and easy in recent years that some underwriters may undertake only cosmetic credit analysis of a new exposure since they do not intend to retain very much of it," the *Financial Times* quoted S&P as saying.

Some welcome these developments. Since credit risk is no longer concentrated in the big, dumb banks but is sprinkled around the financial system, they reason, the world is a safer place. At least, some have claimed, the banks are safer. Consider that no federally insured bank has failed since June 25, 2004. It's been the longest such stretch of industrywide solvency since the establishment of the FDIC in 1933. John C. Dugan, Comptroller of the Currency, has called attention to the many improving vital signs—asset quality, liquidity, earnings and capital. All are on the upswing. But Dugan did not extrapolate these successes all the way out to eternity. Banking is a cyclical business, as we all know.

"With liquidity pouring into the market," Dugan told the Office of the Comptroller of the Currency's Credit Risk Conference last year, "we would expect to see increased competition for loan customers—and we are. With competition intensifying, we would expect to see underwriting standards easing—and we are. And we would expect to find emerging concentrations in some loan categories, such as commercial and residential real estate. We are most definitely seeing that."

Underwriting standards have softened pretty much across the board, Dugan went on to say, especially in real estate. He singled out commercial real estate for special mention. About a third of the nationally chartered banks have commercial real-estate assets equal to 300% or more of Tier 1 capital, he said.

"Such concentrations by themselves would warrant supervisory concern under almost any circumstances," Dugan continued. "But, in order to attract new business and sustain loan volume, banks have made many compromises and concessions to borrowers along the way, resulting in commercial real estate credits with structural weaknesses that go beyond discounted pricing. It should concern us when we see policies governing such things as loan-to-value standards and debt service coverage being relaxed—and then an increasing number of exceptions to those more accommodating policies. We should also take notice when we see lenders routinely adjusting covenants, lengthening maturities and reducing collateral requirements. Those signs of lender laxity concern us just as much as the commercial real-estate concentrations themselves."

Note, please: This was last year, and the lenders did not stop. Small wonder that the dividend yield on the Bloomberg REIT index is setting 10-year lows or that—to quote the October 25 *Real Estate Alert*—"In hotly contested property offerings around the nation, bidders are increasingly trying to stand out by volunteering to sharply curtail the time they spend on due diligence."

There is a margin of safety in paying a low price, of course. And there is a margin of safety in knowing more about one's investments than the market does. So informed, the safe and cheap investor can average down with a minimum of trepidation. I won't say none—not even the best of us can be absolutely sure that Mr. Market doesn't have a trick up his sleeve—but with a plausible minimum of fear.

Relatively speaking, the holders of complex debt securities are uninformed. Not only can't they possibly know, in detail, the myriad of credits inside a collateralized debt obligation or an asset-backed security, but also they can't begin to understand how these credits are likely to be correlated to each other in a downturn. We at *Grant's* have examined CDOs containing more than a million loans. Before an investor could examine each and every one, the bond would be called—or he would be called into retirement. Of course, the asset-backed structures are designed by econometricians and financial engineers. As the residential real estate market boomed and interest rates fell, these quantitative underpinnings appeared unshakable, even if the holder didn't quite understand them. In the down portion of the cycle, the math will seem no more comprehensible. Probably, it will not be so reassuring.

In the old days, banks would work out their own bad loans. They knew more about them than the market (even if it wasn't enough). Nowadays, the CDO or ABS investor knows not much more about his portfolio than does the brokerage-house salesman who sold it to him. I venture that he does not know enough to stand in front of a liquidation. Thus, come the next credit bear market, we may be witness to a fast and indiscriminate off-loading of complex debt instruments, with knock-on effects for all fixed-income securities.

Yes, you may be thinking, it does sound very grave—possibly as grave a threat to our financial well-being as the great postwar bear bond market, the 1966 credit crunch, the 1971 breakdown of Bretton Woods, the subsequent great inflation, the Third World debt crisis or any of the other disturbances that, though heralded by black headlines, never inflicted more than flesh wounds on the safe and cheap investor. And that may be true. Perhaps I'm crying wolf—I have had some practice in that line.

Fortunately, the cost of hedges against monetary and credit disturbances are cheap enough to appeal to even the flintiest of value investors. T-bills pay 5%, and gold is still scarce in the ground. To them, I urge: Read the papers, not forgetting the credit news. It's the overpriced debt market that supports the valuation of your low-priced stocks.

Our Friends, the Creditors

November 17, 2006

Just because the triple-A-rated corporate borrower is nearly extinct doesn't mean there are no triple-A-rated corporate bonds. On the contrary, what nature doesn't provide, Wall Street contrives to invent. Employing the lower-rated materials readily at hand, financial engineers continue to build new lines of triple-A merchandise. The CPDO—constant proportion debt obligation—is the latest to tumble off the assembly line.

No subscriber should stop reading just because he or she would cross the street to avoid encountering a CPDO or its Gyro Gearloose inventor. The very existence of these structures is a marker of the progress of the credit cycle. Only at such a confident juncture as this would investors so cheerfully place their trust in the mathematical models and rating-agency analysis on which the success of such contraptions as CPDOs depend. At some later stage in the cycle, perhaps Speaker Nancy Pelosi or her designate will summon the architects of the structured-product markets to Washington to explain to the Congress and the C-Span cameras why anyone ever believed that so much low-rated dross could be spun into so much high-rated gold. Pending that day of enlightenment, we will guess that money played its part. For the ratings agencies, structured products have become a major profit center. They contributed no less than 38% of Moody's revenues in the latest quarter.

It's increasingly obvious that a fat and happy Mr. Market has talked himself into believing there will never be another bear market in credit. You can infer as much from the concept of "implied equity," now catching on in Europe, as well as from the bright idea of piling debt on a semiconductor business, of which none is more cyclical. Credit bears are in retreat, while the rating agencies enable the brokerage houses and investment banks. When your grandchildren ask you to tell them (over and over and over again) about the Great Structured Products and Debt Crack-Up of 2007, or 2008, or 2009, etc., and how it actually made you rich, you will want to have the facts at hand. The facts follow.

First up, the CPDO. It's the successor to the similar-sounding CPPI, which stands for "constant proportion portfolio insurance." CPPI came to the fore as an equity gimmick a year before the 1987 stock-market crash. No coincidence as to timing; portfolio insurance played a leading role in Black Monday. As for the CPDO, it looks like an ordinary bond, but it isn't. Its promoters believe it is better. Rated triple-A, it pays interest at 200 basis points over the London interbank offered rate, more generous by far than a natural triple-A yield. The secret of the yield is all in the structure, to wit:

1. A bank sets up a special purpose vehicle.
2. The SPV sells the bonds.
3. The proceeds are invested in cash equivalents, which are deposited at the bank.
4. The bank enters the derivatives market to sell options. Specifically, it sells credit default swaps, better known as CDS. More specifically, it sells CDS on investment-grade credit indices. In other words, it lays down bets on the creditworthiness of the indices' constituent companies. This options exposure the bank conveys to the SPV via a total return swap.

Credit bears will be found on the opposite side of this trade. Buyers of CDS, they pay to insure against default or downgrade or a marketwide reappraisal of risk. The premiums they pay go to the bank, and, ultimately, the SPV. And it is these premiums, coupled with interest on the deposited cash equivalents, that go to pay the CPDO's bondholders. The bonds mature, typically, in 10 years. The SPV and the bank settle accounts and roll into a new set of CDS every six months.

To generate the required income, the SPV/bank must sell CDS by the carload. At maximum permissible leverage, CDS exposure may reach 15 times the value of the cash equivalents. So the sale of $1 billion of CPDOs could activate the sale of $15 billion of CDS, a very substantial expression of confidence in the stability of investment-grade credit. For the sellers of credit insurance, the CPDO boosters insist, the ticking clock is a pleasing sound. The indices are refreshed every six months; out go the bad apples, in go the good ones. Really, the promoters ask, what are the odds of a blue-chip borrower hitting the wall in only two fiscal quarters?

Perhaps this confidence is well-founded. But few things are as unstable as a seeming state of stability. Your editor has been reading a book called *Ubiquity*, by Mark Buchanan (Three Rivers Press, 2001). It is a study of the inherent instability, or "upheavability," of man and nature. A key concept is that of the "critical state," i.e., "a special kind of organization characterized by a tendency toward sudden and tumultuous changes. . . " Buchanan argues that the world is forever on a knife's edge. In physics or human society, there is no equilibrium—things teeter on the brink of dramatic change. This insight would help to explain why great events can have such paradoxically trivial causes—or why most things worth forecasting, from earthquakes to forest fires to credit implosions, are never accurately forecasted.

Grand theories aside, events don't stand still just because a CPDO makes a bet on tranquility. If interest rates don't rise and companies don't default and credit spreads don't open, the SPV will build net worth. And as it does, the managers will take money off the table. If things go so well that the liabilities associated with the bond issue are finally and absolutely covered, the managers will take everything off the table. On this happy "cash-in" day, the SPV liquidates its CDS and turns the proceeds over to the bank in exchange for a promise to pay the bondholders their interest and principal. Then it's on to the next deal for the promoters and the ratings agencies, which look like geniuses.

But bad things, too, can happen—defaults, widening spreads, rising rates, etc. If things do go bad, and the SPV suffers mark-to-market losses, the managers take a bite out of the dog that bit them.

That is, they increase leverage, selling more CDS to try to recoup what they've lost—assuming they were not already at maximum permissible leverage. Yet the bank will give them only so much latitude. Once past a certain threshold of mark-to-market pain—typically, less than 10%—the transaction is unwound and the remaining assets are distributed to the bondholders.

To advance its clients' understanding of this innovation, Moody's has drawn a homely analogy. Think of the CPDO as a coin-toss game, it suggests. Heads you win, tails you lose. "The player has an initial stake of 1,000," Moody's proposes, "comprised of 100 from his own pocket and 900 borrowed from a friend. At the outset his strategy is as follows: If he succeeds in converting his stake into 2,000 of winnings, he will stop and reimburse his friend, having thus multiplied his initial investment by 11. This corresponds to the Cash-In Event. At the same time, his friend is concerned about his stake, and thus if the player loses more than 100, he will stop playing. This corresponds to the Cash-Out Event."

We should all have friends like this—good-natured, rich, dim fellows who would lend at a moderate interest rate against a small-ish slice of equity in order to finance the writing of credit insurance at a time of unusually tight spreads and wondrous complacency with regard to the credit cycle. Yet, such friends do exist. These days, they are called "the market."

For those who did business on or around Oct. 19, 1987, one particular aspect of the CPDO will strike them with force. This is the stated intention of putting on more exposure as the market goes the wrong way. That is, as Standard & Poor's puts it, the plan to make oneself whole "by increasing the income from the risky asset to build NAV. At the same time, this could be viewed as 'chasing losses' when it is the risky asset performance that has led to the NAV decrease." The attempt to sell index futures to rebalance dynamically hedged stock portfolios was an unforgettable hallmark of the 1987 stock-market break. For ourselves, we can easily imagine a crash in credit. In such a circumstance, the strategy of selling short the thing that is going up—i.e., credit insurance—could open up the SPV and/or bank to losses not contemplated within the strategy of taking no hit greater than 10%.

The specter of a credit crash is, admittedly, one that is currently invisible to most onlookers. "Credit spreads combine default rates and volatility, and they are both at historic lows," a strategist from Deutsche Bank told the *Financial Times* last week. "So, corporate spreads, also at lows, are where they should be." In the past few weeks, what's crashed is the cost of insuring an investment-grade bond portfolio. Five years of protection on the DJ CDX, the U.S. investment-grade index, stands at 33 basis points per annum, lower by 15%; protection on the European equivalent index, Itraxx Europe, is quoted at 23 basis points, down by 20%. These are rock-bottom prices, so low that Primus Guaranty of Bermuda (ticker: PRS), which makes a business of selling CDS, cut back the rate of its sales in the third quarter, citing the "challenging spread environment."

You could call it that. Whom or what to blame? Some point a finger at the red-hot CPDO market. Perhaps they are right—although no more than $2 billions' worth are believed to have been issued, meaning that no more than $30 billion of CDS sales could be ascribed to them (for reference, the face amount of outstanding credit derivatives tops $26 trillion). A better explanation for the plunge in the cost of investment-grade credit insurance is the pervasive belief that the credit markets have achieved a state of perfect equilibrium.

The kind of generous-spirited creditors who lend to the CPDO promoters do business on both sides of the Atlantic. An October research bulletin from Dresdner Kleinwort, London, chronicles the deteriorating financial condition of European companies that have been through the LBO mill. The promoters are paying more and more for acquisitions, while putting up less and less of their own money to buy them: "[F]alling equity contributions are being compensated for through the use of second lien and mezzanine debt, as opposed to senior debt. We believe this is done to enable LBOs to reach ROE targets, given that purchase-price multiples continue to rise. Indeed, anecdotal evidence from hedge fund investors confirms that it is not just the use of second lien and mezzanine debt that is allowing private equity sponsors to reduce equity contributions. As well as accounting for vendor and shareholder loans as equity (which is not a new phenomenon), private equity sponsors sometimes also use the concept of 'implied equity' in smaller transactions."

Say that you, a private-equity mogul, wish to buy an underperforming division of a big company. You did not get to be a mogul by under-leveraging your acquisitions. So you approach a lender. "Division X of Company Y," you say, "is for sale for $50 million. But its enterprise value—as measured against comparable divisions in related industries—is actually $70 million." So forceful is this presentation that the bank or insurance company advances virtually the entire $50 million, conveniently obviating the need for any but a nominal equity infusion from you. "Debt investors take comfort from the fact that in the event of default, the entity can be sold for the theoretical enterprise value," Dresdner Kleinwort adds, "which should more than cover the debt portion invested." Some comfort.

These days, debt investors mainly take comfort in interest rates, low as they are in comparison to the rates that prevailed in the LBO boom of the 1980s. Investors in the debt of the soon-to-be-private Freescale Semiconductor are said to be taking comfort in a blended rate as low as 8.7%. They will be seeking solace from some other source before very long, we expect.

Freescale is a 2003 spin-off of Motorola Inc. It went public in 2004, and now it is going private again in one of the year's signature LBOs. Freescale has 24,200 employees and $6.2 billion in trailing 12-month revenues. It has a 50-year operating history, more than 10,000 end customers and an intellectual property portfolio encompassing more than 5,600 patent families. Pro forma the LBO, it will be capitalized with $9.5 billion of debt and $5.5 billion of equity. On this debt, which includes senior bank credit, senior

"Yes, it's true, we did lose all your money.
But money's not everything, is it?"

public notes (floating-rate, fixed-rate and payment-in-kind) and senior subordinated notes, it expects to pay $840 million a year.

As the law requires, the preliminary debt prospectus discloses every conceivable risk to the bondholders, except, perhaps, the exogenous consideration that creditors have collectively lost their minds. Numbers are presented to show that, in 2001–03, while Freescale was still a Motorola division, earnings before interest and taxes failed to cover fixed charges and that, indeed, in 2001 and 2002, even EBITDA was negative. "The semiconductor industry is highly competitive and characterized by constant and rapid technological change, short product lifecycles, significant price erosion and evolving standards," allows the section on competition. "If we fail to keep pace with the rest of the semiconductor industry, we could lose our significant leadership positions in the markets in which we compete. Any such loss in market share would have a material effect on our financial condition and results of operations."

But the promoters—Blackstone, Carlyle, Permira Funds, Texas Pacific Group—are plainly not doing the deal on the expectation it will fail. The prospectus wants you to understand that the dismal performance of 2001–03 had something to do with the suffocating Motorola bureaucracy and that, though the semiconductor business might once have been ruinously cyclical—exactly the wrong kind of candidate for an LBO—things are now different. "[P]eak to trough cycles have dampened as the overall semiconductor industry has matured and volatility is expected to decrease further in the future." Yet, we note, even in the newly prosperous 2005–06 period, EBITDA minus capital expenditure has barely covered pro forma interest expense.

It would, of course, be convenient if the now "mature" semiconductor industry stopped devouring itself through incessant innovation. It would be no less convenient if the demand for cellular handsets and automobiles stayed strong and steady, inasmuch as Freescale critically depends on those sources of demand. Such surcease would provide the breathing room necessary for a newly leveraged company to put its financial house in order—paying immense dividends to the equity investors and presenting the good-natured if admittedly dim and undemanding creditors with interest and, at the end of the line, principal—which principal they had at the outset.

We expect that bonhomie will prevail at the closing dinner of this stupendous transaction. Principals and their lawyers and bankers and accountants will drink to the success of the transformed Freescale. But afterwards, when the principals drift away to be alone with a final celebratory bottle of champagne, it would be strange if someone didn't struggle to his feet to offer up a concluding, heartfelt toast: "To our friends, the creditors," he will say with a small smile, "what would we do without them?"

Subprime Companies

February 23, 2007

An address by James Grant before the Harvard Business School Centennial Conference on Private Equity in New York:

What's in a brand? Why, what's not in a brand? Take "private equity." What a beautiful phrase it is! What a dignified and substantial image it connotes! Imagine if, instead, the industry had had to labor under the stigma of the tarnished moniker "leveraged buyout." One shudders. For that matter, where would home prices be today if the confidence-sapping epithet "junk" had been fastened on low-rated mortgage applicants? But "subprime" was the word, and the housing market boomed and boomed.

Brands sell, but numbers count. My thesis today is that the numbers in the U.S. credit markets don't add up. I contend that the private-equity business owes its prosperity to a persistent mispricing of debt. The evolved LBO industry may or may not deliver the net returns it claims—recent academic studies cast some doubt on that. But one thing is indisputable: Cheap debt is the sine qua non of today's deliciously rich, fee-resplendent deals. Without it, private equity would not be the career goal of fully 110% of the Columbia Business School Class of 2007 and 120% of their counterparts at Harvard. The number at Harvard is higher because Harvard is better.

Nominal interest rates are low, and risk rates are pressed close against Treasury rates—too close to afford the lenders anything like a margin of safety. Covenant protection is disappearing even as leverage ratios climb. Rarely have the debt markets been more welcoming to leveraged borrowers. And rarely have they afforded less protection to the lenders. As markets are cyclical, we know that the creditors will eventually reclaim their pound of flesh. We just don't know when. (Actually, I once did know when this crazy cycle would end. It would end in 2005. And having predicted so long, and so emphatically, that it would end in 2005, I have chosen not to change my forecast; 2005 is the year—still.)

On the face of things, the credit markets have achieved a state of perfection. Companies don't default, and banks don't fail—or didn't until the $12 million-deposit Metropolitan Savings Bank of Pittsburgh bit the dust the other day. Until then, no insured bank had failed in 2½ years, the longest such streak since the institution of the FDIC in 1934. And when companies do default, their claims become hot property. For bank debt last year, recoveries averaged 93 cents on the dollar, up from an average of 73 cents for the preceding 19 years, according to Standard & Poor's LCD. But, of course, companies don't default, because their lenders won't let them. Not only are protective covenants becoming eviscerated, but also they are increasingly renegotiated. According to LCD, violations of a coverage or leverage test led to the 36 renegotiations in 2006. If forgiveness is a virtue, the debt markets are going to heaven.

All, that is, except for the $1 trillion subprime mortgage market. The subprime market constitutes an instructive anomaly—or, perhaps, as I happen to believe, not an anomaly so much as a leading indicator. It alone is in a downturn. Nearly 6% of the subprime loans packaged in 2006 are at least 60 days delinquent. The stock market capitalization of the top subprime lenders has melted away (New Century gave up 43% in only three days). And an index of CDS on subprime mortgage loans originated in 2006 recently traded at a hair above 80, down from par only four months ago.

The bulls hadn't banked on sagging house prices. In the boom years, a borrower in arrears could sell his house and walk away with a profit. When house prices stopped going up, late payments and repossessions accelerated. Something else the bulls overlooked was the boom-time collapse in underwriting standards. Defaults were bound to increase because Everyman qualified for a loan. The wave of liquidity in residential mortgage finance, in effect, drowned itself.

It goes without saying that the markets in leveraged loans and subprime mortgages are different and that it is hazardous to reason—or invest—by analogy. Granting those points, I propose to draw an extended analogy between the bear market in subprime borrowers and the bull market in subprime companies.

I leave it to you to draw the relevant comparison in corporate finance to the explosion of so-called innovative, or exotic, mortgages. Or between the virtuous cycles that smiled on both markets (not so much on mortgages these days, of course). Interest rates went down, and asset prices went up. Yield-hungry lenders bid more and more aggressively for loans, bonds, CDOs, CLOs and the rest. Interest rates fell some more. Asset prices rose some more. LCD, which tracks the leveraged corporate loan market day by day and almost minute by minute, gives this picture of the proceeedings: "Going forward, arrangers expect issuers—especially those with a private-equity sponsor—to ride the current wave of liquidity to reprice more and more loans, secure recaps, stretch leverage and wrest additional concessions on covenants."

The breakneck growth in credit derivatives is another large contributor to the widespread view that "liquidity," whatever that ill-defined elixir could be, is limitless. In 2006, no less than $450 billion of synthetic collateralized debt obligations came into the world. You'll recall that synthetic CDOs write credit protection on loans and bonds. The more such protection they write, other things being the same, the tighter credit spreads become and the greater the ease of financing a buyout.

The subprime boom, too, was derivatives enabled. Investment banks swept up hundreds of millions of dollars worth of speculative-grade mortgages. This product they fed into the asset-backed-securities blender, and out it came, almost unrecognizable. Junk no more, it was radiantly transformed into tranches of residential mortgage-backed securities. As much as 80% of these loans now were rated triple-A. And apart from a sliver of equity, none were rated lower than BBB-minus. These days, skeptical investors are beginning to entertain well-founded doubts about the models employed by the rating agencies to anoint these deals. But, in the bull market, the structured-finance machine excited only wonder and gratitude.

As the rise in house prices was off the charts, so is the run of corporate profitability. For the S&P 500, operating earnings grew at a double-digit rate in the second quarter of 2002—and kept logging double-digit gains for the next 17 quarters, right up until today, the longest such run since the data were first assembled in 1989. And net margins for the S&P component companies are the fattest since records began in 1954. No doubt, there are companies in these 50 states that would benefit from the clean broom of new, enlightened, private management. But it is hard to improve on a state of perfection, which not a few U.S. businesses seem rapidly to be approaching even without a management buyout.

The more you look at subprime mortgage finance, the more it resembles the supposedly more sophisticated kind. You'll recall that, before the recent rush of sobriety, lenders gladly fronted 100% and more of the purchase price of a house—80% in a senior lien, 20% or more in a second. Nor did they necessarily disclose the existence of the junior lien to the holder of the corresponding senior claim. So, too, in the land of hedge funds. Hedge funds borrow to enhance their returns. So do funds of funds and so do LBO funds. Do you wonder which central clearinghouse houses records to keep lenders and borrowers properly informed about where risk lies? It doesn't exist.

And as homeowners have (until lately) withdrawn equity from their leveraged assets, so have private-equity sponsors. And as individuals flipped houses and condos back and forth to one another, so have some private-equity promoters. Just the other day, for example, Blackstone Group entered into an agreement to buy Pinnacle Foods Group from CCMP Capital Advisors for $2.2 billion, including $900 million in debt. This transaction was the third involving Pinnacle since that pickle maker and fish-stick producer emerged from bankruptcy in 2001. I wonder how the people who pack the pickles and size the fish sticks manage to keep up with the changing names in the front office.

Well, homeowners don't burn their mortgages any more—and B-quality borrowers don't aspire to an investment-grade debt rating. Thus, again according to S&P, only 7% of rated corporate industrials were rated single-B in 1980. Today, 42% are. "Once upon a time," the agency says in a new report entitled, "The Rise of 'B' Rated Companies and Their Staying Power as an Asset Class," "'B' credits aspired to move up the food chain. After their LBOs, companies would try to improve performance and follow with an IPO. If they were very lucky, they might make it back to investment grade, or at least to the 'BB' category. Well, that kind of thinking sounds nice, but is becoming ancient history. One of the realities facing the 'B' credits today is that of 're-leveraging.' Over the past couple of years, we have seen dividend recapitalizations and related financings allowing equity sponsors and others to take out funds from companies in the 'B' category. The net result is often to weaken the credit. . . . Put another way, 'B' is as good as it's going to get. Any credit upside is taken away from these companies, and the recap often exposes them to downgrades and a higher risk of default. Some folks have characterized this process as moving the patient from the general wing in a hospital into intensive care. On the other hand, as far as the sponsors are concerned, dividend recaps sure beat waiting around for that IPO."

The perceptive sponsor, seeing that his or her prosperity depends on the continued distortions in debt, will take steps to assure that the cycle never turns. How this might be done, I have no idea. To start with, do the thing you can do. Take a lender to lunch. Maybe this kindness will buy you a few more quarters of mispriced prosperity.

Fire the Brainiacs

June 15, 2007

An address by James Grant before the President's Meeting of Fairfax Financial Holdings Ltd. at Niagara-on-the-Lake, Ontario:

Just the other day, Kevin Warsh, a governor of the central bank of the populous country on the other side of Niagara Falls, was singing the praises of financial innovation. Asset-backed securities, derivatives of all kinds, hedge funds etc., he said, have made the world a far, far better place. No more do banks have to retain the loans they make or brokers merely distribute the securities they underwrite. And a good thing, too, said Warsh, who proceeded to quote numbers so fantastic that his London audience must have begun to wonder if they were correctly parsing his American accent.

"Of the $3.6 trillion in net borrowing in U.S. credit markets in 2006," Warsh told them, "$820 billion, or nearly one-fourth, was securitized." He added that the notional value of interest-rate swaps and options has tripled in the past four years to nearly $300 trillion, while the notional value of credit default swaps nearly quintupled in only two years, to $29 trillion. To which startling succession of zeros and commas, I would add that more than $1 trillion of collateralized debt obligations are outstanding.

Warsh was only toeing the company line. The Greenspan Fed blessed the explosion of derivatives, CDOs, etc., and the Bernanke Fed has likewise said "amen." Far from increasing risk, the argument goes, innovative financial techniques have dispersed it. They have rationalized it, too, by affording investors the means to price it. "We, as policymakers," Warsh did concede, "should be careful, and indeed humble, in making definitive judgments in this fast-changing era." But this most optimistic central banker clearly believes that the changes are for the good. Incidentally, the type of the optimistic central banker is another kind of financial innovation.

Warsh went on to say that innovation feeds the wellsprings of liquidity. Now, "liquidity" is a word that can mean everything or nothing. From the mouths of brokerage-house salesmen, it usually means "easy credit," which leads to an easy-to-remember investment recommendation: "buy." To his credit, Warsh—himself a former Morgan Stanley investment banker—did define his term. Liquidity, he said, is the state of felicity in which an investor can move quickly in and out of markets without unduly moving the prices. Confidence is one source of liquidity, financial engineering another. Confidence springs from engineering improvements, as the technicians disassemble securities and redistribute their component pieces. What is a mortgage, after all, except a bundle of options? Break it apart and offer investors the portions and risk profiles they want. "By disaggregating a security into its constituent risk components," said Warsh, "financial innovation can unlock this liquidity."

I am here to take the other side of his argument—not to urge a return to basis books and rotary telephones or even, necessarily, face-to-face encounters between lenders and loan applicants. My mission is, rather, to probe the risks over which Warsh and his Fed colleagues are only too happy to glide. My thesis is that financial complexity poses a clear and present danger. And because I am in

"Fine. Let me try again. Pretty please,
Mr. Margin Clerk sir, may I have a loan?"

the company of value investors, I don't have to spell out the opportunity that this danger presents to liquid and disciplined opportunists. It means lower and better prices down the road. My plan is to describe the dangers, speculate on the opportunities and serve up a modest proposal for reform.

The best critiques of complex finance are the ones delivered by the brainiacs themselves. *A Demon of Our Own Design: Markets, Hedge Funds and the Perils of Financial Innovation* (Wiley, 2007) is a new production of this kind by Richard Bookstaber, an MIT-educated quant, Wall Street risk manager and (currently) hedge-fund manager. How strange, Bookstaber reflects, that stock market volatility has risen these past 20 years while economic volatility has subsided. Engineering has delivered safer airplanes and better skyscrapers, he writes, while financial engineering has brought us more crises. "The fact that the total risk of the financial markets has grown in spite of a marked decline in exogenous economic risk to the country is a key symptom of the design flaws within the system," Bookstaber charges. "Risk should be diminishing, but it isn't."

The author seems to take an almost masochistic glee in exploding the pretensions of the people like himself who dreamt up portfolio insurance in 1987 and the hyper-extended convergence trades of Long-Term Capital Management a decade later; and who, in between, blew up Orange County, Calif., and threw a scare into institutions as large as Procter & Gamble and the mortgage-backed securities market. The complexity of derivatives or asset-backed structures is not, by itself, the whole problem, according to Bookstaber. Nor, alone, would it present insurmountable, unhedgeable risks. The rub is that financial markets are interdependent, or "tightly coupled."

"Tight coupling," explains Bookstaber, "means that components of a process are critically interdependent; they are linked with little room for error or time for recalibration or adjustment." Air-traffic control is one example of a tightly coupled process. The daily functioning of the financial markets is another. "The tight coupling in financial markets comes from the nonstop information flow and unquenchable demand for instant liquidity," the author proceeds. "Information spurs trading, and the trades are entered and executed without a pause. Tight coupling is accentuated by leverage, itself a direct result of liquidity. Leverage and margin are simply loans that use securities as collateral, and the willingness to lend against this collateral is directly related to the lender's ability to quickly sell out the securities if the margin is not posted. The more liquid the securities, the better the leverage terms will be. So tight coupling means higher potential leverage.

"For financial markets, the coupling born of liquidity feeds right back to the source of complexity," according to Bookstaber. "Liquidity is the lifeblood of derivatives; unlike the underlying securities, derivatives are created on the assumption that they can be hedged on an ongoing basis, and so make continuous demands on liquidity. Without liquidity, derivatives markets die."

If Warsh has read Bookstaber's book, he certainly isn't letting on. Financial innovation enhances liquidity, contends the Fed governor. Financial innovation depends on liquidity, lest the ultra-complex structures and options become frozen and untradable, argues the Wall Street hedge-fund manager.

Warsh would have a stronger case to make except for the unavoidable presence of human beings in the markets he idealizes. As it is, people are a constant, intrusive and confounding presence, buying at the top and selling at the bottom and walking into the same doorknobs as their technologically primitive forebears. If any investment enterprise seemed inoculated against the errors of fallible man, it was Long-Term Capital Management, the fund operated, literally, by geniuses. Indeed, as Bookstaber writes, "LTCM had scrupulously modeled and monitored its market risks. It prided itself on having broad diversification across the globe and across markets. The firm's risk models looked at past price variability and provided the partners with assurance that they could survive the financial equivalent of a 100-year flood."

Yet, as John Meriwether, one of the LTCM survivors, ruefully observed in the aftermath, the analogy to floods—he preferred hurricanes—is misleading. Nature doesn't connive, but people do. "The hurricane," said Meriwether, "is not more or less likely to hit because more hurricane insurance has been written. In financial markets, this is not true. The more people write hurricane insurance, the more likely it is that the disaster will happen because the people who know you have sold the insurance can make it happen."

Now I want to quote to you from one of my favorite books on finance—indeed, one of my favorite books. *My Life as a Quant: Reflections on Physics and Finance*, by Emanuel Derman, is, like the Bookstaber volume, a kind of confessional. Before he took up with derivatives, Derman was a physicist, and here is what he says about the difference between the laboratory and the marketplace: "The techniques of physics hardly ever produce more than the most approximate truth in finance, because 'true' financial value is itself a suspect notion," writes Derman. "In physics, a model is right when it correctly predicts the future trajectories of planets or the existence and properties of new particles. . . . In finance, you cannot easily prove a model right by such observations. Data are scarce and, more importantly, markets are arenas of action and reaction, dialectics of thesis, antithesis and synthesis. People learn from past mistakes and go on to make new ones. What's right in one regime is wrong in the next.

"As a result," Derman goes on, "physicists turned quants don't expect too much from their theories, though many economists naively do. Perhaps this is because physicists, raised on theories capable of superb divination, know the difference between a fundamental theory and a phenomenological toy, useful though the latter may be. Trained economists have never seen a really first-class model. It's not that physics is 'better,' but rather that finance is harder. In physics, you're playing against God, and He doesn't change his laws very often. When you've checkmated Him, He'll concede. In finance, you're playing against God's creatures, agents who value assets based on their ephemeral opinions. They don't know when they've lost, so they keep trying."

By claiming that the panics, breaks and near misses of the past 20 years had their principal origin in the complex architecture of the markets themselves, Bookstaber may have overreached. There were financial misadventures enough before mankind discovered that the highest purpose of a mortgage was to be dismantled and reassembled in the form of an asset-backed security, or that a mere bond is a poor substitute for the kind of derivative called a credit default swap. There was no portfolio insurance in 1929 and no Long-Term Capital Management in 1907, yet history records those years as unprofitable ones for the leveraged optimists.

With that reservation, I agree with Bookstaber as heartily as I disagree with Warsh. Leveraged complexity is worrisome. Still more is it troubling in today's markets. Imagine a young man to whom everything has been given—money, family, looks. That lucky fellow is the U.S. dollar-denominated credit markets. He has been spoon-fed low interest rates and vanishingly low corporate default rates. The family retainers have told him stories about the panics and bear markets of yesteryear, but, to our coddled boy, they are only yarns. So when government bond markets fell out of bed last week, neither the junk-bond market nor the leveraged-loan market did more than twitch. The young prince still seems to think he's invincible.

So, of course, the credit markets are highly leveraged. It would defy human experience if they weren't. Low nominal interest rates, high confidence and easy borrowing terms could have had no other result. For the world's stock markets, it's been a very pleasant state of affairs. You will find it concerning only if—like me—you judge that credit risk is broadly underpriced and the structure of credit is shaky. In that case, you will fear for the private equity boom and the real-estate levitation and for the credit markets that underwrite them.

Reading between Warsh's lines, it's apparent that the Federal Reserve carries a torch for the Efficient Markets Hypothesis. Are investors invariably cool and calculating? Are markets friction-less? Is information universally disseminated to all the lucid par-ticipants? Do they act on it? If you answer "yes" to these ques-tions, you, too, may find the Board of Governors of the Federal Reserve System a collegial place to work.

I will meet Warsh halfway. I will concede that markets are just as efficient as the people who operate in them. How efficient is that? Let us turn to mortgage finance to find out. Here is a living laboratory in complexity gone wrong. During the long upswing, lenders were happy to credit a highly counterintuitive proposi-tion. They accepted that a clump of low-rated mortgages could be transformed into a highly rated security. Only very smart people could dream up such a wonderful idea. And only educated people could accept it (they are taught to respect great minds, no matter what cockamamie conclusion those minds arrive at). What was the source of this alchemy? The reordering of cash flows to assure continuous payments to the holders of the senior claims. Risk of nonpayment, such as it was, was borne by the holders of the mez-zanine and equity tranches. They bore it willingly. The ratings agencies lent their imprimatur to the assumptions and calcula-tions on which the projections were based.

Investors bought with confidence. It reassured them to know that the ratings agencies deployed default probability generator models featuring a Monte Carlo multi-step simulation default probability apparatus—whatever that was. Besides, the mortgage scientists and ratings agency quants believed that diversification was their shield and armor. A given residential mortgage-backed security would con-tain mortgages from every region of the country. The diversity of collateral delivered low correlation in credit performance; they could hardly all default at once. As for house prices, the mortgage scientists observed that they almost invariably went up. And all agreed that home ownership was an unalloyed social benefit.

And if the lenders, borrowers, ratings agency analysts, investment bankers, appraisers, etc. hadn't been human, the story might have a happy ending. But it won't, because people in markets neglected to judge the effects of their actions on others. Uniquely uninhibited underwriting practices pushed up house prices and thereby coaxed more borrowers to employ greater leverage. Not wanting to be left behind, lenders competed with one another to offer the easiest terms. Loans tumbled out of the origination mills into the securitization factories, emerging as ABS or CDOs, investment-grade for the most part and thereby suitable for widows, orphans and foreign central banks. Thankfully, too, there were hedge funds and proprietary trading desks to absorb the residual credit risk of the lower-rated tranches. Warsh paid tribute to these social bene-factors in his talk the other day: "By serving as willing counter-parties in a variety of contracts, these institutions, in my view, are serving as a critical linchpin in the development of more complete markets."

Once upon a time, depository institutions not only did the lend-ing but also retained the loans. Nowadays, banks are wont to sell the loans they make, sometimes to hedge funds. In an important new study entitled, "Hedge Funds: The Credit Market's New Paradigm," Fitch Ratings highlights some of the risks of these new arrangements. The Fitch analysts—Roger Merritt and Eileen Fahey—ask, among other things, who will hold the loans in a bear market, when hedge funds face margin calls from their prime brokers and redemptions from their limited partners? Of course, the study allows, not every fund is wild-eyed or overextended.

"Still," the authors go on, "there clearly has been a reduction in lending terms across the credit markets, as well as a trend toward more complex structures with embedded leverage, as evidenced by the tremendous growth in the credit default swap and lever-aged loan markets. Competition among prime brokers, particu-larly from second-tier prime brokers competing for business, also introduces the risk of less lending discipline over time."

Yes, reply the mortgage scientists, but geographical diversifica-tion constitutes an unbreachable wall in the structures they have built. They have done the math: Some pools may go bad, but others will flourish. Correlations are tolerably and safely low.

To which I rejoin, quoting Fitch, "The next credit downturn may very well involve more sudden, correlated declines in asset prices as hedge funds and prime brokers seek to unwind their positions in a more risk-averse market. . . . A deleveraging event is likely to affect most, if not all, sectors of the credit market, resulting in an increase in correlation as hedge funds and prime brokers seek to monetize their most liquid positions first."

My bet is that, come the next bear market in credit, correlations will prove to be shockingly high across the full spectrum of debt instruments. It will turn out that everything was correlated to credit itself—to the ability to borrow on terms over which posterity will shake its head, muttering, "What were they thinking?"

No doubt, the withdrawal of our old friend liquidity will create remarkable opportunities in all markets and time zones. Panicked investors will care no more about value than the euphoric ones did. The bear market in complex mortgage structures may prove espe-

The new banker's hours.

cially confusing and violent. What are the tranches actually worth? In flush times, they were worth what the ratings-agency models said they were worth. In the bear market, they will be worth what a liquid buyer will pay for them. It may turn out that investment-grade tranches will go begging at 50 cents on the dollar when nobody could seem to get enough of them at par.

The philosophical premise of value investing is that the future is unpredictable. Not knowing, and knowing that one can't know, the careful investor insists on a margin of safety in the form of a low price. Of course, in a credit bubble, one can insist until one is blue in the face. Prices won't oblige until the bubble bursts. And maybe—just maybe—the bursting has begun.

Emanuel Derman, the physicist-turned-quant, tells a story about Long-Term Capital Management after the dream had died. He was at Goldman Sachs and joined a conference call with a few of the LTCM partners to discuss the valuation of the deflated swaps portfolio. "The questions they asked us in that brief conversation showed an immediate understanding of theoretical subtleties that was far more insightful and sophisticated than any questions we had been asked by the Goldman traders we knew," Derman writes. "It was a shock to realize that people whose great experience and knowledge straddled both the quantitative and the trading worlds had, despite their sophistication, brought themselves to such a catastrophic state." If the Nobel Laureates at Long-Term could miscalculate, so can we all, not least the mortgage-model builders at Moody's and Standard & Poor's.

Reading Derman, I remembered Warren Buffett's comment on brainpower in his preface to the fourth revised edition of Graham's *Intelligent Investor.* Wrote the Sage of Omaha: "To invest successfully over a lifetime does not require a stratospheric IQ. . . ." I have given this matter some hard thought. Not only does a sky-high IQ not guarantee success, but it also could pose a danger, not only to the genius' own net worth but to the safety and wealth of others. I therefore urge the relevant regulatory bodies of the United States and Canada to incorporate an IQ test into their securities licensing exams. There would be no minimum passing grade. But nobody would be allowed to work in the financial markets in any capacity with a score of 115 or higher. Finance is too important to be left to smart people.

Chapter Eleven

The Fine Art of
Security Analysis

Pariahs' Club

February 4, 2000

THE STOCK MARKET is, by our lights, absurd, but it is becoming slightly more symmetrically absurd. There is a growing list of cheap valuations to complement a considerably larger number of extravagant ones. Possibly, there can be no safety in value until the speculative bubble bursts, but it might be useful to chronicle the arrestingly low valuations attached to some of the companies that, for one reason or another, have been in their own individual bear markets.

We herein offer up three with the understanding that none is an obviously brilliant investment candidate. Each, however, has been badly mauled in the stock market, and each, by some measure, is cheap. Two of the three—Lockheed Martin Corp. and Raytheon

Co.—may legitimately be regarded as indispensable to the national defense. As for the third, not many Dow stocks carry a 9% dividend yield and a mid-single-digit P/E multiple. Then, again, few are branded enemies of the people, as Philip Morris has virtually been. We began our investigation into the tobacco behemoth with a contrary, bullish bias—the valuation vital signs are enticing—but the more we investigated, the less bullish we became. (Maybe that is the truly bullish aspect of the story, although we think we will not dwell on that possibility.)*

The maker of Marlboro cigarettes, Miller beer and Kraft cheese, which, astoundingly, earned almost $2 billion last quarter, spent $902,000 on political lobbying and campaign contributions in New York state in 1999. The size of these outlays was reported in the *New York Times* last Friday, it also being noted that Philip Morris Cos. had been fined $75,000 and seen its chief Albany lobbyist banned from working in New York for violations of lobbying laws. The same edition of the *Times* reported a "startlingly high" incidence of smoking among middle- school students nationwide.

Here, in a nutshell, is the cigarette business. It earns more money than it knows what to do with by making a product that makes you sick. (Possibly, cigarettes have retained their popularity with America's youth because they do make you sick.) It enjoys that rare thing in the year 2000, pricing power, and no matter how high the returns it generates, it is unlikely to elicit new competition. There is no future in smoking—neither for the smoker nor for the tobacco companies—and Philip Morris has been turning the surplus money, after lobbying fees, of course, back to the stockholders. Last year, it paid out $7.7 billion in this way, $4.4 billion in dividends and $3.3 billion in share repurchases. As the tobacco team at Morgan Stanley

---

* Philip Morris changed its name to Altria Group in 2003 to bring "better clarity to the corporate structure." Whatever the subsequent clarity quotient, the company delivered annual returns of 26.7% to its shareholders between February 2002 and June 2008. Over the same span, Lockheed Martin returned 25.1% per annum, Raytheon, 16.4%, as the U.S. defense budget more than doubled following the attacks of September 11.

observes, it was a sum equivalent to about 15% of the current stock-market capitalization. "MO," the stock symbol, is a cruel reminder of the lack of momentum in the share price; at Monday's close, the company was valued at about 6.4 times trailing net income and 0.8 times sales. The dividend yield was exactly 9.17%.

A very cheap stock, indeed, if one is prepared to overlook the risk of oblivion-through-litigation, which one cannot. The bulls contend that the peak litigation risk has passed. One hopeful sign, the argument goes, is the very scale of the Philip Morris share buybacks; unless the company had reason to believe that its legal ground were solid, it would be husbanding its cash. Possibly, but in the language of the old junk-bond prospectuses, there can be no assurance. It is open season on Philip Morris, along with the rest of the tobacco industry, and the companies have been sued by just about everybody, including the Clinton administration (of course), a big class of Florida plaintiffs and aggrieved smokers (or ex-smokers) in Nigeria and the Marshall Islands, among other places. The tobacco companies have won some legal battles, to be sure, but they have also lost some, and the losses only coax forth more litigation, in a pattern that will remind gold bulls of the periodic demoralizing sales of bullion by the world's central banks. In the case of tobacco, the overhead supply is of litigation, not ingots. It may well be that the solvency-threatening legal risk is over, but the risk of a damaging award by a wayward (or, for that matter, a sound and rational) jury is ever present. "Management is unable to make a meaningful estimate of the amount or range of loss that could result from an unfavorable outcome of pending legislation," says page 22 of the latest Philip Morris 10-Q. "The present legislative and litigation environment is substantially uncertain, and it is possible that the company's business, volume, results of operations, cash flows or financial position could be materially affected by an unfavorable outcome or settlement of certain pending litigation or by the enactment of federal or state tobacco legislation." A friend describes tobacco shares as the last remaining assessable stock on earth.

At a price, we at *Grant's* firmly believe, there is value in almost everything, including tobacco companies. In this context, we are glad to be able to observe that shares in General Cigar Holdings, the subject of a bullish piece in the November 5 issue, recently vaulted after Swedish Match tendered for 64% of them. Cigars are no more health-giving than cigarettes, but General Cigar, at the rock-bottom price at which a kind reader called it to our attention, was selling for less than its net current assets.

Philip Morris, as cheap as it is, is not that cheap. Besides, it swims against the tide of the demonstrated tendency of people, when faced with the consequences of their own bad decisions, to hire a lawyer. Nor is this inclination uniquely American. On December 8, a French court held Seita, the maker of Gauloises cigarettes, partly to blame for the death of one of its very loyal ex-customers; so the culture of victimization, if we may use a loaded election-year term, has spread to Europe. The greater *Grant's* family has never been united by politics, and the editor does not mean to impose his philosophy of individual responsibility on the paid-up subscribers. The principal point,

"So who's this Warren Buffett guy?"

of course, is the financial one. It seems rash, not to say unprofitable, to attempt to call a top in the bull market in global litigiousness.

As a purely financial exercise, it is interesting to compare the potential risks and rewards of MO common with those of the tax-exempt bonds of the Tobacco Settlement Asset Securitization Corp., a legal creature of the City of New York. The TSAC's debt is backed by the billions of dollars of future payments earmarked for 46 states (and various other public entities) under the so-called Master Settlement Agreement of 1998. The benchmark 6¼s of 2033, currently priced to yield 6.62%, are rated Aa2 by Moody's, A-plus by Fitch and single-A by Standard & Poor's. Philip Morris, a single-A-rated credit, boasts a taxable 9% dividend yield, as noted—the after-tax equivalent to a well-to-do New Yorker of about 4.5%.

Which to choose? If someone held a cigarette lighter to our head, we would pick the common. The bonds, fully exposed to interest-rate and credit risk, have no claim on a potential bullish turn in MO's fortunes. Alas, so thick is the smoke and haze of litigation that no such surprise is visible, to us. We therefore end this investigation with the same not-quite original observation with which we began it: Philip Morris looks like a very cheap stock.

Next come Lockheed Martin (LTM) and Raytheon (RTN/B), respectively the nation's largest and second-largest defense contractors, and rare examples of high-tech businesses whose share prices have somehow managed not to go up. Indeed, each company has serially and comprehensively disappointed its investors across the range of its capitalization structure, debt as well as equity. Each has choked on a big merger (Raytheon with the defense business of Hughes Electronics, in 1997, and Lockheed with Martin Marietta, in 1995); each has produced massive earnings disappointments; and each has brought anxiety on its creditors. Late last year, Lockheed Martin was found unfit, by dint of poor credit ratings, to issue commercial paper; it turned to its banks and the bond market instead. As for Raytheon, its year-end statement showed a sharp rise in short-term debt, up almost $2 billion from a year earlier. "Thus," comments Carol Levenson, of Gimme Credit, who has been insightfully bearish on the creditworthiness of Raytheon (and of Lockheed Martin, too), "at the same time debt protection measures are slumping (and are expected to slump even further next year), the company is becoming more and more dependent upon its banks for both financing and lenience. This is a worrisome state of affairs, and leaves the company exposed to increasing liquidity risks."

As recently as last July, Raytheon was trading near 1.3 times sales; the current quotation—no less than three disastrous earnings warning announcements later—is 0.38 times sales. To be sure, both Raytheon and Lockheed Martin are leveraged; even adjusting for their debt, however, the valuations are strikingly low—on an enterprise value-to-sales basis, 0.87 and 0.73 times, respectively, for RTN/B and LTM. Raytheon trades at 0.71 times book, Lockheed Martin at 1.12 times book.

Lockheed Martin, itself well practiced at letting the air of hope out of its investors' tires, last month halved its quarterly dividend and reiterated its downward revised earnings forecast of $1 a share for 2000 (about half of what the Street was expecting as recently as last October). Commented the *Washington Post*, "Even at that pessimistic level, the company included a handful of assumptions that could still go sour, such as a contract to sell about $7 billion worth of F-16 fighter planes to the United Arab Emirates. The deal has been in the works for more than a year, with no resolution."

Yet—still—we are inclined to be bullish. Our No. 1 reason is that the companies' main customer needs the companies just as much as the companies need the customer. Senior officials of the Defense Department, indeed, have criticized Wall Street for marking down the companies' share prices; they say they can't understand the market's preference for the kind of high-tech company that has no earnings, precious little revenue and no multibillion-dollar backlog of government business. (The order backlog at Raytheon, in fact, stands at a record $28.4 billion; the backlog at Lockheed Martin, though not a record, is $45.9 billion.) Obviously exasperated, they sound like value investors.

It's not as if the bears were imagining things, of course. However, we agree with the tacit bull argument of the officials' criticisms. Unlike e-Toys, for instance, there will always be a place for Lockheed Martin and Raytheon. Defense spending has plunged over the past decade—according to Under Secretary of Defense Jacques S. Gansler, defense procurement is down by 70% since the Evil Empire shut up shop—but it will, we believe, come back, regardless of who wins the White House next fall. Criticisms of the companies' financial affairs are on the mark, and the two shamed managements can hardly be deaf to them. But even if no new leaf is turned over anywhere, the risk of insolvency, we believe, is insignificant. In techno-talk, the "space" that Raytheon and Lockheed Martin occupy is even more vital than the space occupied by Amazon or Akamai.

We turned to Ed Walsh, longtime authority on the defense industry and owner and editor of *Naval Systems Update*, Occoquan, Va., for a technical briefing on the plight of the two defense giants. Walsh's considered opinion, in brief: Raytheon and Lockheed Martin are unique and irreplaceable; things will get better for the companies, in part because they have to.

"The conventional wisdom in the financial community," Walsh observes, "appears to be that Raytheon and Lockheed Martin have become dinosaurs of the post-Cold War world, trying to postpone an inexorable decline, if not extinction, by resorting to poorly planned acquisitions and ham-handed lobbying. The conventional wisdom is based on facts, but only some of the facts, those almost certain to be overtaken by hard-to-recognize developments in defense systems engineering and systems integration, in which both are the unmatched experts at home and worldwide."

By "systems integration," Walsh says he means the design of the fundamental software and hardware linkages among the combat components of a Navy warship, a Navy or Air Force fighter aircraft, or an

Army or Marine Corps land vehicle. A successfully integrated ship-board computer system, for instance, is one that can track an incoming enemy missile at 3,000 miles an hour and communicate that information to a shipboard gun mount or antimissile system. The sound of success is an explosion that occurs in midair as opposed to inside the ship's hull. To be sure, there have been some embarrassing misses in the business of shooting missiles out of the sky, but the Theater High-Altitude Area Defense System of Lockheed Martin did hit the bull's-eye as recently as last August. Raytheon is the prime contractor for the Navy's ballistic missile defense program, to be deployed on Ticonderoga-class cruisers and Arleigh Burke-class destroyers.

Naturally, in the Information Age, there will be information-based warfare, and the 1997 Quadrennial Defense Review, which forms the foundation for next-generation defense planning, directed the Pentagon to pursue a "joint vision of information superiority—the ability to collect and distribute to U.S. forces throughout the battlefield an uninterrupted flow of information."

This information arena, Walsh winds up, "is dominated by Lockheed Martin and Raytheon. Their roles in defense systems engineering and systems integration are based on the evolution of years of institutional expertise in managing not only weapons-systems production but also the engineering, testing, and logistics services that support highly complex computer-driven systems."

Too big to fail? Never mind Citigroup. Lockheed Martin and Raytheon may just succeed in spite of themselves.

Bearish on Corning

April 12, 2000

Corning Inc., once a maker of casserole dishes and silicon breast implants, and today the world's leading producer of optical fiber and cable, received a multibillion-dollar imprimatur in *The Wall Street Journal* last Friday. The company's stock, according to the paper's "Fund Track" column, is one of the three top holdings of Kevin Landis, who only happens to own the best five-year record in the entire American mutual-fund management industry. Interestingly, the name of Landis's fund is the Firsthand Technology Value Fund. What Corning (GLW) has to do with value, and what value has to do with moneymaking in the year 2000, are the featured topics of the essay just now unfolding.

We start with the observation that Corning trades at 92 times trailing net income (69 times the consensus estimate for 2000). It is quoted at 19 times year-end 1999 book value, and yields 0.4%. It is therefore impossible to claim that the stock is an "undervalued situation," as that phrase has been handed down from generation to generation. It's the apparent irrelevance of traditional valuation criteria to the present-day stock market that causes people to make bar bets. The new new thing is not only the technology, but also the rules of investing.

In what sense is Corning a "value" stock? The bulls have an answer to this question: Corning is a value stock in the sense that it goes up.* A year ago, it was quoted at 65⅞ a share, with a market cap of $16.1 billion. Now it stands at around 170, with a market cap of $46.9 billion. Most investors who participated in this great leap forward are the ones who didn't ask what the P/E was. In the midst of a once-in-a-lifetime technological revolution, they were focused on the technology. Imagine (as true believers in the New Economy sometimes do) the game of tennis without the net. Now imagine a certain section of the gallery at the National Tennis Center in Flushing Meadows, in New York's borough of Queens, in which the fans continue to insist that there is a net, or should be one. That's where the value investors sit.

Grant's turns to Corning for its educational value: It's a case study in the commoditization of the New Economy. A top maker

---

* The Corning share price proceeded to double, then—in response to deepening troubles among Corning's customers—to collapse. In the two years to April 2002, it fell by 87%.

of things that others make, too, though not in such great quantity, Corning is valued in the market is if it were more. It has already assumed the stock-market mantle of a leading maker of the kind of highly engineered communications products, called "photonics," that make the fiber "sweat" and make investors in the successful photonics companies rich. (Last year, Corning's photonics segment showed a loss, owing to "continued research and development.") DWDM, for "dense wave-length division multiplexing," technology is an example of what falls under the photonics rubric. Of course, Corning may do just what it says it intends to do, in the process pushing aside such heavyweights as Lucent and JDS Uniphase. However, at current rich valuations, it seems to us, the market is taking a great deal on faith. If success is built in, how would a disappointment register?

More than a century ago, the Guggenheims became a dynasty by developing the copper with which to build the nation's first electric and telephone backbone. Corning has a silicon-based fiber superior to any produced by the American Smelting & Refining Co., but it's working nonstop to produce a better one. Nobody expected Smelters to create under its own roof a technology that would leapfrog its own copper wire. Creative destruction does, in fact, destroy, yet never in the history of the red metal has a mining company commanded a valuation like GLW's.

Grant's would say that, admittedly. If we had been asked a year ago to pick between a casserole manufacturer at six times earnings (nice little company, clean balance sheet, good margins) and an optical-fiber cable maker trading at 10 or 20 times that valuation, you know what we would have done. We would have ordered up a file on the casserole company.

We concede this freely. However, our interest in valuation is more than a personality defect. A super-high P/E not only constitutes a barrier to a successful investment for the person buying the stock (other things being the same, of course); it also constitutes a beacon for new investment in the high P/E company's major business line. A highly valued company will attract more competition than a modestly valued one. Holding all else constant, extraordinary returns elicit high investment, and Corning last year earned 21% on stockholders' equity. In the old days, as the saying went, 5% would "draw money from the moon." Even in today's jaded Nasdaq stock market, a nearly triple-digit trailing P/E multiple ought to pull funds from Venus or Mars, at least. The wired world is every bit as dynamic and volatile as its acolytes say it is. To us, however, that is not the reason to pay fancy prices for companies that are dedicated to making their own technology obsolete.

It was a Corning research team that in 1970 designed and produced the first optical fiber, a medium capable of carrying 65,000 times more information (also—to be sure!—disinformation) than ordinary copper wire. Corning has dominated the optical-fiber market, and now it is striving to become a leader in photonics as well. DWDM is a technology that makes an optical fiber more productive by splitting a single beam of light into innumerable colors. The more colors, the greater the number of channels that the fiber can transmit. Everybody sees that science is headed toward greater and greater feats of color splicing and greater and greater efficiencies of signal transmission. The issue before the house is whether the demand for bandwidth will grow as fast, or faster, than the capacity to carry it.

The short-form bull case on Corning was given in a March 17 research note by J.P. Morgan Securities:

> We continue to believe that GLW is a cheaper, but effective way to play the growth in optical networking and as such, we reiterate our BUY rating on the stock. . . . We are increasing our 12-month price target to $250 from $200, now using a 79 forward P/E multiple on our 2001 EPS estimate of $3.15 [yes, a P/E multiple]. GLW is currently trading at just over 70 times our 2000 EPS estimate of $2.48, so we do believe that there could be multiple expansion.

And so it came to pass.

For reference, about 63% of Corning's 1999 revenues were derived from telecommunications; the balance was attributable to a range of products including glass panels, microscope slides, funnels and liquid crystal display glass. In 2000, the company expects that about 70% will be communications-related. The biggest contributor to this fast-growing business segment is the fiber-optic division. Corning accounts for as much as 40% of the world's optical fiber production; its 1999 output totaled no less than 28 million kilometers, or 17.4 million miles (meaning that worldwide output reached about 44 million miles, or from here to the top of the Nasdaq 100 Index).

The fundamental bull story on Corning—one so widely and deeply held that it is not always explicitly stated—is that the demand for fiber-optic cable is effectively limitless. "We'll never be done [building infrastructure]," Larry Lang, a vice president of Cisco Systems, recently told *USA Today*, "because the networks keep getting faster, and there's always new technology being developed."

With their DWDM-enhanced transmission capacities, the newer fiber-optic systems are supplanting or augmenting not only the old copper-wire networks but also the semi-new, early-generation fiber-optics networks. Within three years, according to a popular forecast, one billion people will be on the Internet, not just checking their e-mail but doing the kind of bandwidth-intense activities that couldn't be done without high-speed transmission capacity. (To quote from Cisco: Are you ready?) Hence the voracity of demand for the gamut of fiber-optic networking products, fiber-optic cable not least.

Corning, although it makes more than twice as much fiber and cable as its biggest competitor, is very far from a monopolist. Lucent commands an estimated 14% of the market and Alcatel has 12%; five other companies claim 5% or more each: Draka Holding, Fujikura, Furkawa Electric, Pirelli and Sumitomo Electric. Each and every entrant sees demand running away, and many are investing heavily to meet it. Draka, Lucent and Alcatel have all announced substantial increases in production capacity. Corning, which today is operating at full capacity, disclosed a $750 million capital expansion budget on February 3.

"The primary drivers behind our expansion plans," said John W. Loose, Corning's president and COO, "are the strong worldwide demand for Corning fiber, particularly our new, advanced products, and projections for significant growth in Europe, the Far East and other regions of the world. It is the rapid absorption of bandwidth, and the world's seemingly insatiable demand for more, that is creating the opportunity for Corning to meet the requirements of telecommunications service providers as they rapidly deploy optical networks around the world."

Like corn or soybeans, the prices of which tend to fall in parallel with advances in agricultural production methods, optical fiber and cable have been in a technologically induced bear market. "Price declines ranged between 10% and 20% for Corning's optical fiber and cable products in comparison with last year," says the new Corning 10-K report. "However, the weighted average optical fiber and cable price in 1999 declined approximately 5% compared to 1998, due to the higher mix of premium product sales."

Yes, goes the argument, fiber and cable prices have fallen, but the demand is irrepressible. Perhaps, goes the counterargument, but demand was repressed in 1998 when Corning's sales of optical fiber fell by 6% from the levels of 1997 (the result, according to the 10-K, of temporary overcapacity in the worldwide optical cable market). Is it so far-fetched to imagine another decline?

Bulls and bears will disagree on forecasts and valuations, but everyone will gape at the physics. Performance on the optical networks has been doubling almost every nine months. Recently, an article on the bandwidth market that appeared in *Lightwave Fiber Exchange* described the transformation of a particular transatlantic cable, FLAG Atlantic-1, known in the trade as FA-1: "The FA-1 cable at 2.4 [terabits per second] is designed to support 30 times the capacity of the 80 [gigabits per second] transatlantic cables, which in 1999 had been in service for less than a year."

However, none of these miracles changes the fact that Corning is competing to produce a technologically perishable commodity, or that capacity to produce the commodity is fast expanding, or that the price of the commodity is falling. Nor does the excellence of its engineering make Corning any less dependent on the credit-worthiness of its customers, some of which—e.g., Level 3 Communications and Global Crossing—are junk-bond issuers. On April 4, the day of the intraday Nasdaq bear market, it was possible to imagine a setting in which the big, leveraged "bandwidth barons" could not easily obtain the funds with which to purchase the next million miles of Corning's best.

In the February press release disclosing its new capital investment plans, Corning projected that the fiber market would "continue to grow about 20% annually, reaching approximately 100 million kilometers a year by 2002." Is this the stuff of a 69 times forward multiple? No; growth in Corning's market cap has far outstripped the growth in the core fiber business.

What, then, is the source of the great multiple expansion? On the evidence, high hopes for the aforementioned DWDM market, in which—to emphasize—Corning is only beginning to compete. Asked by our colleague Sheila Feerick about its grand design, Corning replied via e-mail, "To become a leading optical layer company, providing the fiber, photonics and optical cable that will enable the development and deployment of an all-optical network." In February, in pursuit of this vision, the company agreed to pay more than $2 billion in stock to acquire NetOptix; in the same month, it spent $66 million to acquire the Photonics Technology Research Center of British Telecom. "Corning's new purchases appear to put it on track to compete directly with its customers," reported the February 17 issue of *Red Herring*.

Companies have tried to change their stripes often enough in business history—Corning, an old hand at invention, established its first research laboratory in 1908. But few have ever had the privilege to be valued at 92 times trailing net income before the experiment panned out.

Risk in a Cheap Stock

January 28, 2002

66 I'll bet if I told you 32 months ago, when we announced the goal [to double earnings per share in five years], that in the fourth quarter of 2001 Fannie Mae would report earnings per share of $1.40, up 59% from the first quarter of 1999, you would have guessed that our stock would be up by at least that amount." So said Tim Howard, CFO of Fannie Mae, on the fourth-quarter conference call Monday.

He went on in that vein:

> I certainly would have. But it's not. At the close of business on Friday, the stock was up just 15%, about a quarter of the earnings growth. But if there is surprise or disappointment in that result, there also is promise. Over the past decade, our stock price has grown faster than our earnings per share. It just hasn't done so evenly. To the contrary, there frequently have been periods when, for whatever reason, the price of Fannie Mae stock has become uncoupled from its fundamentals. This appears to be one of those times. Neither our performance nor our prospects seem to justify our current valuation.

By the sound of it, Howard was singing our song. *Grant's* expects a protracted period of low money-market interest rates, the kind tailor-made for financing a fixed-rate mortgage portfolio. We are soft touches for low valuations, and the nation's top mortgage purveyor is quoted at 15.8 times trailing net income and 13.6 times 2002 forecasts (which management is not shy about

"I'm always bearish?"

predicting it will easily top). When they compare the lowly P/E with a 15-year record of double-digit earnings gains, growth-stock buyers may rub their eyes. Yet, in Fannie Mae, we see another example of a huge financial institution more to be worried about than invested in.

The late Robert M. Bleiberg, thundering free-market editor of *Barron's*, was an unqualified Fannie Mae bull, but he didn't live to see the interest-rate-stunted child of 1981 grow up to share a conforming-mortgage duopoly, or to become an aspiring central bank or virtual Department of the Treasury. We make a clean breast of our prejudice against institutions as lightly capitalized, heavily subsidized and politically ingratiating as this one. Readers with a different set of values can make the proper mental adjustments to the unfolding analysis. However, no reader should not care, as Fannie Mae (along with joint duopolist Freddie Mac) is fast becoming the center of gravity of the interest-rate universe.

Giantism is reason enough to suspect that Fannie is not just another beneficiary of low funding costs and a steep yield curve. Its balance sheet is bigger than the Federal Reserve's. It issued $2 trillion of debt last year. (The Treasury issued $2.9 trillion, but Fannie and Freddie together outborrowed the Treasury by $1.1 trillion.) Fannie has what it calls a "combined book of business." Its net mortgage portfolio plus outstanding mortgage-backed securities (i.e., those held on balance sheets other than its own) ended 2001 at $1,564 billion, up by 19% in a year, the fastest rate of growth in nine years. It is no small thing when a 13-figure number shatters growth records. The company earned 25.4% on its sliver of equity in 2001, and the premium of that return to the yield on the 10-year Treasury note climbed to a near-record height. How will Fannie keep it up? How will it finance its growth and hedge against interest-rate turbulence?

The Fannie Mae front office keeps saying that there's no end in sight to growth. In the short run, the net interest margin will "likely be at elevated levels for a longer period of time than previously anticipated," according to the fourth-quarter press release. Over a longer horizon, rates of household formation, rates of home ownership, loan-to-value ratios and house prices will continue to trend in favorable directions. Residential mortgage debt will grow by 8% to 10% this decade, the company says, but earnings growth will not thereby be capped. In November, Jamie S. Gorelick, vice chair of Fannie, held out a vision of the future before a convention of community bankers in New Orleans. Gorelick cheerfully described the vast amount of mortgage borrowing still to be contracted in America.

"As it has for the past five decades," she said, "the trend of increasing debt-to-value ratios will continue in the current decade. Back in the '50s, the average ratio was just 20%—today, it is 47% [on new loans, it is closer to 80%]. Where might it go? As boomers get closer to their retirement years, some may wish to reduce their ratios. But we expect many others to want to continue using their equity wealth in the golden years. In addition, as more lenders bring more low down-payment mortgages to the market, that will also boost the debt-to-value ratio. So we believe these ratios could grow from 1.3% to 1.7% a year for the rest of the decade."

"Fannie Mae is in a terrific business," said Howard on the conference call. "Unlike most companies, we don't have to sell our product. People demand it." We thought of interest-bearing nicotine.

Fannie's on-balance-sheet mortgage portfolio represents 31% of the Merrill Lynch Mortgage Index; Fannie and Freddie combined hold the equivalent of 52% of the index. Growing faster than the market, the GSEs are annually drawing closer to becoming the market. Mortgages are volatile substances, characterized by what is known in the trade as negative convexity. Let market yields fall, and mortgage durations fall; let market yields rise, and mortgage durations rise. Mortgage investors are forever dissatisfied. In a bear market, they are stuck with the thing they don't want. In a bull market, what they want is called away from them. Great intellects have devoted their professional lives to conquering these design flaws.

Not least of the blessings of the American people is the optionality given free with a typical fixed-rate mortgage. If rates rise, it's the lender's problem. In a decline, the borrower can refinance. The authors of the 1946 Employment Act could not have imagined that a rising burden of mortgage debt would create one of the most potent automatic stabilizers in the nation's countercyclical policy armory.

"Fannie Mae's mortgage portfolio business contributes close to two-thirds of our net income," the company states. "It has considerable room for growth due to its relatively small market share." It is an uncontested fact that, at $705 billion, Fannie's net mortgage portfolio is equivalent to less than 12% of estimated outstanding mortgages. That the company has "considerable room for growth" is, however, a whopper, given the market segment in which Fannie operates, and is expected to have to continue to operate. According to FM Watch, a Washington research organization established to thwart the expansion of the federal mortgage duopoly, Fannie controls 74% of the "conforming" market. That is, it purchased or guaranteed mortgages last year equivalent to 74% of all originations of conforming size (now $300,700 or less). "[W]e figure by 2003 they'll control 91%," says FM Watch director Mike House. "The only way that they can possibly grow is to get into businesses that they're currently not in and [that], frankly, are outside their mission."

Linda Lowell, mortgage analyst at Greenwich Capital (which is not in the business of thwarting the GSEs), seconds the notion that growth options are limited. In this she includes Freddie as well as Fannie: "First, they can increase fee income by increasing the amount of mortgage debt they securitize," Lowell writes in a must-read January 9 *Mortgage Market Roundup*. "Cannibalizing the FHA/VA markets to increase market share has met modest political resistance, while expanding in A– and sub-prime markets generates much stronger political resistance. Growth on this front, then, [it] appears could be limited to the rates at which mortgage debt grows and portfolio lenders retreat. In other words, growth should be slow. By the same token, attempts to expand their mission and venture into new housing-related businesses have met with virulent opposition."*

On this point, Rep. Richard H. Baker (R.–La.), chairman of the House Subcommittee on Capital Markets, gave vehement testimony on November 2. "Fannie Mae and Freddie Mac are not meeting the nation's affordable housing needs," said Baker. "In fact, all indications are Fannie and Freddie have moved predominantly in the direction of refinancing and large down-payment loans—neither of which business activities [have] any beneficial impact on low- to moderate-income first-time homebuyers."

Which would leave portfolio expansion as the most likely avenue of earnings growth, as Lowell proceeds: "If mortgage debt grows at

---

* The government-sponsored enterprises controlled 80% of the residential mortgage-backed securities market in 2001. That share dwindled to 45% at the 2005-06 peak of the housing bubble, but in the bust it went right back up again.

a 6% annual rate (the annual compound rate in 1991–2000), and the securitization rate continues to inch up—as it has in the last four years by less than a point a year—Fannie and Freddie must take increasing shares of their securities for their own account to maintain their portfolio and earnings growth. The limits on this strategy are the cost of the debt sold to finance portfolio growth and how much it costs to hedge, either via more costly debt instruments or in derivatives markets. As the portfolios becomes a more massive weight within the fixed-income markets, we would expect both to rise."

James A. Bianco, founding light of Bianco Research, Barrington, Ill., was among the first to notice that the bond market had fallen into the mortgage force field. Rising and falling interest rates are increasingly exaggerated by the actions taken by the mega-holders of MBS. Rallies move faster and farther than they once did because they are supercharged by duration-seeking MBS investors (falling rates, by increasing prepayments, shorten the duration of a mortgage portfolio; to compensate, mortgage investors buy Treasurys, or take other offsetting action). Similarly, as Bianco points out, selloffs are faster and bloodier than they were in the days of a smaller mortgage market because they are driven by duration-shedding MBS investors (rising rates, by cutting short prepayments, lengthen the duration of a mortgage portfolio; to compensate, mortgage investors sell Treasurys, or the functional equivalent).

Fifteen consecutive years of double-digit returns suggest that Fannie knows something about how to hedge interest-rate risk. Still, it can't be easy. To comply with the new FASB rule requiring that the derivatives portfolio be marked to market, Fannie booked a $7.1 billion charge against its $25.2 billion year-end equity. Fannie protests that disclosure in this manner has "the undesirable effect of marking to market only part of the balance sheet" because the gains on assets being hedged with the derivatives are not shown. Still, to us, the information is eye-opening, because it underscores (a) how big the Fannie Mae portfolio is and (b) how big the price swings are.

As we contemplate a $705 billion mortgage portfolio, we wonder: Who will fund it? Who will enlist as counterparties to hedge it? The bigger the balance sheet, the more of the world's financial capacity it must absorb. As for the funding question, we note that, in the past two years, foreign central bank holdings of U.S. agency securities (Fannie's included) have leapt to $132 billion from $62 billion. Is the domestic market sated? Colleague Peter Walmsley can find no evidence to that effect.

On the hedging question, however, we are not so sure that Fannie won't face constraints. And the authority we cite in support is Robert Dean, senior vice president of market risk oversight at Freddie Mac.

There is no derivatives exchange, Dean points out. The derivatives market is an over-the-counter market, and as banks and dealers consolidate—e.g., J.P. Morgan and Chase Manhattan—"they tend to allocate less capital as a combined entity than they did when they were stand-alone. Not surprisingly, when you get a situation like that, it slightly reduces the capacity of the system. It means that there's a little bit less ability to do derivatives than there was before the merger. Citigroup was another good example. . . . So that's number one.

"So we are very concerned with the liquidity of the derivatives market because, frankly, if the liquidity isn't there, then it's actually not worth using those markets to hedge in. And, quite simply, the reason is that when the liquidity is not there, if you go into the market and try to hedge when dealers don't have enough capacity, you'll just move the market. You'll actually wind up making matters worse for yourself. So we worry about liquidity in terms of consolidation of the system and whether there's still enough capital being allocated to the system. I think that would be our biggest concern. It is fair to say that with the GSEs getting bigger, that we are putting more pressure on the derivatives system, because our rebalancing needs are greater than they were a few years ago."

Which is one of the reasons why Fannie trades at 13.6 times forecast earnings.

Glowworm Will—Eventually—Turn

April 26, 2002

Corning Inc. observed its sesquicentennial year with massive impairment charges, 12,000 layoffs, a $5.5 billion net loss and a $38 billion decline in stock market capitalization. That was 2001."Clearly," wrote then-CEO John W. Loose and chairman James R. Houghton in the just-published annual report, "these results are very disappointing to all of us."

It's a toss-up which group of investors Corning has managed most to disappoint. Before it let down the post-bust bulls, it distressed the pre-bust bears. Now the bulls are heartsick and the bears are stale. A *Grant's* analysis, "Bearish on Corning," dated April 14, 2000, was as right as rain, though it admittedly did not prepare a reader for the subsequent near-doubling of the share price. On the other hand, a subscriber whose copy was lost in the mail for about five months was presented with a unique short-selling opportunity. In those days, the bears called Corning "Glowworm" (that's GLW on the New York Stock Exchange), and they—er, we—said it with a sneer.

Now we return as bulls-in-waiting. The news is horrific, the sentiment is black, yet the technology is as wonderful as it was at the top (more wonderful, in fact, as science doesn't know about the bear market). At the peak, in the fourth quarter of 2000, Corning generated $2,084 million in sales; in this year's first quarter, it produced $878 million, a drop of 57%. Peak to trough, its share price has fallen by 94%. Why are we not bulls-in-fact? The balance sheet is weakening and a debt downgrade looms (current rating: Baa1/BBB). If the *Bloomberg* quote is close to the mark, the Corning 6.85s of 2029 are priced to yield just 7.44%, low pay for the risk. What would the stock price do when (as we expect) the bonds sell off? Not go up. However, to reiterate, we are bulls-in-waiting.

In the bubble, Corning was distinguished, first, by its technology, the very cool business of running voice and data through glass fibers. What it had in addition was almost as rare: an investment-grade balance sheet, a demonstrated record of profitability and a corporate history reaching back beyond 1997. "[W]e have almost a religious belief in bandwidth," said Loose in a February 8 interview with *Bloomberg*. The church of bandwidth was even fuller before the bubble burst. Availing themselves of essentially free capital, Corning's customers overbought, whereupon Corning overbuilt and overbought. Watching the Corning share price bay at the moon, seasoned observers were reminded of the citizens' band radio promotions of the 1970s.

Corning is the premier maker of optical fiber. It makes optical hardware, photonic modules and optical networking devices. It's the No. 1 producer of glass substrates for advanced liquid crystal displays (LCDs) and, for that reason, the leader in the transformation of bulky cathode ray tubes into compact flat-panel monitors. However, for revenue growth, profitability and margin expansion, Corning depends chiefly on the famously unprosperous telecommunications industry. The companies we associate now with desperate debts are the very names that used to figure near the top of the Corning customer list. Telco-generated revenues were 71% of the 2001 total.*

Founded in 1851, Corning made the glass that Thomas A. Edison used in the earliest light bulbs. It developed the red-yellow-green traffic-light system, and the kind of glass you can bake in the oven or scorch in the laboratory. To keep up with the times, it entered into a train of joint ventures. Best known are the alliances with Owens-Illinois in 1938 (fiberglass) and Dow Chemical in 1943 (silicones). The disaster of Dow Corning's breast-implant business forced that subsidiary into bankruptcy in 1995, a crisis that coincided with a sales slump in Corning's lab products sales. Management's response was

---

* Reinventing itself, with emphasis on display technologies rather than telecommunications, Corning delivered annual returns to its shareholders of 27% from April 2002 to June 2008.

reinvention. By 1997, the old Corning Glass Works was a conglomerate no more, but a focused supplier to the broadband revolution.

In the 2001 annual report, management answers some frequently asked questions, such as (in effect), Do you wish you'd never heard of broadband? The exact phrasing is: "If you could change your decision five years ago to focus on telecommunications—would you?"

"No," comes the answer. "We've looked at the market from all possible perspectives. And every single scenario brings us to the same conclusion—the future of optical networking is real and the demand is coming. The only issue is timing."

The colloquy continues:

> Q: What makes you so confident?
> A: We have just begun to see the future demand for bandwidth. Industry forecasts indicate growth of greater than 60% per year for the foreseeable future. Internet growth, expansion of local networks, more effective broadband policies—a lot of unstoppable factors are coming together.

"Foreseeable future," a cliché, is never good usage. It is especially ill-suited to Corning, which found so little of the future foreseeable that, in the second quarter of 2001, it wrote down by $3.2 billion the value of an optical components business it acquired from Pirelli in December 2000 for $4 billion. "As the year began," James B. Flaws, the CFO, was quoted as saying in the first-quarter preannouncement, "we felt we were approaching bottom in the telecommunications sector. Our first quarter performance suggests that has happened." Hopeful, if true.

And the colloquy proceeds:

> Q: If you're so confident, why did you close factories?
> A: Because the near-term outlook in telecommunications is not completely clear. We had more current capacity than current demand. We recognized that early. We moved quickly. And we addressed it.

In fact, nothing could be clearer than the near-term outlook for telecommunications. It is miserable. It is so miserable that, on April 15, with the ink on the annual scarcely dry, management ordered a new round of "restructuring and impairment charges." It is so miserable that Loose announced his "retirement" (succeeded by Houghton, a great-great grandson of Corning's founder). At least the company, unlike some of its customers, can pay its bills. On March 31, it had $1.8 billion of cash and an untapped $2 billion revolving credit line.

In the bubble, bulls disputed that there was, or ever could be, too much optical fiber. They compared the information superhighway to the Long Island Expressway, which was bumper-to-bumper shortly after completion. In the colloquy, management avers that telecom will recover. It will take time, a better economy, cheaper capital and "public policy that supports the bandwidth access this country needs." Which prompts the $64 question: "[I]sn't there enough capacity in place to meet demand for the next several years?"

> A: Yes, in the North American long-haul fiber system, there's a tremendous amount of capacity already in the ground. But as these fibers are lit, demand for photonic and optical network components will increase. And when you look at regional networks and metro networks—the networks that actually bring the Internet together with users—a bottleneck is forming, and it's getting much worse as Internet traffic grows.

The essential bullish case on Corning is that management is correct, that the broadband era has only just begun (less than 2% of the world's population has access to broadband, the annual says) and that Corning will emerge, as it submerged, as the dominant low-cost industry leader.

Warren Buffett admonishes against investing in companies that make things you can't spell. We beg the master's leave to make a conditional and hypothetical exception of Corning. We base our appeal on three sentences in the April 15 press release:

The telecommunications revolution is as real as the industrial revolution. Bandwidth demand is growing, it never stopped growing. When this industry re-emerges, Corning will be the leader of a select group of companies positioned to take advantage of the growth.

Say it's true. Say that the most intractable problem Corning faces—a shortage of solvent customers—will be cured. Say that timing a telecom revival will prove just as problematical as timing the preposterous preceding top. Assuming these things, how should an investor proceed?

Cautiously, and mindful of credit risk. From an April 15 Moody's bulletin: "While recognizing Corning's leadership position in the markets it serves and its current strong liquidity position, Moody's noted that the rapid falloff of business in the telecommunications sector will curtail internal cash generation more severely than originally anticipated, while its debt protection measures have weakened considerably, and will remain weak over the near-to-intermediate term."

Citing points of vulnerability, the agency mentioned, among others, potential contingent liabilities (involving possible superfund and asbestos costs) associated with the April 2000 bankruptcy filing of Pittsburgh Corning. And it continued: "Corning's credit metrics have weakened and will not show meaningful improvement until 2003. In year 2001, Corning had an operating loss of about $275 million before impairment and restructuring charges of about $5.7 billion, down from about $710 million the prior year. Meanwhile, interest coverage for the period deteriorated to −1.5 times from 7.7 times, and leverage rose to about 47% from 28% at the end of 2000, mainly due to charges associated with goodwill and impairments." So saying, Moody's reiterated its warning that the company is vulnerable to a downgrade.

Carol Levenson, nonpareil debt analyst (and founder of Gimme Credit), anticipates a two-notch downgrade. That would demote the 151-year-old icon to within one notch of junk. "We noted in February that management asserted the company still had access to the commercial paper markets," Levenson wrote last week, "but we doubt this is still the case since the Moody's action. On the bright side, the company had less than $250 million in commercial paper outstanding at the end of the year and an untapped $2 billion credit line. Still, it's always better to have access to the commercial paper markets than not to have it, especially when your free cash flow is decidedly negative, as Corning's is. Its cash position has deteriorated since year-end, standing at $1.8 billion at the end of the first quarter, down $400 million."

Corning is getting cheaper. It isn't cheap. The stockholders are paying 30 times trailing cash flow, 4.7 times peak, bubble-intensity cash flow. What if there were no equity, or more exactly, if the bondholders inherited the keys from the stockholders? In that case, at existing prices, the bondholders would be paying 12.4 times trailing cash flow, 1.9 times peak. (These are multiples of enterprise value—debt and market cap minus cash, if any, to earnings before interest, taxes, depreciation and amortization.)

Glowworm will shine again. Not at these multiples, perhaps, and not tomorrow in any case. But the bears have had their turn.

Three Years Later and Still Not Cheap

March 14, 2003

Benjamin Graham, the man at whose feet Warren Buffett sat, once laid out seven criteria for conservative stock selection. A deserving company should have (1) "adequate" size, (2) a good balance sheet, (3) 10 consecutive years of net profits, (4) 20 years of uninterrupted dividend payments, (5) a modicum, at least, of earnings growth, (6) a P/E ratio no higher than 15 and (7) a ratio of price to book value no higher than 1.5:1. These criteria he commended to the "defensive" investor, i.e., "one interested chiefly in safety plus freedom from bother." They pertained to industrial companies, not to utilities or banks.

Now unfolding is the application of Graham's seven criteria to the present-day stock market and to the bear markets, panics and corrections of yesteryear, starting with 1974. David Schiff, editor of *Schiff's Insurance Observer*, set the project in motion by musing that probably few, if any, public companies would meet the Graham test today, even though the millennial bear market is celebrating its third birthday. He turned out to be right. Compustat, commissioned by *Grant's Interest Rate Observer*, searched the S&P 500 and found exactly two Graham-compliant names, Limited Brands (Victoria's Secret, Limited Stores, Express, etc.) and Scientific Atlanta (maker of television set-top boxes).*

Investment principles aren't timeless but changeable, as Graham himself acknowledged. The seven criteria just quoted are from the fourth edition of *The Intelligent Investor*, which appeared in 1973. The first edition, published in 1949, presented four rules only, including a maximum P/E of 25 times earnings. Then, again, one should not make too much of the heterodoxy of a 25 P/E multiple (or, as Graham called it, "multiplier"). The corporate earnings against which the higher multiple applied were those at the close of the unprosperous 1930s.

Rules bear the impress of the era in which they are written. For example, Graham's second principle, concerning financial strength, stipulates a current ratio of 2:1 or better (i.e., current assets at least twice as large as current liabilities). And he decrees that no eligible company shall run up long-term borrowings greater than working capital (i.e., current assets minus current liabilities).

The master wrote before the dawn of just-in-time inventory management and before the capital markets opened so many opportunities to borrow against so many different kinds of assets (or none at all). And, of course, he wrote before leveraged balance sheets

---

* Limited Brands returned 12.4% per annum to the stockholders between March 2003 and June 2008, a hair better than the S&P 500 (which, though it might not have been "cheap," nonetheless proceeded to rally). Scientific Atlanta was acquired by Cisco Systems in February 2006, yielding a windfall to its value-minded holders.

"I've lost track. This time around,
are we going public or private?"

became de rigueur. "Working capital aside," advises Schiff, "in the 1970s and 1980s, I remember seeing many companies with stable earnings, cash, no debt, that were selling for near—or well below—their tangible book values. LBOs, buybacks and modern financial management have changed that. Most companies, in the quest for ROE and growth, WANTED to be more leveraged."

Graham, who took his lumps in the 1929 Crash, could not help but share in the crisis-induced financial conservatism of his generation. In a poll conducted by the Federal Reserve in 1948, 90% of the respondents said that they opposed investing in common stocks, about half calling them inherently unsafe, the remaining portion of the 90% admitting to not paying very close attention. (On August 28, *The Wall Street Journal* reported on a poll of Japanese investors that found 83% "have no interest in investing in stocks—even though savings accounts pay them virtually no interest and Japanese stocks are the cheapest in more than a decade." Make that two decades.)

It's easy to see that they don't make bear markets like they used to. At the 1974 low ebb, 85 out of 500 S&P companies met Graham's seven-rule test. The number dwindled to 62 in August 1982, 14 in post-crash October 1987 and six in January 1991, when another president named Bush took aim at Saddam. That only two S&P companies pass the test at the third anniversary of this bear market is a fact deserving of wonder and scrutiny.

Some will say that the shrinking number of undervalued stocks is only a measure of the improvement of the monetary system and the evolution of the species. Because inflation is dormant, interest rates are minuscule. "Stocks will never get as cheap as they did in 1974 because rates are so low," they say.

But low rates are no more inherently bullish for equities than high rates are inherently bearish. It seems to depend on why rates are low, or high, and how fast they are falling or rising. Thus, for example, long Treasury yields fell to 2.19% from 3.60% between 1929 and 1946, but U.S. equities didn't go up. And Japanese bond yields have fallen to 0.73% from 5.73% in 1989, and Japanese stocks haven't gone up, either. And if those facts weren't inconvenient enough, the S&P 500 vaulted to 80.3 from 15.3 between 1946 and 1966, while long Treasury yields climbed to 4.66% from the aforementioned 2.19%. It is notable how much milder was the 1982 bear market than the 1974 slump (as measured by the number of companies that met Graham's seven-point test), even though the long bond yielded 12.81% in August 1982, 502 basis points more than it yielded at the October 1974 stock-market low. Professional observers of interest rates, we are prepared to assert that low interest rates are bullish for equities, and rising interest rates are bearish for equities—except when they aren't.

If not interest rates, what explains the increasing paucity of Graham-worthy bargains? We positively rule out the hypothesis that present-day investors are shrewder and more panic-resistant than their forebears. How could they be? They have the same nervous system. Borrowing from Richard Russell, we suspect that posterity will identify 1975-2000 as a great bull market that culminated in the 1996-2000 CNBC updraft. Accordingly, the setbacks of 1982, 1987 and 1991 will go down as corrections to a trend that was stopped in its tracks on March 10, 2000.

Jeremy Grantham, chairman of the Boston money management firm of Grantham, Mayo, Van Otterloo & Co., contends that the 1996-2000 phase of the U.S. bull market was a bubble, for which he has an exact definition. A bubble, says Grantham, is a once-in-40-year, two-standard-deviation event. There were 27 in history before the one just named, and each and every one ended up where it started. "There were no exceptions, no survivors, no new eras, no new economies, Alan dear," Grantham told the fall 2002 *Grant's* conference, addressing the chairman of the Federal Reserve, who wasn't in the room. Grantham has proposed that 680 on the S&P represents "fair value," which implies a fall of at least 15% from Tuesday's close. However, he notes, it would be rash to count on the averages stopping short at fair value when they flew so high over that mark.

The Compustat results will answer some questions and provoke others. In response to the recurrent question, "Is the stock market cheap yet?" the answer comes: "No, not by the lights of Benjamin Graham." Which will prompt another question: "Are those lights bright or dim, timely or dated?" To which we reply, "They are bright enough and timely enough."

Many will quibble about specific Graham criteria: dividends, for example (Graham stipulated 20 years' worth, paid without interruption), earnings consistency (10 years without a miss) or minimum company size. By setting these tests, the master eliminates from consideration micro caps, small caps, turnarounds (to be turned around, a company must have been facing in the wrong direction), growth stocks, distressed securities and companies that, like our good friend EchoStar, don't pay a dividend because they think they have something better to do with the money.

But these are Graham's criteria, stipulated only yesterday, in 1973, when Helen Reddy was singing "I Am Woman" and Richard

Nixon was telling fibs and instituting the pure paper dollar. So we will not try to improve on them, except for one or two suggestions later on because there's nothing wrong with progress. "It's actually a pretty good list if what you're trying to do is invest the South Carolina State Teachers' Pension Fund, which is what really matters in this world," says A. Alex Porter, founder and principal of Porter Felleman, New York asset-management company, of the Graham seven. "If I were doing that, this is the kind of list I'd want."

As you may not remember, 1974 was a year of double-digit inflation, surging oil prices and monetary turmoil. On October 11, *The Wall Street Journal* published an advertisement for a book entitled, *How to Beat the Depression That Is Surely Coming*, by a certain "Professor of Economics and Director of Finance at a large Eastern University." At about the same time, according to author John Rothchild (*The Davis Dynasty*, Wiley, 2001), Graham advised the investor Shelby Davis, "Sonny boy, you're looking at one of the great buying opportunities of your generation."

Not just any bear market dropped 85 big-cap stocks into Graham's value list. The Dow had peaked at 1,000 in 1966. Eight inflation-plagued years later, it closed at 577.6. Few could bear to watch, but James H. Farrell Jr., research director of Provident National Bank of Philadelphia, exactly saw things Graham's way. For the first time since 1942, the Dow was selling below book value, Farrell told *The Wall Street Journal's* "Abreast of the Market" column. At that, it was selling at 85% of book vs. 91% of book in 1942 (this was before the Battle of Midway was won). The market was trading at 6.3 times 1974 earnings, the cheapest, said Farrell, since 1949.

So it was that the American Broadcasting Co. was quoted at 86% of book value and 7.75 times trailing three-year earnings per share; Nabisco at 147% of book and 9.24 times trailing three-year EPS; Time Warner at 85% of book and at 7.39 times trailing three-year EPS; and Wrigley at 127% of book and 9.39 times trailing EPS. Absent from the list of Graham-approved industrial-company bargains was Graham's biggest personal holding, the

Government Employees Insurance Co. Geico, one of the great postwar growth stocks, had plunged into scandal and loss, with a stock price to match. From a high of 42 a share in 1974, it found its way down to 4⅞ before Buffett and Jack Byrne mounted their now-famous 11th-hour rescue in 1976. Even then, it was sawed in half; Buffett paid 2⅛ for 500,000 shares in the month of the U.S. bicentennial.

Before leaving 1974, it is well to record that "one of the greatest buying opportunities of your generation" did not appear that way to most of the people caught up in it. That stocks were cheap was not so obvious as the reasons given for why they were cheap, and for every James H. Farrell Jr., the "Abreast of the Market" column quoted innumerable members of the brokerage-house tribe, who can always be counted on to say such things as "investors would feel a lot more comfortable if the oil-consuming countries could somehow bring oil prices down...."

For those who partook, the 1974 lows provided a valuation benchmark that subsequently spoiled them for life. Reminiscing about the great stocks they bought for nothing, the aging bulls sound like the old forty-niners lying about the tomato-size gold nuggets they picked up off the ground at Sutter's Mill. Not even the 1982 low, with its shrunken list of Graham value candidates, quite measured up. ABC was back, but now quoted above book value and with an eight-handle P/E ratio; Nabisco had actually gotten a little cheaper (1.3 times book and 7.7 times trailing three-year EPS) and Wrigley was valued almost as it had been in 1974. But Time Warner was missing—out of value range, apparently.

The 1987 low was a panic low, not really a proper liquidation, and its shortcomings are betrayed in the paucity of Graham names on the list. The 1991 low was, of course, worse, although we might have picked up more eligible stocks had we set the search for October 1990 rather than for the month the war began, January 1991. For a snapshot of comparative valuations, Bush I vs. Bush II, we note that Merrill Lynch traded as low as 52% of book in the fall of 1990, compared to a 30% premium today; Bear Stearns was at a 10% discount to book value then, compared to a 50% premium today.

The main lesson we draw from the Compustat findings is that stocks can get very cheap, even absurdly cheap, although the absurdity is obvious mainly in retrospect. Knowing this, we are no closer to knowing how cheap they may become in this bear market. January 1991 yielded precious few bargains but proved the start of the greatest levitation in American financial history.

The question before the house is whether the reduction in value-laden equities at successive bear-market lows is a trend to be extrapolated or a trick meant to snare us. The latter, we believe, knowing Mr. Market as we do. So we are in no hurry to declare a bottom because we are tired of the sound of our own foreboding voice. We will continue to look for bargains but try not to settle for non-bargains, even though they are cheaper than they were at the top.

In the first edition of *The Intelligent Investor*, Graham takes to task those who would believe that stocks excel unconditionally, at any price, in the long run or short: "The extreme depth of the depression of the early 1930s was accounted for in good part, this writer believes, by the insane height of the preceding stock-market boom. Naturally there was a great revulsion of feeling toward the investment merits of common stocks." It is food for thought that the March 2000 highs towered above the 1929 peak, whether measured by average P/E, the cost of a dollar of dividend income or market cap to GDP.

Graham made no claim that his seven criteria would deliver optimum investment results. Rather, he suggested that they would deliver a satisfactory combination of financial reward and peace of mind. The half-dozen names netted in the January 1991 survey returned an average of 20% per annum from that time to the present (or to their acquisition), but there were only six of them. Much less productive were the 14 Graham candidates that surfaced after the 1987 panic; to date or acquisition, they returned 8.2% a year.

And, probably, even those 14 names are too small a set on which to base a generalization. Some enterprising scholar should test the returns generated by the 85-member class of 1974.

Which brings us to another topic for future research, the possible amendment of Graham's seven tests. Colleague Peter Walmsley, although a self-described strict Graham constructionist, has dreamt up two suggestions, which the management of this publication endorses. First, a quality-of-earnings test. Calculate the variance between "normalized" earnings (known less pejoratively as "EPS from continuing operations") and plain-old 10-K GAAP earnings. "Go back over every quarter in the last 10 years," Walmsley suggests, "and compare the earnings per share on the income statement to earnings per share from continuing operations. An average variance of more than 15% is a red flag. It won't catch out companies that smooth earnings using pension accounting, excessive reserves or financial subsidiaries that can time gains and losses as they please. What it will weed out are companies that have been taking 'nonrecurring' charges for every quarter since early in the Clinton administration."

The second suggested modification is to substitute debt-to-equity for debt-to-working capital. The beauty of this improvement, Walmsley notes, is that it's true to Graham's belief that an investment candidate should be financially strong. At the same time, it serves to unmask companies that use big-bath accounting to depress book equity in order to inflate future ROE (the Street, looking only at "recurring" earnings, thinks none the worse of them for it). What this debt-to-equity ratio should be, we have not yet settled on. Something low enough to warrant financial strength across the business cycle, but something high enough to exclude the minimum number of deserving companies from the Benevolent Protective Order of Value.

Bullish on Tata

July 2, 2004

The U.S. Interstate Highway System, under construction since 1956 and still not finished (works in progress include the I-95 interchange with the Pennsylvania Turnpike outside of Philadelphia), was a boon to the automobile and to the autocentric U.S. economy. The Indian economy is not now, and may never become, autocentric, but 8,873 miles of highway are planned or under construction to connect the major metropolitan centers of Delhi, Bombay, Calcutta and Madras. In scale and economic significance, India's "Golden Quadrilateral" project (slated for completion in 2007) is fully a match to the one put in motion by President Dwight D. Eisenhower.

All of which is preface to a bullish essay on Tata Motors Ltd., India's top commercial-vehicle manufacturer and second-ranking passenger-vehicle maker. "Up with India," the headline over our review of Reliance Industries (*Grant's*, May 21), is also the subtext for Tata, a likely beneficiary of the constellation of bullish forces that lifted India's real GDP by 8% in 2003, second-best in Asia after China.

There are more than one billion Indians, but not even one in 1,000 bought a passenger car last year. Sales toted up to just 900,000 vehicles for a rate of only 0.7 per 1,000 people, lower than Indonesia's 1.5 cars per 1,000 or Thailand's 2.9 cars per 1,000, even though Indonesia and Thailand, when measured by per-capita income, were as poor or poorer than India only a half-decade ago. However, neither India nor Tata is standing still. The national passenger-vehicle market grew by 27.4% in 2003, while Tata's sales were up by 34.4%.

The "Tata" in Tata Motors is not some branding consultant's confection but rather one of the oldest names in Indian business. Jamsetji Tata founded a textile company in Bombay in 1868 from which 80 existing Tata businesses are descended. The Tata subsidiaries invest in one another, but Tata Motors enjoys a special sign of grace: In the past two years, Tata Group, the corporate parent, has boosted its investment in Motors to 33.4% from 25%. (Foreign institutional investors constitute another important ownership bloc, holding 39%.)

You might suppose that no car and truck manufacturer in the world would be so single-mindedly focused on domestic opportunities as Tata. Even with only 2,241 of the aforementioned 8,873 miles of new highway completed, top-line growth is soaring. However, management harps not only on the opportunities ahead but also the disasters behind, notably fiscal 2000, the first loss-making year in the company's 58-year history. "[T]he commercial vehicle sector is one of the barometers of the economy of a country," writes Ratan Tata, chairman, in the new annual report, "and we have in the past seen unprecedented growth in commercial vehicles in India and other parts of the world, followed by a collapse of demand. The passenger car sector is also cyclic and while this sector is showing growth today, it is only two years ago that this growth in passenger cars was flat. The company is addressing this challenge by taking steps that will ensure viability even during downturns, through expansion in international markets and constant attention to holding down costs."

Maruti Udyog Ltd., India's No. 1 passenger-car maker, also suffered a millennial spin-out. The difference between No. 1 and No. 2 is that Tata has fully recovered, and, indeed, has gone on to set new financial and operating records, whereas Maruti's earnings languish well below the 2000 peak.

Still, as a hedge against weather, politics and other indigenous hazards, Tata is building up its export business. Its five-year plan is to boost export volumes to 20%–25% of total sales, up from 5%–6%. China, South Africa, Russia, Sri Lanka and Bangladesh are among the countries earmarked for the opportunity to purchase—for instance—the Tata Indica (rebranded in some countries as the Tata

CityRover, a mini-car). To fill out its product line, Tata last year paid $102 million for the commercial-vehicle division of South Korea's Daewoo.*

In India, the monsoon is an annual imponderable, the Communist Party of India (Marxist) a cyclical one. To appease the far-left members of the 14-party governing coalition, the newly installed prime minister, Manmohan Singh, has abolished the Ministry for Privatization. And the "Common Minimum Program," the hot-off-the-press position paper of the coalition government, endorses the perpetuation of India's capital-repelling labor laws. Musing on India from our Wall Street aerie, *Grant's* envisions a dawning of enlightened public policy and profitable enterprise, all of it leading to higher share prices, among other social blessings. However, it can't be denied that India presents risks. If Tata's own management is worried about them, we—the truly distant outsiders—can hardly afford not to be.

Every investor needs a margin of safety, and the passive, public, distant investor needs one most of all. An excellent margin of safety was available in the shape of a depressed share price in 2000–02, at the very time when management was restoring Tata's cash-flow margins (to 12.8% in the just-ended fiscal year from 6.1% in fiscal 2000) and nearly doubling its revenues (to Rs162.8 billion in the just-ended fiscal year from Rs81.6 billion in fiscal 2000). Today, the share price is back up, but only to where it was quoted in the summer of 1997. However, on the eve of the Asia crisis, book value was 47% lower and net income was 23% lower than on March 31. At Rs381.6 a share (that's $8.80 a share on the GDRs), Tata is valued at 14 times trailing net income and 9.8 times the fiscal '05 estimate. The balance sheet is in good repair, and inventories and receivables have both been significantly reduced over the past three years.

---

* Continuing to expand internationally, Tata Motors bought Jaguar and Land Rover from the Ford Motor Co. in March 2008. From press date to June 2008, the Tata share price, quoted in Rupees, had risen by 42%.

If Ford and General Motors are finance companies that also happen to manufacture cars and trucks, Tata is a truck and car manufacturer that also happens to lend—a little bit. Last year, through a tie-in with Tata Finance, it financed 16% of its domestic sales. Auto loans in India were formerly very hard to get. Now they are a little less hard to get—but only a little. To qualify for a loan, one must have a gross annual salary of the equivalent of $2,175, roughly four times GDP per capita. With highways to drive on and finance companies to borrow from, the Indian vehicle market may be entering a golden age.

If so, the Indica, Tata's largest-selling and best-known product in the passenger-vehicle line, would become one of the subcontinent's mainstays. "The newly refurbished Tata Indica V2 is a better option than the Fiat Uno diesel or the Maruti Esteem diesel taking into account such factors as resale value, maintenance costs, contemporariness, and fit and finish quality." So applauded The Hindu Business Line in March.

Quarterly results are expected in mid-July, advises a knowledgeable Indian analyst we know. "The most important number to watch will be the EBITDA margins," our authority reports. "The first-quarter margins have risen on a year-over-year basis for the last four years. Also, the margins have now consistently risen quarter to quarter since the first quarter of fiscal 2004 [i.e., one year ago]."

The market would take it amiss if there were no improvement from the 13.3% margin registered in the year-earlier period, our source speculates. On the other hand, construction on the Golden Quadrilateral proceeds apace. Long-term investors were well advised not to be shaken out of GM in the early going of the great Eisenhower road-building project. Patience will pay in India, too.

Swing and a Miss

May 16, 2008

The chance to invest at a knockdown price in a humbled blue chip doesn't come along every day. It presents itself, almost by definition, when people are too frightened to avail themselves of it. In general, fears pass. It's an investor's low entry point that keeps on giving.

Now under way is a reappraisal of AIG and Fannie Mae, the humblest blue chips in North America. *Grant's* had staked out a bullish position on the former while maintaining a bearish stance on the latter. Lining them up together, however, we detect an analytical inconsistency. In most important respects, the two are more alike than not. They are both highly leveraged, packed with mortgage assets of miscellaneous quality (Fannie has nothing but) and prisoners of events over which they have no control. Their stocks can almost be said to represent warrants on the trend in house prices.

Grant's was wrong on AIG (February 22 and March 7). We acknowledged the likelihood of additional mark-to-market writedowns in a portion of the insurance giant's structured-finance portfolio (in fact, we flagged $16.3 billion, much more than the company disclosed last week), but we failed to plumb the true depths of the credit problems. Neither did we appreciate that the management was just as confused as we were. "The Strength to Be There," the AIG corporate mantra, turns out to be a reference to yesteryear, not to the present or, probably, the immediate future. The insurer will be "there" only on the sufferance of the residential real estate market. Otherwise, it—and, of course, Fannie Mae—may be elsewhere, and their shareholders will be nowhere.

In our analyses of AIG, we had invoked the spirit of Benjamin Graham. The truth is that leveraged financial institutions are rarely value investments worthy of the name. They may turn out to be successful speculations, as Citicorp common was from the lows of the early 1990s and as AIG will almost certainly be from the bottom of this cycle (of which more below). But the buyer of a bank, broker-dealer or insurance business, no matter how diligent, can almost never know enough to secure for himself a true margin of safety. The acid test of a value is whether an investor possessing no more than ordinary moral courage can buy it confidently on the way down. We belatedly see that AIG affords no such confidence. That it affords no such confidence to just about everyone may be its saving grace. Possibly, there is no one left to lose faith in it.

AIG is a proverbial black box, and into that box Fannie Mae throws some helpful, reflected light. In a particular sense, things have never been better for the bigger of the government-sponsored mortgage enterprises. After years of losing market share to the yes-men of Countrywide and Washington Mutual, Fannie, along with Freddie Mac, has come roaring back into its own. In the first quarter, Fannie copped a 50.1% share of new-mortgage business, double its share in the year-earlier period. At the peak of the mortgage bubble, GSE-eligible originations amounted to 37% of all originations; they stand today at 81%. The evidence of this growth is stamped on the first-quarter income statement. Net interest income jumped by 42%, to $1.69 billion, while guaranty fee income leapt by 60%, to $1.75 billion. Looking at the revenue line alone, one would have to concur with CEO Daniel Mudd, who told the *New York Times* the other day that "right now I'm seeing the best opportunities since I've been in this business."

Fannie's is a simpler business than AIG's. It comes in two parts, guaranty operations and on-balance-sheet activities. In the first, Fannie stamps its brand and guarantee on bundles of mortgages refashioned into bonds. In the second, it earns a spread on the difference between the cost of its liabilities and the yield on its assets. In the three months to March, Fannie Mae hummed. Compared to year-earlier readings, guaranty fees rose to 29.5 basis points from 21.8 basis points, while what amounts to the net interest yield jumped to 86 basis points from 64 basis points. Average earning assets reached $833.2 billion, up by $35.6 billion from a year earlier. And the new business came with tighter underwriting standards: higher FICO scores (728 vs. 716) and lower loan-to-value ratios (70% from 73%).

The trouble, of course, is that the first quarter of 2008 is not Day 1. The legacy of the mortgage mess is what plagues Fannie and AIG alike. Fannie today supports $723 billion of mortgages held on-balance sheet and $2.25 trillion in off-balance-sheet guarantees on $43 billion of core capital. Most of those loans and guarantees date from the wine, women and song portion of the cycle. Hence, the disappointing first-quarter results (along with the near certainty of more disappointments, and equity dilution, to come): a loss of $2.2 billion, or $2.57 a share, a 29% cut in the common dividend and a subsequent $4.5 billion financing.

AIG, of course, shares every one of those legacy risks, though not Fannie's immediate business-building opportunities. For AIG, to judge by the indictment served up Monday by Hank Greenberg, the deposed chairman and CEO, the immediate future is as problematic as the profitless present. "Core businesses are. . .deteriorating," Greenberg writes in an open letter to the AIG board. "U.S. life operations are stagnant. The company has lost its leading and unique market positions in China and Japan. The life business in Asia had been a crown jewel, but now the company's position has eroded." And it puzzled Greenberg—as, indeed, it did nearly everyone else—that AIG, in disclosing its miserable first quarter, chose to raise the common dividend, not to reduce or omit it.

Greenberg, AIG's largest individual shareholder, may be management's idea of a pain in the neck, but Fannie Mae has the federal government looking over its shoulder. From Capitol Hill come persistent demands to "do something" about the housing situation. Rep. Barney Frank, Democratic chairman of the House Banking Committee, was quoted in the *New York Times* the other day as saying of the GSEs, "I want these companies to help with affordable housing, to help low-income families get loans and to help clean up this subprime mess."

Lending a hand in this projected work of re-liquefaction, the Office of Federal Housing Enterprise Oversight, Fannie's regulator, has reduced its ward's surplus capital requirement to 20% from 30%. A further reduction to 15% appears to be in the cards when Fannie completes an additional $6 billion of fund-raising ($4.5 billion of the $6 billion was rounded up last week). When all is said and done, Fannie could be left with $12.6 billion in excess core capital. This is a fair sum of money, but nothing like the additional exposure to risk assets it can support. Leveraged fully, it could undergird $440 billion in new on-balance-sheet assets or $2.44 trillion in additional off-balance-sheet guarantees.

With private-sector lenders largely hors de combat, Fannie and Freddie hold a commanding competitive position in residential mortgages. It would be even more commanding except for their own boom-time overreaching. For Fannie, comeuppance is taking many forms, including, most directly, high and rising credit costs. In the just-ended quarter, Fannie set aside $3.24 billion in credit expenses, up from $321 million a year earlier. Reserves against loan and guaranty losses total $5.2 billion, equivalent to 18 basis points of Fannie's overall exposure, on-balance sheet and off-, up from four basis points a year ago. As we judge the situation, that $5.2 billion sounds bigger than it actually is.

AIG and Fannie would have been well served by going into corporate hibernation from 2002 through 2007. By the end of 2005, AIG had seen enough of boom-time underwriting practices to decide to stop insuring subprime-blighted super-senior CDOs. But neither it nor Fannie actually came in out of the rain. "Fifty-seven percent of Fannie's book of business is 2005-and-newer vintage," colleague Ian McCulley advises. "Included in Fannie's overall exposure, i.e., its book of business—and these are not mutually exclusive categories—is $20.6 billion of negative amortization loans, $215 billion of interest-only loans, $128 billion of loans with

FICO scores below 620, $268 billion of loans with original loan-to-value ratios of 90% or more and $30 billion of loans with both sub-620 FICO scores and 90%-plus LTVs.

"The Fannie Mae book of business incorporates, in addition, $51.2 billion of subprime exposure and $344.6 billion of Alt-A exposure. And again, some of the above risk factors probably fit into these categories," McCulley goes on. "Fannie holds $25.8 billion of private-label Alt-A securities and $25.2 billion of subprime residential mortgage-backed securities (RMBS) on its balance sheet. The Alt-A RMBS are carried at 85 cents on the dollar and the subprime at 83 cents. All of the Alt-A RMBS are rated triple-A, although 15% of that is on watch for downgrade. Of the subprime RMBS, 42% is rated triple-A, 48% between double-A and triple-B and 10% below investment grade."

Counterparty relationships also play their part in the Fannie Mae credit drama. Twenty-one percent of the company's book of business consists of mortgages backstopped by such credit enhancement as private mortgage insurance. Delinquencies on these assets, at 3.15%, tower above the average delinquency rate on the non-credit-enhanced balance of the portfolio, at 62 basis points. Fannie's top three mortgage-insurance counterparties are MGIC ($27 billion), PMI ($17 billion) and Genworth Mortgage ($16 billion).

Level 3 assets are the kind that are valued not by opening up *The Wall Street Journal* to look up the appropriate prices, but by "valuation techniques that use significant inputs that are unobservable," to quote the latest AIG 10-Q report. If that description does not fill you with confidence, neither will the companies' respective Level 3 exposures: $48.5 billion, or 60.8% of shareholders' equity, for AIG; $56.1 billion, or 144.5% of shareholders' equity, for Fannie Mae.

It's an admissible oversimplification to say that AIG and Fannie are highly leveraged financial institutions exposed to a currently fast-depreciating asset. According to the 20-city Case-Shiller index, house prices have fallen by 14.8% from their July 2006 peak and, over the past three months, have dropped at an annualized rate of

24.9%. Signs of stability in the residential real estate market will be welcomed by one and all, but the stockholders of Fannie and AIG should greet the news, when it finally comes, with hosannas.

Whether or not the bottom in credit is in, the market wants to believe that it is. Fondly do seasoned hands recall the opportunities left in the wake of the synchronized crack-up in junk bonds, commercial real estate, commercial banks and savings-and-loan institutions in the early 1990s. In AIG and in Fannie, they strain to see the distant shadow of one of the left-for-dead New Hampshire thrifts or of Citicorp before it was taken in hand by Prince al-Waleed bin Talal.

Sweet is the memory, but just try to recreate the experience. A clairvoyant will invest as a matter of course in the junior-most instrument of the most-leveraged, least-creditworthy financial institution. Knowing the hour, day, month and year of the absolute lows, he or she can afford to buy (as the adepts say) the most upside optionality. For the rest of us, a portfolio approach is advisable: some of each of the strong, the weak and the (evidently) hopeless. We non-clairvoyants are a little like emergency-room doctors, except that our patients are susceptible to new strains of illness introduced from outside the hospital.

So which company, AIG or Fannie, is the more complete hostage to the mortgage situation? A glance at the table suggests that it's Fannie. The GSE is the undisputed leader in Level 3 assets (both absolutely and in comparison to stockholders' equity), although AIG is foremost in monoline risk. AIG's portfolio of RMBS is rated higher than Fannie's, and it is also smaller (absolutely and as a percentage of equity). In terms of the ratio of price to the downwardly mobile metric called book value, the market appraises the two companies almost identically. AIG is cheaper on the basis of estimated 2009 earnings, for whatever the estimates are worth.

"AIG's most valuable asset," a sell-side analyst posited the other day, is "its unmatched global footprint in foreign life insurance. AIG has the unique position of being an early entrant and/or market leader in many of the world's fastest-growing and most attractive life insurance markets." It's a fact that, somewhere behind the black headlines, there is a real business. But it's no less a fact that a company supposedly expert in risk analysis failed to see the crisis coming, then couldn't seem to recognize it on its own balance sheet.

Examining that balance sheet two months ago, *Grant's*, too, was overly sanguine. In our February 22 piece, we estimated the potential loss on AIG's $93.1 billion portfolio of RMBS investment at $1 billion (the securities were highly rated, after all; either GSE-issued or certified double-A or triple-A). In fact, the company, in its first-quarter filing, disclosed a net realized capital loss of $6.1 billion, of which $5.6 billion was of the "other-than-temporary," i.e., permanent, variety. The quarter also delivered an unrealized loss of $10.6 billion. Unrealized losses do not run through the income statement (as the "other-than-temporary" impairment did) but reduce shareholders' equity on the balance sheet through the comprehensive income (loss) account. If house prices continue to slide, however, as

colleague Dan Gertner observes, a portion of those unrealized losses will likely be redefined and recast as other-than-temporary impairments. The threat hangs heavily over future conference calls.

The line we took in February and March is that a meaningful portion of such unrealized losses will one day be reversed. And so they will be, come the turn in housing, but that moment seems not yet to be at hand. What is front and center is the demonstrated failure of the AIG front office to analyze the risks entailed in structured mortgage finance.

AIG is, of course, in the CDO insurance business (management judged it to be not so very different than the excess-casualty insurance business). All in, the company insures $77.5 billion of exposure to what are known as multi-sector CDOs, of which $60.6 billion hold some subprime assets. The subprime-tainted segment can be further broken down into mezzanine and high-grade. Mezzanine CDOs typically own triple-B-rated assets, high-grade CDOs double-A-rated ones. Of the $60.6 billion of subprime-infected CDOs insured by AIG, $43.1 billion are high-grade and $17.5 billion mezzanine.

What are they worth on the Street? The April 14 edition of *J.P. Morgan's U.S. Fixed Income Markets Weekly* ventures an educated guess. The publication reports that 147 structured-finance CDOs had suffered technical default as of April 7; 15 of these contraptions had been liquidated and 14 were in the process of liquidation. By Morgan's estimate, the average recovery on the super-senior portions ranged from 52% for high-grade CDOs to 18% for mezzanine-grade CDOs to 8% for CDOs of CDOs (i.e., "CDOs-squared"). Applying these recovery rates to AIG's super-senior CDO portfolio would result in a loss of no less than $43.4 billion.

It would, that is, if AIG had not already marked down its exposure by $19.3 billion. Subtracting that sum from the hypothetical $43.4 billion of loss yields a slightly less horrifying $24.1 billion. But, so far, the horror is all in the imagination. No AIG-insured CDO has yet suffered an event of default. "In fact," Gertner advises, "the three largest ratings agencies still rate 69% of AIG's $60.6 billion CDO book with subprime exposure as triple-A. Unfortunately, triple-A doesn't mean what it used to."

By the law of compensation, markets that overdo it on the upside tend to underdo it on the downside. And in the midst of underdoing it, distraught investors project the worst imaginable case on the most out-of-favor securities and institutions. It is hard to conceive of an institution more out of favor today than AIG, nor an asset class more scorned than structured finance. One day, house prices allowing, AIG will likely prove a brilliant investment, or, rather—because it is a leveraged financial institution—speculation. *Grant's* swung and missed. We'll swing again.

Postscript

The Close of the Era of Peace and Quiet

May 2, 2008

FINANCIAL EPOCHS COME and go on little cat feet. Nobody issues a press release to herald their arrival. And no one rings a bell to toll their departure. One day, people wake up to discover that the world has changed. "How did that happen?" they wonder.

Professionals in the change-anticipation field fare little better than the amateurs at divining the big turns, possibly because the experts overreact to the little turns. They labor under the occupational hazard of the itchy trigger finger. To be the first to spot the outlines of a looming secular change is a glorious thing, they muse. So, starry-eyed, they mistake a cyclical turn for the career-enhancing, secular kind. We ourselves have erred in that fashion (among others). This acknowledgement out of the way, however, we make bold to serve up a forecast. Higher interest rates and higher inflation are the coming things. The Great Moderation, so called, is history.

High time, too, we say. Low interest rates and low volatility may please most of the people most of the time. But they bring no joy to the editor of a journal devoted to the Sturm und Drang of interest rates and credit cycles. Not long after the founding of *Grant's* 25 years ago, a kind of macroeconomic peace settled over the world. A great bond bull market had begun in 1981. A new era of fast-cycle logistics had got under way, approximately, in 1982 (the year when the inventory-to-sales ratio for the U.S. economy put in its late-20-th-century high). The pace of deregulation in finance and transportation accelerated, and the Berlin Wall came tumbling down. Before very long, the North American Free Trade Agreement, outsourcing, the worldwide wage-arbitrage movement and a revolution in financial structures and institutions made their respective contributions to the new order. Along the way, recessions became shorter and milder, expansions longer and cooler. Inflation seemed to give up the ghost, while lending and borrowing (and the splendid profits accruing therefrom) went up and up. A few years ago, the phenomenon got its name. Central bankers agreed that they themselves deserved no small credit for this, the Great Moderation.

"Over the past 25 years," Janet Yellen, president of the Federal Reserve Bank of San Francisco, declared in March at a Paris symposium convened to explore the interaction of globalization, inflation and monetary policy, "the level and volatility of domestic inflation rates have declined significantly worldwide. The decline began in industrial countries in the early 1980s and then occurred in many developing countries in the 1990s. In addition, the inflation process has changed noticeably over this period. Inflation expectations have declined and become better-anchored, shocks to inflation have become less persistent and there is less pass-through of shocks to energy and exchange rates into the overall inflation rate."

What alignment of stars was responsible for these happy circumstances? Yellen considered monetary policy, deregulation, a global "savings glut" and globalization itself. She invoked the relative ease with which businesses could substitute low-cost, nonnative work-

ers for the high-cost, local alternative. Altogether, national bound-
aries seemed to count for less and less in the inflation equation.
Citing research by the Bank for International Settlements, she
noted that "domestic inflation [is] increasingly sensitive to foreign,
rather than domestic, output gaps. This phenomenon could reflect
an intensification of the degree of effective competition between
domestic and foreign workers in the labor market due to globalization and might explain why inflation movements are so highly correlated across countries."

That "inflation movements" are today less correlated to the
American business cycle than to events outside the 50 states is
the kind of news that, in the days of the old Dow Jones ticker,
would have set bells to ringing. Along the U.S. Treasury curve,
only the 30-year yield is pitched higher than the year-over-year
rise in the headline CPI. The funds rate is half of that inflation
measure. On the face of it, government securities are the very
"certificates of confiscation" that their embittered holders mis-
took them for a generation ago in the midst of a once-in-a-lifetime buying opportunity. Worry not, however, today's bond bulls
counsel. The United States is in recession, the recession will persist and—on well-documented form—the rate of inflation will
dwindle, pushing market yields even lower.

"Over the past five cyclical downturns," relate Van Hoisington and Lacy Hunt, hugely successful buyers of long-dated Treasurys, "the year-over-year increases in the [standard inflation
barometers] did not peak until the economy was in recession. In
all these situations, major reductions in inflation occurred in the
early stages of the ensuing recovery." Inflation rates diminish in
the early phase of economic recovery because output rises much
faster than unit labor costs do.

That the sixth time may be different is the thrust of this essay. Naturally, the burden of proof falls on any who would presume to call
the turn in a quarter-century trend. Reverencing the father of chaos
theory, Edward Lorenz, who died last month at the age of 90, one

might go so far as to say that the burden of proof falls on any who would venture an opinion about the future, period. "Predictability: Does the Flap of a Butterfly's Wings in Brazil Set Off a Tornado in Texas?" was the title of a 1972 paper by Lorenz on the inherent limits of accurate weather forecasting. It's a cinch that, as hard as it is to forecast the weather, it would be still harder if the butterflies read the Brazilian press. In the bond market, the participants not only read the forecasts, but they also adjust their behavior to confound them.

Another trouble with the bond market, we think, is that so few forecasts take into account the inflation roaring in the formerly low-cost, low-wage precincts of Asia. Inflation rates are rising in the rich nations of the West, too, but Western central banks are ballooning their balance sheets to paper over the mortgage mess. Meanwhile, the global supply chain has suffered some broken links, and the bond vigilantes of yesteryear are conspicuous by their absence. Central banks could never seed a new inflation because a cynical bond market would never again suffer silently in the face of negative real yields. So said the theorists at what proved the start of a quarter century of falling bond yields. But the long bull market lulled the former doubters to sleep, or sent them off to early retirements. If past is prologue, a new bear market in fixed-income securities will raise up a new generation of cynics. Sell-offs in government securities markets worldwide in recent days suggest that a reappraisal might be under way.

Because financial cause is so frequently confused with financial effect, the would-be diagnostician of a change in trend must proceed with caution. The fact is that a cluster of bullish developments had their origins with the fall of inflation in the early 1980s. In ways not fully explained, or, perhaps, explainable, these good things reinforced one another over the course of the succeeding two-and-a-half decades. If Paul Volcker, the inflation-slaying Federal Reserve chairman, was the author of the feast, he had plenty of collaborators. Eight years ago, Fred Smith, the founder and CEO of Federal Express, reflected on some of the nonmonetary causes of low everyday prices. "[T]he movement to fast cycle logistics," wrote Smith, "combined with the deregulation of the transportation industry in the late 1970s, has had truly profound effects on our economy. In 1980, logistics costs—including the carrying costs of inventory, plus warehousing and transportation costs—were about 17% of GDP. Last year, they were about 10%. We've had a 7% productivity improvement in our economy as a result of the deregulation of transportation and the adoption of fast cycle logistics."

Boeing, as much as any company in the world, took the related ideas of fast-cycle logistics and the globally integrated supply chain and ran with them. It had meant to fly with them, but the Boeing 787 Dreamliner is yet unbuilt on account of a cluster of supply-chain snafus (some of which were noted in the previous issue of *Grant's*). In a recent letter to the editor of the *Financial Times*, Philip Lawrence, a professor at the U.K.'s Aerospace Research Center, asserted that there is a limit to outsourcing and that Boeing had run up against it. No doubt, the just-in-time model of logistical management is here to stay. But, as Lawrence suggested, that does not mean the savings obtainable through the outsourcing of complex manufacturing work are somehow limitless.

Even the savings obtainable through the outsourcing of low-tech manufacturing work are getting hard to come by. American clothing companies import textiles and apparel valued at close to $100 billion a year from such low-wage sanctuaries as Bangladesh, Vietnam and Pakistan. But strikes, civil unrest and supply-chain disruptions are on the rise in those places as inflation robs the low-wage workers of what little they earned in the blessed days of disinflation. Striking for higher wages, *Women's Wear Daily* reports, 19,000 workers recently walked off the job at a Nike plant at Ching Luh, Vietnam. The Vietnamese government ordered a 13% rise in the minimum wage in January, but the officially acknowledged inflation rate is 19%, with food and energy prices tripping along at 40%. Management settled the strike with a 10% salary increase and the promise of a free lunch for all hands. "The deflationary price advantages that companies enjoyed have dissipated," Women's Wear quoted an apparel consultant as saying. "Apparel prices have firmed."

You know the world has changed when China is regarded by a growing number of manufacturers as a high-wage nation. Six weeks ago, *Der Spiegel* favored its readers with an account of the plight of companies like Adidas, which went to China in search of fatter margins but now faces considerably thinner ones. The disappointed ex-pats blame the rising renminbi exchange rate, the rollback of tax preferences for exporters and a draconian new labor law, among other Chinese measures intended to put a lid on domestic inflation. The labor law, the paper reported, "requires companies to provide employee benefits including pensions; to guarantee collective-bargaining rights; and to hire for the long term. It's 'wreaking havoc,' says Ben Schwall, president of Aliya International, a Dongguan company that does quality inspections for China's lighting industry. The law is raising operating expenses by as much as 40% when you add spiraling wages in almost every sector. 'We knew it was going to be a more difficult year, but no one foresaw 40% more in costs,' says Willy Lin, vice-chairman of the Textile Council of Hong Kong."

Manufacturing refugees from seaboard China are not without alternatives. The trouble is that the lower-cost regions to which they repair—western China, Vietnam, etc.—are not so handy as coastal China. Reduced wage costs are offset, in part, by higher logistical costs. Altogether, the world seems to be running out of uninflated cost structures.

The implantation of the capitalist gene in formerly resistant peoples helped to make the Great Moderation all that it was. Between the early 1980s and the late 1990s, an estimated two billion new pairs of hands had joined the global labor force. Employers never had it so good, especially so in countries like the United States, where relocation to the low-cost meccas of the East was no idle threat but an actionable business plan. Hoisington and Hunt, the bond bulls, remark on the "unprecedented deceleration in the increase in [real wages] during the past three years of economic expansion. . . ." The counterargument is that, as globalization giveth, so globalization taketh away. The president of the World Bank, Robert Zoellick, speculates that inflation has pushed 33 countries to the edge of civil insurrection. If globalization has made one world economy out of a myriad of national economies, it follows that inflation is a world problem, not a localized one. From which it follows, in turn, that low nominal bond yields are a kind of 21st-century fool's gold.

Colleague Ian McCulley, who did the analytical heavy lifting for this essay, observes that, in finance, there is often no sure way to distinguish the dependent variable from the independent one. Thus, one can't be sure that the financial boom that tracked the progress of the Great Moderation is the cause of that benign cycle or merely an effect of it. Whichever, he notes, "financial profits as a percentage of domestic U.S. corporate profits grew from a low of 12% in 1984 to 37.6% in 2007. This period of massive growth in financial earnings coincides nicely with a big burst of deregulation, starting with the easing of Regulation Q in 1980 and continuing to the Gramm-Leach-Bliley Act in 1999, which moved the center of financial gravity away from the traditional banking system towards capital markets, investment banks and hedge funds—the so-called shadow banking system. The secular decline in interest rates as a result of lower inflation and a more predictable macroeconomic environment was a powerful tailwind for most financial companies."

Nothing enlarges the financial share of the national income like furious lending and borrowing. So it has been in the United States. Over the past quarter century, at compound annual rates, total debt climbed by 8.4%, household debt by 8.7% and financial debt by 12.2%. Over the same span of years, the personal savings rate plunged to 0.4% from 11.2%. Adapting to an era of low inflation and seemingly certain growth, Americans pushed the ratios of debt service to incomes to all-time lows. Financial innovation helped to make it possible.

In her remarks at the Paris symposium, Yellen took credit, on behalf of her colleagues at the Federal Reserve, for the fact that, so far, upside jolts to commodity prices have not disturbed the reigning complacency toward inflation (or formerly reigning complacency; the Conference Board on Tuesday reported that household inflation expectations now match the "all-time high" reached after Hurricane Katrina). "In the U.S. case," she said, "it is the credibility of monetary policy that, in my view, has helped to insure that the inflation shocks resulting from energy, food, materials and exchange rates do not spill over into inflation expectations and wage-setting, and thus have only transitory effects."

From the vantage point of the hopeful holders of low-yielding Treasury obligations, it would be good if Yellen were right. We think, however, that she is flattering herself. Creditors are settling for negative real yields because bond prices have, for the most part, been going up since 1982. It's not so much that creditors trust the Fed; rather, they believe in their hearts that past performance is indicative of future results. They are backward-looking investors. After a quarter century of mainly profitable experience, most people would be.

As for the Fed, it is asking the holders of its uncollateralized paper dollars to take a great deal on faith. In the face of a headline rate of inflation almost as high as the one that prompted the Nixon administration to impose wage-price controls in 1971, the Bank of Bernanke continues to trim, not to raise, the federal funds rate, weakness in the dollar-exchange rate notwithstanding. At least the Fed, in its wholesale exchange of Treasurys for mortgage-backed securities, has taken care to manage the growth of its balance sheet. Not so on the Continent, where the footings of the European Central Bank are expanding at 20% a year while euro-zone M-2 is growing by 11.3% a year. Across the English Channel, the Bank of England, savior of Northern Rock, is expanding its assets by 22.7% per annum, while U.K. M-4 is rising by 12% per annum.

"However," notes McCulley, "in the new, globalized world, decisions that affect inflation are no longer made only in Washington, Frankfurt or London. The People's Bank of China has a $2.4 trillion balance sheet, about three times bigger than the Fed's. The PBOC's assets, which include most of the country's foreign exchange reserves, mushroomed by about 31% in 2007. If media leaks regarding the growth in forex reserves so far in 2008 are accurate, that growth has continued, if not accelerated, despite the appreciation of the renminbi. The Central Bank of Russia has a $550 billion balance sheet growing at 43% a year. The balance sheets of the central banks of Brazil and India are chugging along at year-over-year rates of 17% and 38%, respectively. Each one of these monetary institutions is trying to beat back inflation by raising its intervention interest rate or by stiffening reserve requirements. But each is expanding its assets—a.k.a. 'printing money'— much faster than local nominal GDP is growing."

No small contributor to the smooth sailing of the past quarter century was the readiness of foreign central banks to absorb

"Well, I think that $100 million is a lot of money."

dollars and invest them in Treasury and federal agency securities. Exemplary cases in point are the monetary authorities of Singapore and Hong Kong. Each has bought, and continues to buy, dollars to stabilize its own currency. Hong Kong implements a hard peg, Singapore a crawling, or adjustable, one. To effect these linkages, each monetary authority must mimic the monetary policy of the Federal Reserve. In times past, the dollar peg proved a source of safety and soundness. Now it is an engine of debasement, with measured rates of inflation in the city economies running at 4.2% and 6.7%, respectively.

As *Grant's* goes to press, the Fed is weighing its next interest rate decision. Dollars to doughnuts, a sympathetic discussion of the inflationary burdens borne by the dollar-shadowing nations of the world—from China to Saudi Arabia—will not figure much in the minutes. Neither will speculation that the post-1971 experiment in paper currencies is ending in a gust of debasement, or that the non-monetary contributors to the Great Moderation are falling away, one by one. If we are wrong about all this, we will have touted our readers off a possible move in Treasury securities to dramatic new lows in yield. But that risk we judge to be far less costly than a move to much higher yields on the back of an inflation rate not much higher than the one the market is ignoring today.

Index